T0203581

3D Game Development with Unity

3D Game Development with Unity

Franz Lanzinger

CRC Press
Taylor & Francis Group
Boca Raton London New York

CRC Press is an imprint of the
Taylor & Francis Group, an **informa** business

First edition published 2022
by CRC Press
6000 Broken Sound Parkway NW, Suite 300, Boca Raton, FL 33487-2742

and by CRC Press
2 Park Square, Milton Park, Abingdon, Oxon, OX14 4RN

© 2022 Franz Lanzinger

CRC Press is an imprint of Taylor & Francis Group, LLC

Library of Congress Cataloging-in-Publication Data
Names: Lanzinger, Franz, author.
Title: 3D game development with Unity / Franz Lanzinger.
Other titles: Three D game development with Unity
Description: First edition. | Boca Raton: CRC Press, 2022. |
Includes bibliographical references and index. |
Summary: "This book teachesbeginners and aspiring game developers how to develop 3D games with Unity.
Thousands of commercial games have been built with Unity. Blender, the top open source 3D modeling and animation package, is also introduced"—Provided by publisher.
Identifiers: LCCN 2021045810 | ISBN 9780367349219 (hbk) |
ISBN 9780367349189 (pbk) |ISBN 9780429328725 (ebk)
Subjects: LCSH: Computer games—Programming. | Three-dimensional display systems. | Unity (Electronic resource)
Classification: LCC QA76.76.C672 L36338 2022 | DDC 794.8/1526—dc23
LC record available at https://lccn.loc.gov/2021045810

ISBN: 9780367349219 (hbk)
ISBN: 9780367349189 (pbk)
ISBN: 9780429328725 (ebk)

DOI: 10.1201/9780429328725

Typeset in Minion
by codeMantra

Contents

Acknowledgments

A BIG THANK YOU TO THE MANY PEOPLE AND ORGANIZATIONS who made this book possible.

First and foremost, thank you Atari Coin-Op! That's where I got my start in the game industry at the ripe old age of 26 in 1982. Unfortunately, Atari Coin-Op no longer exists, but the unparalleled influence of that small group of pioneers continues to this day. I was fortunate to be a part of it. Coin-Op was indeed the real Atari.

A *huge* thank you to the thousands of people who built and continue to build Unity, Blender, GIMP, Audacity, and MuseScore. This book relies heavily upon their contribution and their generosity for making this valuable software available at no cost to indie developers such as myself.

Thank you to the 3.1 billion players who play video games. Without you none of this would exist, not the games, the game companies, nor the countless jobs and careers in game development.

A special thanks to Dave O'Riva, Steve Woita, John Newcomer, Brian McGhie, Mark Alpiger, Ed Logg, Aaron Hightower, Mark Robichek, Eric Ginner, Joe Cain, and Todd Walker. You taught me how to play games and how to make them. To the Valley Chorale, the Serendipity Choir, Cathy Beaupré, and Lisa Egert-Smith, thank you for the songs and the music.

If I forgot to thank you, please insert your name here. You know who you are.

Finally, a big hug and thank you to my wife Susan for your love and support.

Author

Franz Lanzinger is an independent game developer, author, and pianist. He is the owner of Lanzinger Studio located in Sunnyvale, California. His game development career spans almost 40 years starting with the coin-op classic *Crystal Castles* at Atari in 1983, continuing with *Ms. Pacman* and *Toobin'* for the NES, published by Tengen in 1990.

Franz has been an indie game developer since 1991. He worked on SNES *Rampart, Championship Pool,* and *NCAA Final Four Basketball,* as well as *Gubble* for the PC, Mac, and PlayStation. This is Franz's third book about game development. He is currently working on a remaster of *Gubble*. In his spare time, he is the piano accompanist for the Valley Chorale and the Serendipity Choir. Go to franzlanzinger.com for the latest news about Franz as well as resources for his books.

Introduction and Overview

Hello dear reader and fellow game developer. In this book you'll learn to develop 3D games using Unity. *3D Game Development with Unity* combines a practical, hands-on, step-by-step approach with explanations of the theory and practical aspects behind it all. You'll use Blender for 3D modeling and texturing, GIMP for 2D art, Audacity for sound effects, and MuseScore for music composition and notation. Most important, Unity will allow you to put all these assets together and code C# scripts to make games.

Along the way, you will use Unity's Asset Store to download additional art and code resources. All of this astounding software is free to use for students, independent (indie) game developers, and small commercial game studios. Much of it is open source. If you carefully work through this book, you'll be ready to make your own original games, whether as a solo developer, a contributor to a small team, or as an employee at a large game company.

2D Game Development with Unity (CRC, 2021) and *3D Game Development with Unity* are both written by Franz Lanzinger. While it is helpful to work through these books in order, that is not required. For this, the second volume, you need to have some coding background, preferably in C# or some other C-like language such as C++ and a basic knowledge of algebra, geometry, and physics. If you're brand new to coding you should definitely start with the first book.

This book, just as the first, is divided into two parts. In Part I you will become familiar with the necessary software tools. You'll develop a small introductory game followed by a 3D remake of the 2D maze game *DotGame* from the first book. Then, in Part II, you'll build a new 3D FPS adventure game complete with many of the features typically found in commercial games.

As you work through each step, you'll experience the joys and occasional frustrations of game development: the awesome feeling of making your character move for the first time, and the pain of thinking it's going to work only to discover that it doesn't, and you have no clue as to why. It's all part of the process, and there's nothing quite like it.

You are strongly encouraged to follow along with each step and thus build the games and assets as you're reading this book. That is the best way for you to learn. Actually, for most mortals, it's the only way! In this book many assets are created "from scratch." All game assets, code, color figures, and project files are available for download at franzlanzinger.com, so you won't really need to type in the code or draw anything, but you'll learn much more if you build and type everything yourself along with this book. If your copy of this book is presented in monochrome (i.e., not in color) you may wish to refer to the color figures at franzlanzinger.com using a color monitor.

Of course, you'll always have the opportunity to branch out and do things a bit differently from this book. This way you have total control over your game. As your knowledge and skill improve, you'll soon know enough to make that next awesome, original hit game.

Game development can be a daunting, exciting, and highly rewarding endeavor. It can be a lifelong career, a hobby, or a steppingstone toward becoming an artist, musician, or software engineer. There's a lot to learn, and some aspects may seem difficult at first. Don't let that stop you! It's incredibly fun and satisfying, so go forth and make games!

I

Basics of 3D Game Development

CHAPTER 1

Software Tools

I N THIS CHAPTER YOU'LL install the principal software tools used in this book and test them out to make sure that they run: Visual Studio, Unity, GIMP, Blender, and Audacity. In the following chapter you'll use these tools to make a small 3D game. You'll continue to use these tools throughout this book. Later on in this book you'll install MuseScore for music composition and notation. Your main hub for all of this will be Unity.

This book was written to let you follow along with a series of steps. By doing so you will experience firsthand what it's like to be a game developer. There are hundreds of numbered steps in this book, requiring you to pay very close attention and to do them in order, one by one. Most of the steps are followed by additional explanations, descriptions, or screen shots.

When coding, making just the wrong kind of mistake can have devastating consequences for your project. The devastation can occur immediately, but if you're unlucky it'll be days, months, or even years later. This is the nature of the beast. Some mistakes can come to haunt you decades later. Really. The best way to avoid this painful embarrassment is to test early and often. Type carefully, and make very sure that you don't skip any steps. If you only have a few bugs along the way, you'll be doing better than most. Simply accept that this will happen to you, and when it does, fix the problem, learn from it, and move on.

YOUR COMPUTERS

You'll need to have access to a PC or Mac to follow along with the steps in this book. Your system needs to meet the development system requirements for Unity. In the spring of 2021, the Unity company released the 2020.3.0f1 LTS version of Unity, the version used for this book. LTS stands for long-term support, which means Unity will support this version for 2 years, fixing bugs but not changing it otherwise. So, you should be OK when using the latest version of 2020 LTS Unity, for example, 2020.3.3f1. Here is a summary of the system requirements for 2020 LTS:

DOI: 10.1201/9780429328725-2

- OS: Windows 7 SP1+, Windows 10, 64-bit versions only; or macOS High Sierra 10.13+.

- CPU: X64 architecture with SSE2 instruction set support.

- DX10-, DX11-, and DX12-capable GPUs. For Macs Metal-capable Intel and AMD GPUs.

Look at unity.com for details. It's in the Unity Manual under System requirements for 2020.3. While not strictly necessary, it's highly recommended that your screen has at least 1920x1080 resolution. Some laptops or older desktop systems might have lower native resolutions. If that is your situation you should seriously consider upgrading or replacing your display. You should probably get at least one 4K monitor because many of your players will have one. A two or three monitor setup with a fairly recent graphics card is recommended in order to maximize your game development productivity and enjoyment. If you don't have multiple monitors, Virtual Desktops in Windows and Mission Control on your Mac are very useful and workable alternatives. If you wish to support real-time ray tracing in your project, then search the web for high-end graphics cards or laptops that support real-time ray tracing and get one. Yes, they are expensive as of 2022, but prices are decreasing, and availability is improving. This book contains an optional section on ray tracing in the lighting chapter (Chapter 21).

If your system meets the requirements for Unity, it will be more than adequate for the other software tools used in this book. And yes, you really should have fast internet access. If you don't know the speed of your internet connection, this would be a good time to find out. Run a speed test and check that your download speed is at least 10 Megabits per second, the faster the better. 30 Megabits per second is recommended for an enjoyable experience. Some of your downloads will be large and time consuming, but once everything is downloaded and installed, you'll be able to work on your project with slow or even no internet access. In case you're curious, the author uses a three-monitor setup with a 75 Mbit internet connection.

This book assumes that you have a three-button mouse and a numpad. There are workarounds but your life will be much easier if you connect these devices to your system when needed.

Most serious game developers have access to several systems, old and new, laptops and desktops, maybe even both PCs and Macs. Really old systems may not be compatible with Unity development, but they can sometimes be used for doing Visual Studio projects or for the creation of graphics, sound, or music. They may also be good enough for testing your games, so by all means, keep your old systems if you can deal with storing them and keeping them updated. It's important to test your games on a variety of systems before releasing them to the public and to your external testers.

As stated in the title, this book focuses on the development of 3D games for PCs and Macs. If you're interested in developing non-game applications, this book may also be for you. Unity got its name from its ability to allow for the creation of games once and to then deploy them to many targets such as desktops, consoles, and mobile devices. An early slogan for Unity was "Author once – deploy everywhere." That was and still is a noble sentiment, though in reality it's somewhat more complicated than that. All games in this book will run on PCs and Macs, and most of them can be modified to run on consoles and/or mobile devices with some effort.

The process of taking a game from an existing platform to another one is called *porting*. Porting is easy in Unity when compared to writing your own game engine and getting it to work on all of your target platforms. Even when using Unity, be aware that each platform has a long list of specific requirements, especially if your goal is to produce a commercial release. The number of supported platforms for Unity stands at approximately 20 as of 2022. You'll need to do your own research on the current details of porting to and developing for your intended target platforms.

NOTES FOR MAC USERS

If you are following along with this book on a Mac, here are some important notes. Macs can be wonderful development machines, so by all means, continue to use your Mac if that is your preferred computer and you don't have access to a decent Windows machine. You can skip this section if you're only using Windows.

All of the software tools used in this book are available both for Windows 11 and for macOS. There can be slight differences between Mac and Windows versions, but for the most part they are close to the same. The devil lies in the details. The keyboard shortcuts may differ, and the screenshots do not match exactly, or in some rare instances not at all.

From here on in, this book will usually assume that you're using Windows 11. You can still follow along on your Mac, but you will need to adjust the keyboard shortcuts, and you'll have to live with the slightly different screen shots. Occasionally the Menu structures are different, but the same set of choices is always available. It helps to use the same software version numbers as the corresponding Windows version number recommended in this book. Also, be sure to go to www.franzlanzinger.com for the latest compatibility notes and additional help for Mac users.

In the next section you'll start things off by installing Visual Studio.

VISUAL STUDIO

Visual Studio is Microsoft's suite of development tools. It supports a plethora of programming languages, among them C#, the language used by Unity. In this section you'll install the free version of Visual Studio 2019. If you have a free or paid version of Visual Studio 2019 installed on your system already you may safely skip this section. Visual Studio 2019 Community is free and may be downloaded at visualstudio.microsoft.com/vs/community/. Go ahead and proceed with the installation. The author installed Update Version 16.8.5. Feel free to use a more recent version, and to periodically update as prompted by Microsoft. If you are installing Visual Studio 2019 for the first time on your system, under Workloads select "Universal Windows Platform development." If you have an earlier version of Visual Studio 2019 installed, follow the installation instructions and you will still have all of your old projects available. On a Mac, follow the specific instructions for Mac installation. This is a somewhat large install, so check that you have enough disk space and time to do the download and install.

TYPOGRAPHIC CONVENTIONS

You will soon start following step instructions. Please make a note of the following typographic conventions used in the step instructions. These conventions are designed to help you follow along more easily.

- Step indicators are **bold**, for example **<Step 23>**, sequentially numbered, with the count restarting within each section.

- When referring to something to be typed, **bold** is also used. For example, when asked to type the word "hello" the instructions will read: Type **hello**.

- Special keys are surrounded by angle brackets like this: **<shift> <ctrl> <alt> <enter>** or **<spacebar>**.

- Numpad keys are shown like this: **<numpad>3**, or **<numpad>+**.

- Mouse-click instructions are bold as well, such as **right-click**, or **middle-mouse-button**. **LMB**, **MMB**, and **RMB** are abbreviations for the left, middle, and right mouse buttons.

- Menu and button selections are bold, possibly separated with a long dash, such as **File – Save**. Long dashes indicate submenu selections or popups.

- On-screen text may be in bold, in a different font, or quoted, depending on the context. For example **Exit**, Exit or "Exit."

- When items are in quotes, ignore any punctuation at the end, for example, at the end of the previous bullet point ignore the period at the end within the quotes. That's just the period at the end of a sentence, not part of the quoted text.

- Usually, but not always, there is a period at the end of step instructions to indicate the end of a sentence. When a period might cause confusion it is omitted, for example **<Step 53>** type **42** won't have a period after the 42 to avoid having the reader type it.

- Step instructions may use bold for emphasis, for example: **Move** the **robot** to the **right** to match Figure 12.3.

- C# code is generally displayed using a smaller font with syntax color highlighting. The text colors in this book won't necessarily match the text colors seen on your screen.

It's difficult to consistently follow these conventions when producing a large, complex manuscript, so the author apologizes in advance for breaking these conventions on occasion. Following the steps in this book takes a diligent eye for detail. Take your time and double check complex steps, and don't skip any of the steps. You will probably make a mistake or two along the way, so be prepared to restart from previously saved project files if things go awry.

HELLO WORLD!

To test out the installation of a programming language, the first step should always be to write a "Hello World!" program. Traditionally, this is a minimal program that only displays the text "Hello World!" as pioneered in the seminal 1978 book *The C Programming Language* by Brian Kernighan and Dennis Ritchie. C#, the programming language used in this book, is one of many successors to C.

\<Step1\> Run Visual Studio 2019.

\<Step 2\> Sign in or create a Microsoft Account, if necessary. This is only needed the first time you run Visual Studio.

\<Step 3\> **Click** on Create a new project in the Get started panel. On a Mac, **click** on New.

On a Mac this interface looks different, but you'll also see a way to create a new project.

\<Step 4\> **Click** on `All languages` and select C#. Also **select** `Windows` for the platform and `Console` for the Project type,

If you're getting the message "No exact matches found" click on `Install more tools and features` and install Universal Windows Platform development, and when you're finished installing, try this step again.

\<Step 5\> **Click** on **Console Application**.

\<Step 6\> **Click** on **Next**.

\<Step 7\> Enter the Project Name **Hello World**.

On a Mac, use the project name "HelloWorld" without the space. On Macs, project names may not contain spaces nor an exclamation mark.

\<Step 8\> Optional: Enter a project location.

This would be a good time to set up a folder on your system for all the projects for this book. It's up to you to name and create that if you wish.

\<Step 9\> **Click** on **Next** and then **Create**.

\<Step 10\> Check that you have this line of code inside of the Main function:

```
Console.WriteLine("Hello World!");
```

Your screen should now look similar to Figure 1.1.

\<Step 11\> **Debug – Start Without Debugging** to compile and run it.

This step automatically saves your work, compiles it, and runs it. When running the console app, a popup window appears and prints `Hello World!` in the window followed by `Press any key to close this window . . ..`

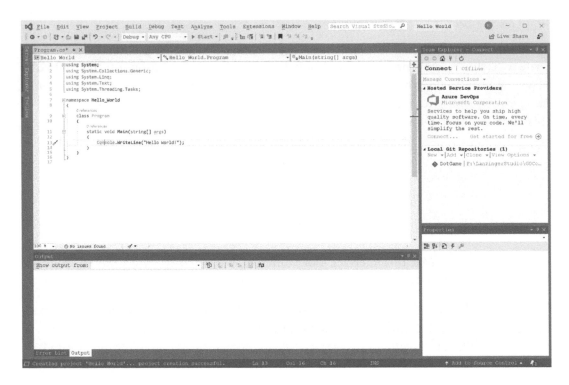

FIGURE 1.1   Hello world program in visual studio.

<Step 12> Exit Visual Studio.

You are now set up to use C# in Visual Studio 2019.

C#

C# (pronounced C Sharp) is the programming language used in this book and by Unity. C# is one of the many descendants of the granddaddy of them all, C. As of 2022, C# is one of the top programming languages both in terms of job demand and popularity. As a side benefit to reading this book you'll learn some basics of C#, and improve your programming skills as well.

To get started with game development it's helpful to first learn your programming language well enough to do the job. C# is a large language, but only a relatively small subset of C# is necessary to make games in Unity. It's perfectly OK to learn the advanced features later on and only as needed.

This book assumes that you know the basics of C# as shown, for example, in the companion book *2D Game Development with Unity* by Franz Lanzinger. If you worked through the first few chapters of that book, you're good to go. Here's a summary of C# features that should be familiar to you:

- Numbers: int, float, double

- Math Operators: +, -, *, /, %

- Bitwise Operators: |, &,!

- Math Functions: Math.Sqrt, Math.Sin, Math.Cos

- Control: if, else, switch

- Classes and Methods

Most introductory books or courses for C# will cover this material. If you know C++ well and are making the switch to C#, search the web for "C# for C++ developers" to find a summary of the differences between C# and C++.

In the rest of this book, you won't be creating standalone C# applications as you just did with the HelloWorld program in the previous section. Instead, you'll create C# code with Visual Studio connected to Unity, with both running in separate windows. You'll see that in action in the next chapter.

UNITY

In this section you'll install Unity and take it for a quick spin. Go to www.unity.com and install the Personal, Plus, or Pro edition of version 2020.3.0f1. You'll need to check the financial eligibility conditions to see which edition is right for you. This book is compatible with all three. This book was produced and tested with the Personal Edition, version 2020.3.0f1. Check the author website www.franzlanzinger.com for the latest compatibility information if you are interested in following along with this book using a more recent version of Unity.

This book was originally written and developed using a Windows 10 system. Almost all the figures are screen captures produced using a 4K monitor, so you'll notice differences if you're using a smaller screen. On a Mac, your screen might look a little different from the corresponding Windows screen captures. Also, make sure to read or reread the earlier section entitled "Notes for Mac Users."

Unity is a real-time development platform for making games and similar applications for a wide variety of targets. With Unity you can develop games as well as non-game apps for PCs, Macs, game consoles, VR, and mobile devices. The name "Unity" implies that you can develop your game once and then deploy it to many platforms. It is without a doubt the world's most popular game engine with half of all released games developed using Unity, according to a rough estimate by Unity's CEO in 2018. Only a few very large game development studios have the resources to develop, use, and maintain custom game engines for their games. Also, you should be aware of the major competing engines such as Unreal Engine and Godot. You have chosen well to go with Unity, but it's educational to learn about other game engines occasionally.

Now that you've installed Unity, your logical next goal will be to create a "Hello World!" project. This will be quite a bit different from the Hello World project for Visual Studio. No coding will be necessary. Instead, you'll create a GUI object with the text "Hello World!" Follow the next few steps to do this:

<Step 1> Run Unity, **click** on **New**. Use the name **HelloUnity, 2D Template**, select **Location, Create Project**. Wait about a minute or two while the project is set up by Unity.

<Step 2> **GameObject – UI – Text**. Set **Pos X** and **Pos Y** to **0** in the inspector panel.

<Step 3> **Click** on the **Play** arrow, middle top of the window, to play the game.

You should see a blue screen with "New Text" in the middle. This "game" is just a static screen. The paragraph you are reading right now is an explanation for Step 3, and not considered part of Step 3 itself. It is often good to read such explanatory paragraphs before doing the corresponding steps.

<Step 4> **Stop** playing the game by **clicking the Play arrow** again, then **change the text** from New Text to Hello **World!** in Inspector Panel.

<Step 5> **Play** and then **stop**.

<Step 6> **File – Save. File – Exit**. (On a Mac it's **Unity – Quit**).

Special instructions for Mac users such as in the previous step may or may not be included in the remainder of this book. Please read the earlier section for Mac users if you haven't done so already.

GIMP

GIMP is a 2D graphics program that you will use on occasion for the creation of 2D assets such as textures or GUI elements. GIMP is a cross-platform image editor available for Macs, Windows, and Linux. It is open-source software and may be freely used for any purpose, including commercial projects.

If you haven't done so already, please install GIMP as follows. Go to www.gimp.org/downloads for instructions. This book uses GIMP 2.10.14, released in October 2019. You may wish to use a more recent version of GIMP, but be aware that the user interface and feature set might be slightly different if you do that.

You'll try out GIMP by drawing a sketch of a toy car. You'll use this sketch later on when creating a toy car in Blender.

<Step 1> Open GIMP.

Before you start using GIMP, you're going to set up the user preferences to match what's used in the book.

<Step 2> **Windows – Single Window Mode**.

Do this several times to see what this does. For the purposes of this book, it's better to use Single Window Mode, so please use that.

<Step 3, Windows> **Edit – Preferences**.

<Step 3, Mac> **Gimp-2.10 – Preferences**.

This opens a Preferences dialog. It's quite extensive and worth exploring once you're familiar with the basics of GIMP. For now, you're going to try to match the settings in the book.

<Step 4> **Window Management – Reset Saved Window Positions to Default Values.**
You're doing this in case you have moved the windows. You can do this in the future if you'd like to have the default window positions again.

<Step 5> **Exit** and **relaunch GIMP.**
This relaunch is necessary to activate the windows position reset.

<Step 6, Windows> **Edit – Preferences – Theme – Light.**

<Step 6, Mac> **Gimp-2.10 – Preferences – Theme – Light.**
The book uses a light theme because that looks better on paper.

<Step 7> **Icon Theme – Color – OK.**
This is the author's personal preference. Feel free to use a different theme if you wish.

<Step 8> **Go back** to **Preferences**, then use **Icon Size** from the **Theme – Custom Icon Size.**
Pick a **size** for the icons that you like.
Because this book was produced with a 4K monitor, the author used **Huge** to make the icons large enough. If you too have a 4K screen, you may wish to match the author's 200% setting in the Scale and Layout Display setting in Windows 11.

<Step 9> **Adjust** the window size and panels on the left and right of the window, if necessary. Compare with Figure 1.2.

FIGURE 1.2   GIMP setup with light theme, color icon theme, Huge icons on 4K monitor.

Your screen may look slightly different depending on your monitor resolution and any previous usage of GIMP. You are now ready to use GIMP. Just to make sure that you're set up the way you want, do the following:

<Step 10> **Exit** GIMP and **launch** it again.

As you can see, the window size and layout were preserved when you exited and launched again.

You are now ready to use GIMP to draw something. You'll create a sketch of a toy car. You'll use this sketch in the Blender section as a reference image for creating a 3D model of a toy car.

<Step 11> **File – New** and **choose** an **Image Size** of **1920×1080 pixels – OK**.

In the next step you are going to immediately save the project and the image. This is a good habit to cultivate. The reality is that you're going to get interrupted when working, so this way you'll be able to quickly save your work and shut down your system when necessary without having to think about it. While you're at it, create the following folder in an easily accessible place on your system: **3DGameDevProjects**. You plan to store all of your projects for this book in that folder. This might be a good time to place this folder into cloud storage, if you have access to that. If you don't have cloud storage, go and explore that at some point. There are several free cloud storage plans available such as OneDrive or Google Drive with more than enough storage space for the projects from this book. By using cloud storage your projects will be automatically backed up and will be easily accessible on multiple systems, such as your main development system, your laptop, and your old test system. You'll also be ready to make your projects and builds available to coworkers and testers.

If you find that cloud storage activities are slowing down your system you may wish to have a working folder on a fast local drive, and a separate backup folder, with just the backup updating to the cloud.

<Step 12> **File – Save As…** and use **toycar.xcf** for the name, **3DGameDevProjects** as the folder. Then **click** on **Save**.

Make sure you're able to find the 3DGameDevProjects folder that you just created.

<Step 13> **File – Export As…** with the name **toycar.png** and then **click** on **Export**.

In case you haven't noticed, those three dots after "Export As" indicate that you'll get a pop-up when clicking on that selection. You used the existing settings for exporting to a png image.

<Step 14> **Exit** GIMP.

<Step 15> Use your operating system to look at the **3DGameDevProjects** folder.

You should have two files in that folder, toycar.png and toycar.xcf. The png file is the image itself in png format, the xcf file is the GIMP project file.

The png file should have a size of 9KB, the xcf file 11KB. The size of the png file is so small because it's getting compressed. You'll see that the size will increase as you work on the image, or if you turn off compression for some reason. It's important to always be aware of the size of your project files and to have a sense of what is considered small, large, or huge. Huge files should be avoided when possible in order to keep your game running smoothly and to speed up loading and saving of those files.

\<Step 16\> Launch GIMP and do **File – Open Recent – toycar.xcf**.

Your goal now is to draw something similar to Figure 1.3. You'll start by drawing the outline using a black brush.

This next step is only necessary if the active foreground color isn't black.

\<Step 17\> Click on the **Active Foreground Color**, the upper left rectangle as shown in Figure 1.4. Then **select** a black color using the Change Foreground Color dialog. Then **click OK**.

To quickly get a solid black color you can click on the black preset and check that the HTML notation is in fact 000000.

\<Step 18\> Select the **Paintbrush Tool**, the one that looks like a paintbrush. **Adjust** the **Size** to about **20**. Then **draw** the black outlines of the car.

FIGURE 1.3   A sketch of a toy car, drawn in GIMP.

FIGURE 1.4   Foreground and background color selection box.

<Step 19> **Change** the **Active Foreground Color** to a **shade of red**.

<Step 20> **Select** the **Bucket Fill tool**, the one that looks like a bucket with paint pouring from it.

<Step 21> **Click** on the interior of the car to make it red.

<Step 22> Make the **tires grey**.

Congratulations! You did it. Your drawing may not match Figure 1.3 but that's OK. You now know enough about GIMP to make some sketches. You won't actually use this image, so if it's ugly, don't worry about it.

<Step 23> **Export** the image to **toycar.png**, and then **save** the project.

This step will overwrite toycar.png and toycar.xcf in your project folder.

It's time to move on to your next game development tool, Blender.

BLENDER

Blender is a truly remarkable open-source application for creating 3D graphics. It is an incredibly powerful program. It compares favorably with its very expensive competition, especially for indies and small studios. Before you dive in, go to https://www.blender.org/about/projects/ and watch some of the movies to get an idea of what Blender can do. Start with The Daily Dweebs, in 4K if possible, if you are short on time, as it is only 1 minute long, or Spring for something more realistic and recent.

As most open-source applications, Blender is completely free and can be used for any purpose. Go to www.blender.org and download Blender 2.92, which is the version used in this book. You will likely find that version at download.blender.org/release. You can go to franzlanzinger.com for compatibility information regarding more recent Blender versions.

<Step 1> **Launch Blender 2.92**.

If this is the first time you're running this version of Blender, you'll get a dialog which allows you to select various options. Use the defaults and dismiss this dialog as well as the splash screen.

<Step 2> **File – Defaults – Load Factory Settings**.

For this book, you'll be using the Factory Settings for Blender 2.92 with the light theme.

<Step 3> **Edit – Preferences… Click** on **Themes**, then on **Presets**, and then **select Blender Light** and **Close** the popup window.

The light theme looks better when printed on paper, so that's the reason for this choice. If you prefer you may select another theme, but be aware that if you do that you may encounter some cosmetic and potentially confusing differences when comparing your screen with the figures in this book.

<Step 4> **File – Defaults – Save Startup File** (Figure 1.5).

<Step 5> To test this setup, **exit Blender**, then **launch it again**.

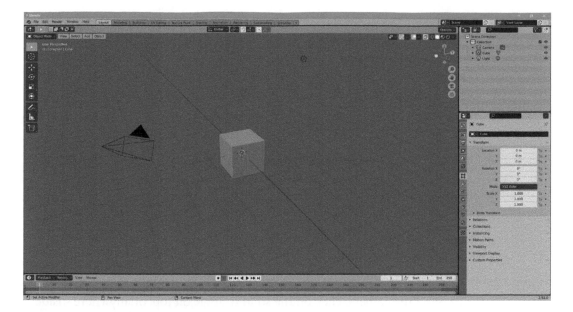

FIGURE 1.5   Factory default scene for Blender 2.92, light theme.

You're now ready to create a simple toy car in Blender. Blender uses the blend file type to store its projects. Just as you did with GIMP, you'll immediately save your project in the 3DGameDevProjects folder.

\<Step 6\>   **File – Save As…**

\<Step 7\>   Navigate to **3DGameDevProjects**, use the file name **toycar.blend**, and **save** your project.

\<Step 8\>   **Exit Blender, launch Blender, File – Open Recent, toycar.blend**.
You are now set up to work on the project. If you need to shut down your system, you can do a File – Save (or \<ctrl\>s) and then close Blender. Yes, as with all of your game development tools, you need to explicitly save your work before exiting, but if you forget to save Blender will show you a reminder popup. Before working on making your simple toy car you're going to experiment a little with the user interface of Blender. After that you'll once again reload the toycar project.

\<Step 9\>   Look at the top row of tabs, starting with Layout. **Click** on the other tabs in turn, then **click** on Layout again.
Each of these tabs sets up your workspace suitable for a particular task, for example, Animation.
Doing this gave you an overview of just some of the capabilities of Blender.

\<Step 10\>   **Hold** the \<**shift**\> key, then let go. Notice the very bottom of the Blender window when you do this.

The bottom of the Blender window displays the current actions of your three mouse buttons. If you don't have a three-button mouse, say on a laptop, you will need to get one and connect it to your system. This book assumes that you have a three-button mouse with a scroll wheel. Those mice are inexpensive and can be attached to any PC, Mac, laptop, or desktop via USB. And yes, it works to use multiple mice simultaneously.

Now, getting back to the Blender window, let's take your mouse for a spin.

<Step 11> **Left-click** on the **background**, then **select** the default **cube** by **left-clicking** on it.

The cube highlights with an orange outline when you select it. Note: Blender released version 2.8 in 2019. Before 2.8 Blender used the right mouse button for selecting. Your current version of Blender, 2.92, uses left-clicking, just as you would expect. Keep this in mind when watching Blender tutorial videos from 2018 or earlier.

<Step 12> In turn, **click** on the **camera** and the **light**, then **click** on the **cube** again.

To select the camera, click on the solid triangle on top, or anywhere inside the pyramidal icon for the camera. The default light is shown as a small circular icon.

<Step 13> **Drag** the **middle mouse button**, then **let go**.

This will change the 3D view of the scene while rotating around the center of the scene.

<Step 14> **Hold <shift>**, then repeat the previous step.

This pans the view.

<Step 15> **Hold <ctrl>** and **drag MMB**, the middle mouse button. Alternatively, **let go of <ctrl>** and **turn the mouse wheel**.

This last step allows you to zoom the view in and out. These mouse actions will become second nature to you as you gain experience with Blender.

Next, it's time to explore the numpad. This book assumes that you have a numpad. Blender was designed for use with that. If you don't have a numpad, say on a laptop, try this optional step:

<Step 16, optional> **Edit – Preferences. Input. Check Emulate Numpad.**

This setting allows you to use the numbers on top of the keyboard instead of the numpad numbers. This doesn't fully emulate the entire numpad, just the digits. It may be worthwhile for you to connect a keyboard with a numpad, or an external numpad if you use Blender a lot.

<Step 17> **<numpad>1**.

This shows your scene using the Front Orthographic view, as shown in Figure 1.6.

Your screen shows the cube as seen from the front, using an orthographic view, not perspective as before. Try the other numpad numbers and see what they do if you wish.

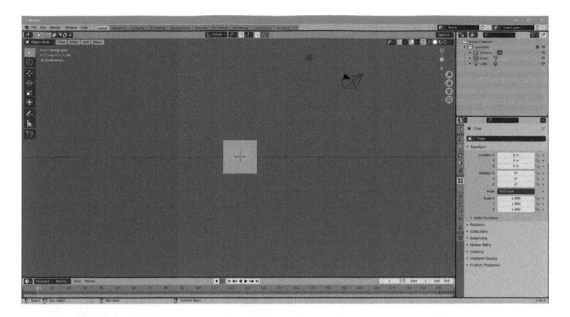

FIGURE 1.6   Front orthographic view in Blender.

<Step 18> **File – Open Recent – toycar.blend** and don't save your changes when prompted.

You're now ready to start modeling. Over the years the user interface of Blender has evolved from esoteric to eminently usable. The learning curve can be daunting for beginners, but it's much better now than in the early Blender days. For experts, the Blender user interface allows for a very efficient workflow. You can see this in action in the numerous YouTube videos where artists quickly build highly detailed models. It can be exhilarating to quickly build something in Blender. To see what's possible, check out a few of the "10 minute modeling challenge" videos. Thank you Imphenzia!

Modeling involves creating the 3D geometry of your object. You will use *box modeling*, a common modeling technique where you start with a box or another simple primitive, such as a torus, and then build from there. After that you do texture painting to give your car some color. You'll make the body of the car red, the windows light blue, and the tires grey.

<Step 19> **Select** the cube, then type **gz1<enter>**.

This moves the cube up one unit, so it rests on the coordinate plane.

<Step 20> **sy3<enter>**.

The cube has now stretched along the y-axis by a factor of 3. Compare with Figure 1.7.

<Step 21> **Click** the **Modeling** tab at the top.

This has the side effect of putting Blender into edit mode. Compare your screen with Figure 1.8.

FIGURE 1.7   Stretched cube in Blender.

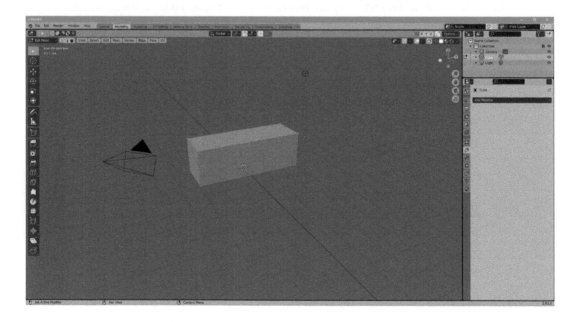

FIGURE 1.8   Modeling workspace in Blender.

The screen looks a little different now. You have more tool icons on the left, the cube is shaded light orange, and you are in *edit* mode. In edit mode you are able to change the geometry of the selected object or objects. The mode is displayed at the top left.

You are going to do a loop cut with two cuts.

<Step 22> **Click** on the **Loop Cut** icon, the ninth icon from the bottom on the left.

As your mouse hovers over the tool icons you should see tool tips with the names of the tools. You can do this until the tool tip shows "Loop Cut" as another way to find the loop cut icon.

<Step 23> **Move** the mouse near the center of the cube until you see the loop cut highlighted.

Compare with Figure 1.9.

<Step 24> **Left-click**, then **click** on Loop Cut and Slide, bottom left corner of the window.

<Step 25> **Select 2** for the number of cuts.

<Step 26> **Click** on the **Select Box** tool icon, the first of nine tool icons on the left.

<Step 27> **Click** on the **Face select Icon**, the third icon to the right of the "Edit Mode" indicator.

If you have trouble finding this icon, hover the mouse over the icons to the right of the "Edit Mode" indicator and read the tool-tip popups until you find it.

<Step 28> **Click** on the top middle face, type **e2<enter>**.

The letter "e" is short for *extrude*. It takes the selected face and moves it along its normal, and then creates a new box.

<Step 29> Type **a**.

This selects all geometry in the object. You are still in edit mode, so the Camera and light aren't selected.

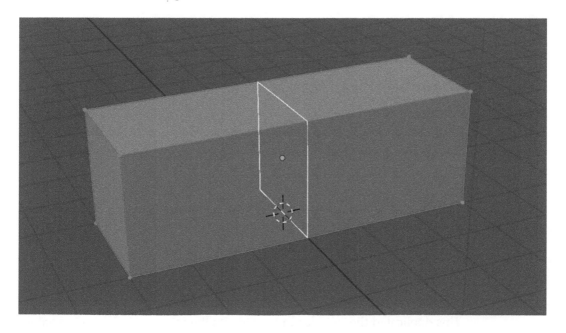

FIGURE 1.9   Loop cut in Blender.

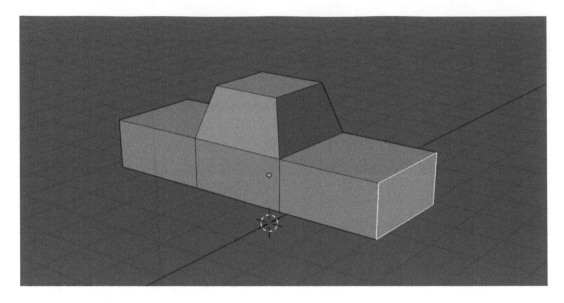

FIGURE 1.10   Selecting the back face of the car.

<Step 30> **sz0.5<enter>**

> This scaled the box by a factor of 0.5 in the z direction. It's starting to look like a car, albeit a very boxy car.

<Step 31> **Select** to **top face**, then type **s0.7<enter>**.

<Step 32> **Hold MMB** and **turn the view** so you can then select the back face, then **select** it as shown in Figure 1.10.

<Step 33> **gy-0.7<enter>**

> This makes the back section of the car shorter. It's hard to see, but be sure to type that minus sign.

<Step 34> **Edge Select** and **select** the front edge of the hood of the car.

<Step 35> **gz-0.2<enter>**

> This lowers the front of the hood, making the model look a bit more like a car. Next you're going to add wheels.

<Step 36> **<numpad>7**

> This got you into the Top Orthographic view.

<Step 37> **<Shift>A Cylinder. Click** on **Add Cylinder** if necessary. Radius **0.4m**, Depth **3m**. Location Y **3m <enter>**

<Step 38> **ry90<enter>**

<Step 39> **<shift>Dy-4**

> This duplicated the cylinder and moved it along the y-axis. Yes, you need to type that minus sign.

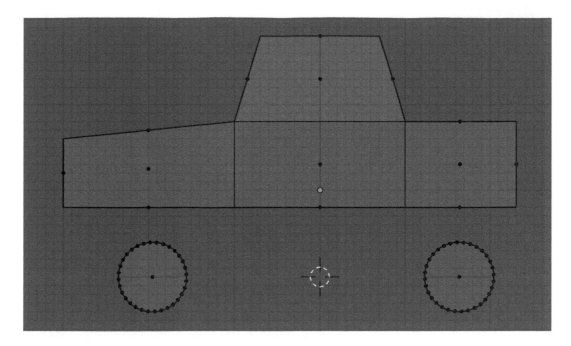

FIGURE 1.11   Car floating above wheels.

<Step 40> **gy** and adjust the wheel position with your mouse, then **left-click.**

<Step 41> **Toggle X-ray** (use the shortcut **<alt>z** or click on the icon)

<Step 42> **Draw a box** around the top cylinder with the **left mouse button.**
This is called box selecting.

<Step 43> **gy** and **adjust** the wheel position, then **left-click.**

<Step 44> **<numpad>3, Select – None, Face Select.**
If you did all of these steps correctly your car should look like Figure 1.11.
You're almost done!

<Step 45> **Box Select** the wheels.

<Step 46> **<numpad>7**

<Step 47> **sx0.8<enter>**

<Step 48> **<numpad>3** and then use **g** to **adjust** the wheel position.

<Step 49> **Select all** by typing **a** and then **g** and move the car down to the floor. Turn off X-ray.

<Step 50> **Adjust the view** to look at your brand new car! Compare with Figure 1.12.
That's actually not bad for a very minimalistic mesh. The wheels aren't realistic, but they look OK from above. This will be good enough for prototyping the car game in the next chapter.

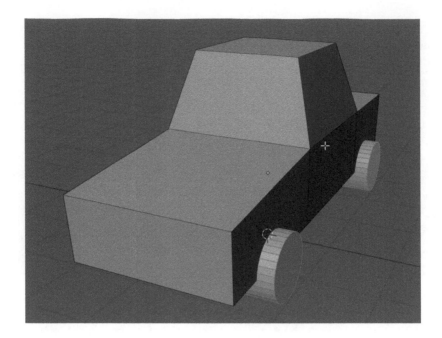

FIGURE 1.12   A brand new car!

<Step 51> **File – Save** and **exit Blender**.

This chapter had a lot of steps, but you're just getting warmed up. In the next chapter you'll test out your car in Unity.

AUDACITY

Audacity is free, open-source, cross-platform audio software. It's an easy-to-use, multi-track audio editor and recorder for Windows, macOS, and other operating systems. You'll start by installing Audacity from audacityteam.org. This book was written using Audacity 3.0.2. A newer version will be available when you're reading this, for example, 3.0.3. Feel free to install this newer version instead. Alternatively, you may find the 3.0.2 version at audacityteam.org in the download – Windows section under alternative download links. Audacity doesn't change all that much from version to version, so the steps below will likely continue to work in future Audacity versions.

In this section you'll create an engine sound effect for your car.

<Step 1>   Download, if necessary, and **launch** Audacity 3.0.x and compare with Figure 1.13.

The microphone and speaker listings will likely differ for you. Be sure to have some audio working on your system. Speakers or headphones are OK. You won't be using the microphone.

<Step 2>   **Generate – Chirp…**

<Step 3>   Waveform: **Sawtooth**.

<Step 4>   Frequency (Hz): Start **90** End **75**

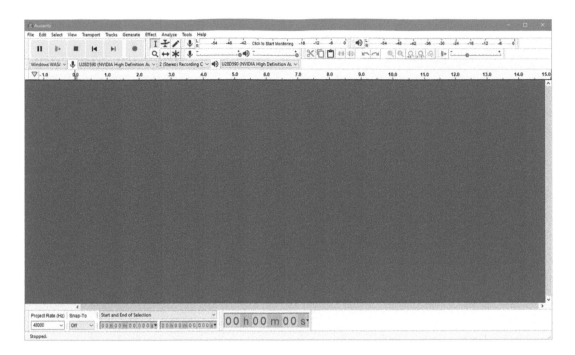

FIGURE 1.13   Starting Audacity.

<Step 5>   Amplitude (0–1): Start **0.8** End **0.6**

<Step 6>   Interpolation: **Linear**

<Step 7>   Duration: **00h00m03.000s**

<Step 8>   **Preview**
> Listen to the somewhat annoying sound. It should sound like a racecar driving by. Feel free to experiment with these settings.

<Step 9>   **Click** on **OK**.
> You now see the waveform in the Audio Track window.

<Step 10>   **File – Export – Export as WAV**. Use the name **toycarsound.wav**.
> Store the file in your usual 3DGameDevProjects folder. You can enter the Metadata Tags as you wish.

<Step 11>   Type **<shift><spacebar>** to listen to a looped playback, **<spacebar>** to stop.
> You would normally save the project here, but you're not going to bother because this is just a short experiment, and it's probably going to be replaced with something better.

In this chapter you installed and tried out Visual Studio, Unity, GIMP, Blender, and Audacity. In the next chapter you'll use them to make a game.

CHAPTER 2

A 3D Game

I N THIS LONG CHAPTER you'll make a simple 3D racing game. You'll use assets from the previous chapter, as well as a newly created terrain and other game objects. Your goal is to continue to learn how to use your chosen game development tools and see how they interact with one another.

A quick side note: If you find yourself fighting a bug or two between here and Chapter 13 you may wish to skip ahead to Chapter 13, "Testing and Debugging," and work through it. That chapter is a standalone beginner tutorial about Visual Studio and Unity debugging tools. To help with debugging, be sure to save your work often.

PROJECT SETUP IN UNITY

It's usually a good idea to set up your project in Unity, even if you're not going to work in Unity right away. You made an exception in Chapter 1 and created various toycar files directly in your top folder before setting up the Unity project. You'll be moving those files into the Unity project shortly.

<Step 1>   **Launch** the **Unity Hub** and **click** on **New** 2020.3.0f1.
　　　　　If you have more than one version of Unity installed, click on the arrow next to "New" to select 2020.3.0f1, or your preferred Unity version.

<Step 2>   Type in the Project Name, **toycar**.

<Step 3>   Navigate to the Location, the **3DGameDevProjects** folder.

<Step 4>   Check that you have the **3D Template** selected, then **click** on **Create**.

<Step 5>   **Right-click** in the Assets panel and **Create – Folder**, then immediately type the name of the folder, **Sound** and then **<enter>**.

<Step 6>   Create an **Art** and a **Scripts** folder as you did in the previous step.
　　　　　Your Assets folder should look like Figure 2.1.

DOI: 10.1201/9780429328725-3

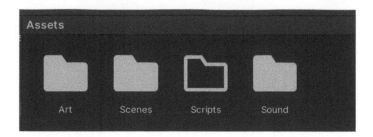

FIGURE 2.1   Assets folder for the toycar Unity project.

<Step 7> In your operating system, **open** the **3DGameDevProjects** folder. **Drag** toycar. blend into the Art folder, then **drag** toycarsound.wav into the Sound folder.

This step is easier if you have two monitors. If you don't, you can arrange two vertical windows next to one another so that you can do the drag operation. Another way to do this is to right-click in the Art folder, choose "Import New Asset..." and then navigate to toycar.blend.

<Step 8> In the Assets panel, **double-click** on the Art folder, if necessary.

The Assets panel should now show the toycar.blend file as in Figure 2.2.

<Step 9> **Click** on toycar in the Assets -> Art panel.

This doesn't really do anything other than show the import settings for toycar in the inspector. The inspector is a panel on the right side of the Unity window. The importing of .blend files is quite complex with dozens of options, but for now the default settings are OK.

In the next step you will change the theme for Unity. This is an optional, cosmetic step, but if you wish to have your screen match the printed figures in this book you will need to do this.

<Step 10> **Edit – Preferences... General – Editor Theme – Light. Close the Preferences pop-up**.

FIGURE 2.2   toycar.blend imported into Unity.

You just used the preferences popup to make the Unity screen lighter. This makes printed screen shots more readable in the paper version of the book. For example, look at Figure 2.3.

Many developers prefer the default dark theme, so by all means keep that if you don't like the light theme.

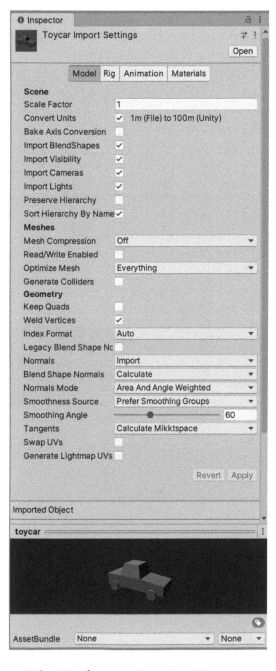

FIGURE 2.3   Inspector panel showing the toycar import settings.

IMPORTING THE TOY CAR

In this section you will put the toycar into the Scene panel. Technically speaking, the toy-car is already imported into Unity, but right now it's simply in your Assets folder and not actually being used in any scene. First you're going to create a floor for your car.

<Step 1> **GameObject – 3D Object – Plane**.
This created a small, white plane.

<Step 2> In the inspector, **change** the Transform to **Position (0,0,0)**, **Scale (5,1,5)**.
The (x, y, z) notation is shorthand for setting the X coordinate to x, Y to y, and Z to z in the Transform. For the position, the default setting may already be (0,0,0) when you create a new GameObject. The default position is the center of the scene as shown in the scene panel, so if perchance you moved the scene view the center might have moved away from (0,0,0). The change in Scale from (1,1,1) to (5,1,5) makes the plane larger by a factor of 5.

<Step 3> **Drag** the **toycar** from the Art folder into the **Scene** panel. Then change the position to (0,0,0) if necessary.
Compare your Scene panel with Figure 2.4.
Of course, this isn't a game yet, rather it's a test that Blender and Unity are working together.

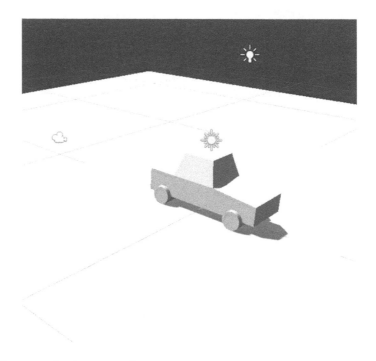

FIGURE 2.4 Toycar in the Scene panel.

<Step 4> File – **Save** and then **exit Unity**.

In the following section you'll make a world for the toycar. The word "world" is somewhat of an overstatement. This world will consist of some terrain, a track, and some buildings.

MAKING THE WORLD IN BLENDER

The world-building approach for this game will be a combination of modeling and texturing in GIMP and Blender. After that you'll put the resulting blend files together in Unity. In this section you'll go back to Blender and make some mountain terrain as well as a track for the car.

You'll prepare for all that by painting the track in GIMP.

<Step 1> **Launch** GIMP.

<Step 2> File – **New. Select** a size of **256 × 256 pixels**.

The idea here is to import this file into Blender, turning the color values from the image into a heightmap. You see a smallish white square in the middle of the main GIMP window.

<Step 3> Type **<numpad>**+ a few times to make the image larger on your screen.

If you don't have a numpad you can experiment with typing the digits 12345 or doing View – Zoom: Fit Image in Window.

<Step 4> Look at the active foreground/background color icon as shown in Figure 2.5.

Make sure that the foreground color is indeed black, and that the background color is white. If you previously used GIMP these colors may be different. If so, explicitly set them by clicking on the respective rectangles and use the color dialog to make them black and white.

<Step 5> **Click** on the **Exchange foreground and background colors** icon, or type **x**.

It's the small, crooked double-arrow icon to the right of the white square and above the black square.

<Step 6> File – **New**, use **256×256** again.

FIGURE 2.5 Active foreground color black, background white.

This will make a black square image. You need the background to be black because the black pixel color will translate into low values on the heightmap, whereas white pixels will translate into tall values.

<Step 7> **Zoom** in on the image again as you did before with the white image.

You still have the old white image in another panel, but you plan to only use the black image. You can see all existing images near the top. You should see a small white square and a small black square.

<Step 8> **Select** the **paintbrush tool, set** the **size** to **21, hardness 75,** and **draw** a track similar to the one in Figure 2.6 by dragging the mouse.

Your drawing doesn't need to match Figure 2.6 exactly, but you'll want a white loop of some kind.

<Step 9> **File – Export As ...** and use the name **track.png** in **toycar/Assets/Art.**
You may use the default settings for the export.

<Step 10> **File – Save As...** and use the name **track,** also in **toycar/Assets/Art.**

<Step 11> **Exit** GIMP.

Next, you will use the file track.png in Blender to make a 3D mesh for the track.

<Step 12> **Launch** Blender.

You've seen the splash screen often enough now, so it's time to turn it off.

<Step 13> **Edit – Preferences. Click** on **Interface**, if necessary, and **uncheck Splash Screen.**

<Step 14> **Exit** Blender and **launch** it again.

That's right, the user preferences are automatically saved, and now, when you start up Blender again there's no more Splash Screen. You can get it back, of course, by changing the preferences.

<Step 15> **Select** the default **cube** and type **<delete>** to delete it.

FIGURE 2.6   Drawing the track for the toycar game.

<Step 16> **Save** the project in **track.blend** in the usual **Art** folder.

<Step 17> **Select** the **Modeling** Workspace.

<Step 18> **<shift>A Mesh Plane**.

<Step 19> **<tab>** to get into Edit Mode.

<Step 20> **Right-click Subdivide**.

<Step 21> **Open** the **Subdivide panel** on the lower left and change the **number of cuts** to **63**.

  You do that by clicking on the 1 and then typing **63 <return>**.

<Step 22> **Click** outside of the plane and type **a** to select it again.

<Step 23> **Subdivide** again, this time with **3** cuts.

  You should now have exactly 65536 faces, that's 256x256. You can check this yourself by turning on the Scene Statistics display in the Status Bar in the Blender Preferences panel. You like knowing these statistics, so you'll keep this preference.

<Step 24> **Layout** Workspace.

<Step 25> **Select** the **plane**.

<Step 26> **Double-click** on **Plane** in the outliner panel (top right) and change the name to **Track**.

  It's a good habit to name your objects to something meaningful as soon as possible. As your scenes become more complex you can quickly get lost among all those default names.

<Step 27> Locate the properties panel.

  This is the panel on the bottom right of the Blender window. On the left side of that panel you'll find a vertical strip of 14 icons.

<Step 28> **Click** on the **Modifier** Icon, the one that looks like a wrench. The properties panel should now look like Figure 2.7.

<Step 29> **Click** on **Add Modifier** and **select Displace**.

<Step 30> **Click** on the **Texture Properties Icon**, the checkerboard icon at the bottom.

<Step 31> **Click** on **New**.

  The Track just moved lower. You can ignore that for now.

<Step 32> **Click** on **Open** and select **track.png** in the Art folder. **Zoom** into the track with the mouse wheel.

  Compare your screen with Figure 2.8.

  It's time to take a break. This is optional, of course.

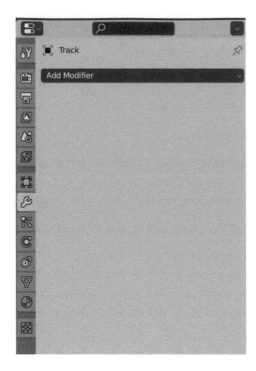

FIGURE 2.7   Blender properties panel with modifier icon selected.

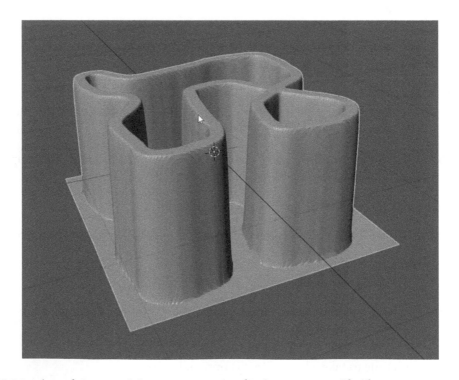

FIGURE 2.8   A track imported from an image as a displacement into Blender.

FIGURE 2.9   Displaying the displacement modifier in edit mode.

<Step 33> **File – Save, File – Quit**.

When you're ready to resume, just launch Blender and reload the track blend file from the recent files list.

<Step 34> **Modeling** Workspace.

The track is gone! Never fear, this can be easily fixed.

<Step 35> In the **properties panel**, **select** the **modifier** icon. **Click** on the **Edit Mode icon**, as shown in Figure 2.9.

The screen now shows both the original plane and the modified plane. That's not really what you want. The following steps make the modifier permanent, or as Blender calls it, you're applying the modifier. You need to do that in Object Mode.

<Step 36> **Layout** then **click** on the **Modifier icon**.

<Step 37> **Click** on the **downward arrow**, the fifth icon to the right of "Displace" and then **click** on **Apply** in the drop-down menu.

<Step 38> **Modeling**.

Wow, that's quite an image. Compare it to Figure 2.10.

You don't really want the track that tall, so you'll scale it down some.

<Step 39> **sz0.3<enter>**

<Step 40> Use **edge select** mode.

The quick way is to type 2 on the keyboard, but this only works if you have a numpad. Otherwise, click on the edge select icon as you learned to do previously.

This is a good start for the track. Later, you'll give it a color material in Unity, so you can now move on to making some terrain.

<Step 41> **File – Save File – New – General**.

This is going to be quick. First you'll load a terrain add-on into Blender.

<Step 42> **Edit – Preferences: Add-ons**. Then search for landscape. Install **A.N.T. Landscape**.

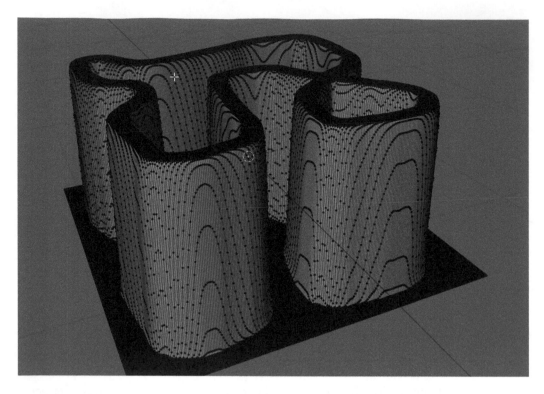

FIGURE 2.10   The track in edit mode after the displacement modifier is applied.

<Step 43> Delete the default **cube. <shift>a – Mesh – Landscape. Zoom** in using the mouse scroll wheel.

<Step 44> File – Save As… terrain.blend in the **Art** folder.

Well, that was quick and easy, but you just want to see what this looks like in Unity, and then work on giving the terrain color and the proper scale, all of which you can do in Unity.

<Step 45> Exit Blender.

You don't really need to exit Blender, but it's a good habit to clean up after yourself or else you'll have a bunch of programs running simultaneously on your system, using up resources. If you plan on switching back and forth between Unity, Blender, and GIMP, for example, then yes, keep them open. Unity is particularly good at this, and allows you to make changes in Blender, save the file in Blender, and it will automatically detect that you updated the file, so it will import the new version without you having to do that explicitly. You'll see that in action a bit later.

MAKING TEXTURES IN GIMP

In this section you'll make two textures: a grass texture and a road texture. Textures are usually 2D images that are attached to the surfaces of 3D models to make the models look more realistic. Textures work particularly well for flat parts of models, such as roads or walls. GIMP has some built-in patterns that can work as textures, so this is going to be quick and easy.

<Step 1> **Launch GIMP**. Make a **new image** of **128x128 pixels** and zoom in on it to make it larger.

<Step 2> On the top right, **click** on **Pattern**, then **click** on the dark grey **Slate Pattern** as shown in Figure 2.11. You will need to click on it to see the name.

<Step 3> **Select** the **bucket fill tool** and in **Fill type**, select **Pattern Fill**. Then **click** on the inside of the image to get something similar to Figure 2.12.

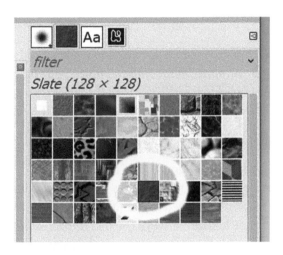

FIGURE 2.11 Selecting the slate pattern in GIMP.

FIGURE 2.12 Road texture.

\<Step 4\> **Export** the image to the file **roadtexture.png** in the **Art** folder.

\<Step 5\> **Choose** the **Pattern 3D Green,** the first green pattern, and **create** the file **greentexture.png** in the **Art** folder using the same method as for the road texture.

> This last texture isn't very good, but it's OK as a placeholder.

\<Step 6\> **Exit** GIMP.

> You're done with GIMP for now, and you didn't bother to save the GIMP project files. Next, you'll take a look at the Unity project and bring in the terrain, the track, and the textures.

MATERIALS IN UNITY

In this section you'll use Unity to create materials for the toycar, the terrain, and the track. Materials can be as simple as a single color, or as complex as a combination of multiple textures and settings. While you're at it, you'll arrange the toycar, track, and terrain relative to one another in the scene, which is easier said than done. You'll start by making the car red.

\<Step 1\> **Open** the **toycar** project in Unity.

\<Step 2\> **Select** the **Art** folder. Compare with Figure 2.13.

> The folder contains the two textures from the previous section; the terrain, toycar, and track files created in Blender; and the track image file used for modeling the track, together with the GIMP project file for the track. You may have a file with the name track, which is somewhat of a mystery. The following step is only possible if you have this mystery file. Skip the step if you don't have this file.

\<Step 3, optional\> Right-click on the mystery track file (the one with the white rectangle icon) and select "Show in Explorer" (or Finder on a Mac). When you're finished looking at that, close the Explorer window.

> You'll see that the file has the full name of track.blend1. This is a backup file automatically generated by Blender under certain conditions. You can safely ignore these backup files, or even delete them if you feel that you won't need them. The web has more info about blend1 files.
>
> Moving on, it's time to create a red material for the car.

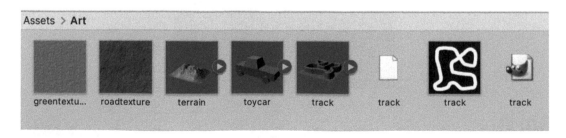

FIGURE 2.13   The art folder in the toycar Unity project.

<Step 4> **Right-click** inside the Art folder panel, then **Create – Material**. Immediately type **carmat<enter>**.

You have just created a material to be used for the toycar object. By the way, if you want to rename an icon, Unity has a strange interface for that. You click on the name, wait about a second or two, then click on it again without moving the mouse. Then you can edit the name. To try this, **rename carmat** to **carmatnew,** and then back again to **carmat**.

<Step 5> In the inspector panel, **click** in the white square next to **Albedo**, then select a bright red color in the color selector popup as shown in Figure 2.14. Close the color popup.

You're almost there.

<Step 6> **Drag** the carmat material into the scene panel and observe how the plane and the toycar change to a red color as you hover the mouse on them. **Release the left mouse button** when the toycar is red.

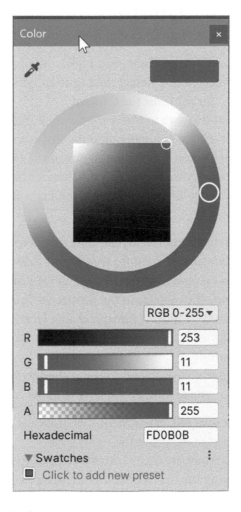

FIGURE 2.14   Selecting a red color.

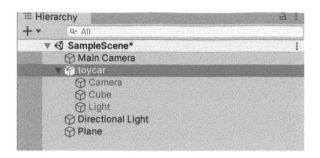

FIGURE 2.15   The toycar object, expanded in the Hierarchy panel.

<Step 7>   In the hierarchy panel, **click** on the triangle next to toycar and compare with Figure 2.15.

You just expanded the toycar object, which revealed three child objects: Camera, Cube, and Light. These three objects were imported from Blender. You probably should have renamed the Cube to toycar, and not included the Light and Camera in the blend file, but for now you'll live with it. First, you'll take a closer look at these three children of toycar.

<Step 8>   In turn, **click** on **Camera**, **Cube**, and **Light** and observe the effect in the scene panel and in the inspector. **Select** the **Light** and **disable** it in the inspector by unchecking. Do the same for the Camera.

The Camera and Light are where they were in Blender, the Cube is the car model. You can see the red material in the inspector for the Cube.

You don't want to use the Blender light nor the camera so that's why you disabled them. You will be changing the Blender file for toycar very soon, so you'll clean things up then by removing the Light and Camera and renaming the Cube.

<Step 9>   **Select** the **Cube** inside of the **toycar** object and type **f**. See Figure 2.16.

That **f** is a keyboard shortcut for the "Frame Selected" command in the edit menu. This command frames the scene view around the selected object. Try it with some other objects in the hierarchy. This is a quick way to look at objects that may be hidden someplace in a large, complex scene. There is a similar command in Blender with the same name and the shortcut <numpad><period>.

This is a good time to learn more about shadows. Unity will automatically cast shadows for you as long as you have shadow casting enabled.

<Step 10>   With the **Cube selected**, experiment with the **Cast Shadows** and **Receive Shadows** settings in the inspector.

The default settings are Cast Shadows On and Receive Shadows selected. Also, try changing the Receive Shadows setting for the Plane. When you're finished experimenting, be sure to turn on the shadow settings the way they were when you started.

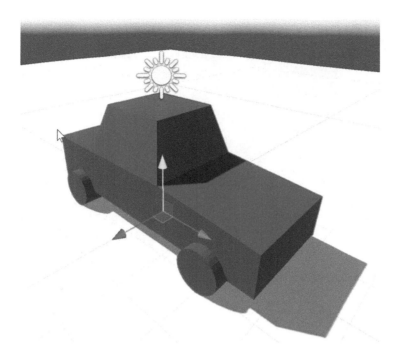

FIGURE 2.16   Red toycar with shadows.

<Step 11> **Select Directional Light** in the hierarchy. **Change** the X and/or Y coordinates of the rotation setting of the transform in the inspector.

You can do this by dragging the letters X or Y with the mouse. Of course, you can just type numbers into the fields as well. Watch the effect on the shadows and the lighting on the car and the plane.

Also, try changing some of the many settings for the light to see what's available. These settings can have a dramatic effect on your scene. It's also important to be aware of possible performance problems if you turn on expensive lighting features. The book will explore these issues in Chapter 21, "Shaders and Lighting in Unity."

<Step 12> Do a **frame selected** for the **Plane**.

You're now going to bring the track into the scene. In order to see the track better, you'll create a temporary track material for it with a blue color.

<Step 13> **Create trackmat**, a blue material, in the **Art** folder.

<Step 14> **Drag** the **track** Blender file (the one with the triangle attached to the icon) into the hierarchy.

Well, you can't see it. This is a common problem when bringing objects into a scene. First, select the Track child object as follows:

<Step 15> In the hierarchy, **expand** the **track** object, then **select** the **Track** child object.

<Step 16> Type **f** in the scene panel to do a "frame selected." Compare with Figure 2.17.

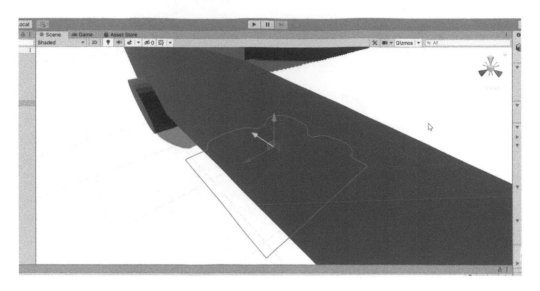

FIGURE 2.17   Trying to look at the track. Where is it?

You can see the outline of a very small track and the origin Gizmo underneath the track. Next, you'll turn off the plane.

<Step 17> **Select** the **Plane** object in the hierarchy, then **uncheck** it in the inspector.
The checkmark is to the left of the text **Plane** near the top of the inspector. Part or all of the track is now visible.

<Step 18> **Drag** the **trackmat** material onto the **Track** child object in the hierarchy.
The track is now blue, and easier to see. Clearly you want the track to be larger. A good place to do that is in the import settings.

<Step 19> **Click** on the **track** Blender object in the Assets/Art folder. In the inspector, **change** Scale Factor to **30**. Then **click** on **Apply** at the bottom.
It can take a few seconds for Unity to apply this new import setting. The track is now 30 times larger.

<Step 20> Do a **frame selected** for the track, then **zoom** in a little with the mouse wheel. Compare with Figure 2.18.
Next, you'll move the toycar so that it is sitting on top of the track rather than floating in space.

<Step 21> **Select** the **toycar** object in the hierarchy and **move** it by dragging the arrows in the scene. Stop when the toycar is approximately on the track. Compare with Figure 2.19.
This toycar is far too large for this track. You'll fix this by scaling the car down.

<Step 22> In the import settings for toycar, **change** the **scale factor** to **0.25**, **apply**, do a **frame selected** and **adjust** the position of the toycar if necessary.

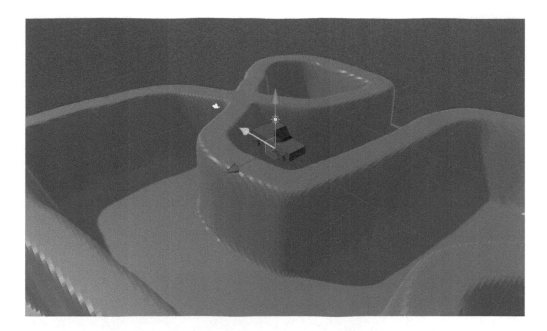

FIGURE 2.18   Result of scaling the track by 30.

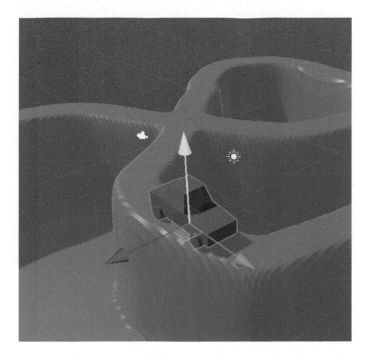

FIGURE 2.19   The toycar is now sitting on the track.

That's much better. Take a look at Figure 2.20.

It's looking like a game! It's not playable yet, but often when creating a new game, just having something that looks like a rough sketch of your vision is the first breakthrough. Let's keep going and bring in the terrain.

FIGURE 2.20   A smaller toycar.

FIGURE 2.21   Tiny terrain.

<Step 23> **Drag** the **terrain** into the hierarchy.

This looks weird. Maybe it has to do with lighting?

<Step 24> **Expand** the **terrain** in the hierarchy, **select** the **light and camera**, and **uncheck** them in the inspector.

That's better. You have a tiny terrain visible in the middle of your scene view. Compare with Figure 2.21.

Before you scale up the terrain you're going to give it a material.

<Step 25> **Create** a **material** in the **Art** folder, call it **terrainmat**, give it a dark green color, and **assign** it to the **landscape** child object in terrain.

Your goal is to move the terrain into the background, just for decoration.

<Step 26> **Hover** over the 3D Gizmo in the top right corner of the scene panel, then **right-click**, select **Top**, and **uncheck Perspective**.

Compare your screen with Figure 2.22.

<Step 27> **Select** the **Landscape** and **set** the Z position to −150.

This moves the landscape out of the way, ready to be scaled up.

<Step 28> **Change** the **scale factor** for the terrain import settings to **100**, then **apply**.

In Figure 2.23, notice the relative positions of the track and the landscape. You'll need to zoom out to see this on your screen.

<Step 29> Make **three copies** of the **terrain** object in the hierarchy.

You do this by **right-clicking** on **terrain**, then **select Duplicate**. Repeat for each copy. You'll end up with four terrain objects: terrain, terrain (1), terrain (2), and terrain (3).

<Step 30> **Select terrain(1)**, and then **move** it to the left and up. **Arrange** the four terrains as shown in Figure 2.24.

<Step 31> Resurrect the **plane** object by **selecting** it and **checking** it in the inspector.

<Step 32> **Assign** the **terrainmat** material to the **plane**.

<Step 33> In the inspector, **adjust** the X scale and Z scale to cover the center region as shown in Figure 2.25.

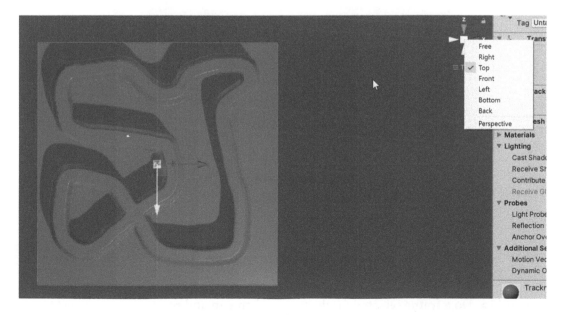

FIGURE 2.22 Setting up the top view for a Unity scene.

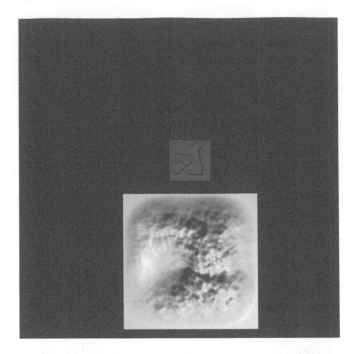

FIGURE 2.23   Green terrain and blue track from above.

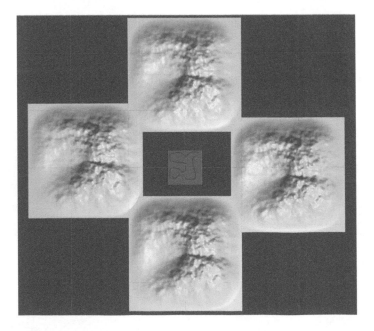

FIGURE 2.24   Four copies of the terrain, arranged to surround the track.

<Step 34> **Adjust** the Y position of the plane to be about -8 so that you can see the top of the track.

<Step 35> Do a **frame selected** for the toycar. Then **pan** and **rotate** the view to get something like Figure 2.26. See below on how to pan and rotate in Unity.

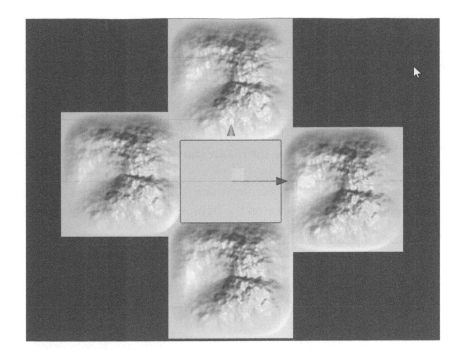

FIGURE 2.25   Patching the center with a plane object.

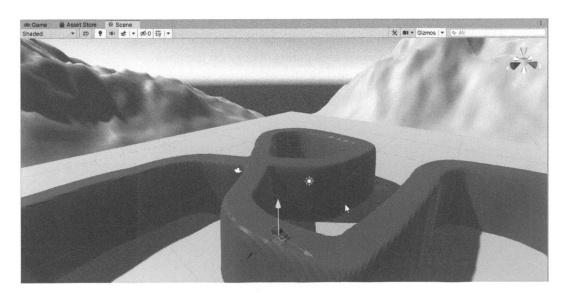

FIGURE 2.26   A perspective view of the scene.

To pan the view, simply hold the middle mouse button and move the mouse. To rotate, first unlock rotation by clicking on the tiny lock in the upper right corner of the scene. Then hold the right mouse button to rotate. If you get lost, use "frame selected" to point at the car again. This can take a little getting used to, especially since this interface is different from the one in Blender.

After dozens of steps, you're finally ready to bring in those textures from GIMP. This is the easy part.

<Step 36> **Select terrainmat**, then **drag** the **greentexture** on top of the **square** to the **left of Albedo**.

Wow, the terrain looks quite a bit better. Compare your view with Figure 2.27. Bringing in the track texture is only slightly more difficult.

<Step 37> **Select trackmat** and **drag** the **roadtexture** to the **square** on the **left of Albedo**.

The road is now a dark purple, which is not what you want. Apparently the Albedo combines the color on the right with the texture map on the left.

<Step 38> **Change** the **Albedo color** to **white**.

That's better, but the texture is too coarse. To make it finer, do this:

<Step 39> In the Main Maps section in the inspector, **change Tiling** to **5** for both X and Y.

Compare with Figure 2.28.

You're going to do two more things to make the scene look better. First, that tiling is still not fine enough.

<Step 40> **Change** the **tiling** in the previous step to **10** and **10**.

<Step 41> In the **track import settings**, **change Normals** to **Calculate** and **Apply**. **Move** the view around to see the lighting change on the track.

Compare with Figure 2.29.

You're happy with the scene so far, but there's much more to do. Before you forget, save your work!

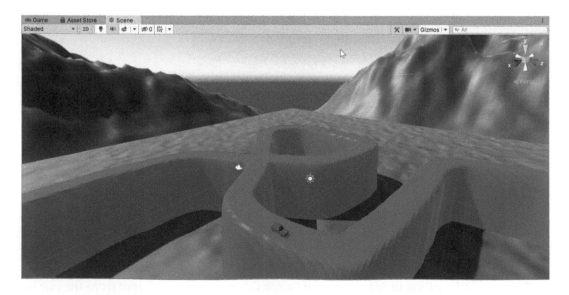

FIGURE 2.27 Terrain with a simple texture map, created in GIMP.

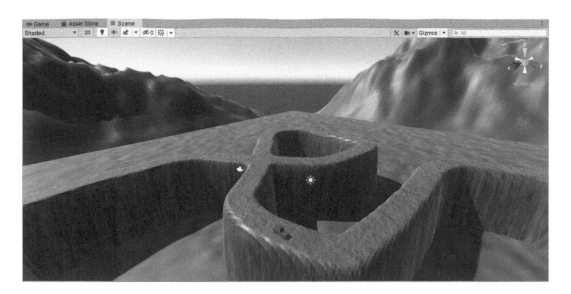

FIGURE 2.28 Applying the road texture.

FIGURE 2.29 Normals calculated in Unity resulting in better lighting and smoother track mesh.

<Step 42> File – Save to save the scene.

Unity has separate save systems for projects and the scenes associated with the project. This can be confusing at first. For now, simply save the Scene, which automatically saves everything, including the project. That feels backwards somehow, but that's how Unity does it. For a more detailed explanation, please refer to "Saving your Work" in the Unity Manual. Go to the Unity documentation for 2020.3 and search for "Saving your Work" to find the relevant manual section.

IMPROVING THE CAR

In this section you'll use Blender to improve the toycar.

<Step 1> **Launch Blender** and **load toycar.blend**.

You can leave Unity running while you're doing this.

<Step 2> **Rename** the **Cube** to **carmodel**.

To do this, **double-click** Cube in the outliner and then type **carmodel<return>**.

Note that renaming works differently in Blender when compared to Unity.

<Step 3> **File – Save**.

<Step 4> **Minimize Blender**, then **open** the Unity project.

You'll now see that the Cube is called carmodel in Unity. The extra light and camera are still there. You now have both Blender and Unity open simultaneously. This can be very useful. Let's try removing the light in Blender.

<Step 5> In Blender, **delete** the **light**, **save**, and look at the project in Unity.

Amazingly, this works. You don't have to tell Unity to reimport. It just automatically detects that a newer version showed up in the folder and reimports. The toycar object now has only two child objects: camera and carmodel.

Now you might think that it would be a good idea to delete the Blender camera as well. It turns out that this would change the export process with the effect of rotating the car. So, it's best to just leave the camera there. If you try to delete the camera in Unity, you'll get a very strange error message. You're just going to follow the age-old adage: If it ain't broke, don't fix it!

<Step 6> In Unity, do **File – Save**. Then **minimize** the Unity window.

You're going to go back to Unity soon enough, so it's OK to just leave it running. This is much faster than exiting Unity and then starting it up later. If you have two monitors, you can skip the minimizing and just leave both windows on separate monitors.

<Step 7> Back in Blender, go to the **Modeling** Workspace.

You're going to make that car look a little more detailed, and with multiple colors. You're also going to fix the wheels so that they no longer look like steamrollers.

<Step 8> **Select** the **toycar**, then type **<tab>** if necessary to go to **Edit** Mode.

<Step 9> **Turn on X-Ray** and **select wireframe viewport shading**.

<Step 10> Choose **edge select** mode and type **<numpad>7** to go to top ortho view.

<Step 11> **Box select** the top wheel cylinder, then **hold <shift>** and **box select** the bottom wheel cylinder.

Your screen should now look like Figure 2.30.

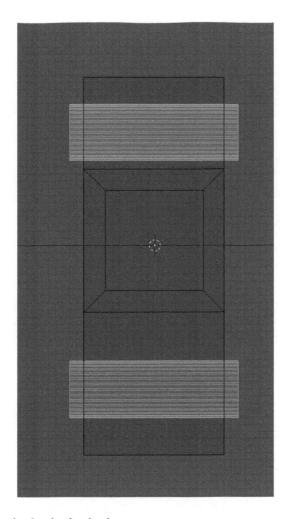

FIGURE 2.30   Selecting both wheel cylinders.

<Step 12> Type the **<delete>** key and **select Edges** in the pop-up panel.

You just removed the wheels because you're now going to redo them in a better way. Your plan is to create a wheel and use it to carve a wheel well in the car body, and then shrink the wheel to fit the wheel well. After all that you'll repeat the process for the other wheels.

<Step 13> **<tab>** to go to Object Mode, **<shift>A – Mesh – Cylinder**.

You now have two separate objects in the 3D view.

<Step 14> **Rename** the **Cylinder** to **wheel** in the outliner.

<Step 15> **Hover** the mouse in the 3D viewport, then **ry90<enter> sx0.4<enter>**

You now have something that looks like a wheel, but it's too large.

<Step 16> **s0.5<enter>**

<Step 17> **<numpad>3** and compare with Figure 2.31.

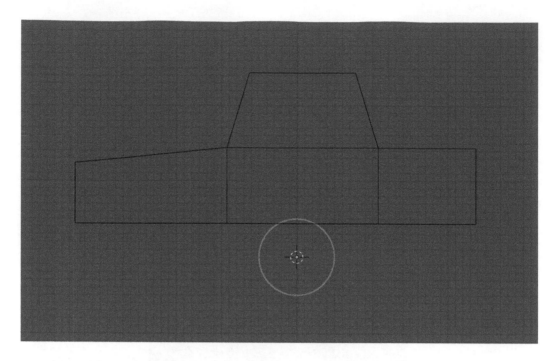

FIGURE 2.31   Car with wheel.

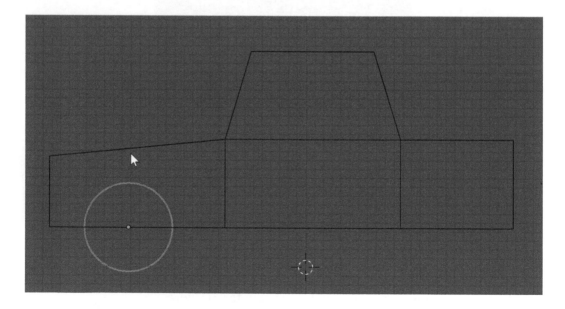

FIGURE 2.32   Car with wheel in front.

<Step 18> **Type g** and **move** the **wheel** to the front as shown in Figure 2.32.

<Step 19> **<numpad>7 gx** and move the wheel to the right as shown in Figure 2.33.

<Step 20> **Select** the **carmodel, Add Modifier – Boolean**
     The Boolean modifier will be used to make the wheel wells.

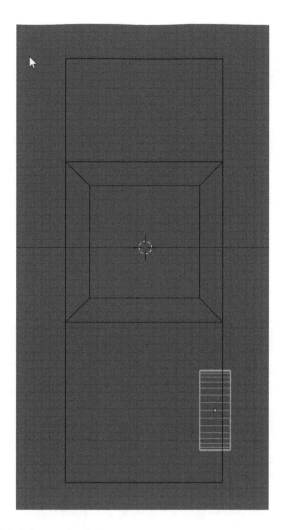

FIGURE 2.33   Car with left front wheel in position.

<Step 21> **Select Difference, click** on **Object** (not the Object Type), and **select wheel** (your only choice). Compare with Figure 2.34.

First, you're going to test if this modifier worked to your satisfaction. The easiest way is to apply the modifier, move the wheel out of the way, then rotate the carmodel to look at the result.

<Step 22> **Apply** the modifier, **select** the **wheel, move** it to the right with **gx**, then **rotate** the scene with the middle mouse button. **Toggle X-Ray** and compare with Figure 2.35.

<Step 23> Make three more wheel-wells using the Boolean modifier. Look at the car from below and compare with Figure 2.36.

Next, you're going to make a better wheel and put it into position. After that you'll copy the wheel. That way you end up with four wheels.

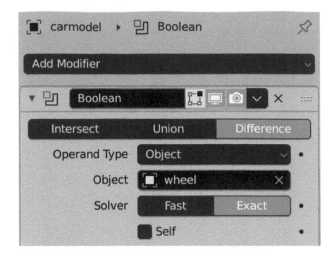

FIGURE 2.34   The Boolean modifier.

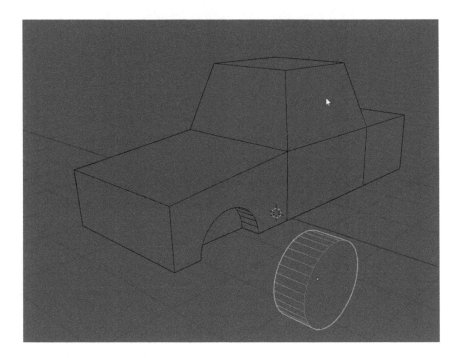

FIGURE 2.35   The effect of the Boolean modifier.

<Step 24> Select the **wheel, <numpad>7, turn on X-Ray** and line it up with the top right wheel well.

<Step 25> <numpad>3 and then **s<shift>X0.8<enter>**
The <shift>X restricts the scale command to just the y-z coordinate plane. In other words, the scale doesn't apply to the x-axis. This makes the wheel a little smaller so that it fits into the wheel well.

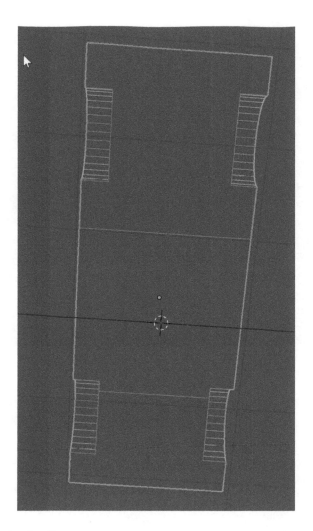

FIGURE 2.36   Four wheel wells.

\<Step 26\> **\<numpad\>7**, then **move** the wheel out slightly to separate it from the carbody.

> You're going to add some detail to the wheel before duplicating it.

\<Step 27\> **\<tab\>** to go into edit mode. **Turn off X-ray. \<numpad\>3, face select**, and **select** the outer face of the wheel.

\<Step 28\> **i0.2\<enter\>e-0.1\<enter\>**

\<Step 29\> **Rotate** the scene to look at your wheel. Compare with Figure 2.37.

\<Step 30\> Use the **top view**, use **object mode, duplicate**, and **move** the **duplicate wheels** to get **four** wheels in position.

> Hint: you'll have to rotate the wheel duplicates by 180 degrees on the z-axis at some point.

\<Step 31\> Adjust the front and back of the car to match Figure 2.38.

FIGURE 2.37 **A better wheel.**

FIGURE 2.38 Toycar with improved front and back.

<Step 32> **Edit Mode, face select, select** one of the car windows.

<Step 33> **i0.05<enter>e-0.05<enter>**

These are the inset and extrude commands. You're doing this to add detail to the windows.

<Step 34> **Repeat** for the other three car windows.

FIGURE 2.39   Final model for toycar.

You are now done with modeling for the car, finally. Along the way you got much more familiar with Blender. You only used a few of the commands but you made quite a bit of progress.

<Step 35> Try out the different Viewport Shading settings and rotate the view to look at your creation from all angles. Compare with Figure 2.39.

You could add much more detail to this low poly model and still call it low poly. For your purposes here this is more than adequate.

<Step 36> **Save**.

<Step 37> Switch over to **Unity** and look at the new car model there. **Select** the **toycar** object and type **f.** Compare with Figure 2.40.

As you can see, the wheels are now white because they are separate objects, and no material has been assigned to them. You also notice that the wheels don't look smooth enough.

<Step 38> Back in **Blender**, in **object mode**, **select** all the wheels, then **right-click** in the 3D editor and **select Shade Smooth**.

The wheels now look more like rubbery tires, which is what you want.

<Step 39> **Save** in Blender, **exit Blender** and switch to **Unity**.

That worked. Now the tires, though they are still white, are also shaded smoothly in Unity. You closed Blender because you won't be using it for a while.

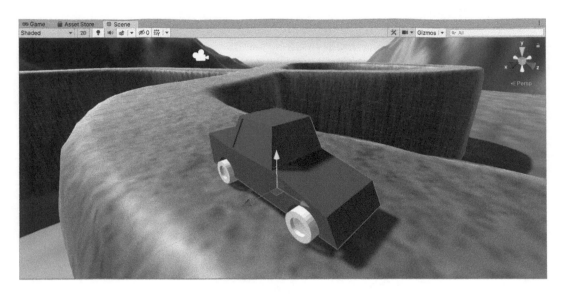

FIGURE 2.40   Updated model for toycar.

<Step 40> Make a **dark grey material** in the **Art** folder, call it **tiremat**, and **assign** to
each of the four wheels.

You've spent enough time on this model. Those windows should really be
grey, but you'll live with that and move on.

<Step 41> **Save.**

In the next section you'll introduce gameplay into your Unity scene.

GAMEPLAY

Your goal in this section is to move the toycar on the track, and have it fall off the track and
drop down below if the player steers the car off the track.

<Step 1> In Unity, **press play**, that icon shaped like a triangle at the middle top of the
Unity window. Compare with Figure 2.41.

That's not what you expected. You thought you would see the view from the
Main Camera when pressing play. It turns out that there are other cameras
hiding in this scene, and one of them, the one associated with the track, is
taking priority.

<Step 2> **Press Play** again to stop play mode.

<Step 3> **Select Main Camera** in the hierarchy panel and look at the small camera
popup as shown in Figure 2.42.

<Step 4> Find the other cameras in the hierarchy and **select** them, one at a time.

If you expand the track and the four terrain objects, you'll see that all of
these objects have child cameras. Those cameras got imported from Blender.
You're going to turn off their import since you won't be needing them.

FIGURE 2.41   Why are you seeing the scene from so far away?

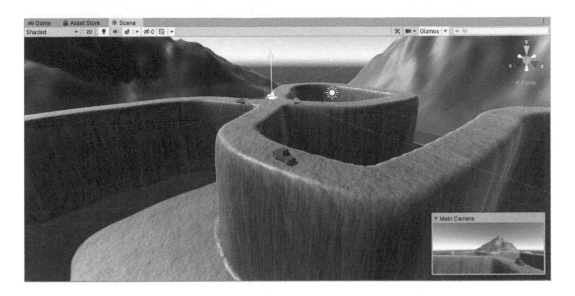

FIGURE 2.42   Camera pop-op for main camera.

<Step 5> In the import settings for the **track** and the **terrain** assets, **turn off Import Cameras** and **Import Lights** in the inspector. Be sure to **Apply** those changes.

<Step 6> In **scene** panel, **select** the **main camera**, and **move** it so that it is behind the car as shown in Figure 2.43.

<Step 7> When you **press Play** now you'll get the main camera view. **Press Play** again to stop play mode.

FIGURE 2.43   The main camera behind the car.

Play mode is a wonderful thing, but it can be dangerous. The problem is that Unity allows you to experiment in play mode by making temporary changes. You have no way of saving changes made in play mode, and when you finally stop it all those changes are lost. To avoid this potentially unwanted situation do Maximize on Play as follows:

<Step 7> **Play** again, click on the **Maximize On Play** button at the top right of the play panel, then **stop Play**, followed by **pressing Play** yet again.

Be sure to have the "Maximize on Play" setting turned on except when you're in experimental mode and aware that your changes will be lost during play mode.

<Step 8> Toggle play mode by typing **<ctrl>p**.

This shortcut is worth remembering because you'll be doing this a lot.

<Step 9> **Click** on the **Game** tab, the one that looks like a controller with the text label Game.

You're now looking at the view from the main camera. You are not in play mode.

<Step 10> **Select** the **Main Camera** and in the inspector, **drag** the letter **X** in the **Rotation** section. **Drag** the **Y Position** as well and adjust the camera to a good over-the-shoulder view.

The X rotation will likely be about 10 degrees. Your goal is to set up the Main Camera at a good initial configuration when starting the game.

Now it's time to add controls and physics to this game. You'll start by lifting the car up.

<Step 11> **Click** on the **Scene** tab to get back to your usual Scene view.

<Step 12> Do a **frame selected** for the toycar object and lift it up about 1.5 units.

<Step 13> **Play** then **stop Play**.

Nothing happened. The toycar is floating in air. You're now going to add physics so that the car drops down.

<Step 14> With the toycar still selected, **click** on **Add Component** in the inspector. Clear the search field if necessary. Then **click** on **Physics – Rigidbody. Set Mass to 0.3. Test** (Play, observe, stop Play).

This time the car fell down, right through the track. It's a start. You're missing collision detection. No, you won't have to write collision detection code, as was the case in the good old days. You'll just add collider components for the track and the toycar.

<Step 15> **Select** the **carmodel** child object of toycar.

<Step 16> In the inspector, **click** on **Add Component**, then **Physics – Box Collider.**

<Step 17> **Select** all four wheels in the hierarchy.

You do this by **selecting** one wheel, then you **<ctrl>select** each of the other three wheels. If the wheels are next to each other, you can select the top wheel and <shift>select the bottom wheel in the hierarchy list, which automatically selects everything in between.

<Step 18> In the inspector, **add** a **Box Collider component** as you did earlier.

That's right, you can add components to multiple objects simultaneously. And yes, a box collider for each wheel may seem wrong, but for this game it's what works.

<Step 19> **Select** the **track** object in the hierarchy, expand, and **select** the **Track** child object.

<Step 20> In the inspector, **Add Component**, and then do **Physics – Mesh Collider.**

The track is a complex object, so you need to have a mesh collider rather than a box collider for it. Mesh colliders are expensive, so you'll want to only use them where necessary.

<Step 21> **Test**.

The car drops down and stops on the track. That's what you wanted.

<Step 22> In the inspector, adjust the Y-position of the toycar so that it is on the track, then **test**.

The time has finally come for you to try and control that toycar. You'll do a very simple control scheme. You steer left or right with the arrow keys and assign the <spacebar> key to the gas pedal. Maybe you'll add a brake later. You'll start with steering.

<Step 23> In the Assets folder, **double-click** on **Scripts**, and then **right-click Create – C# Script**. Immediately type the new name for this script: **toycarscript<return>**.

<Step 24> **Select** the **toycar** object in the hierarchy, then **drag** the **toycarscript** on top of it.

The inspector shows a new component for toycar: the toycarscript.

Notice that the inspector capitalizes the script name, but this is just cosmetic and doesn't change the name, as you will see in the next step.

<Step 25> **Double-click** on toycarscript in the **Scripts** folder. If prompted, choose Microsoft Visual Studio 2019 as the editor. Wait a little while and then look at the new Visual Studio window.

You will see the initial script as created by Unity. Compare with Figure 2.44.

As you can see, the name of the class in the script is still lower case: toycarscript. The class has two members, Start and Update, both empty. This script does nothing. You may wish to check that by testing the game. Your next goal is for the script to rotate the car in response to the arrow keys.

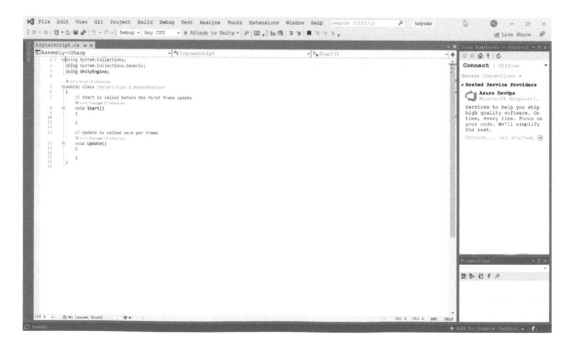

FIGURE 2.44   Visual studio displaying the Unity default script for toycar.

<Step 26> Replace the toycarscript class with this code:

```
public class toycarscript : MonoBehaviour
{
    void FixedUpdate()
    {
        Rigidbody rigidb = GetComponent<Rigidbody>();

        if (Input.GetKey("right"))
        {
            transform.Rotate(Vector3.up, 0.5f);
        }
        if (Input.GetKey("left"))
        {
            transform.Rotate(Vector3.up, -0.5f);
        }
    }
}
```

You're using `FixedUpdate` instead of `Update` because you want the calculations to happen at fixed intervals rather than every frame. This will, hopefully, make this code work on different systems regardless of their frame rates.

As you type this into Visual Studio you will notice that the colors will be set automatically, and the editor will try to help you out with smart completion. Often, you won't have to type everything, but just enough letters to tell Visual Studio what you had in mind. For example, you only need to type tr<return>R<return> to enter transform.Rotate.

There's a chance that, due to the way you installed Unity and Visual Studio, that code completion won't work for you. To fix this, do **Edit – Preferences… External Tools – External Script Editor** and select **Visual Studio Community 2019.** Then restart Unity and try again.

<Step 27> **<ctrl>s** in Visual Studio to save your edits.

You will be doing this a lot. No, Visual Studio doesn't automatically save your edits, so you'll have to remember to manually save in Visual Studio before testing your changes in Unity. And yes, you *will* forget to save, and wonder why your changes didn't work. It helps to know that if you have unsaved changes in a file in Visual Studio, you'll see an asterisk next to the file name. When you save, the asterisk disappears.

<Step 28> **Click** on the Unity window to bring focus back to it. This loads the new script. Then **test**.

You can now rotate the car using the left and right arrow keys.

<Step 29> Insert the following code at the end of the Update function:

```
if (Input.GetKey("space"))
{
    if (rigidb)
        rigidb.AddForce(
            10.0f *
            (transform.rotation * Vector3.forward)
        );
}
```

That factor of 10.0f is an experimental power factor related to the car's engine. You may need to change this factor on your system.

<Step 30> Insert the following line of code before the first GetKey call:

```
rigidb.freezeRotation = true;
```

No, this doesn't freeze your ability to steer, but it keeps the car from tumbling out of control.

<Step 31> Save with **<ctrl>s** in Visual Studio, then **test** in Unity.

You can now drive the car, but the camera isn't following yet. The following code will do that:

<Step 32> Create a script with the name **camerascript** in the Scripts folder. **Drag** the script onto **Main Camera**. Then enter this code for the camerascript class:

```
public class camerascript : MonoBehaviour
{
    Vector3 camoffset;
    // Start is called before the first frame update
    void Start()
    {
        camoffset =
        transform.position -
        GameObject.FindGameObjectWithTag("Player").transform.position;
    }

    // Update is called once per frame
    void Update()
    {
        transform.position =
        GameObject.FindGameObjectWithTag("Player").transform.position
        + camoffset;
    }
}
```

This code moves the camera to a position in the back and up relative to the car.

<Step 33> **Save** in Visual Studio and **test** in Unity.

No, it doesn't work yet. You will have to add a tag to the toycar as follows:

<Step 34> **Select toycar** and in the inspector, **select** the tag **Player** in the Tag dropdown.

<Step 35> **Test**.

You now have a game, in a manner of speaking. It's not easy, nor fun, but you can drive the car around the track while carefully avoiding falling off the track. Can you complete a lap? If you have trouble, you may want to reduce the power factor in the toycarscript and try again.

<Step 36> **Save** in Unity and **exit** Unity. Also exit Visual Studio, if necessary.

In the next section you'll create some additional game objects: low-poly buildings.

CREATING BUILDINGS WITH THE ARRAY MODIFIER

In this section you'll make two low poly buildings to add to your game world and make it more interesting.

<Step 1> **Launch** Blender, and **save** a file called **building.blend** in the usual **Art** folder.
You will use box modeling to make a building.

<Step 2> **Select** the **default cube**, then **type gz1<enter>**.

<Step 3> **Modeling** workspace, **face select, select top face, gz-1.3<enter>**.

<Step 4> **Select** the **front left face** and **type gy-1<enter>**.
You just created a box that will serve as the bottom floor of your building. Compare with Figure 2.45.

<Step 5> **Zoom** closer to the building.

<Step 6> **Select** the **Loop Cut icon** on the left side of the screen.

<Step 7> **Change** the **Number of Cuts** from **1** to **8** in the dialog at the top left.

<Step 8> **Enter** three loop cuts, one in each direction, as shown in Figure 2.46.
These loop cuts create extra geometry to help you put in windows and doors. You're not going to worry about inefficiency here. Your 3D hardware can easily handle it.

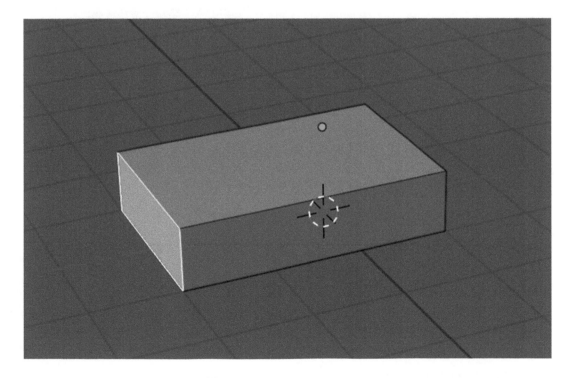

FIGURE 2.45   Bottom floor of building.

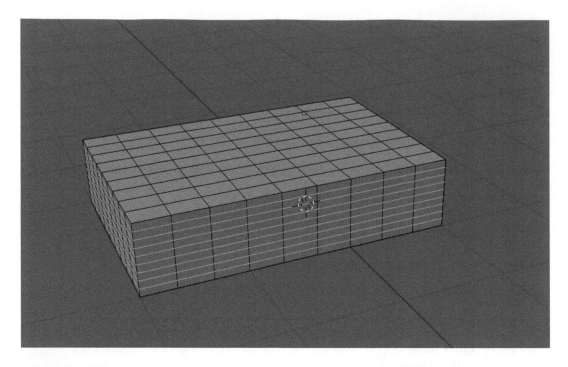

FIGURE 2.46   **Loop cuts**

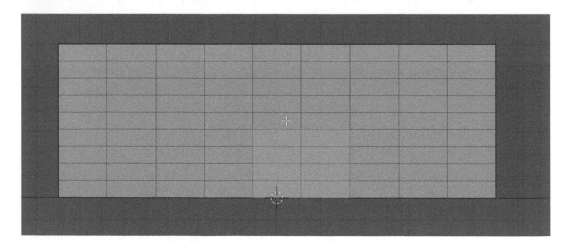

FIGURE 2.47   Box selecting eight rectangles to form the outline of a door.

<Step 9> Go to the front orthographic view with **<numpad>1** and **zoom in** with the scroll wheel.

<Step 10> **Face Select. Select** a door by selecting **eight rectangles** as shown in Figure 2.47.
You do this by choosing the Select Box icon at the top left, then box selecting the eight rectangles using face select mode.

<Step 11> **Type i0.03<enter>.**

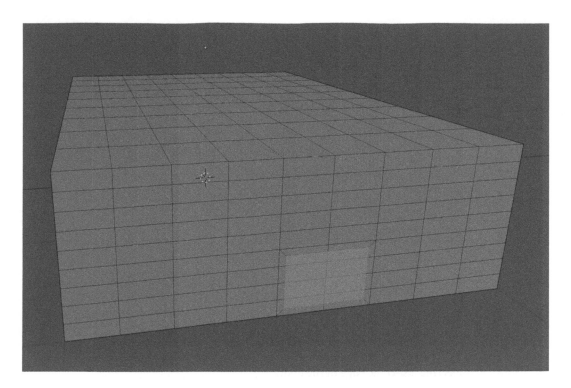

FIGURE 2.48   Result of inset faces command.

<Step 12> **Middle Mouse drag** the view down a little bit to match Figure 2.48.

<Step 13> With the eight central faces still selected, type **gy0.02<enter>**. Then **e-0.04<enter>**.

<Step 14> **<numpad>1** to go back to the front ortho view. **Edge Select, Turn on X-Ray, zoom** in on the door, and **box-select** the **edges** shown in Figure 2.49.
Yes, that looks like a single edge, but you actually selected seven edges. Take a look at your selection from another angle, if you wish, but then go back to the front ortho view.

<Step 15> Type **gz, move the mouse down** and **click** to bring the edge almost to the bottom. You just completed a door. The next step is actually a bunch of steps.

<Step 16> Add three windows near the front door as shown in Figure 2.50. Turn off X-ray first.
This is a good time to save your work.

<Step 17> **Save**.

<Step 18> Make a balcony for the level above by **extruding** as shown in Figure 2.51.

<Step 19> Add some windows to the other three sides of this floor. You can decide how many. Use the inset and extrude method that you used for the other windows. You can do insets and extrudes for multiple windows at a time.

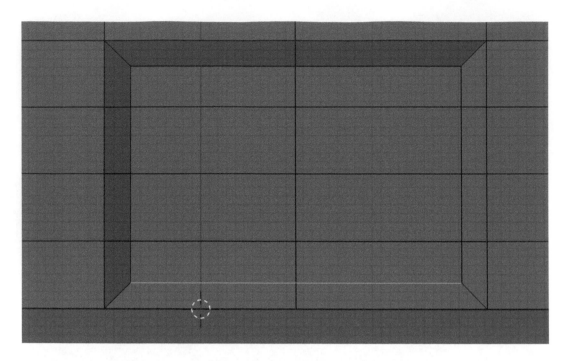

FIGURE 2.49 Selecting a specific edge of the door.

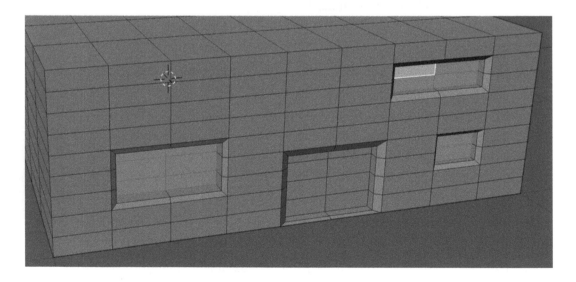

FIGURE 2.50 Three windows and a door.

<Step 20> Go to the **Layout** workspace and examine your model. It should look somewhat like Figure 2.52.

You're now ready to stack floors on top of one another. You can do this with the array modifier.

<Step 21> **Rename** the **cube** to **buildinglevel** in the outliner panel at the top right.

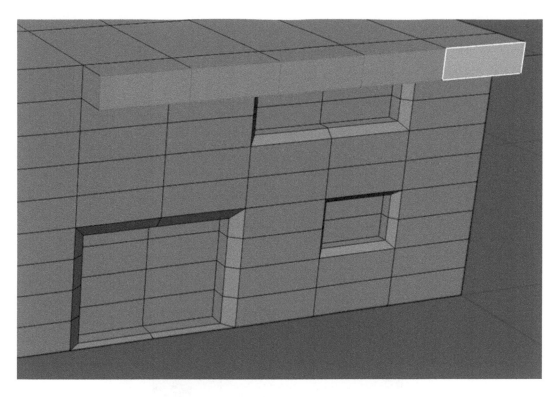

FIGURE 2.51   Making a balcony.

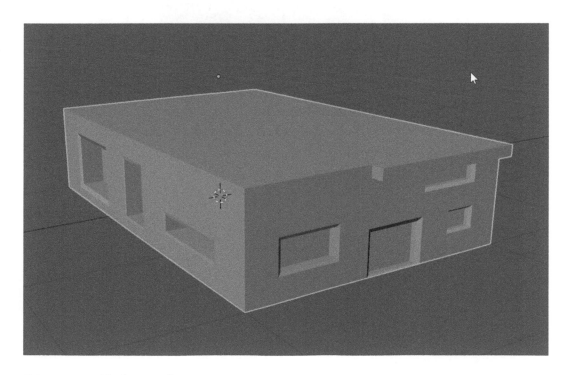

FIGURE 2.52   The bottom floor.

<Step 22> **Click** on the Modifier icon, the eighth icon from the top in the properties panel. Then **click** on **Add Modifier** and select **Array**.

<Step 23> **Change** the Factor to X=**0.000**, Y=**0.000**, Z=**1.000**.

<Step 24> **Change** the count to **10** and zoom out. Compare with Figure 2.53.

<Step 25> **File – Save**.

<Step 26> **Change** the **Count** to **5** in the Properties. Then add a second array modifier. Use the defaults.
You now have a wider five-story building.

<Step 27> **File – Save As** with the name **buildingwide**.

<Step 28> **Exit Blender**.

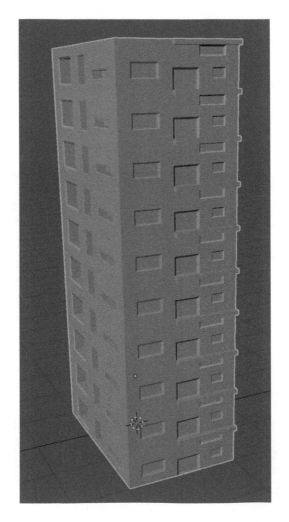

FIGURE 2.53   A ten-story building.

<Step 29> In **Unity**, find the buildings in the Art folder and **select** one of them. **Turn off Import Cameras** and **Import Lighting** for it, **apply**, and then do the same for the other building.

<Step 30> **Drag the buildings** into the hierarchy and move them so they don't conflict with the track.

      The buildings are too small, so do this:

<Step 31> **Select** a building in the Art folder, change the **scale** factor in the inspector to **2**, **apply**, and do the same for the other building.

<Step 32> **Move** the **buildings down** and adjust their positions to look like Figure 2.54.

<Step 33> **Test**. Try to move the car so you can see the buildings as you drive by. Compare with Figure 2.55.

<Step 34> **Save**.

It's looking pretty good now. If this were a real product, this would be a very early prototype, something to show basic gameplay. There is, of course, lots of room for improvement. Here's a list:

- The car has red windows, they should at least be grey, or maybe transparent.

- The feel of driving the toycar is very wrong. Yes, it works, but it's not at all realistic.

- The toycar should tumble and crash when falling off the track.

- There's no sound at all.

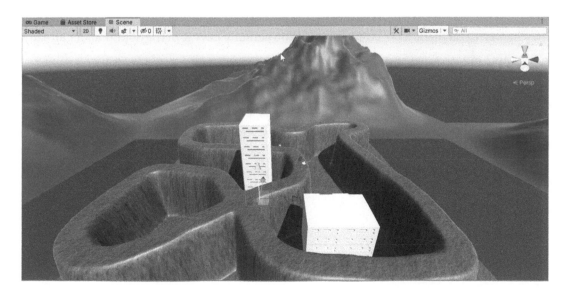

FIGURE 2.54 Buildings in Unity.

FIGURE 2.55   Looking at the tall building while driving by.

- There is no game structure such as starting the game, scoring, a game over message, etc.

- There should be a timer for the race.

- Where are the other cars for you to race against?

You're not going to do all that. This chapter is getting way too long as it is. But you made a game engine sound effect for this game in Chapter 1, and it'll be very easy to put it in and have it respond to the speed of the toycar.

SOUND

In Chapter 1 you made a car engine sound. You actually have it in the Sound folder already.

<Step 1> In the project panel at the bottom, go to Assets/Sound.
You should see the toycarsound asset as the only asset in the Sound folder.

<Step 2> Look at the import settings in the inspector. **Click** on the **Play** icon near the bottom of the inspector above the waveform and listen to the sound.
This is to test that the import is working. If you don't hear anything, chances are that your speakers aren't on for your system, or maybe you have zero volume. Test this by going to your browser and playing a video with sound, for example.

<Step 3> **Test**.
That's right, there's no sound when playing the game right now. Why is that? Yes, you need to bring the sound into the scene.

<Step 4> **Drag toycarsound** into the **hierarchy** and look at it in the inspector.

There you will see the Audio Source component for toycarsound. It's that component that will make the sound in the game.

<Step 5> In the inspector **check Play on Awake** and **Loop**.

The Play on Awake will start the sound when the scene starts running. If you don't have Loop checked then the sound will just play once and then stop.

<Step 6> **Test**.

This is, of course, very wrong. What you want is to have the engine sound for the car respond to the movement of the car. A simple and cheap way to do this is with the following script:

<Step 7> **Add** the following script, called **soundtest**, to the toycarsound object:

```
using System.Collections;
using System.Collections.Generic;
using UnityEngine;

public class soundtest : MonoBehaviour
{
    AudioSource m_source;
    Rigidbody rb;
    // Start is called before the first frame update
    void Start()
    {
        m_source = GetComponent<AudioSource>();
    }

    // Update is called once per frame
    void Update()
    {
        rb = GameObject.FindGameObjectWithTag("Player").
            GetComponent<Rigidbody>();
        m_source.volume = 0.3f * rb.velocity.magnitude;
    }
}
```

This code needs some explanation. In the Start method you obtain the AudioSource component. In the Update function you get the rigid body component of the player, which then allows you to get the speed, i.e., the magnitude of the velocity vector. The 0.3 is an experimental factor that translates the speed to the volume of the engine sound.

One more thing: the rb calculation is spread out over two lines for the purposes of printing this code in this book. It can all fit on a single line inside of Visual Studio.

<Step 8> **Test**.

That works, but you'd like a sound for an idle engine, so do the following:

<Step 9> At the end of the Update function, add the following line:

```
m_source.volume += 0.2f;
```

This line adds a base level of volume so that you'll always hear the engine.

<Step 10> **Test** and **save**.

You've done enough for this prototype. There's much more that could be done to improve the sound, but it's good enough for getting a taste of what it's like to work on sound effects in a Unity game.

In the next chapter you'll take a closer look at the 3D concepts used in game development.

CHAPTER 3

3D

I N THIS CHAPTER YOU'LL explore various 3D aspects of game development. First, there's the basics of 3D coordinate systems. Then, you'll look at how Blender and Unity deal with 3D mathematical concepts. You'll learn about cameras, both in Unity and Blender, and then you'll take a closer look at 3D assets.

Thousands of books have been written about 3D math, so this chapter will necessarily cover just some of the basic concepts. If you're ambitious, look at gamemath.com. There you get free access to the book *3D Math Primer for Graphics and Game Development, 2nd Edition* (Fletcher Dunn, 2011, CRC press). The word "primer" is a bit of an understatement since the book is 850 pages long! No, you don't need to know everything in that book to develop 3D games, but it's a good reference if needed. With Blender and Unity doing much of the difficult work for you, you'll do just fine with the basics.

3D COORDINATES

It all started with René Descartes (1596–1650), the famous philosopher, mathematician, and scientist. Descartes is best known for these three Latin words: cogito ergo sum, in English: I think therefore I am. This raises the question: do video game characters think, and if so, do they exist? You'll get to that question later. Meanwhile you're getting oriented in the artificial 3D worlds inside of Unity and Blender, and it all depends on 3D coordinates.

Descartes' 3D coordinate system locates points in space by listing three numbers, the x, y, and z coordinates. A good way to better understand 3D coordinates is to create a box in Blender and look at the coordinates of the corners.

<Step 1> **Launch** Blender. **Select** the default **cube**.
Next, you'll move the default cube forward, up, and to the right.

<Step 2> Type **gx1<enter>gy1<enter>gz1<enter>**.
This moves the cube so one of the corners coincides with the origin of the coordinate system.

<Step 3> **Modeling** workspace.

DOI: 10.1201/9780429328725-4

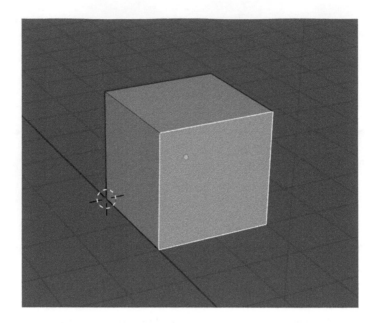

FIGURE 3.1   Selecting the front face of the default cube.

<Step 4> **Choose face select** mode.

<Step 5> **Select** the **front face** as shown in Figure 3.1.

<Step 6> Type **gx1<enter>**.
This stretches the cube forward.

<Step 7> **Select** the **top face**. Then type **gz-1<enter>**.
This squashes the cube down by 1 meter. Yes, that's a minus one.

<Step 8> Type **n**, a mnemonic for "numbers," to show the properties panel.
The n key toggles the display of the properties panel.

<Step 9> **Vertex select** mode, then **select** the vertex that is farthest from the origin.
This is the upper vertex of the right-most edge of the cube.

<Step 10> In the Properties panel, **select Global**.
Compare your screen with Figure 3.2.
Look at the X, Y, Z coordinates of the Vertex in the Properties panel. One way to think of this is to take an imaginary walk toward the vertex, starting at the origin. Move 3 meters along the x-axis, 2 meters along the y-axis, then jump 1 meter up along the z-axis. You arrive at your goal, the vertex with coordinates (3,2,1).

<Step 11> In the Properties panel, change the X, Y, and Z coordinates of the Vertex and observe the result. Then **type <ctrl>z** to undo. Also, select a few other vertices, determine the 3D coordinates, and then check your answer in the Properties panel.

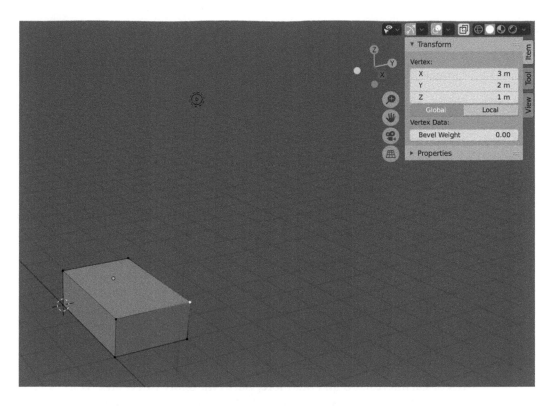

FIGURE 3.2 Selecting a vertex of the default cube.

<Step 12> In turn, **type <numpad>1**, **<numpad>7**, and **<numpad>3** and look at the result.

In the top view you'll see the x and y coordinates, In the front view the x and z coordinates, and in the right view the y and z coordinates.

<Step 13> Exit Blender, and don't bother to save.

You are now ready to do an optional side quest. Search the web for "Vector Math Tutorial for 3D Computer Graphics." At chortle.ccsu.edu you'll find the Fourth Revision of this tutorial, dated July 2009. Take a look at the table of contents, and work through some or all of the 16 chapters. You may know this content from a linear algebra course, or an analytic geometry course. Yes, it's OK to skip this, or to work through it at your own pace on the side.

In the next section you'll take a closer look at 3D in Blender.

3D IN BLENDER

In the previous section you examined the 3D coordinates of vertices in Blender.

As an aside, the proper usage is "vertex" for a single point, and "vertices" for multiple points. You'll sometimes encounter the non-word "vertice" as an invalid alternative to "vertex." Don't write or say "vertice," it's not a word!

Blender is a vast program. You will be using Blender to make 3D objects and animations, ready for export to Unity. You may benefit by exploring the 2D parts of Blender, such as the recently improved grease pencil features, for example. In this section you'll look at some of the 3D concepts used in Blender.

<Step 1> **Launch** Blender, **delete** the default **cube**.

<Step 2> **Create** all the built-in default meshes by typing **<shift>A – Mesh** and then **clicking** on every one of the meshes, one by one. Then arrange them in the scene somehow. Compare with Figure 3.3.

Blender can create additional meshes using add-ons. You'll try that next.

<Step 3> **File – New – General**, and once again **delete** the default **cube**.

<Step 4> **Edit – Preferences – Add-ons**. Select "**Community**" if necessary. Then enable the "**Add Mesh: Extra Objects**" add-on. Close the pop-up.

<Step 5> **<shift>A – Mesh – Extras – Teapot+** and compare with Figure 3.4.

<Step 6> **Expand** the "**Add Teapot**" menu at the bottom left, and then **drag** the **Resolution** with the mouse to look at the different available resolutions for the Teapot, ranging from 2 to 15.

This is an example of a *procedurally generated* mesh. Feel free to explore the many other add-ons and meshes available in Blender. This teapot is here for historical interest. To find out more, watch the short video "The World's Most Famous Teapot: The Utah Teapot." It's also a great example of how one page

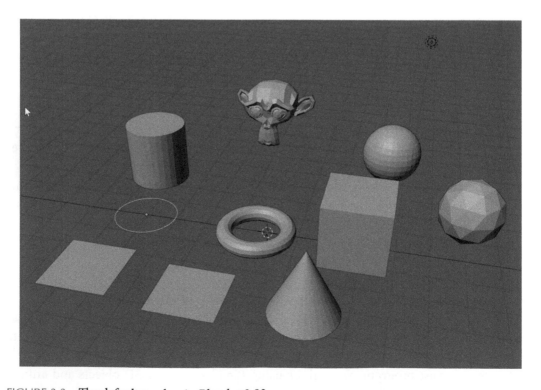

FIGURE 3.3 The default meshes in Blender 2.92.

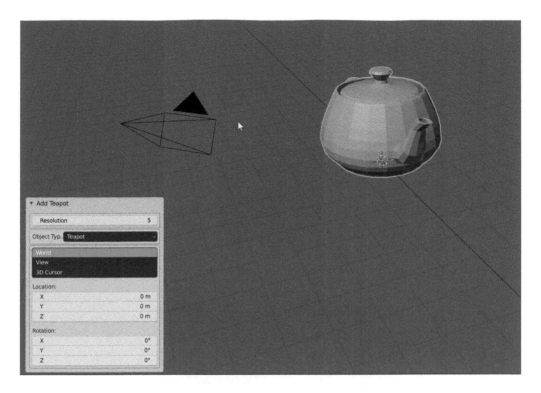

FIGURE 3.4   Teapot generated in Blender.

of numbers can describe a realistic-looking teapot. Those numbers are the 3D coordinates that you just learned about in the previous section.

Moving on, you'll take a closer look at the three axes used in Blender.

<Step 7>   **File – New – General** and look at the top right axis gizmos as shown in Figure 3.5.

There, you can see the three axes: x in red, y in green, and z in blue. In the 3D viewport, you can also see a long red line, the actual x axis, and perpendicular to it a long green line, the y axis. The z axis is not getting displayed, by default.

<Step 8>   To turn on the z axis overlay display, **click** on the **Overlay drop-down menu** as shown in Figure 3.6 and **click** on Z.

You can now see a vertical blue line. This setting isn't permanent, so if you leave Blender and start it up again the Z coordinate line will no longer be displayed.

Unfortunately for us, the coordinate systems of Blender and Unity differ. The Blender system is right-handed. When looking down using the Top Orthographic View, x goes to the right, y up, and z out at the viewer. In the default view, x points down, y to the right, and z up. This is the usual x-y-z coordinate system used in mathematics.

Unity, on the other hand uses a left-handed coordinate system, with x to the right, y up, and z away from the viewer. This is the coordinate system

FIGURE 3.5   Axes in Blender.

FIGURE 3.6   Viewport overlays in Blender.

commonly used in computer graphics. For more information about left- vs. right-handed coordinate systems in Unity and Blender, search the web.

<Step 9> **File – New – General**.

You're now going to continue to examine the gizmos located at the top right of the 3D Viewport.

<Step 10> Try out the zoom, hand, camera, and perspective gizmos.

The zoom gizmo simply moves the view in and out, similar to the mouse wheel, but smoother. The hand gizmo pans the view, just like

<shift><MMB>drag. The camera gizmo switches to the camera view, just like <numpad>0. Finally, the perspective gizmo switches between perspective and orthographic view.

Blender defaults to perspective view, which means that objects farther from the camera appear smaller than equally sized objects closer to the camera. You can also quickly see this effect when looking at the grid lines.

<Step 11> **Hover** the mouse over the **axis gizmo**. Note that a shaded circle appears. Then **left-click-drag** the mouse to rotate the view. Compare with MMB-drag. Both of these actions do the same thing.

<Step 12> **Hover** the mouse over each of the colored circles and note the keyboard shortcuts for them, and try them out, both with the gizmo and with the <numpad> keys.

You've been using <numpad>1, <numpad>3, and <numpad>7, so this is familiar territory. If you don't remember which <numpad> command is which, using the gizmos is a good alternative.

Finally, let's make an object in Blender and carefully follow its coordinates when it is exported to Unity.

<Step 13> **Delete** the default **cube**.

<Step 14> Create Suzanne, the default monkey like this: **<shift>A – Mesh – Monkey**.

<Step 15> Go to **Front Orthographic view**, **zoom** in on **Suzanne**, **edit mode**, **point select mode**, **select** top of the right ear (that's on the left from your viewpoint), type **n** and compare with Figure 3.7.

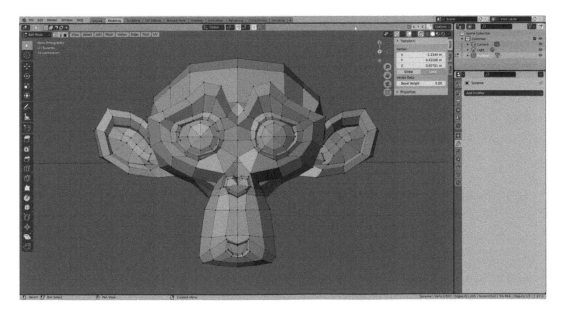

FIGURE 3.7   Suzanne.

You should see in the transform panel that the selected vertex is at (−1.2344, 0.42188, 0.50781). You will make a note of those coordinates and look at them in Unity later on.

<Step 16> **File – Save As…** Use the file name **Suzanne** in the **Art** folder for the toycar project as usual.

In the next section you'll look at how Unity deals with 3D.

3D IN UNITY

In the previous section you saved the built-in Suzanne model in a blend file and looked at one specific vertex on the right ear of Suzanne. You're now going to import Suzanne into Unity and check to see if the coordinates match.

<Step 1> **Create** a new Unity Project with the name **3Dtest**. Leave Blender open for now but minimize the window if you need it out of the way.

You just remembered that you put Suzanne into the toycar project, so do this:

<Step 2> **Move Suzanne.blend from toycar/Assets/Art to 3Dtest/Assets**.

You can do this in your operating system while leaving Blender and Unity running.

<Step 3> Back in Unity, notice that Suzanne has shown up in the Assets folder.

<Step 4> **Click on Suzanne** in the Assets folder. Look at the inspector panel.

The inspector, as usual, lists many options. You'll leave them alone for now.

<Step 5> **Drag Suzanne** into the **hierarchy** panel. Verify that the position and rotation are 0 in the inspector.

<Step 6> **Expand Suzanne** in the hierarchy and **select** the **Suzanne** child object. Note that the X Rotation is −89.98.

<Step 7> **Right-click** on the **coordinates gizmo** at the top right of the Scene Panel, **check Front** and **uncheck Perspective**. Type **f** to do a "frame selected" on the Suzanne child object. Compare with Figure 3.8.

Your goal was to match the view in Blender. Both views are looking at Suzanne from the front. Looking at the coordinates gizmos, Unity shows the x-axis pointing to the left, y-axis up, and the z-axis is missing. In Blender, x is to the right, z is up, and y is missing. To find the coordinates of the right ear point, do the following in Unity:

<Step 8> **GameObject – Create Empty. Move** the origin of this object to match the ear point as shown in Figure 3.9.

<Step 9> Look at the inspector.

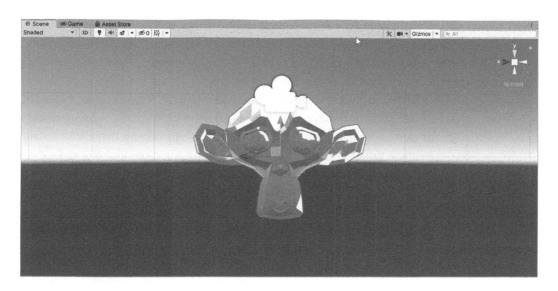

FIGURE 3.8   **Suzanne in Unity.**

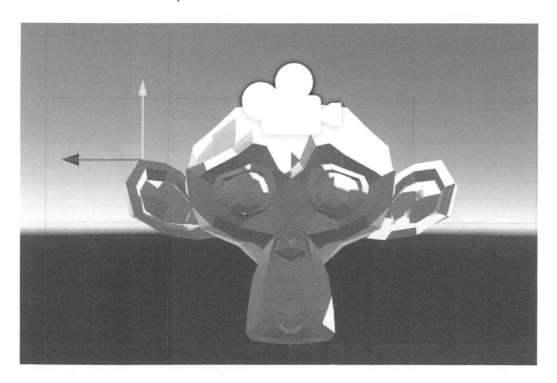

FIGURE 3.9   Empty GameObject lined up with Suzanne's ear.

There you find that in Unity, the coordinates of the GameObject are (1.213, 0.505, 0). Those numbers are close to the Blender coordinates of the ear point. That zero coordinate for z isn't right.

<Step 10> In Unity, **select** the **right orthographic view**, and **align** the empty GameObject with the top of the ear by sliding it along the z axis.

You should now get a z-coordinate close to −0.424. The final Unity coordinates are (1.213, 0.505, −0.424). When compared to the Blender coordinates, you can see that the sign is reversed for the x-coordinate, y and z are switched, and the z coordinate also has the sign reversed.

Why did you just go through this exercise? Well, it's important to realize that Blender and Unity have different 3D coordinate systems. When writing code for moving objects in the scene you'll be manipulating these coordinates, and it helps to know how the coordinate axes are arranged and aligned.

In the next section you'll examine the cameras in Blender and Unity.

CAMERA VIEWS

Cameras are virtual objects in the sense that you can't see them, neither in Blender nor in Unity, at least not in rendered scenes. In the next few steps you'll review your knowledge of basic Blender commands by building a simple scene featuring Suzanne.

\<Step 1\> In Blender, **create a new file**.

\<Step 2\> **Delete** the default **cube** and **create Suzanne**. **Move Suzanne** up by **1m**.

\<Step 3\> **Create** a **plane** with a size of **20m**.

\<Step 4\> **Move** the light to location **(3.8, −2.3, 3.7)**.

\<Step 5\> **Select rendered viewport shading**. Compare with Figure 3.10.
          You moved the light in front of Suzanne to improve the lighting and show the shadow.

FIGURE 3.10   A simple scene featuring Suzanne.

\<Step 6\> Go to the camera view by typing **\<numpad\>0** or clicking on the camera gizmo.

As usual, those numpad commands only work when the mouse is hovering in the 3D Viewport editor. Also, the Blender window needs to have focus. It's easy to just hover the mouse over an inactive Blender window and to then wonder why the keyboard shortcut command doesn't do anything. If you haven't done that yet, guess what, you will. Worse, that shortcut might end up typing into your Visual Studio window and corrupt your code. You have been warned!

This is a good time to review the concept of Blender editors. The Blender window always consists of several editors. You may think of them as panels or windows, but the official terminology is "editor." They aren't always easy to find when they are long and skinny. Know that the upper left corner of each editor has a dropdown which displays a cryptic icon, unique to that type of editor. Figure 3.11 highlights the four icons for the four editors currently operating in your Blender window.

\<Step 7\> Hover the mouse over each of the four editor icons and compare their names with this list:

- 3D Viewport

- Outliner

- Properties

- Timeline

This is the default editor setup for the Layout Workspace.

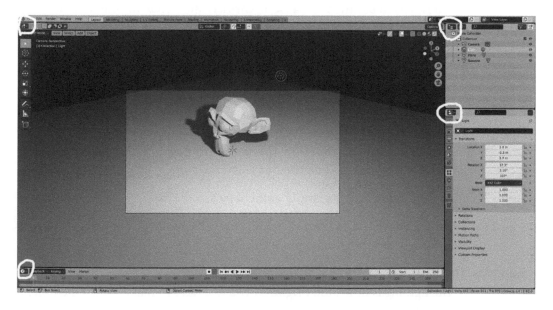

FIGURE 3.11   Four Blender editors.

<Step 8> Try out some of the other workspaces and examine the editors for them. Then come back to the Layout workspace.

This exercise doesn't do anything, but it's worth your time to get more familiar with Blender.

<Step 9> After this detour, **select** the **camera** in the **outliner** editor, then go to the **properties editor** and experiment with the location and rotation coordinates for the camera. Use **<ctrl>z** to undo your experiments.

This warrants some discussion. The X location for the camera starts at 7.3589m. You can drag that number left-right. As you increase and decrease this number the camera moves along the red x-axis. Similarly, the y location controls movement along the y-axis. It's the same for z. To get a better view, move the plane down a little to reveal the axes and grid below Suzanne.

The rotation settings are currently at (63.6, 0, 46.7). The x rotation turns the camera left-right, the y rotation twists the camera, and the z turns it up and down. In aircraft terminology, x is yaw, y is roll, and z is pitch. Although these coordinates have the names just like the coordinate axes, they are not 3D coordinates, but rather Euler angles, measured in degrees in Blender. Euler angles are named after the Swiss mathematician Leonhard Euler (1707–1783). Pronounce his last name oiler, just like the ex-Houston American football team. No, it's not "you-ler."

Euler angles are the default numbers used by Blender to describe 3D rotations. In computer graphics, quaternions are often a preferred method for describing rotations. You will encounter them in Unity when dealing with rotations of game objects. No, you don't really need to understand Quaternions to use them because all the necessary code for them has already been written for you in Unity.

Moving on, you will save your work and go to Unity

<Step 10> **File – Save As cameratest.blend** in 3Dtest/Assets.

<Step 11> **Exit** Blender.

<Step 12> **Open** the **3Dtest** project in Unity.

You still have the old Suzanne and the empty gameobject there, so you'll delete them as you won't be needing them anymore.

<Step 13> **Delete Suzanne** and the **empty gameobject** in the hierarchy.

<Step 14> **Select cameratest** in the Assets folder. You will import the lights and cameras, one of each, to look at them more closely in Unity.

<Step 15> **Drag cameratest** into the hierarchy.

The lighting is much too bright, so you will have to make some adjustments to see what's happening.

<Step 16> **Expand cameratest**.

You see that the imported light is there, plus you also have the default Unity directional light.

<Step 17> **Turn off** the **Directional Light**.

As usual, all you need to do is to uncheck it near the top of the inspector panel, after you select it, of course. The lighting is still too bright.

<Step 18> **Select** the **light** in the **cameratest** hierarchy and look at the light properties in the inspector. You see that the intensity is 1000. Whatever that means, it feels like that's too much. **Set** the **intensity** to 1, 10, and 100, then choose **10**.

<Step 19> **Select** the **Game tab**.

Aha! You have something that looks similar to the camera view in Blender. There is a bluish tinge, and the aspect ratio is different. First, let's fix the aspect ratio.

<Step 20> **Change** the **Aspect ratio** to **16:9** in the **Game** panel as shown in Figure 3.12.

Next, you're going to remove the bluish tinge for the light.

<Step 21> **Window – Rendering – Lighting, click** on **Environment**, then change the Source for Environment Lighting to Color and then back to Skybox. Close the Lighting window.

As you can see, the game now appears in black and white. The blue coloring was generated by the Environment Lighting Setting. As you just saw, lighting can be a somewhat complex issue. You will explore more about lighting in Unity later in Chapter 21.

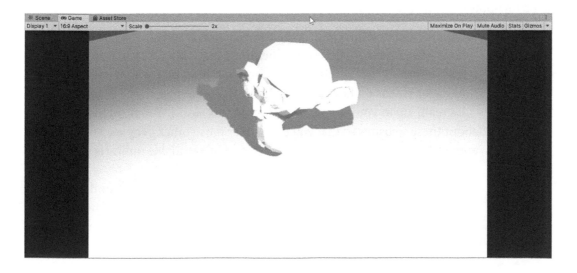

FIGURE 3.12   Suzanne in Unity with adjusted lighting.

\<Step 22\> **Select** the **Camera** in the **cameratest hierarchy** and look at the position and rotation values in the inspector. Experiment with changing those values just as you did in Blender.

As you quickly found out, conceptually these numbers work similarly to the Blender numbers, but they are somewhat different. For example, the roll for the camera is Z in Unity, but it's Y in Blender. This is a consequence of the differing coordinate systems in Unity vs. Blender.

\<Step 23\> **Save**.

In this section you examined some of the 3D aspects of Unity and Blender and compared the subtle differences between the two applications. Next, you'll look at some of the 3D assets available to you online. You don't need to build every asset in your game from scratch when countless free and low-cost assets are just a few clicks away.

3D ASSETS

In the early days of game development there was no market for game assets. The vast majority of assets were built from scratch by the developers themselves. This approach has advantages. You have full control, you own it, and you, or other people at your company were the only ones with access. Once the internet became widely used, all that changed. Websites are now selling or giving away everything from textures, stock photos, 3D models, and even entire collections of assets ready to be easily turned into a professional-looking game.

The reality, as of 2022, is that most developers use at least some premade assets for anything from background objects to grass textures. You name it, it's out there for a price, and often for free. In this section you'll look at two of the main sources of 3D assets for game development: the Unity Asset Store and the internet in general. As an exercise you'll try to get a low-poly computer monitor.

\<Step 1\> Search the web for "low poly computer monitor Blender."

Your search results will be overwhelming. Not only will you find offerings from companies that specialize in 3D models, but you'll also see tutorial and time-lapse videos on how to make monitors in Blender.

It's really up to you how far to delve into this world. You need to know about these websites so that you can find and use other people's work when appropriate. For now, just being aware of what's available online is a good start.

It helps to expand your horizons and learn how to import models from other file formats, not just. blend. Many of the other common file formats such as .obj or .fbx can be imported into Blender and Unity. Two particularly good websites with .fbx and .obj files are turbosquid.com and sketchfab.com.

Another very popular way to get 3D assets into your project is via the Unity Asset Store. The Asset store used to be tightly integrated into Unity, but it's now accessible only through your browser or via the package manager. To try it out, do this:

<Step 2> Go to assetstore.unity.com and search for "computer monitor." Sort by Price (Low to High).

You'll find the Low Poly Office Props – LITE among other interesting free items. Feel free to explore and try out a few of the free assets in the 3Dtest project.

In Chapter 4 you'll start your first of the two large projects in this book: DotGame3D.

Designing a 3D Remake

I N THIS CHAPTER YOU'LL begin development of DotGame3D, a 3D remake of DotGame. Unity makes this fairly easy because the 2D version was also developed using Unity. You'll start with that version from Volume I from this book series. You'll take the 2D project and make it into a 3D game by replacing the sprites with 3D models, updating the code, and making any other necessary changes. You'll also add more levels and features, time permitting.

THE 2D GAME: DOTGAME

In this section you'll download the game DotGame from franzlanzinger.com. Even if you have this project on your system you should download the version from the website to make sure your steps will be compatible with this book. You'll play the game to get a feel for it. You'll also take a closer look at the DotGame assets within Unity, Blender, GIMP, and Audacity.

<Step 1> In your browser, go to **franzlanzinger.com**, and **click** on the **BOOKS** tab.

<Step 2> **Click** on **Click here for Resources for 2D Game Development with Unity**.

<Step 3> **Click** on **Projects and Videos**.

<Step 4> **Click** on the link for **Final DotGame Project** and wait for the download to finish.
It's about 130 MB, so it should take roughly about a minute to download with your fast internet connection.

<Step 5> **Move** the downloaded zip file to the **3DGameDevProjects** folder and extract it there.

<Step 6> **Rename** the newly extracted DotGame folder to **DotGame_Old**.

<Step 7> **Move** the **DotGame subfolder** up one level to the **3DGameDevProjects** folder.

DOI: 10.1201/9780429328725-5

<Step 8> **Delete** the **DotGame_Old** folder as it is empty now.

Your 3DGameDevProjects folder should now have the following subfolders: 3DTest, DotGame, toycar, and the downloaded zip file. You're keeping the zip file just in case something goes wrong, and you need to start over. If you still have a toycar file or two in this folder, move them into the toycar folder.

<Step 9> **Launch** the **Unity Hub**, **click** on **Add**, and **select** the **DotGame** folder.

The project you just downloaded uses Unity version 2019.3.0f6. You're now going to update that old project to your current Unity version, 2020.3.0f1.

<Step 10> **Change** the **Unity version** for **DotGame** to **2020.3.0f1**.

You do that by simply selecting 2020.3.0f1 in the dropdown menu.

Changing the Unity version in the Unity hub requests to update to the new version when you open the project within Unity in the next step.

<Step 11> **Click** on **DotGame** in the **Unity Hub** to launch Unity with the DotGame project. You will be asked to upgrade the project to 2020.3.0f1. **Confirm** and wait for the upgrade process to finish.

<Step 12> In the Assets folder, **double-click** on **Scenes** and then **double-click** on **TitleScene**.

<Step 13> **Turn off** "**Maximize On Play**" in the Game panel, and then **play** the game.

The game should show the TitleScene as in Figure 4.1.

After the Title Scene completes, the game then automatically goes to the Menus Scene.

<Step 14> **Hover** the mouse over **Play DotGame** and **click**.

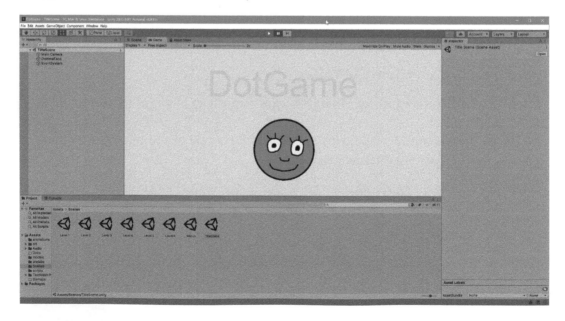

FIGURE 4.1   DotGame title scene in Unity.

The game was designed to be played on a larger screen, so you've decided to start over with Maximize on Play turned on. Also, if you're new to this game, there's an obvious problem: What are the controls? They are simple, but if you don't know you'd be stuck pretty soon. The main character is called Dottima, and you move her with the keyboard arrow keys, and shoot arrows with the space bar. You can also pick up bombs by running into them and drop them with the space bar to start the bomb fuse.

<Step 15> **Stop playing**, turn on **Maximize On Play**, and **play** again. **Stop playing** after you get to Level 3.

You were playing the game within Unity, but of course, these games are designed to be played outside of Unity. The zip file doesn't contain a build, but the project is already set up to create one.

<Step 16> **File – Build Settings**. Click on **Build**, and **create** a new folder called "**builds**" as a folder for the new build. Then proceed with the build.

<Step 17> **Exit Unity** and **run DotGame.exe** in the **builds folder**.

This time you'll try to finish the game. Observe the different game objects, how they look, and how they act. Even if you don't quite get through all six levels, you can always try again later. Yes, there are six levels, and the only level that's somewhat of a challenge is level six. Once you finish level six it's game over.

In the next section you will plan how to bring this simple 2D game into 3D.

REMAKING DOTGAME

DotGame 3D is going to be a *remake* rather than a *remaster*. There's a subtle difference. A remaster takes an older game, leaves the gameplay mostly alone, and improves the assets. For example, a remaster might take an old PS3 game and improve the textures and 3D models for a PS4 release, as was done for several AAA PS3 titles. It's also fair game to improve the lighting, shadows, and sound quality. It's questionable whether it's acceptable to change the gameplay for a remaster. Minor gameplay changes are typically considered OK, but the main goal is to recapture the old game as it was, warts and all. Of course, fixing old bugs is usually recommended, but even this can be a judgment call.

Remakes, on the other hand, have more freedom to change the game, sometimes drastically. The author's *Ms. Pacman* from 1990 for the NES, SNES, and Genesis, published by Tengen, is a remake of the original arcade Ms. Pacman but added dozens of brand-new levels beyond the original four, plus multiplayer, speedups, and more. At some point, when the game is completely different, you really shouldn't call it a remake anymore, but rather a sequel.

When the hardware of the original game is substantially different when compared to the new version, the new game is often called a *port*. Ports from arcade to consoles were common in the 1990s, sometimes with poor results, especially when the console was less powerful than the original arcade hardware. Nowadays, ports to less-powerful hardware

are rare, though you can sometimes find them on mobile devices when the original game was on a more powerful console or PC.

So, should DotGame3D be a sequel, a remake, or a port? It really depends on how much the game changes along the way, and if you want to port DotGame3D to a mobile device, for instance. To keep things simple, you'll shelve porting to mobile for now and revisit the idea later. Regarding remake vs. remaster, you consider the original 2D game much too short and simple, so you'll definitely aim for a remake with extra bonus levels.

CONTROLS

The controls for 3D games are, by the very nature of 3D, more complex than a joystick and a button or two. You will need to support a modern game controller, usually called gamepad, and possibly require one. If you, the developer and reader of this book, don't have a gamepad for your development system, this would be a good time to get one. Search for a gamepad that is compatible with all of your systems while you're at it. With a little persistence you can find controllers that work for both PCs and Macs.

You'll keep it simple and control the movement of Dottima with the left and/or right joystick and shooting with the A button. You might add vibration support for when Dottima takes damage.

Typically, the feel and details of the controls are best developed via experimentation during development. You're planning to support mouse and WASD keyboard controls as well as gamepads, at least during development. You'll finalize the controls only after trying out a few alternatives during testing.

THE CAMERA

Dealing with the camera in a 3D game can be tricky. Bad camera coding can ruin a 3D game, so extra care should be taken here. Before you get started, you'll need to think about which of the basic camera systems you'll want for this game: first person or third person?

Some of the early 3D games only supported first person, a view where the camera is located near the head of the player character. This means that you can't see the player, which is certainly not what you want in DotGame. The main character is an integral part of this game, so she shouldn't be invisible.

There are three basic third-person camera schemes: fixed, follow, or user-controlled. A fixed scheme would simply put the camera in a fixed position. A follow camera moves in response to the movements of the player character. Third, a user-controlled camera allows the player to control the camera in various ways, typically by orbiting the camera around the player to allow for views on the side or behind the character. Finally, some games allow for multiple camera schemes, chosen by the player from an options menu.

You're not sure, at this point, which of these camera schemes will work best for DotGame3D, so you plan to try them all out, time permitting, and choose the best one later on. So, without further ado, let's get to work! You'll begin by creating Dottima as a 3D character and setting up the project. You'll do that in the next chapter.

CHAPTER 5

3D Dottima Character

I N THIS CHAPTER YOU'LL develop a 3D version of the Dottima Dot character from the 2D version of the game. Before you do anything else you need to set up the Unity project. Then, you'll use Blender to model Dottima. Finally, you'll export Dottima into Unity and move her during the title animation.

SETTING UP THE PROJECT

You already have the 2D project, so your plan is to make a copy and start there by changing the name and turning on the 3D settings where appropriate. You'll keep the original 2D project around as a reference.

<Step 1> In your operating system, **copy** the **DotGame** folder to a new folder called **DotGame3D** in **3DGameDevProjects**.

<Step 2> In the **Unity hub**, **click** on **Add** and select the newly created **DotGame3D** folder. Then **click** on it to launch it.

<Step 3> **Test**.
     You're making sure that the copy is still working properly. The only new thing so far is the title of the project. The game itself still has the DotGame name in the title scene. You're going to start your remake by updating the title.

<Step 4> In the hierarchy, **select DottimaFace** and **scroll** down in the inspector until you see the script for DottimaFace.
     You can see that the Inspector lists a script called Dottima Title (Script).

<Step 5> In the **Assets** folder, **double-click** on **Scripts**. **Double-click** on **DottimaTitle**.
     This will open the script in Visual Studio, as usual. At the bottom of the script, you'll see where the title is generated using the GUI.Box function call.

DOI: 10.1201/9780429328725-6

FIGURE 5.1 The Title Screen for Dottima 3D.

<Step 6> **Change** the title text from "**DotGame**" to "**DotGame 3D**" in Visual Studio. Then type **<ctrl>**s to save.

In the title you'll have a space before 3D, but usually you'll omit the space when referring to the game.

<Step 7> **Play** in Unity. Compare with Figure 5.1.

<Step 8> **Stop Play mode**.

Once again, remember the importance of exiting play mode when you're finished playing. To help with this, make sure that "Maximize On Play" is turned on.

<Step 9> Look at **Assets/models** in the Project panel.

There you see five Blender models. That's right, Blender was used to make some of the graphics in the 2D game. You'll be able to reuse these! This is the folder where you'll create and store the 3D version of Dottima. You'll do that in the next section.

<Step 10> **Save** and **exit** Unity.

You didn't actually have to save because you only changed that script file. If you forget to save, Unity will remind you when it's necessary. It's not a good idea to just leave Unity running without saving while going off and doing other things. That's a recipe for losing your changes.

MODELING 3D DOTTIMA IN BLENDER

Now that you've set up the project you have a place to store the blend file for 3D Dottima. In this section you'll model 3D Dottima by creating a thin disk with the face of Dottima textured on one side. You'll animate the facial features in the next section.

<Step 1> **Launch** Blender and save with the name **Dottima** in **Assets/models** in the **DotGame3D** project.

The 2D version of Dottima is called DottimaFace, the 3D version Dottima.

<Step 2> **Delete** the default **cube**.

Notice that you're in the Layout workspace with the default 3D viewport.

<Step 3> Type **<shift>A – Mesh – Cylinder**.

<Step 4> Type **gz1<enter>**.

<Step 5> **<numpad>1**. Compare with Figure 5.2.

You are looking at the cylinder in the front orthographic view. Your plan is to squash the cylinder and rotate it. First though, you need to rename the cylinder so as to not confuse it with the other cylinders that you will create later.

<Step 6> **Rename** the cylinder to **Dottima** in the outliner panel.

The next step is to rotate Dottima to face you. When you look at the axis gizmo at the top right you see that the x-axis is aligned horizontally, so that's the axis you'll rotate around by 90 degrees to achieve the desired effect:

<Step 7> Type **rx90<enter>**.

Perfect, except that the disk is still too thick. Look at it from above:

<Step 8> Type **<numpad>7**.

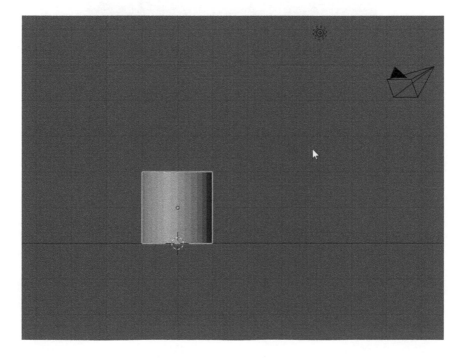

FIGURE 5.2 Starting with a cylinder to model Dottima.

Checking the axis gizmo again, you see that the y-axis runs along the cylinder, so you'll need to scale down along that axis as follows:

<Step 9> Type **sy0.2<enter>**.

<Step 10> **Move** the **view** to approximately match Figure 5.3.

The 0.2 scale factor was an educated guess. You can always use the mouse to adjust the scale factor instead of typing it in. In an attempt to keep your project in sync with the project in the book you're going to refrain from making your own adjustments, at least for now.

You notice that the edge of the disk isn't smooth enough, so you'll turn on smooth shading:

<Step 11> Make sure that Dottima is still selected and then **right-click – Shade Smooth**. Compare with Figure 5.4.

Next, you're going to model the eyeballs and pupils using smaller disks. You've decided to not be all that faithful to the original artwork. As long as your new 3D Dottima character will be recognizable as Dottima, or Dottima's 3D cousin, you'll be OK with that. You will use Figure 5.1 as a rough reference. This is where it's very useful to have two screens, with the reference image on one and the Blender window on the other.

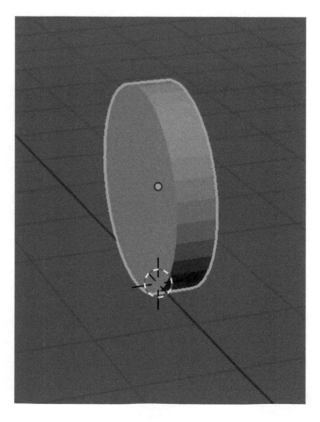

FIGURE 5.3 Thin disk on the way to becoming Dottima.

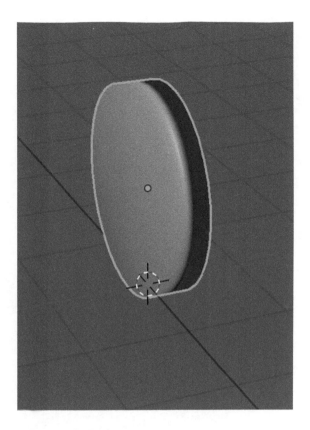

FIGURE 5.4   Dottima with smooth shading.

<Step 12> In the **Layout** workspace use **wireframe viewport shading** and **turn on X-ray** if necessary. Compare with Figure 5.5.

<Step 13> Type **<numpad>1<numpad><period>**.
This zooms the view so that Dottima appears very large and centered.

<Step 14> Type **<shift>Ds0.2<enter>**.
This duplicates Dottima and scales her by a factor of 0.2.

<Step 15> **Rename Dottima.001** to **right eye** in the outliner.

<Step 16> **Move** the **right eye** to approximately match Figure 5.6.
Of course, you did that with the "g" command. You placed the eye to be approximately in the same position as in the reference image in Figure 5.6.

<Step 17> Type **<shift>Dgx1<enter>**.

<Step 18> **Rename right eye.001** to **left eye**.

<Step 19> Make a **fine adjustment** of the left eye position to be symmetric with the right eye.
To make that adjustment you type gx and then use the mouse. Take a close look at the grid lines to make sure the eyes are laid out symmetrically.

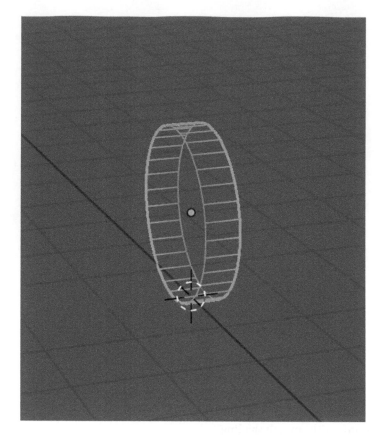

FIGURE 5.5   Wireframe viewport shading with X-ray turned on.

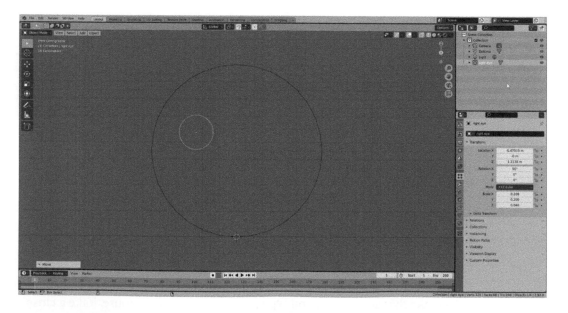

FIGURE 5.6   Right eye in position.

<Step 20> Change the hierarchy in the outliner by moving the eyes to be part of the Dottima mesh. Do that by **<shift>dragging** the **eyes** on top of **Dottima** in the outliner.

<Step 21> **Expand Dottima** and the **eyes** in the outliner. Compare with Figure 5.7.
Those cylinder objects don't need to be renamed.

<Step 22> **Hover** the mouse in the 3D viewport and type **<numpad>7**.
The top view shows that the eyes are inside of Dottima. You will now move them forward so that you'll be able to see them.

<Step 23> **Select** one eye and **<shift>click** the other so that both are selected.
When you do that the newly selected eye turns yellow, the old eye turns red. This shows you that you have both eyes selected.

<Step 24> Type **gy, move** the **mouse**, then **left-click** when the eyes are mostly outside of Dottima as in Figure 5.8.
Remember that you can always type <ctrl>z to Undo, possibly multiple times and try again.

<Step 25> **Front Ortho view**, make pupils with **<shift>D, scale 0.35**. Move them forward as shown in Figure 5.9.

<Step 26> As above, fix the outliner hierarchy by **renaming left eye.001** to **left pupil**, similar for the **right**. Then **shift-move** the **pupils** to their respective eyes in the outliner.
The expanded hierarchy should now look like Figure 5.10.

<Step 27> **Turn off X-ray**, use **solid viewport shading**.

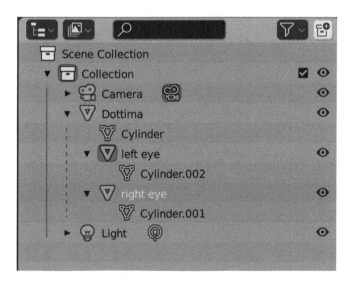

FIGURE 5.7   Hierarchy for Dottima with eyes.

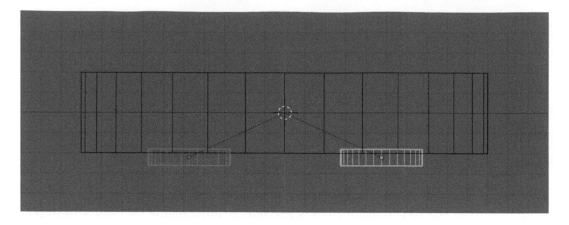

FIGURE 5.8   Dottima with eyes in correct position.

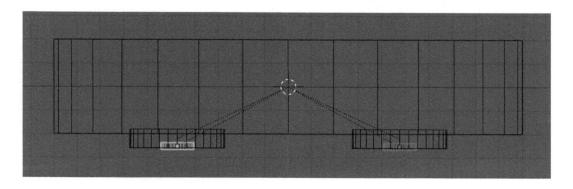

FIGURE 5.9   Dottima's eyes with pupils.

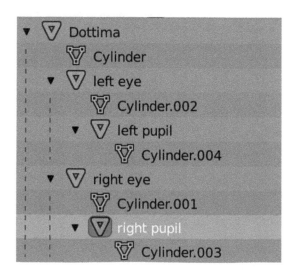

FIGURE 5.10   Hierarchy for eyes with pupils for Dottima in Blender Outliner.

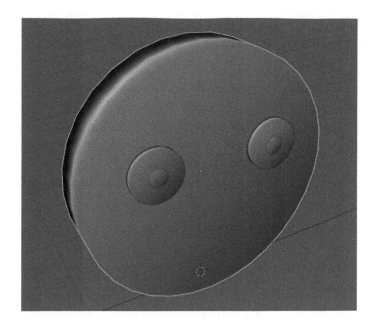

FIGURE 5.11   Dottima with eyes and pupils.

<Step 28> **<numpad>442222** to get a better perspective view of Dottima.

<Step 29> **Select Dottima** and compare with Figure 5.11.

It's about time to bring in better colors for Dottima. First though, save your work.

<Step 30> **Save**.

In the next section you'll learn about textures and texture painting in Blender. In your previous project you created materials and colors for Blender objects in Unity. This time around you'll do that in Blender and export the materials and textures to Unity.

TEXTURE PAINTING DOTTIMA

Your plan is to paint the facial features in the texture for Dottima, and to color the eyes yellow and the pupils black. You'll do the eyes and the pupils first. To get started you'll create a yellow material for the eyes.

<Step 1> Select **left eye** in the outliner.

<Step 2> In the **properties editor click** on the **material properties icon**, near the bottom of the icon column.

If you haven't done this before, it's educational to click on all of the property icons, one by one, starting at the top with "Active Tool and Workspace Settings" and working down the list until you get to the last one, "Texture Properties." The material properties icon is immediately above the texture properties icon.

The material properties section shows the name of the currently selected object, and below it a currently empty list of materials.

<Step 3> **Click** on **New**.

You immediately get a default material with the name Material.001. In case you're wondering where those 001 digits came from, it's not at all obvious. It turns out that the default cube has a material, and when you delete it that material is still present. This causes any new material to get an initial name of Material.001. After that, it's Material.002, etc.

To keep things organized, you're going to rename Material.001 to "yellow material".

<Step 4> **Double-click** on **Material.001** in the material list and **rename** it to **yellow material**.

Notice that the reference to the yellow material also changed its name automatically. Next, you'll actually make the material yellow.

<Step 5> **Change** the **Base Color** to a **yellow** color of your choosing as shown in Figure 5.12.

To actually see the yellow material in the 3D viewport, do this:

<Step 6> **Select material preview viewport shading.**

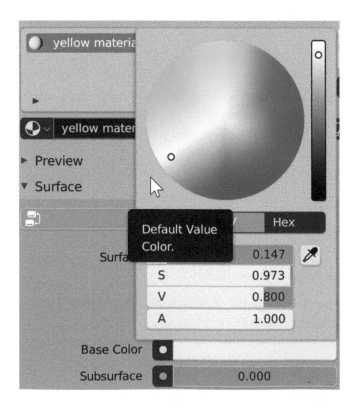

FIGURE 5.12   Color picker in Blender for choosing the Base Color of the yellow material.

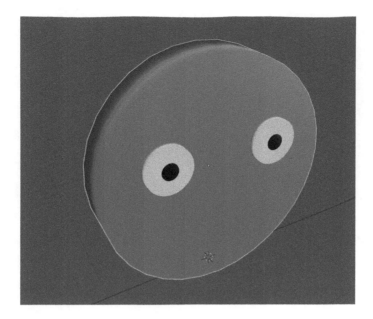

FIGURE 5.13   Dottima with purple, yellow, and black materials.

<Step 7> **Select** the **right eye**, and link the **yellow material** to it by using the drop-down menu called **Browse Material to be Linked** to the left of the New button.

<Step 8> Make the pupils black and Dottima purple using the same technique you just used to make the eyes yellow. Make a black material and a purple material when doing this. Compare with Figure 5.13.

You could conceivably leave well enough alone, but Dottima just doesn't look like herself. You'll use texture painting to paint a texture for Dottima, which will have the eyelashes, the nose, and the mouth drawn using black ink.

<Step 9> **Select Dottima** if necessary, then **select** the **UV Editing workspace**. Compare with Figure 5.14.

Zoom in if you wish. If you accidentally deselect Dottima, type **a** in the right panel to get her selected again.

As you can see, you have two panels now. The left panel is a UV editor, the right panel the usual 3D Viewport in edit mode. The 3D Viewport shows Dottima using solid viewport shading. The UV editor shows how Blender takes the faces of Dottima's cylinder mesh and maps them to a square texture. That texture doesn't exist yet, so you'll need to set it up.

<Step 10> In the **UV editor**, do **Image – New, name Dottima Head, uncheck alpha, purple color, OK.**

The UV editor now shows the Dottima Head image, a solid purple color, underneath the UV faces. The image has also zoomed in.

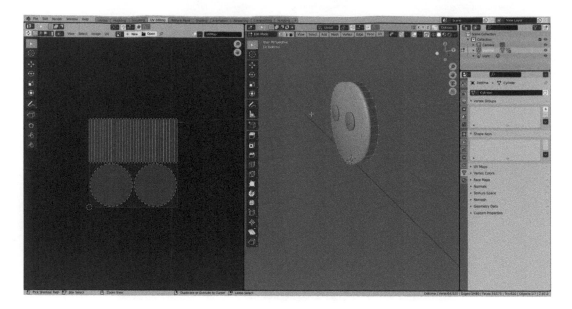

FIGURE 5.14   UV editing Dottima.

<Step 11> Image – Save As… dottima_texture.png in **Assets/models** of the **DotGame3D** Unity project.

    You didn't really have to save this image here, but it's good to set up where this texture is going to go as soon as possible. You're using the.png file format, which is your preferred image format for textures when given a choice. The png format is widely used, non-proprietary, and has all the features you will need, including lossless compression and support for transparency via an optional alpha channel.

    You are now ready to go to the Texture Paint workspace.

<Step 12> Choose the **Texture Paint** workspace.

    The left panel shows the Image editor in Paint mode for drawing in 2D directly onto the texture. The right panel shows the 3D viewport editor in texture paint mode for drawing onto the 3D mesh directly. You are not yet set up, but you're almost there.

<Step 13> In the image editor on the left, find the **"Browse Image to be Linked"** drop-down, and choose **Dottima Head**. Make sure you're still in Paint mode.

    You can now draw in the image editor. Try it out, if you wish by drawing with a large white brush using your mouse, but then <ctrl>Z to undo your test. As you can see, the 3D model didn't change at all. That's because it's not set up yet.

<Step 14> Select **Material Properties** in the **properties panel**.

    You should have a purple material there from Step 8.

<Step 15> **Click** on the **yellow dot** to the left of the purple Base Color, **select Image Texture,** then link it to **Dottima Head**. Finally, select the top icon in the properties panel, called **Active Tool and Workspace Setting.**

Congratulations! You are now set up for Texture painting.

<Step 16> **File – Save.**

You're saving so you can do some experimentation and then reload when you're done.

<Step 17> **Try** the different paint tools in the **2D image panel** and the 3D viewport panel. When you're finished, load the save file from the previous step, or do multiple undos.

<Step 18> **Hover** the mouse in the 3D viewport panel, then type **<numpad>1**.

<Step 19> Zoom in on Dottima to approximately match Figure 5.15. **Use the mouse wheel** to zoom and **<shift>MMB** to pan.

<Step 20> **Select** a **black color** in the color picker in the properties panel and **draw** the **eyelashes**, **nose**, and **mouth**. When doing that adjust the brush radius as necessary. Try to match Figure 5.16.

<Step 21> **Decorate** the back. Type **<ctrl><numpad>1** to show the back.

This is really up to you. You can draw most anything there. How about a red bow as in Figure 5.17? Do draw something other than a red bow. Here's your chance to be creative.

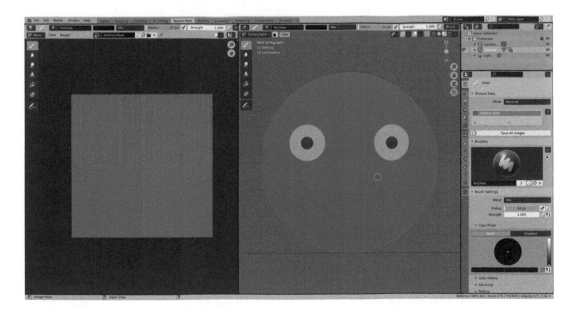

FIGURE 5.15   Setup to texture paint facial features for Dottima.

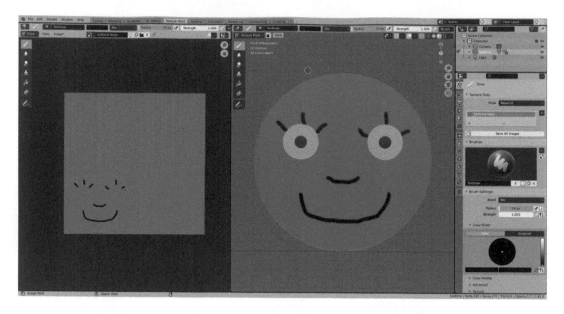

FIGURE 5.16 Dottima facial features.

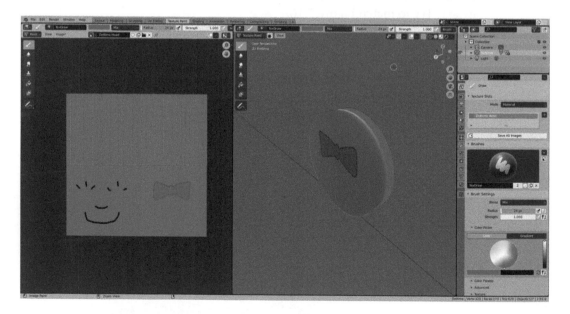

FIGURE 5.17 A red bow for Dottima?

Now notice in the Paint panel the asterisk next to "Image". This means that the image file needs to be saved.

<Step 22> Image* – Save.

This saves the image file associated with the Paint panel. Blender uses the asterisk convention here as well to indicate that the image has been altered and needs to be saved.

<Step 23> **File** – **Save** and **exit** Blender.

> If you should forget to save the Image, the File – Save command doesn't remind you, but if you try to exit Blender with unsaved changes in the image file, Blender does remind you and gives you a chance to do that.
>
> You're now ready to try out Dottima in Unity.

CONTROLLING DOTTIMA IN UNITY

Now you'll import Dottima into Unity and control her movement in the title scene.

<Step 1> **Load DotGame3D** in Unity.

> You should have the TitleScene in the Hierarchy, and the Game panel selected.

<Step 2> **Select** the **Scene panel**.

> You should see the 2D Dottima sprite on the left. Your first goal is to import the 3D model of Dottima and replace the DottimaFace game object with it.

<Step 3> In the **Assets/models** folder, **select Dottima.**

> You can also see the dottima_texture.png asset, the image that you just saved in Blender as a result of texture painting. You won't be using that texture directly because the Dottima blend file will reference it for you.

<Step 4> In the Dottima Import Settings, **uncheck Import Cameras** and **Import Lights**, and then click on **Apply**.

> You won't be needing those cameras and lights.

<Step 5> **Drag Dottima** from the Assets/models folder into the **hierarchy**. Compare with Figure 5.18.

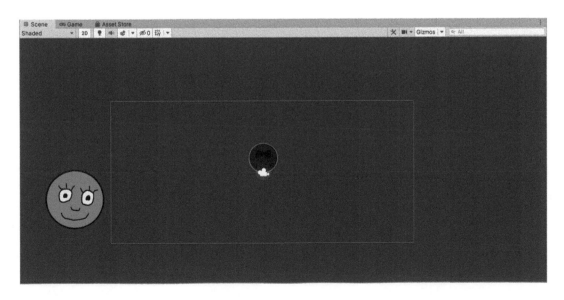

FIGURE 5.18   Dottima imported into Unity, needs work.

The 3D Dottima is dark, too small and facing away. You'll fix these problems one at a time.

<Step 6> **GameObject – Light – Directional Light**.

That's better. You can see Dottima a little better. To improve the lighting even more, edit the Rotation for the light in the Inspector as follows:

<Step 7> **Change** the **Rotation** of the **Directional Light** to **(0, 0, 0)**.

This has the effect of pointing the directional light directly away from the camera. Dottima is about one half of the desired size, so change the scale factor during import as follows:

<Step 8> **Select Dottima** in **Assets/models**, then **change** the **scale factor** in the inspector to **2** and **apply.**

Dottima is now about the same size as the 2D DottimaFace game object. Next you'll turn Dottima around to face the camera.

<Step 9> **Select Dottima** in the hierarchy, expand it, **select** the **Dottima child object**, then change the **Y rotation** in the inspector to **180**.

Next, you're going to replace DottimaFace with Dottima. When you look at DottimaFace in the inspector you can see that it has a script component with the script DottimaTitle. You will try to use that same script with Dottima. If you're lucky it'll just work.

<Step 10> **Select Dottima** in the hierarchy, and with the move tool, **move** it on top of DottimaFace.

<Step 11> **Select DottimaFace** and **disable** it in the inspector. Compare with Figure 5.19.

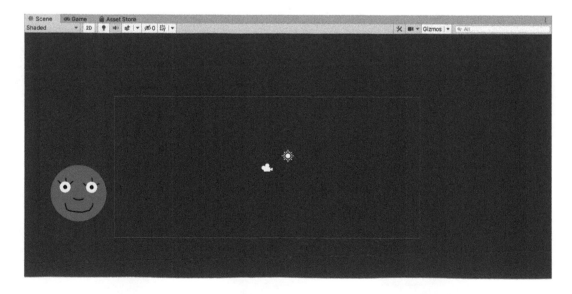

FIGURE 5.19 Dottima setup in the TitleScene.

<Step 12> Go to **Assets/scripts** and **double-click** on **DottimaTitle**.

The script opens in Visual C. This is the same script you modified at the beginning of this chapter in order to update the title of the game to DotGame 3D. This is a good time to look at this script more carefully.

```
using System.Collections;
using System.Collections.Generic;
using UnityEngine;
using UnityEngine.SceneManagement;

public class DottimaTitle : MonoBehaviour
{
    float timer = 7.0f;
    // Start is called before the first frame update
    void Start()
    {

    }

    // Update is called once per frame
    void Update()
    {
        float delta;
        delta = Time.deltaTime;
        gameObject.transform.Translate(
            new Vector3(delta * 4.0f, 0.0f, 0.0f));
        timer -= delta;
        if (timer < 0)
        {
            SceneManager.LoadScene(GameState.MenuScene);
        }
    }

    private void OnGUI()
    {
        GUI.backgroundColor = Color.clear;
        GUI.color = Color.yellow;
        GUI.skin.box.fontSize = (int)(Screen.width / 9.0f);
        GUI.Box(new Rect(
            0.0f,
            Screen.height * 0.1f,
            Screen.width,
            Screen.height * 0.3f),
            "DotGame 3D");
    }
}
```

As you can see, there is a timer variable initialized to 7.0f, and that should still work. The OnGUI function simply draws the title of the game, so again, this should work as is. The Update function moves the gameObject by calling the Translate function until the timer reaches zero. It then causes the scene to exit and move on to the MenuScene.

<Step 13> **Drag** the **DottimaTitle** script on top of **Dottima** in the hierarchy.

Time to dive in and run it.

<Step 14> **Test**.

This appears to work. Just so you can understand what's happening you'll look at the game in the scene panel while it's running.

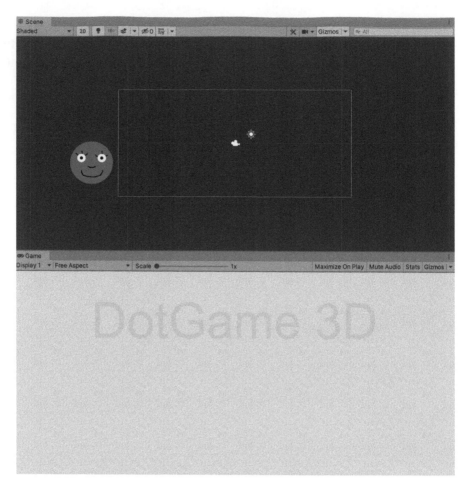

FIGURE 5.20   Running DotGame using the 2 by 3 layout.

<Step 15> In the game panel, **turn off Maximize On Play**, if necessary. **Change** the **Layout** to **2 by 3** and **test**. Compare with Figure 5.20.

In this 2 by 3 layout, you can see the scene and the game panels simultaneously. Dottima moves across the screen just as her 2D cousin. The only difference is that the squashing animation is now missing.

<Step 16> Use the default layout.

<Step 17> **Save** and **exit** Unity.

So far you just brought Dottima into the TitleScene, but of course you'd very much like to have her in the game itself. You're not quite ready to do that yet. Those levels are set up for 2D at the moment. You'll bring Dottima into the level scenes later on when they are set up with 3D meshes and a perspective camera.

In the next chapter you'll remake the DotRobot character from the 2D game in 3D.

CHAPTER 6

Blender Modeling and Animation

So far, you've started with the 2D game DotGame and converted the main character to 3D. You updated the simple title scene animation to 3D, but the game itself will need substantial changes to remake it in 3D. Your overall plan is to upgrade all the characters in the game to 3D, then rebuild the level scenes in 3D, and finally update the code to make the game work using your new 3D assets.

In this chapter you'll continue with upgrading the art assets of DotGame3D. You'll focus on the DotRobot character. Fortunately, that character was built using the *prerender* technique. Prerendering is a computer graphics technique where you build and optionally animate an object in 3D and use the 3D program's rendering engine to generate 2D sprites. This can result in realistic-looking sprites and tends to be easier than drawing the sprites in a 2D paint program. For the DotRobot character you'll be able to use the 3D model, ignore the sprite generation, and run the animation of the character directly in Unity instead. That sounds easy, but it does take some effort.

REMAKING DOTROBOT FOR 3D

You are half way there because there's a 3D model already. That's the theory.

<Step 1> In Blender, load **DotRobot.blend** from the **Assets/models** folder. Compare with Figure 6.1.

As you can see, you're using the Animation workspace.

<Step 2> Type **<spacebar>** and watch the animation. Then type **<spacebar>** again to stop it.

This is a simple walk animation. The Blender window has two 3D viewports, a dope sheet, and below it a timeline, as well as the usual outliner and properties panels on the right.

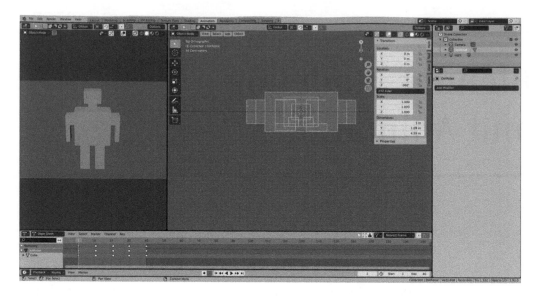

FIGURE 6.1   DotRobot model and animation in Blender.

<Step 3>   **Hover** the mouse over each of the **six Editor Type icons** and verify that you can find them and have all six of them displayed.

It's important to know where all the editor panels are and what they do, especially when you're switching workspaces.

<Step 4>   In the 3D Viewport on the right, switch to **Rendered Viewport Shading**, and type **<numpad>442222**. Compare with Figure 6.2.

The robot has a light blue color. Where is that coming from? Is it the material?

<Step 5>   Change the **viewport shading** to **Material Preview**.

That makes the robot white, so it appears that the blue tint comes from the lighting. In Blender, the material preview shading renders the viewport with lighting turned off, so that way you can see the true colors of the materials.

<Step 6>   Go to the **layout workspace** and **select** the **light** in the Outliner panel.

Indeed, you can now see that the color is set to a light blue shade in the properties panel. This robot can be used as is, but since you're here you'll take a small detour and texture DotRobot.

TEXTURING DOTROBOT

In this section you'll find a texture for DotRobot and then use it to make DotRobot look like he's made out of metal. A good resource for free textures is the website ambientCG.com. The content on this site currently uses CC0 licensing, which allows you to use the associated assets for any purpose without attribution. This means you don't need to give credit, but if you are so inclined, credit is appreciated. For ambientCG.com the suggested credit is:

```
Contains assets from ambientCG.com, licensed under CC0 1.0 Universal.
```

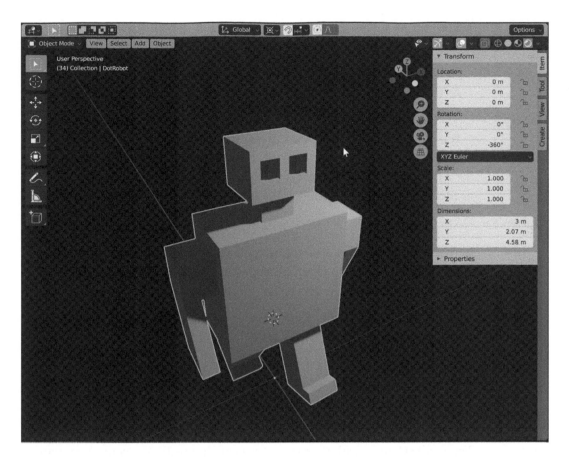

FIGURE 6.2 Walking DotRobot.

Of course, the internet has thousands of free textures, but this website gives you at least some assurance that their assets are in fact free to use and don't constitute copyright infringement.

<Step 1> Go to **ambientCG.com** and browse the site.

You don't even have to create a username. This website specializes in PBR textures. PBR is an acronym for Physically Based Rendering. These types of textures achieve excellent realism. You don't really care about realism in DotGame3D, as long as the textures look good to you.

<Step 2> Search for **Metal 038**. **Select** it and **click** on the **1K-JPG download.**

<Step 3> Copy the zip file from your download folder to the Assets/models folder in the DotGame3D project. Extract the folder there.

When you look at the unzipped folder titled Metal038_1K-JPG you will find five maps: Color, Displacement, Metalness, Normal, and Roughness. You won't be using all of those maps. You're just interested in the Color map.

When you get more advanced you'll learn about the other maps and how to incorporate them into your materials.

<Step 4> Open **DotRobot.blend** in Blender.

As usual, when texturing an object in Blender, the first step is to UV Edit it.

<Step 5> Open the **Layout** workspace. In the Timeline editor set the **current frame** to **0**.

You can do this by editing the current frame indicator on the left of the Start and End indicators. Alternatively, you can drag the blue frame gizmo to the left until it's at 0. The effect is that the robot is now standing upright. You needed to do that before doing UV editing.

<Step 6> Go to the **UV Editing** workspace.

<Step 7> In the **UV Editor** panel, click on **Image – Open** and select **Metal038_1K_ Color.jpg**. Then **click** on **Open Image**. Compare with Figure 6.3.

The robot in the 3D Viewport isn't selected, so do that next:

<Step 8> In the 3D Viewport, **select DotRobot** by clicking on it. The robot gets an orange outline.

<Step 9> Switch to **Edit Mode** in the 3D Viewport.

Something very strange just happened. You're only seeing the legs. This is the result of a "hide" operation left over from the creation of the original DotRobot. To unhide, do this:

<Step 10> **Type <alt>H** and **a** with the mouse hovering in the 3D Viewport. Compare with Figure 6.4.

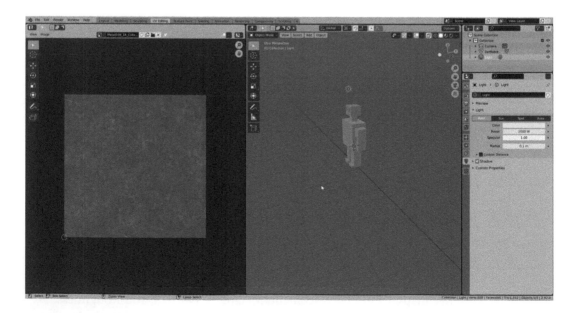

FIGURE 6.3   UV editing DotRobot.

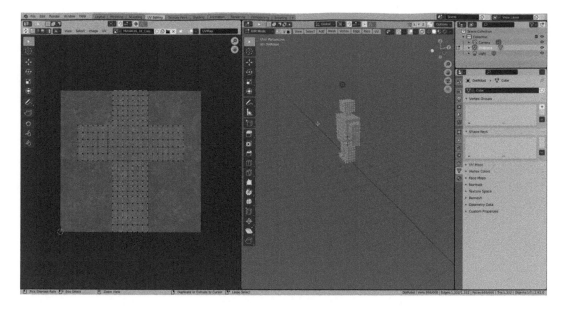

FIGURE 6.4   Unhiding DotRobot in edit mode.

<Step 11>   Go to the **Texture Paint** workspace.
You won't be doing texture painting just yet, but this workspace is useful for setting up the material for DotRobot.

<Step 12>   Select the **material properties** icon in the properties panel.

<Step 13>   **Click** on the small yellow dot next to Base Color, then **click** on **Image Texture**.

<Step 14>   **Click** on the **Browse Image to be linked** dropdown and **choose** the **Color map**.
Take a look at Figure 6.5.
The robot is now textured, but it's not quite what you had in mind. The legs and arms have very distorted textures. To fix this, do the following:

<Step 15>   Go back to the **UV Editing** workspace.

<Step 16>   In the 3D Viewport, type **U** and then select **Smart UV Project** in the pop-up menu.

<Step 17>   Select **Rendered Viewport Shading, Object Mode,** and zoom in on the Robot. Compare with Figure 6.6.
That robot looks good like that. Time to save.

<Step 18>   **Image – Save As** and save the image in **Assets/models**.

<Step 19>   **File – Save**.
You're ready to try out DotRobot in Unity.

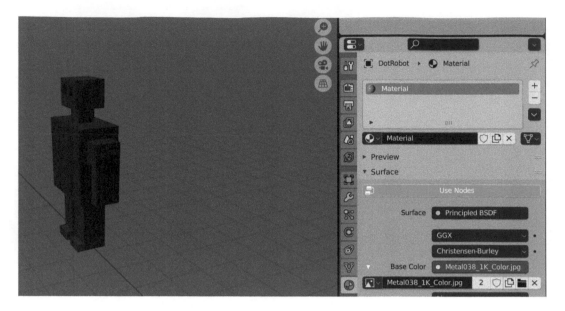

FIGURE 6.5   Using the downloaded color map for base color.

IMPORTING TO UNITY, PART 1

In this section you'll look at DotRobot in Unity. You're going to create an experimental scene that you will use to display .blend files. You'll call that scene the "Staging" scene. You won't be using that scene in the game itself. Rather, it will be a useful tool during development. First, you'll set up that scene.

<Step 1>   Open **DotGame3D** in Unity

<Step 2>   **Click** on the **2D** icon at the top of the scene panel. This turns off 2D mode for the Scene panel.

<Step 3>   **Edit – Project Settings…** which opens the Project Settings pop-up.

<Step 4>   **Editor** and in the **Default Behaviour Mode** section select a mode of 3D. Close the pop-up.
    This puts the entire project into 3D mode. Both this step and Step 2 are necessary when converting a 2D project to a 3D project.

<Step 5>   Go to **Assets/Scenes** in the Project panel.

<Step 6>   **Create** a **new scene** there, with name **Staging**, and **double-click** on it to **open** it.

<Step 7>   **Edit – Preferences – Scene View** and **check Create Objects at Origin**.
    Without this setting Unity creates new objects at the scene pivot point, which can be confusing.

<Step 8>   **GameObject – 3D Object – Plane** and then type the name **Stage<enter>**.
    Zoom in and compare with Figure 6.7.

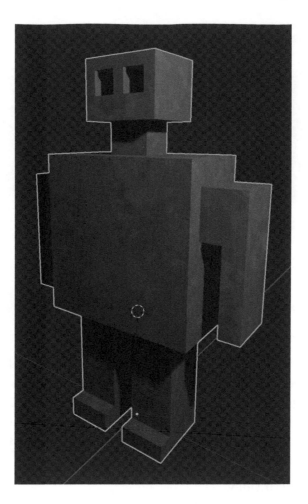

FIGURE 6.6   Textured DotRobot.

It is useful to have a stage object when testing out the look and placement of other objects. Note that the 2D icon is not highlighted and that the transform for the stage is (0, 0, 0), (0, 0, 0), (1, 1, 1).

<Step 9>   Go to **Assets/models** and click on **DotRobot**.

<Step 10>   In the inspector, look at the import settings for DotRobot. Select **Model** and change the **scale factor** to **0.1**. Uncheck Import Lights and Import Cameras and **apply**.

When you look at Rig, Animation, and Materials you discover that there is no animation data for this model. That is bad news. Why is there no animation data?

<Step 11>   **Drag DotRobot** to the **hierarchy** and **zoom in** on it in the scene panel.

The robot is there, and when you zoom in on it you can see the texture, but it's not animating, as you would expect when there is no animation data. As it turns out, Unity cannot import this animation because the model isn't rigged.

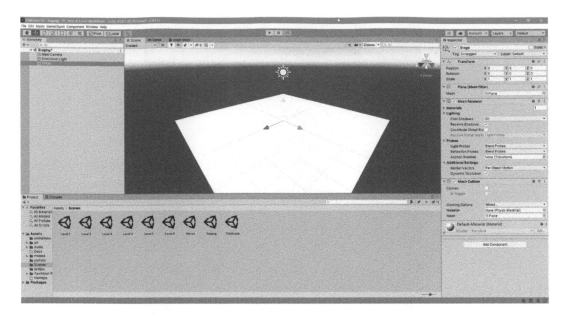

FIGURE 6.7   Setting the stage.

You now need to take a detour in your development and learn about rigs
and rigged animations. Yes, you'll need to redo the animation in Blender by
building a rig for DotRobot and then animating the rig. Only then will you be
able to import the animation into Unity. Furthermore, you'll need to use.fbx
format instead of .blend format. None of this is obvious, so it's worth testing a
simple example first before tackling DotRobot itself.

<Step 12> **Save** and **exit** Unity.
   Strictly speaking, you don't need to exit Unity here, but you'll be using
   Blender for a while, so you decided to shut down Unity while working in
   Blender for an extended time.

EXPERIMENTAL RIG

In this section you'll create a simple test mesh in Blender, then you'll make a rig for it,
animate it, and then export it to Unity using fbx format. This is a simple but educational
exercise. This way you'll be more comfortable when doing the more complex rigging and
animation for DotRobot in the next section.

   This is an example of a problem-solving method used by mathematicians for centuries:
when working on a difficult problem, find a similar simpler problem and solve that first.

<Step 1> In Blender create a **new file** with name **testrig.blend** in the usual **Assets/
   models** folder.

<Step 2> **Select** the default **cube** and rename it to **tower**.

<Step 3> Type **sz4<enter>gz4<enter>**, **modeling** workspace, **<numpad><period>**.

<Step 4> **Loop cut** the **tower** with **5 cuts**. Use **extrusions** to match Figure 6.8.

FIGURE 6.8   Test mesh for the test rig in Blender.

Pretend that the tower is the robot body, and the extruded section is an arm. You're going to try to swing that arm using a rig, similar to the arm motion in DotRobot.

A rig, sometimes called a skeleton, is a set of bones that influence an associated mesh. Animating the mesh is accomplished by animating the bones of the rig, which in turn change the positions of nearby vertices. The advantage of doing animations this way is that just a few bones can control a complex mesh containing hundreds or even thousands of vertices.

<Step 5>   **Layout** workspace. **<numpad><period>**.

Next you'll add the *armature*, a set of bones that animate the mesh. You need to be in object mode to create the armature.

<Step 6>   **<shift>A – Armature. Turn on X-ray** to see the armature.

You now see a small bone at the bottom of the stretched cube.

<Step 7>   <tab> to switch to Edit mode.

<Step 8>   **Select** the **top of the bone**, then type **gz2<enter>ez3<enter> <numpad>3** and compare with Figure 6.9.

<Step 9>   **Extrude three** additional **bones** as shown in Figure 6.10

<Step 10>   Select the **bottom bone**, the first one you created, and type the function key **<F2>**. Enter **root** as the new name.

     You may need to find out how to enable the function keys on your keyboard if this doesn't work for you. The internet can help if you search for "function keys" and the name of your keyboard or laptop.

     It's recommended that you name all the bones in a rig, especially the root bone. For this test you'll ignore that advice somewhat and just rename one other bone.

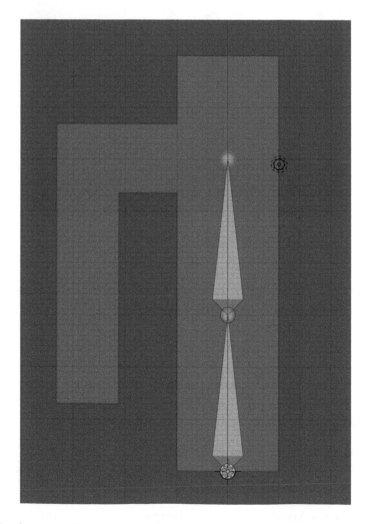

FIGURE 6.9   Two bones for the test rig.

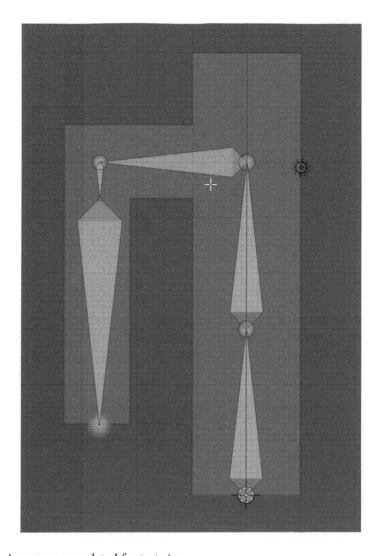

FIGURE 6.10   Armature completed for test rig.

<Step 11> **Rename** the last bone in the chain to **armbone**.

<Step 12> In the outliner, **expand** the **armature** until it looks like Figure 6.11.

<Step 13> **Select** the **root bone** in the outliner, then in the properties editor below, click on the **bone properties** icon, the bottom icon in the column of icons. **Uncheck Deform**.

    Bones, by default, have the ability to deform their associated mesh. The root bone is usually used just to position the mesh rather than deform it.

<Step 14> **Uncheck Deform** for **all other bones**, **except** for the **armbone**.

    In this test you will only use the armbone to deform the arm and leave everything else as is. Next you will make the armature the parent of the tower mesh. This needs to be done in object mode.

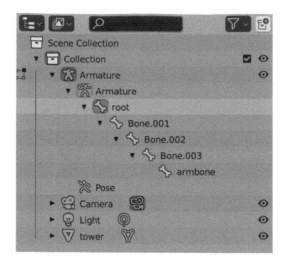

FIGURE 6.11   Armature expanded in the outliner.

<Step 15>   Type **<tab>** to get object mode. **Select** the **tower** in the outliner, then **<ctrl>-select** the **Armature.** Hover the mouse in the 3D viewport, then type **<ctrl>p** and select **Armature Deform with Empty Groups** as shown in Figure 6.12.

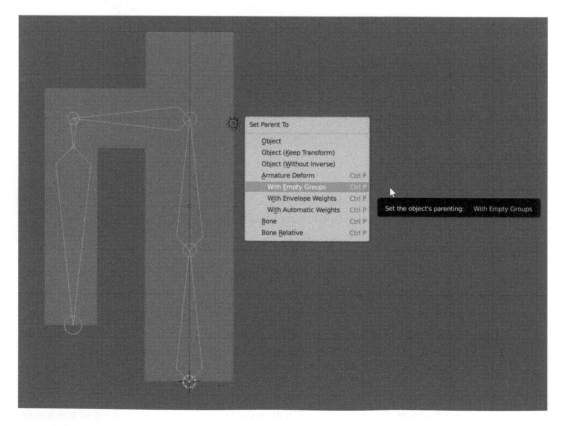

FIGURE 6.12   Parenting the armature with empty groups.

The "with Empty Groups" phrase refers to the vertex groups associated with each of the five bones. Each bone is only capable of deforming the vertices in its vertex group. You now have all of those vertex groups empty.

\<Step 16\> Select the **tower** object in the outliner, now a child of the Armature.

\<Step 17\> Click **Object Data Properties** and look at the Vertex Groups. You see just one group, called armbone.

\<Step 18\> Switch to **edit mode** and select the **bottom four vertices of the arm.**

\<Step 19\> Click on the **Assign** button below the Vertex Groups list.
The vertex group now consists of those four vertices. You can check that it worked by unselecting everything and then clicking on the Select button. You're finally ready to test out the rig.

\<Step 20\> **Object mode, select Armature**.

\<Step 21\> **Pose mode, select the armbone**, type **ry** and move the mouse. Compare with Figure 6.13.
Because this took a while, time to save your work before doing the animation.

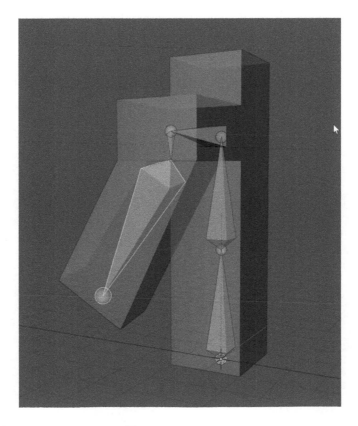

FIGURE 6.13   The arm bone is moving the arm.

\<Step 22\> **File – Save**.

Now that you have an armature, the rest is a lot easier.

\<Step 23\> Go to the **animation** workspace.

\<Step 24\> **Turn on Auto Keying** by clicking on the small round icon in the Timeline editor, middle bottom of the Blender window.

\<Step 25\> Change the **number of steps** of the animation from **250** to **20**, bottom right.

\<Step 26\> **Change Dope Sheet** to **Action Editor**. Select **frame 1**.

\<Step 27\> In the right 3D viewport, **\<numpad\>1**. **Turn on X-Ray**.

\<Step 28\> With the **armbone** still selected, type **ry** and adjust the arm for a swing to the left. Compare with Figure 6.14.

\<Step 29\> At **frame 10**, **swing arm to the right**.

\<Step 30\> Select the **key** at **frame 1**, **\<shift\>D** to copy, **click** at **frame 20** to copy it there.

\<Step 31\> **Press** the **play triangle** in the Timeline to test out the animation.

\<Step 32\> **File – Save**.

Unfortunately, you now need to export the animation to Unity using fbx format, rather than just using the .blend format. Fortunately, it's only slightly more complex than saving to .blend.

\<Step 33\> **File – Export – FBX**. **Click** on **Armature, shift-click** on **Mesh** in the Object Types section. Then do **Export FBX**, making sure that the filename is **testrig.fbx**.

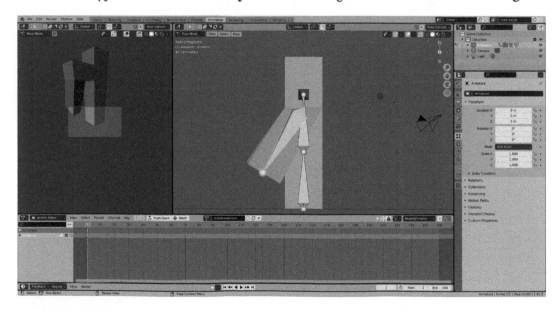

FIGURE 6.14   Arm bone swings to the left, autokey inserts keys at frame 1.

The fbx file format is commonly used for storing and transferring 3D data. Both Blender and Unity have good support for this format.

<Step 34> **File – Save**.

That's not really necessary, except this way you save your fbx export settings too. You're leaving Blender open for now.

<Step 35> Open **DotGame3D** in **Unity**.

Bringing animations into Unity from Blender takes a few steps. You should still be in the Staging scene with the stage and DotRobot in the center. As you recall, the DotRobot animation didn't work, so now you're bringing in the testrig

<Step 36> In Assets/models, **click** on each of the **testrig icons** and **find** the one with the **fbx** extension in the name. You will have at least two testrig icons and you can see the full name displayed at the bottom. Click on **testrig.fbx**.

The other testrig icons will have .blend, .blend1,… extensions. You won't be using them.

<Step 37> **Expand** the **testrig** icon in the Project panel.

You will see two Armature icons, two tower icons, and a Material icon, as shown in Figure 6.15.

<Step 38> **Click** on **testrig** and inspect the import settings in the inspector. Click on all four buttons one by one as you did before with DotRobot: **Model**, **Rig**, **Animation**, and **Materials**. Note that you now have an animation!

<Step 39> **Test** the **animation** in the inspector by clicking on the **play** button for it, as shown in Figure 6.16.

The animation loops and matches the Blender animation, just what you wanted. You can make that animation appear larger by dragging the double line. You're now ready to put this animation onto the stage.

<Step 40> **Drag testrig.fbx** into the **hierarchy**.

OK, that is way too big, but you don't care, it's just a test.

<Step 41> Play the game, then stop.

That didn't work. You still need one more step.

<Step 42> **Drag** the **armature** on the right (the one with the triangular icon) on top of **testrig** in the hierarchy.

FIGURE 6.15   Expanded testrig.fbx file in Assets/models.

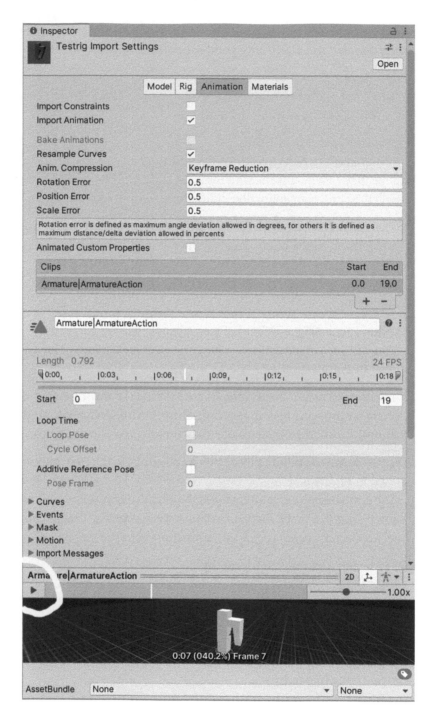

FIGURE 6.16 Test animation in the inspector.

\<Step 43\> Test.

The animation will play just once, and then freeze. To loop it do this:

\<Step 44\> Select **testrig.fbx** in the Project panel. In the inspector, click on **Animation**, and then **check Loop Time**, then **Apply**.

\<Step 45\> Test.

Finally! The animation is running and looping. This wasn't exactly easy, but you'll be repeating the steps in this section in the future. Eventually they'll become easier. This section is a good example of a *workflow*. Game developers, animators, programmers, even composers all develop workflows over time. A good workflow will serve you well and become much faster as you repeat it over and over, sometimes for years. As your tools evolve your workflows will also change, sometimes drastically. You'll put your new workflow to the test in the following sections when you apply it to DotRobot.

\<Step 46\> Save and **exit** Unity.

In the following section you're going back to Blender where you will rig DotRobot.

RIGGING DOTROBOT

In this section your goal is to duplicate and maybe improve the non-rig animation that's in the project already.

\<Step 1\> Load **DotRobot.blend** into Blender.

In the Animation workspace choose the Dope Sheet and review the keyframes for the DotRobot animation. Note that you have only one animation for DotRobot, a simple walk cycle. At frame numbers 0, 20, and 40 the robot is standing upright. At frame 10 the right leg and left arm are extended forward, and the left leg and right arm are extended backwards. For frame 30 right and left are switched.

Clearly, you will need bones for the arms and the legs. While you're at it, it might be fun to animate the head as well. You will do that by slightly turning the head left and right during the walk. Other possibilities would be to animate the body and the feet, but you're going to leave well enough alone and keep it fairly simple for this character.

As it turns out, the current animation in DotRobot.blend needs to be removed in order to put in an armature and create an animation with that armature. The easiest course of action will be to rebuild the robot mesh, texture it, create an armature, and then animate. Sometimes it's better to just start from scratch, and this is one of those times. Think of it as a learning experience.

\<Step 2\> Create a new .blend file entitled **DotRobotRigged.blend**.

\<Step 3\> Examine Figure 6.17, which will serve as your reference image.

This is a good review exercise. You will start with a cube and then use loop cuts, extrusions, and scaling to build the mesh in the Modeling workspace. Along the way you'll allow yourself the freedom to make slight improvements when compared to the original.

The following steps will have few comments. This should be familiar territory for you.

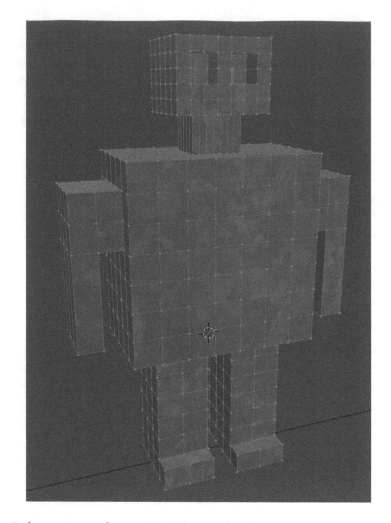

FIGURE 6.17   Reference image for new DotRobot mesh.

<Step 4> Select the default **cube**, rename it to **DotRobot**, go to the **Modeling** workspace, **hover** the mouse in the 3D viewport, **gz1<enter>**.

<Step 5> Type **sy0.4<enter> <numpad><period>** and **zoom out** a little with the mouse wheel.

<Step 6> **Face select, select** the **top face, e0.1<enter>s0.4<enter>sx0.5<enter>e0.3 <enter>**. Compare with Figure 6.18.

<Step 7> Type **e0.1<enter>s2<enter>e0.5<enter>**.
     You just built the body, neck, and head. Next, you'll add some loop cuts to prepare for adding the limbs.

<Step 8> Create **three loop cuts** as shown in Figure 6.19.

<Step 9> **Select six faces** for **each leg** at the bottom of the body, then do **e1.5<enter>**.

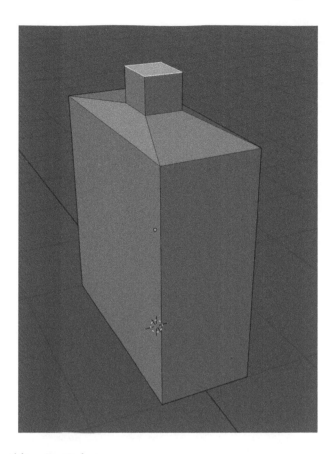

FIGURE 6.18   Rebuilding DotRobot.

<Step 10> Type **a** to select all and do **gz1.5<enter>**.

<Step 11> Create **five loop cuts for each leg. Extrude** the feet by **0.2 meters** as shown in Figure 6.20.

<Step 12> **Create** the **arms** as shown in Figure 6.21. The upper arm is **extruded** by **0.5**, the lower arm by **1**. You'll also need to put in a single loop cut.
    Only one more thing to do, add the eyes.

<Step 13> **Add four loop cuts** on the **head**, and **extrude two 2 × 2** eyes, using a negative extrusion by **0.25 units**.
    This robot looks slightly different from the reference. Mainly, the head is smaller, and the shape of the head and shoulders is tapered. Now, you're going to save a backup, just in case.

<Step 14> **File – Save. File – Save As… with name DotRobotModelBackup.blend. Exit Blender. Launch Blender** and load **DotRobotRigged.blend.**
    The next few steps will texture your freshly made model, very similarly as you did in the texturing section earlier in this chapter.

<Step 15> Go to the **UV Editing** workspace.

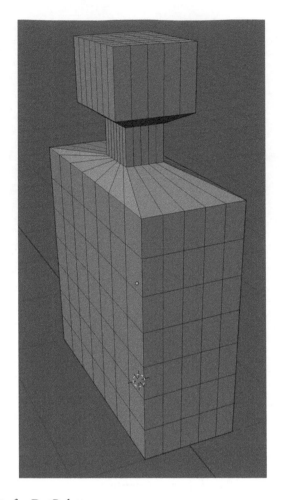

FIGURE 6.19   Loop cuts for DotRobot.

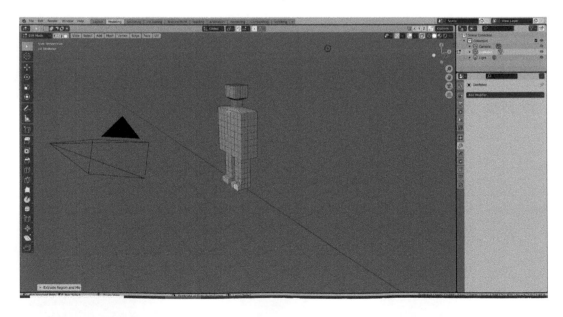

FIGURE 6.20   Extruding the feet.

<Step 16> In the UV Editor panel, click on **Image – Open** and open **Metal038_1K_ Color.jpg**.

<Step 17> In the 3D Viewport, go to **object mode** and **select DotRobot**, if necessary.

<Step 18> Back to **edit mode**, and type **a** to select all.

<Step 19> **Right-click – UV Unwrap Faces – Smart UV Project**. Click **OK**.

<Step 20> **Texture Paint** workspace, click on **Material Properties**.

<Step 21> **Base Color – Image Texture**.

<Step 22> **Browse Image to be Linked – Metal38_1K_Color.jpg**.

<Step 23> **Layout** workspace. Use **rendered viewport shading**. **Zoom out** if necessary so you can see DotRobot. **Move** the **light** with the **g** command to light the front of DotRobot.

　　This is just to make sure that DotRobot looks OK.

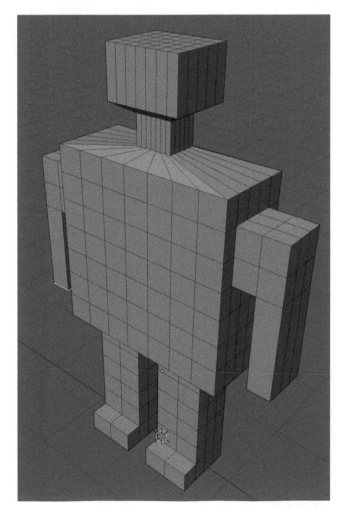

FIGURE 6.21   DotRobot, missing eyes.

<Step 24> **File – Save.**

You're now ready to put in the armature.

<Step 25> In the **Layout** workspace, select **DotRobot** if necessary,
<shift>A – Armature.

<Step 26> Type **<numpad>1**, select **DotRobot**, **<numpad><period>**, **solid viewport shading**, and compare with Figure 6.22.

<Step 27> **Select Armature**, switch to **edit mode**, **wireframe viewport shading**, and **build the armature** shown in Figure 6.23 using extrusions (**ex** and **ez**) and move commands (**gz**).

<Step 28> Still in **edit mode** name the **root bone, armr, arml, legr, legl**, and **head** bones using the **<F2>** function key. You can leave the names of the other bones as is.

<Step 29> In **object mode, select DotRobot**, **<ctrl>-select** the **armature, hover** the mouse in the **3D viewport, <ctrl>p with empty groups**. Then **select DotRobot**.

<Step 30> Switch to **edit** mode, select **Object Data Properties**. Select the **head** bone in the Vertex Groups list. You may need to scroll the list to find it.

You will now start the process of manually assigning vertices to vertex groups.

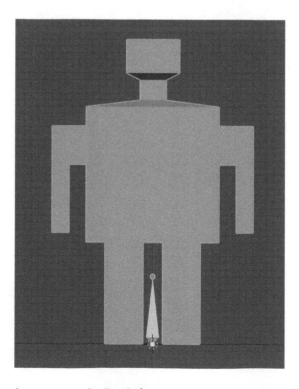

FIGURE 6.22   Starting the armature for DotRobot.

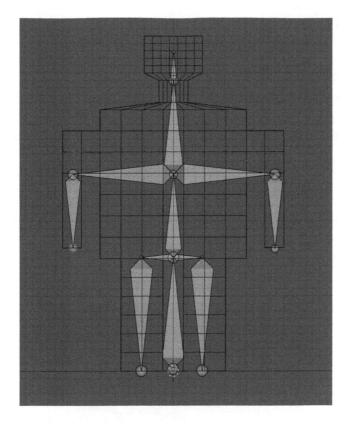

FIGURE 6.23   Armature for DotRobot.

<Step 31> **Turn on X-Ray, vertex select mode** and **box-select the head vertices.**

<Step 32> Click on **Assign** below the vertex group list.

<Step 33> For the **arms**, select the **end vertices,** for the **legs** select the **entire legs.**

<Step 34> **Check your assignments** by clicking on the relevant bones in the vertex groups list and using the select and deselect buttons to see if the correct vertices get highlighted in response.

<Step 35> **Object mode, select armature, pose mode. Check** that the arm, leg, and head bones work by rotating them with **rx** or **rz**.
    Now that the bones are working you will save and move on to the next section where you will set up the walk animation for DotRobot.

<Step 36> **File – Save. Exit Blender.**

REANIMATING DOTROBOT

In this section you'll animate the armature of DotRobot in Blender. This works similarly to animating meshes directly. You will put DotRobot into pose mode and manipulate bones to put DotRobot into poses of a simple walk cycle. In later chapters you will encounter a more realistic and complex walk cycle for humanoid characters.

<Step 1> **Load DotRobotRigged.blend** in Blender.
DotRobot is in pose mode, ready to be animated.

<Step 2> Go to the **Animation** workspace.

<Step 3> Type **<ctrl><numpad>3** with the mouse hovering in the 3D viewport on the right.
This gives you the left orthographic view of DotRobot facing to the right.

<Step 4> **Wireframe viewport shading**.

<Step 5> Type **<numpad>866** to get a better view.

<Step 6> In **object mode**, **select** the **armature** in the outliner, mouse in right 3D viewport, then type **<numpad><period>**.
Compare with Figure 6.24.

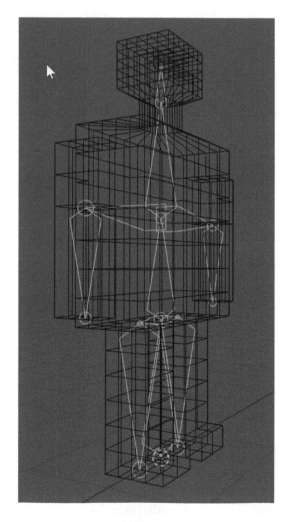

FIGURE 6.24   DotRobot armature, ready to be animated.

<Step 7> In the **timeline editor** at the very bottom right, **change the end frame** of the animation from the default 250 to **40**.

Your walk cycle will have 40 frames of animation, which will be plenty of frames.

<Step 8> **Click** on the **Auto Keying icon**, a black dot near the middle of the timeline editor.

This mode automatically adds appropriate keyframes whenever you change anything at a frame. You'll start by moving the arms and legs into extended positions at frame 1. Frame 1 should be highlighted in blue.

<Step 9> In the right 3D viewport, go to **pose mode, turn on X-ray**, use **rendered shading**.

<Step 10> Type **a** to select all the bones. Compare with Figure 6.25.

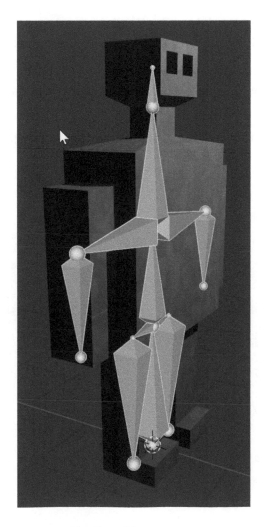

FIGURE 6.25 DotRobot armature with selected bones.

<Step 11> Type **i** with the mouse hovering in the right 3D viewport and choose **Location & Rotation**.

The Dope sheet now fills with keyframes for each bone. With the mouse hovering over the dope sheet, you can type **<ctrl><spacebar>** to have it fill the entire screen. Then, type **<ctrl><spacebar>** again to restore the original layout.

<Step 12> Move to frame **21** and **41** and do **Step 11** there as well.

Moving to different frames can be done by dragging the current frame number, or by typing the desired frame number into a textbox at the bottom right next to the start and end boxes.

<Step 13> With the mouse hovering on the dope sheet, type **<ctrl><spacebar>** and compare with Figure 6.26. Your order of the bones may differ, which is fine.

<Step 14> Type **<ctrl><spacebar>** to restore the animation workspace layout.

<Step 15> Go to **frame 11** and then **pose DotRobot** as shown in Figure 6.27.

You do this by typing **rx30** or **rx-30** after selecting the **arml**, **armr**, **legl**, and **legr** bones.

<Step 16> Go to **frame 31** and **pose DotRobot** with the arms and legs swinging the other way.

<Step 17> **Play** the animation by clicking the right-facing triangle at the bottom middle of the timeline editor.

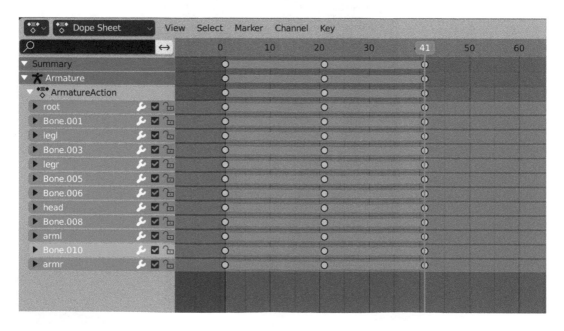

FIGURE 6.26 Dope sheet with keyframes for frames 1, 21, and 41.

FIGURE 6.27　DotRobot walk cycle at frame 11.

The animation plays, but there is a hiccup when it loops back from frame 40 back to frame 1. This happens because the keyframes at frame 41 and frame 1 need to be set to cyclic mode to achieve a smoother transition. Here's how to do that so that the interpolation algorithm knows not to slow down the animation when looping.

<Step 18> **Stop** the **animation**, then in the right 3D viewport, type **a** to select all the bones.

<Step 19> **Change** the **editor type** to **Graph Editor**. Type **<shift>E** and **select Make Cyclic** as shown in Figure 6.28.

You won't try to learn the graph editor at this time. You're just using this one feature of it to fix that annoying hiccup. Did it work?

<Step 20> Go back to the 3D Viewport and **play** the animation.

That should have done it and gotten you a very smooth animation. You're going to do just one more change to the animation, just for fun.

\<Step 21\> At **frame 11** turn the head to the left, at **frame 31** to the right, and **test** that animation.

That turning is done by selecting the head bone, typing **rz**, and adjusting the angle with the mouse. Your animation is now complete, ready for export.

\<Step 22\> Do the usual **fbx export** with **Mesh and Armature selected**.

\<Step 23\> **File – Save** and **Exit Blender**.

IMPORTING TO UNITY, PART 2

In this short section you'll test out the DotRobotRigged.fbx file in Unity.

\<Step 1\> In **Unity**, open the **DotGame3D** project.

You should still have the Staging scene in the hierarchy, just like you left it.

\<Step 2\> In Assets/models, select **DotRobotRigged.fbx** and look at the import settings in the inspector.

\<Step 3\> For the model, **change** the **scale factor** to **0.1**.

\<Step 4\> In the **Animation** section, **test** the **animation** as follows: increase the size of the playback section, check the Loop Time checkbox, and play it.

To increase the size of the playback window, grab the **Armature|ArmatureAction** text and drag it up. The window should now look like Figure 6.29.

\<Step 5\> In the **Staging** scene, **remove** everything except the main camera, the directional light, and the stage game objects.

\<Step 6\> In the **Console** panel, look at the Warning message about Vertices not having weight or bones assigned. This is OK and can be ignored because that's exactly

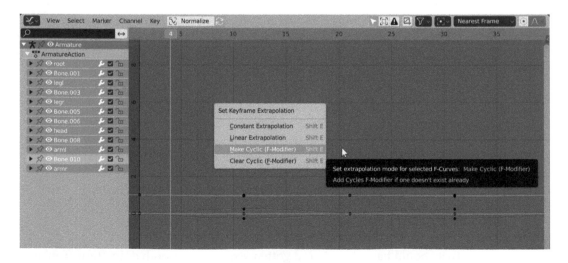

FIGURE 6.28   The graph editor used to make the animation cyclic.

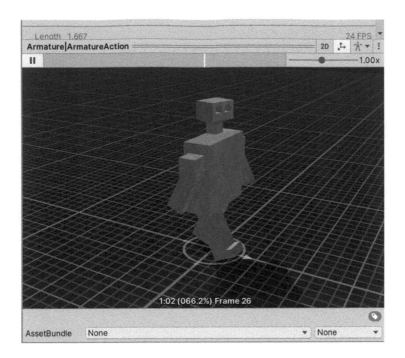

FIGURE 6.29   DotRobot animation in Unity.

what you wanted to do. Usually, all vertices will have bones assigned to them, but you're not doing that in this instance.

<Step 7>   Back in the **Project** panel, **drag** the **DotRobotRigged.fbx** icon into the hierarchy. You will get a message about applying changes to the import settings. Go ahead and apply the changes.

The DotRobot mesh appears at the center of the stage.

<Step 8>   **Expand** DotRobotRigged.fbx if necessary. You will see two Armature icons. **Drag** the **triangular** one into the **DotRobotRigged game object** in the hierarchy.

<Step 9>   **Test** the game.

You should see a small animated DotRobot in the middle of the stage.

<Step 10>   **Adjust** the **camera**, the **lighting**, the **color** of the **stage**, and **turn on shadows** in the **project settings**. Your result should look like Figure 6.30.

The shadow setting is in Edit – Project Settings – Quality in the Shadows section. You will need to turn on Shadows for most of the quality levels. The shadows are set to "disable shadows" presumably because this project was created as a 2D project on an older version of Unity.

<Step 11>   **Save and exit Unity**.

You're hoping that converting the other objects from DotGame will be easier. In the next chapter you'll continue to do that.

FIGURE 6.30 Rigged DotRobot on stage.

CHAPTER 7

More Art Assets

IN THIS CHAPTER YOU'LL import assets from the Unity Asset Store and incorporate them into DotGame3D. You'll explore other places on the web for grabbing free art assets, including meshes and textures. Finally, you'll upgrade most of the other art assets in DotGame to 3D.

THE UNITY ASSET STORE

The Unity Asset Store is a great thing, allowing you to vastly expand Unity's functionality. It's also a good place to hunt for free assets. In this section you'll acquire several free assets from the Unity Asset store and incorporate them into DotGame3D. You're going to look for most anything that could be useful for the game and put it into the Staging scene.

<Step 1> Load **DotGame3D** into **Unity**.

<Step 2> Rename **DotRobotRigged** to **DotRobot** in the hierarchy, if necessary.

<Step 3> **Window – Asset Store**.
In version 2020.3.0f1 of Unity you will see a message telling you that the Asset Store has moved. In earlier versions of Unity, the Asset Store was integrated into the Unity editor directly. In order to improve the performance of the Editor the Unity company has decided that the Asset Store will only exist on the Web.

<Step 4> Click on the **Search online** button.
This will open your default browser and go to the website assetstore.unity.com. You may also be automatically signed in. If not, sign in.

<Step 5> **Search** for **book** in the top search area. You will find an item by VIS GAMES called **Books. Click** on it.

<Step 6> **Browse** that page and look at the four images.
You will discover that this asset includes four books.

<Step 7> **Click** on **Add to My Assets. Accept** the EULA.

DOI: 10.1201/9780429328725-8

EULA stands for "End User License Agreement." Please read it and accept it if you agree. If you don't agree you'll need to find an alternative way to create or find similar placeholder assets.

<Step 8> Go to **My Assets**.

You will see a list of all the assets that you obtained from the Asset Store with your current user account. The new asset will appear at the top.

<Step 9> **Click** on **Open in Unity**.

In Unity the Package Manager pop-up will open and list "My Assets."

<Step 10> **Click Books**.

On the right you will see a detailed description of this Asset. If you don't see Books in the list of assets, click on "My Assets" in the Packages dropdown.

Note: These steps depend on your particular download history from Unity, and the interface currently implemented on the Asset Store website.

<Step 11> Click on **Download**, then on **Import**, and then, in the "Import Unity Package" pop-up, click on **All** and then **Import**. **Close** the Package Manager pop-up.

<Step 12> In the Assets folder, **double-click** on the newly created **Books** folder.

<Step 13> **Double-click** on **example_scene** and look at the scene. Compare with Figure 7.1.

These books can be useful for building levels. Next, you'll try to put the books into the staging scene.

<Step 14> Go to **Assets/Scenes** and **double-click** on the **Staging** scene.

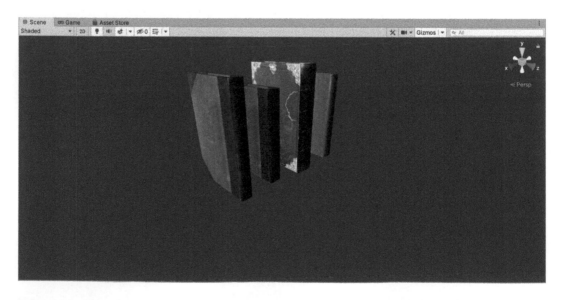

FIGURE 7.1   Four books from the Unity Asset Store.

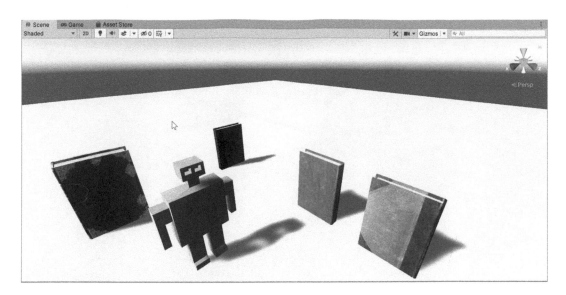

FIGURE 7.2   Robot with books.

<Step 15>   Go back to the **books folder** and then **double-click** on **Prefabs. Drag book_0001a** into the staging scene. **Drag** the **other books** into the scene as well, **change** the **y-rotation** for some of them to **90**, and change the **scale** for all of them to **(3, 3, 3)**. Try to make something like Figure 7.2.

You're going to need a floor, so how about searching for one? You now have an Asset Store tab, so you'll use that in the next step.

<Step 16>   In the Asset Store, **search** for **floors**, click on **Free Assets** in the **pricing** section. Browse around for a while, then select, or search for **Five Seamless Tileable Ground Textures** by **A3D**.

These textures can be applied to a simple plane game object. Try it out as follows:

<Step 17>   Click on **Add to My Assets** and bring it into Unity as you did before. **Download** and **Import.**

<Step 18>   Go to the **Assets** folder, then to the new **Five Seamless Tileable Ground Textures Folder**. Try out the example scene and compare with Figure 7.3.

You won't need all those textures. You'll try out the Grey Stone texture on the stage.

<Step 19>   In the **staging** scene, select the **stage, expand Materials** in the inspector, and **click** on the tiny bullseye icon on the right of the Element 0 Material, as shown in Figure 7.4.

<Step 20>   In the **Select Material** pop-up, search for **Grey Stones** and **select**.

The tiling for this material is much too small. This results in the stones being much too large in this scene.

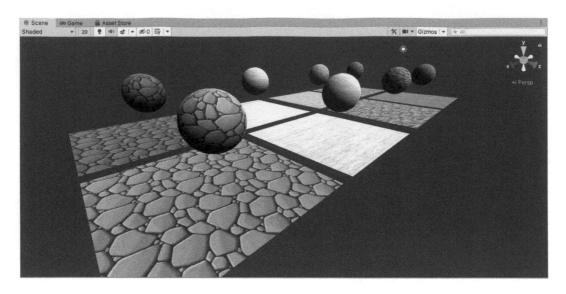

FIGURE 7.3   Five Seamless Tileable Ground Textures from the Unity Asset Store.

<Step 21>   Back in the Materials **section** of your new Asset, **click** on the **Grey Stones** material and in the inspector, change the **Tiling** setting from (3, 3) to (**20, 20**), or other large values of your choosing. Compare the staging scene with Figure 7.5.

FIGURE 7.4   Changing the Material for the Stage.

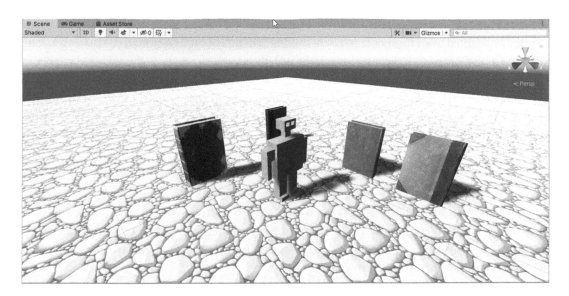

FIGURE 7.5   A whole new floor.

With the thousands of free and inexpensive assets available in the Unity Asset Store you can very quickly build beautiful, complex scenes. Also, along the way, you can learn a few things from your fellow game developers.

<Step 22> File – Save.

The Unity Asset Store isn't the only game in town. There are other possibilities for acquiring just the right assets for your masterpiece.

MILLIONS OF MESHES ON THE WEB

To search the entire internet for meshes, search for **Free 3D models**. This book isn't large enough to adequately discuss all the websites, companies, and individual 3D artists who make their amazing art available to you. In such a situation, the internet itself comes to the rescue. Search for **best websites for 3D models** and use some of those reviews and lists as starting points.

Before you start downloading too many assets, here are some basic guidelines:

- Know the origin of these assets. Find out the name of the artist or artists who created them.

- Give credit even if you don't have to.

- Find out the details of the license, especially if the asset is free. If there is no licensing information available, don't use that asset. Exception: public domain assets.

- Check the polycount. You probably need to keep the polycount reasonable because these assets are going into a real-time game-engine. It's possible to reduce the polycount yourself in Blender, but it's a lot easier to avoid this problem in the first place.

For DotGame3D you're going to limit yourself to the Unity Asset Store and the assets that you created or adapted from this book. Many of the assets in this book, and from franzlanzinger.com, use the CC-BY or the CC0 license. Search the web for more information about these licenses.

The term polycount is an abbreviation of polygon count. Typically, the only polygons in 3D models are triangles and quadrilaterals, also referred to as quads. Keep in mind that quads will be converted to two triangles by the game engine, so the real limitation is the resulting number of triangles. As of 2022, a typical total maximum polycount per scene is 100,000 for mobile and 1 million and up for PC and consoles. When possible, keep that polycount much lower. This will allow for shorter download times and better frame rates on low-end devices.

You may wish to plan ahead 10 years when these limitations will be much higher. To do that, create highly detailed meshes and high-resolution textures when creating your assets at first, then use automatic tools to reduce the polycounts and resolutions of these assets when using them in your present-day game.

FREE TEXTURES

If you are using 3D assets created by someone else, generally you'll get textures as part of the package. When creating your own 3D assets, you may need to create or acquire textures to use in your models, unless, of course, your models look good without textures or with a texture from your own texture library. Typically, you'll model the mesh first, then bring in the textures, just as you did for DotRobot earlier in this chapter. It's particularly easy and at the same time overwhelming to attempt to find and use textures on the web.

Just as you did for 3D meshes, search for **best websites for free textures**. You will find an article at thegraphicsassembly.com about free PBR (physically based rendering) textures. Another good article is at makeitcg.com about **20+ best websites to download free textures**. Of course, you'll also find textures in the Unity Asset Store. Just as for meshes, be aware of the licensing issues that you will face when using these textures or any other asset from the web.

Whatever you do, do not screen grab images from the web and use them as textures. This is the game development equivalent of illegally sampling another musician's copyrighted song. A good way to stay away from court is to create and copyright your own assets from scratch. The next best thing is to carefully document where all of your external assets originated, and to pay for them when necessary.

In the next section you'll get back to working on DotGame3D and converting the remaining 3D assets left over from the 2D version.

3D MODELS FROM THE 2D GAME

In Assets/models you have four additional 3D models to convert: Blockade, QuestionMark, bomb, and Spiker. You'll start with Blockade.

<Step 1> Load **DotGame3D** into Unity.

<Step 2> **Drag** the **Blockade** model into the **staging** scene.
Obviously, that Blockade model is too large.

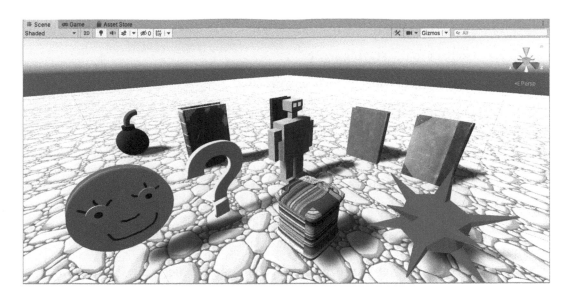

FIGURE 7.6   The Stage is set.

<Step 3>   In the import settings for Blockade, **change** the **scale** to **0.1** and **uncheck Import Cameras** and **Import Lights**.

<Step 4>   **Move** the **Blockade** so you can see it better.
    You'll probably make some adjustments to this object later on. You really should stretch it vertically and fix the UV mapping, but that can wait for now.

<Step 5>   For the **QuestionMark,** the **bomb,** and the **Spiker, fix the import setting** just as you did in Step 3.

<Step 6>   **Drag** a **Question mark**, **bomb**, and **spiker** into the staging scene.
    All that's missing is Dottima. She will also, at first, appear to be much too large for this scene, but you already adjusted her scale for another scene. You'll adjust her scale in the transform instead of the import settings.

<Step 7>   **Drag Dottima** into the scene, and then **change** the **transform scale** to **(0.07, 0.07, 0.07)** in the inspector. Compare with Figure 7.6.

<Step 8>   **Save**.
    Yes, this isn't quite complete. You're still missing a few graphical elements: the arrow, the bomb explosion, and the fuse animation. You will bring those into the game later on. Next, you'll lay out a level so that you can start playing the game.

3D PLAYFIELD WITH COLLISIONS

The playfield for the first level will consist of a floor and some books. Just as in the 2D version, the goal for Dottima is to find the exit. Along the way you'll get used to the controls for Dottima's basic movement. You won't worry about obstacles or enemies along the way. You'll start by creating yet another scene.

<Step 1>   Go to **Assets/scenes. Create a new scene** with the name **3DLevel 1.**

<Step 2>   Go back to the **staging scene.**

<Step 3>   In the Project panel go to **Assets/prefabs.**

<Step 4>   **Drag** the **Stage** game object into the **prefabs** folder.

This creates a prefab called "Stage," which you can use in **3DLevel 1.** In the prefabs folder you can see eight prefabs left over from the 2D game. These prefabs are templates for creating game objects in your various scenes. The game objects are inherited from the prefabs, so you'll be able to make changes to the prefabs and have those changes appear in all of the inherited game objects. The act of dragging a game object into the Assets folder or one of the subfolders creates a new prefab automatically.

<Step 5>   Back in **3DLevel 1 drag** the **Stage** prefab into the hierarchy. Compare your Scene view with Figure 7.7.

You may need to adjust your view of the scene. Choose a free, perspective view, and drag MMB so you can see the gizmo for the Stage in the center of the screen. This would be a good time for you to read or reread the "Scene view navigation" section of the Unity manual. If you're not familiar with those controls, try them out on this very simple scene.

<Step 6>   **Rename** the **Stage** prefab to **floor**. Also rename the **Stage** game object to **floor**.

That's right, renaming a prefab doesn't rename the inherited game objects, so you need to do that manually if you want that.

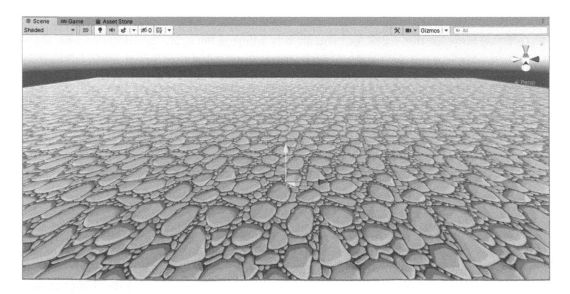

FIGURE 7.7   Rebuilding Level 1 in 3D: The floor.

<Step 7> Back in the **Staging** scene, make a **prefab** out of **Dottima**, stored in Assets/ prefabs.

<Step 8> In **3DLevel 1 create** an instance of the **Dottima** prefab. Change **Position** to **(0, 0, 0)**, **Rotation** to **(0, 180, 0)**. Place an instance of **book_0001a** to the **left of Dottima**. Compare with Figure 7.8.

This doesn't look like much of a level. Before you start putting in more books, you'll try to get Dottima to move around and collide with the book. By colliding you mean that the book will remain stationary and Dottima won't be able to move through the book. You'll also make the book somewhat larger.

Just as in the 2D game, you will need to put in colliders and rigid body components. You'll also put in a simple character controller so you can move Dottima in response to your controls. You'll do the simplest thing first: moving Dottima with the four keyboard arrow keys.

<Step 9> With **Dottima** selected, click on **Add Component** in the inspector. Add a **Box Collider** from the Physics section.

Note that in the 2D version, game objects have colliders, etc., from the Physics 2D section. Make sure to avoid those 2D components in 3D games such as this one.

You may wonder why you should be using a box collider for a circular object. The simple answer is that it's good enough for this game, and easier to deal with than the alternatives. Box colliders are computationally very efficient, so it's a good idea to use them whenever possible. Another,

FIGURE 7.8 Dottima and a book.

perhaps more important advantage is that box colliders allow you to quickly adjust the geometry of the collider in order to fine-tune game play. Often, making the box collider slightly smaller than the associated object makes the game feel more forgiving.

Next, you'll adjust the box collider for Dottima.

<Step 10> Adjust the scene view by **selecting the non-perspective Back view**, then do **frame selected** by selecting **Dottima**, if necessary, and then typing **f**. Zoom out to show all of Dottima.

Compare your view with Figure 7.9.

That small green square, the box collider, will need some adjusting.

<Step 11> In the inspector, click on the **Edit Bounding Volume** icon next to **Edit Collider**.

You now see five small green squares at the bottom of Dottima. Only the outer four squares are movable.

<Step 12> Carefully **drag** the **outer four squares** to **fit** the green box to **Dottima**.

<Step 13> Go to the **Top view** and **adjust** the **collider** there as well.

You only had to adjust the top square by dragging it down somewhat. Compare with Figure 7.10.

<Step 14> **Add** a **Rigidbody** component to **Dottima**.

<Step 15> **Turn off Gravity**. In the Constraints section, **freeze all three rotations**.

You won't be using gravity for Dottima, at least for now. You may turn it on again on later levels.

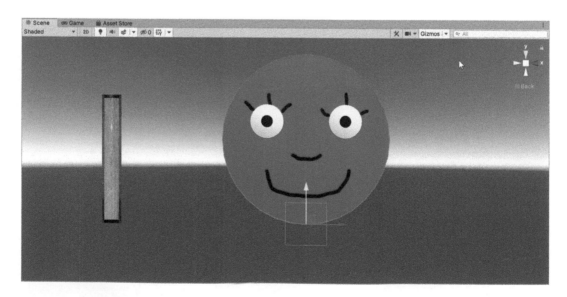

FIGURE 7.9 Dottima with box collider.

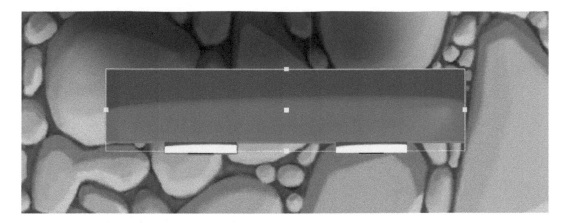

FIGURE 7.10   Dottima box collider adjustment from the top.

Your next simple goal is to move Dottima when playing the game. You'll do that by writing a short script. This script will eventually replace the DottimaController script from the 2D game.

<Step 16>   In the **Assets/scripts** folder create **DottimaScript** and **assign** it to **Dottima**.

<Step 17>   **Edit DottimaScript** in Visual Studio to look like this:

```
using System.Collections;
using System.Collections.Generic;
using UnityEngine;

public class DottimaScript : MonoBehaviour
{
    private Rigidbody rb;
    // Start is called before the first frame update
    void Start()
    {
        rb = GetComponent<Rigidbody>();
        rb.velocity = new Vector3(0.0f, 0.0f, -0.5f);
    }

    // Update is called once per frame
    void Update()
    {

    }
}
```

This script accesses the rigid body component and sets the velocity vector to (0.0f, 0.0f, −0.5f). Remember that those f's at the end of the numbers indicate to Unity that the numbers are floats rather than doubles. In general, you will be using floats throughout this Unity game, so you will need to type f's at the end of fractional constants. For consistency you added the f at the end of 0.0. The z component is negative because the z-axis points away from the camera, and you wish to move Dottima toward the camera.

Once you've correctly typed in this code and aren't getting error messages in Unity, you'll be ready to test the code.

<Step 18> **Test.**

During the test you should see Dottima move toward you. Compare with Figure 7.11.

You presumably still had "Maximize on Play" turned on, so it was easier to see the very small Dottima moving toward you and getting larger along the way. Next, you'll move the Camera closer to Dottima's initial position.

<Step 19> Select the **Game** tab, select the **Main Camera** in the hierarchy, and **experiment** with the Z position of the camera in the inspector.

Initially the Z position is the default −10. You can drag the Z letter with the mouse as shown in Figure 7.12.

As you can see, in this figure the Z position is −1.78, which will give you a closer view of Dottima and the book. You are also going to tilt the camera down.

FIGURE 7.11 Dottima moving toward the camera.

▼ ⟟ **Transform**			❼ ᵈ⁺ ⋮
Position	X 0	Y 1	⬉−1.78
Rotation	X 0	Y 0	Z 0
Scale	X 1	Y 1	Z 1

FIGURE 7.12 Dragging the Z position of the Main Camera.

<Step 20> Set the **Z position** of the **main camera** to **-1.78**. **X rotation** to **15**. **Test**.

This time you can see that Dottima slowly moves down and out of view of the camera. Next, you'll put in the controls using the keyboard arrow keys.

<Step 21> In **DottimaScript change** the **Start** and **Update** functions to this:

```
void Start()
{
    rb = GetComponent<Rigidbody>();
}

// Update is called once per frame
void Update()
{
    float speed = 2.0f;
    Vector3 moveInput = new Vector3(
      Input.GetAxisRaw("Horizontal"),
      0.0f,
      Input.GetAxisRaw("Vertical"));
    rb.velocity = moveInput.normalized * speed;
}
```

You removed the velocity initialization from the `Start` function because it's no longer needed and put in a simple velocity calculation, which takes the horizontal and vertical axis inputs and converts them to a velocity for Dottima.

<Step 22> **Test** the game with the **arrow keys**, **WASD keys**, and a **game controller**.

That's right, Unity automatically lets you use the game controller as well as the arrow and WASD keys. This turned out to be much easier than anticipated. You can even plug in and unplug game controllers while the game is running, and everything will continue to work as expected. Try this if you have multiple game controllers. If your game controllers are being used for the first time while running the game you may need to exit the game, finish setup, and then run the game again in order for that game controller to work.

You're now ready to tackle collision detection. As you probably noticed, Dottima runs right through the book, which isn't what you want.

<Step 23> For the **book** game object, **add** a **Mesh Collider** and a **Rigidbody**. In the **Rigidbody, uncheck Use Gravity** and **check Is Kinematic.**

While it may be more efficient to use a box collider for the book, the book mesh is simple enough and easier to set up.

<Step 24> **Test**.

Well, that was fun. Speaking of fun, try the following.

<Step 25> **Uncheck** the **Y freeze rotation** and test that.

Now, Dottima can spin on the y-axis, but is otherwise well behaved. You're going to undo this for now, but maybe in the future you'll allow y rotation in some situations.

<Step 26> Undo the **previous step**.

<Step 27> **Save**.

> Even though you're in the middle of a section, this is a good place to save. Next, you're going to actually do what this section is all about: build a playfield.
>
> First things first: That book is just too small in relation to Dottima.

<Step 28> In the **scene** view, **change** to the **Back Orthographic view**.

> In other words, turn on Back and turn off Perspective in the view gizmo.

<Step 29> Do a **frame selected** for the **book** (book_0001a).

<Step 30> With the **book** selected, **change** the **scale** from (2, 2, 2) to **(4, 4, 4)** in the Inspector. Zoom out and compare your scene view with Figure 7.13.

<Step 31> **Rename book_0001a** to **booka**.

> This is just to make the naming of the four books more compact.

<Step 32> **Drag booka** to the **prefabs** folder, thus creating a prefab. Choose **Original Prefab** in the popup window.

> When creating a prefab using a prefab instance you get this popup. The alternative choice, creating a prefab variant, isn't necessary here. You can read more about prefab variants in the Unity manual if you wish. You won't be using prefab variants in this project.
>
> To keep things simple, you'll only be using the "booka" prefab when making this level. Later on, you'll bring in the other books. You'll try to create a maze that is similar to Level 1 in the 2D game, but it's OK to not be authentic in your recreation. After all, this isn't a remaster, it's a remake. You still

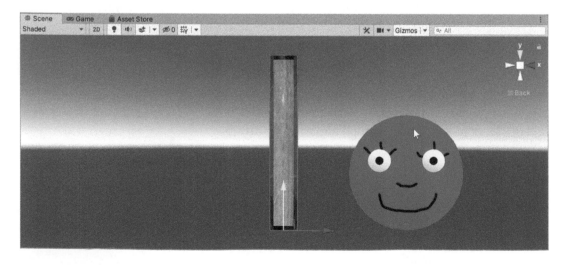

FIGURE 7.13 **Book enlarged.**

have Level 1 available in the Assets/scenes folder, so if you wish, take a look at the old scene as a reminder. You'll need to turn on 2D mode in the Scene panel when you do that. When you're finished looking at Level 1, go back to 3DLevel 1.

<Step 33> In the **scene** panel, **select** the **top orthographic view**, and do **frame selected** for **booka**.

<Step 34> **Drag** additional **books** into the scene and arrange them as shown in Figure 7.14.

<Step 35> **Test**.
   The game feels OK, except that Dottima sometimes gets stuck when moving along a wall. You're not going to worry about this problem just yet. This has to do with the somewhat loose placement of the books. You may revisit this later on, once the game is actually playable.
   Next, you'll create a prefab for a rotated book.

<Step 36> **Create** a **booka** instance in the middle, below the 12 books, and **change** the **y rotation** to **90**. Change its name to **bookar** and create a **prefab** from it. Compare with Figure 7.15.

<Step 37> Use the new prefab to **create three more rotated books** and **arrange** the **four rotated books** as shown in Figure 7.16.

<Step 38> **Test**.
   So far, so good. To create a full level, you'll be adding many more books. As you can see, this will cause the hierarchy to become unwieldy. To fix this you will create a playfield object and make all the books and the floor child objects. That way you can easily hide all the books when working on other parts of the scene.

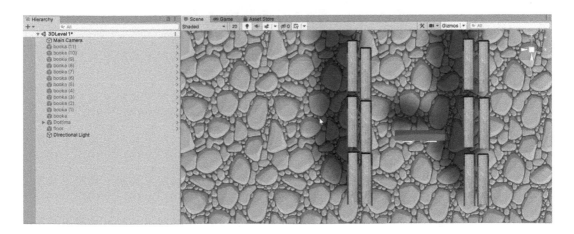

FIGURE 7.14   Arranging 12 books.

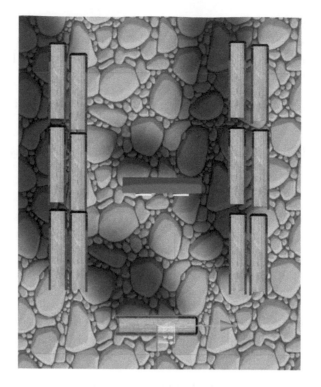

FIGURE 7.15   A rotated book at the bottom.

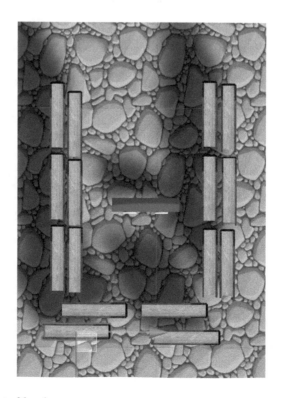

FIGURE 7.16   Four rotated books.

<Step 39> **Create** an **empty game object**, name it **playfield**.

<Step 40> **Drag-select** all the **books** and **drag** them on top of the playfield object in the hierarchy.

<Step 41> Put the **floor** into the **playfield** game object as well.
The new hierarchy should look like Figure 7.17.

<Step 42> **Test**.
You are continuing to follow the philosophy of testing early and often. The huge advantage of using a system such as Unity for game development is the ability to immediately test your game after making changes, whether they are large or small. This way, when a problem appears you get a hint about what might have caused the issue: It was most likely that change you just made.

In the prehistoric days of game development, it was common and often necessary to write code for days or even months without testing. This made testing and debugging much more difficult. Today, you can spend just a few seconds making a change, and then you can test it right away.

Getting back to business, you have noticed that Dottima is difficult to see among all of those books. You will need to move the camera up.

<Step 43> **Select** the **Main Camera**, use the **Game** view, and **experiment** with the position and rotation transforms for the camera. You can also try **changing** the **field of view**.

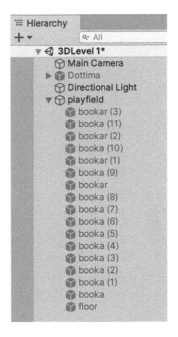

FIGURE 7.17 A better hierarchy.

You are going to have to decide what to do with the camera. Before committing, a reasonable stationary camera will allow you to lay out the level and test basic movement.

\<Step 44\> **Change** the **main camera transform** to **position (1, 2, −1.7)**, **rotation (35, 0, 0)**, **field of view 60**. Compare with Figure 7.18.

\<Step 45\> In the **scene** panel, using a **top orthographic** view, **place** horizontal and vertical **books** approximately as shown in Figure 7.19. Use box-selecting and **\<ctrl\>d** to duplicate sets of books. This will keep them as children of the playfield game object.

\<Step 46\> **Test. Save.**
It looks like it works, so far. It's fun to have the books be free-standing and not arranged in a rigid grid as in the 2D game. You'll continue to place the rest of the books in the next step.

\<Step 47\> **Place** more **books** as shown in Figure 7.20.
Before you test this, you may need to move the floor to the right.

\<Step 48\> If necessary, **center** the **floor** to the right by adjusting its x and z positions. **Zoom out** your top view of the scene and compare with Figure 7.21.
Your new floor position should be about (2.6, 0, 2.0).

\<Step 49\> **Test** the game. Compare with Figure 7.22.
Clearly that camera is out of position.

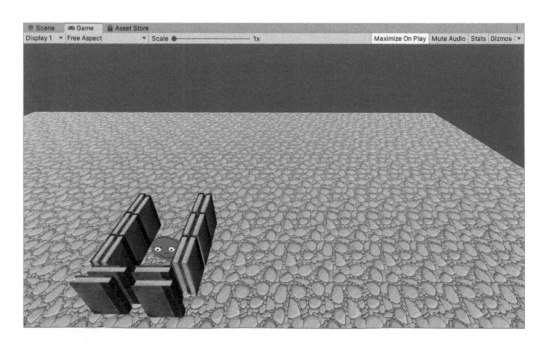

FIGURE 7.18 New main camera settings.

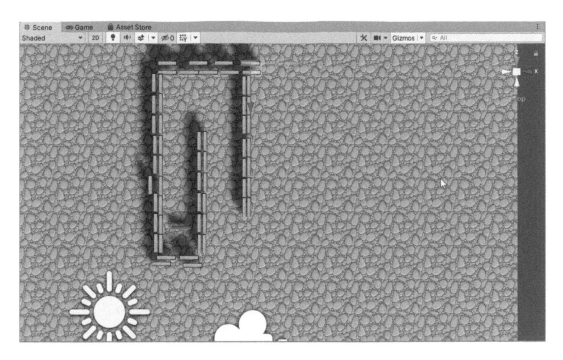

FIGURE 7.19   Starting to build the playfield.

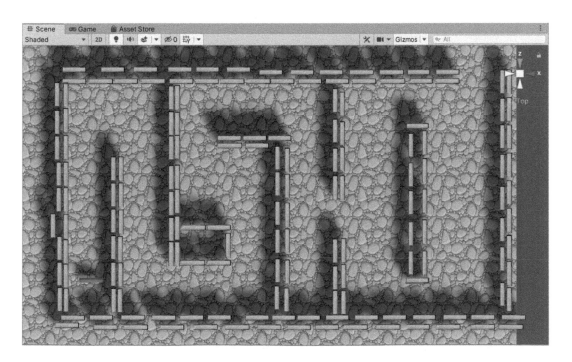

FIGURE 7.20   Top view of the first 3D level.

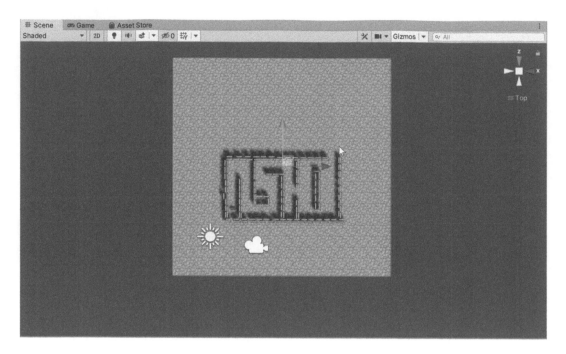

FIGURE 7.21   Centering the floor.

FIGURE 7.22   Testing the playfield.

<Step 50> **Change** the **X position** of the **main camera** to **2.7**, and the **field of view** to **80**. **Test** again. If necessary, adjust the main camera position to center the maze and have all of it visible.

For now, this is acceptable. You can see the entire playfield and you are able to move Dottima from her starting position to the exit. You can almost call this a playable game, although there are a lot of missing elements. It's time to take a break and think about how to bring in enemies and make the camera movable. You will do that in the next chapter.

<Step 51> **Save** and **exit** Unity.

CHAPTER 8

First Playable

I N THIS CHAPTER YOU'LL make the game playable for the first three levels. It is often an important milestone to have your game playable. Getting a feel for how the game plays is invaluable. In a way, the current version of the game is playable already, except that it's not much of a game when all you can do is to move the main character around. You really need to add the arrow weapon and some enemies to shoot at. You won't have sound yet, and the graphics won't be final, but having something resembling a real game will definitely help.

MOVING THE CAMERA

In this section you'll work on making the camera follow Dottima around, thus allowing for a nicer view of the game.

<Step 1> Load **DotGame3D** into Unity. **Select** the **Main Camera**.
Your goal here is simple: Move the camera to a suitable location where the player can see Dottima and her immediate surroundings.

<Step 2> **Select** the **Game** tab and **move** the **X position** of the camera to **0**.
This lines up the camera with the initial position of Dottima.

<Step 3> **Change** the **field of view** to **40 degrees**.
Earlier you made the field of view much larger so you could see the entire playfield. This smaller field of view is better for a moving camera.

<Step 4> **Change** the **X rotation** to **50**.
This lets the player have a less obstructed view of Dottima. Compare with Figure 8.1.
It's time to write a short script for camera movement.

<Step 5> Create the following script with name MainCamera, attach it to the main camera, and move it to the scripts folder.

DOI: 10.1201/9780429328725-9

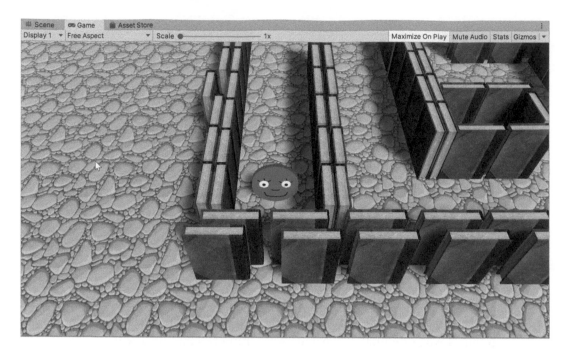

FIGURE 8.1   Main camera setup to make it movable.

```
using System.Collections;
using System.Collections.Generic;
using UnityEngine;

public class MainCamera : MonoBehaviour
{
    GameObject player;
    // Start is called before the first frame update
    void Start()
    {
        player = null;
    }

    // Update is called once per frame
    void Update()
    {
        if (!player) player = GameObject.Find("Dottima");
        if (player)
        {
            transform.position = new Vector3(
                player.transform.position.x,
                2.0f,
                player.transform.position.z - 1.6f
                );
        }
    }
}
```

The player variable is initialized to **null** at the start so that Update works. The update code tries to find the player, and if successful it places the camera at a fixed offset from the player. The calculation for the y component assumes that the y position of the player is 0. It's important to realize that if you wish to use this code where the y position of the player may be nonzero.

FIGURE 8.2 Dottima nearing the exit.

<Step 6> **Test** and **Save**.

This is looking much better. When you bring Dottima near the exit, compare your screen with Figure 8.2.

It may feel that the camera is a little too close to Dottima, but you can easily adjust that later depending on what else is happening in the game. In the next section you'll expand the game to three levels with enemies and a weapon for Dottima.

THREE LEVELS

In this section you'll create two additional levels by copying the first level twice, introducing spikers on level two, and a blocker on level three. You'll adapt the 2D code for the spikers and blockers to work in 3D. You'll also put in code for detecting when Dottima reaches the exit and code for then moving to the next level.

<Step 1> **Select** the scene **3DLevel 1**. In the hierarchy, **click** on the **three dots** on the right of **3DLevel 1** and select **Save Scene As**. Compare with in Figure 8.3.

<Step 2> **Save** the scene with the name **3DLevel 2.unity** in the **Assets/Scenes** folder.

<Step 3> **Create level 3** in a similar manner.

You now have three levels that are identical except for their names. You may wish to test all three levels to make sure that they run, just in case something really bad and unexpected happened. Testing, even when you "know" it's not necessary, can save you lots of grief during development.

<Step 4> **Go to 3DLevel 2. Select** the scene view.

<Step 5> **Adjust** the view to **approximately** match Figure 8.1.

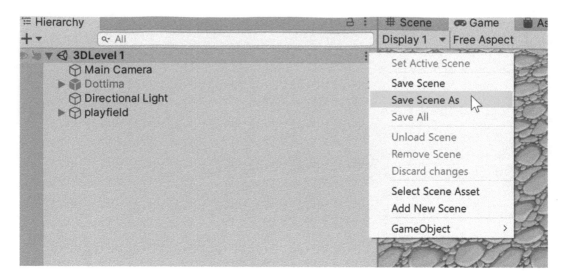

FIGURE 8.3　How to copy a scene.

You do that by selecting the free and perspective view in the Scene gizmo in the upper-right corner of the Scene view. Then adjust the view by dragging the right mouse button and moving with the keyboard arrow keys, or by dragging the middle mouse button.

Your next step is to add spikers to the scene and to make them work. To keep the prefabs organized a little better create a new folder: Assets/3dprefabs.

<Step 6> **Create** the folder **Assets/3dprefabs**.

Your plan is to put the 3D prefabs for spikers, blockades, etc., into this folder. You will leave Dottima and the books in the old prefabs folder, even though they are 3D prefabs. This is perhaps not the best way to organize your prefabs, but that's what you're doing for now.

<Step 7> Go the **Staging** scene.

<Step 8> Select the **3dprefabs** folder.

<Step 9> **Create prefabs** for the **Spiker, Blockade, DotRobotRigged, bomb**, and **QuestionMark**, all in the **3dprefabs** folder. Create **original prefabs**, not variants.

<Step 10> **Save** the staging scene, then go to **3DLevel 2**.

<Step 11> **Drag** the **spiker** into the scene, as shown in Figure 8.4.

This spiker looks to be too large when compared to the 2D version, so you're going to change the scale in the prefab.

<Step 12> **Select** the **spiker prefab** in **3dprefabs**, and change the **Scale** to (**0.7, 0.7, 0.7**) in the inspector.

FIGURE 8.4   Spiker in level 2.

<Step 13> Test the game.

You can see the spiker, but it's not animated and Dottima moves right through it. To make this playable you'll need to put in collision detection and kill Dottima when she collides with the spiker. You'll also need to add the arrow so that Dottima can attack the spikers. You'll do that in the subsequent section.

3D SPIKERS

In this section you'll animate the spikers and put in collision detection for them. The animation will be done using code. You'll also port the movement code from the 2D game.

<Step 1> Select the **Spiker** game object in the hierarchy.

<Step 2> Add a **rigidbody** component, **turn off gravity**.

<Step 3> Add a **sphere collider** and **edit** the **collider** to fit. Compare with Figure 8.5.

It's OK, and in fact encouraged to have the sphere collider be slightly smaller than the spiker mesh.

<Step 4> Test.

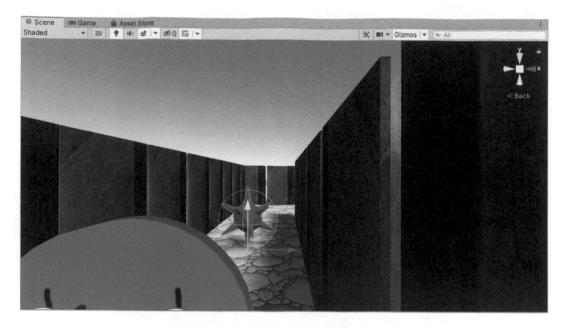

FIGURE 8.5 Adding a rigidbody and sphere collider to the spiker.

You can push the spiker around by colliding Dottima with it. This next step may not really be necessary. You know that the spiker y position should always be zero, so you're going to constrain the rigidbody as follows:

\<Step 5\> With the **spiker selected**, **check** the **Freeze Position Y** box in the Constraints section, Rigidbody section, in the inspector panel.

This will ensure that the spiker will stay on the floor and not go airborne for some reason.

Next, you'll add the rotation animation.

\<Step 6\> **Create** the following script with the name **Spiker3D** and **assign** it to the **spiker**.

```
using System.Collections;
using System.Collections.Generic;
using UnityEngine;

public class Spiker3D : MonoBehaviour
{

    private Rigidbody rb;
    private Vector3 eulervel;

    // Start is called before the first frame update
    void Start()
    {
        rb = GetComponent<Rigidbody>();
        eulervel = new Vector3(0, 100.0f, 0);
    }

    // Update is called once per frame
    void FixedUpdate()
```

```
    {
        Quaternion deltaRotation =
          Quaternion.Euler(eulervel * Time.fixedDeltaTime);
        rb.MoveRotation(rb.rotation * deltaRotation);
    }
}
```

This code is very similar to the code in the Unity Manual in the MoveRotation section. If you're interested, read that section for an explanation.

<Step 7> **Test**.

You see the spiker rotating just like in the 2D game. The big difference is that the rotation is accomplished by rotating the rigidbody using Unity code, rather than prerendering several frames in Blender and then looping through those animation frames. The resulting animation is much smoother, takes less memory, and can easily be adjusted. For example, you can make the spiker rotate at a very slow rate by changing the eulervel vector to (0, 10.0f, 0). Try it!

Your next goal is to port the 2D spiker script to 3D.

<Step 8> Take a look at the **Spiker.cs** script in **Assets/scripts** and try to understand that code.

If you worked through the book *2D Game Development with Unity* you might remember this code. It sets up a direction vector variable used to keep track of the current direction of motion of the spiker. When the spiker collides with something the direction is changed and there is a small bounce back.

Upon reflection, this code should work in 3D as well, with some minor adjustments. The rigidbody2D component will have to be changed to a rigidbody. The Vector2 items will be changed to Vector3 with a zero y component.

You could combine this code with the existing Spiker3D code, but it's a little cleaner to just make this into a separate script. Yes, it's possible to have multiple scripts for game objects. When you do that all the scripts run simultaneously.

<Step 9> **Edit Spiker.cs** in Visual Studio and save it as **SpikerMove.cs**.

<Step 10> **Edit SpikerMove.cs** to match the following code listing:

```
using System.Collections;
using System.Collections.Generic;
using UnityEngine;

public class SpikerMove : MonoBehaviour
{
    public float speed;
    private Rigidbody rb;
    private int direction; // four directions 0,1,2,3
                           // down, left, up, right

    void Start()
    {
        rb = GetComponent<Rigidbody>();
```

```
            direction = 0;
    }

    private Vector3 dirVector;

    private void FixedUpdate()
    {
        if (direction == 0) dirVector = new Vector3(0.0f, 0.0f, -1.0f);
        if (direction == 1) dirVector = new Vector3(-1.0f, 0.0f, 0.0f);
        if (direction == 2) dirVector = new Vector3(0.0f, 0.0f, 1.0f);
        if (direction == 3) dirVector = new Vector3(1.0f, 0.0f, 0.0f);

        rb.velocity = dirVector.normalized * speed;
    }

    private void OnCollisionEnter(Collision collision)
    {
        Vector3 newPosition = new Vector3(
            transform.position.x - dirVector.x * 0.07f,
            0.0f,
            transform.position.z - dirVector.z * 0.07f);

        rb.MovePosition(newPosition);
        direction = (direction + 1) % 4;
    }
}
```

In addition to removing the 2D references, you removed the 2D animation code and changed the name of the class to `SpikerMove`. You also changed the bounce offset to `0.07f` in the collision enter code. That 0.07 was found via experimentation. The `OnCollisionEnter` is tricky. Make sure to change the `dirvector.y` to `dirvector.z` and the same goes for `transform.position.y`.

<Step 11> **Attach SpikerMove** to the **Spiker** gameobject.

<Step 12> In the inspector, **type** in a **speed** of **1** in the **Spiker Move** section.

<Step 13> **Test.**

The spiker is now bouncing off the books and changing direction when that happens. Before you put more spikers out there it's time to update the prefab.

<Step 14> **Drag** the **Spiker** on top of the **Spiker prefab** in **Assets/3dprefabs**.

<Step 15> **Instantiate two** additional **spikers** someplace on the playfield.

<Step 16> **Test.**

The spikers are working well enough for now. They can get stuck in a corner sometimes, but that's OK for now. They're not damaging Dottima just yet. That code will be put in a little later.

<Step 17> **Save** and **exit** Unity.

In the next section you'll create the 3D arrow weapon for Dottima in Blender.

3D ARROWS FOR DOTTIMA

In this section you'll create a 3D model for the arrow weapon. Then you'll port the code that shoots arrows and handles the collisions of arrows with spikers.

<Step 1> **Launch Blender** and **save** the project with the name **arrow.blend** in **Assets/ models**.

You'll use the familiar box modeling technique to make a 3D model of your arrow. It will look similar to the arrow in the 2D game.

<Step 2> **Rename** the **cube** to **arrow** in the outliner.

<Step 3> Type **s<shift>y 0.2<enter>**.

The <shift>y command scales the other two axes, thus the scale happens along the x and z axes, leaving the y-axis unscaled.

<Step 4> **Zoom** in to get a better view.

<Step 5> Type **sy2<enter>**.

<Step 6> **Select** the **Modeling** workspace. Then **select** the **Select Box** icon on the top left. Zoom in again.

<Step 7> Hover the mouse over the arrow, type **<ctrl>r,** and then move the mouse wheel to get seven loop cuts. Then **Left-click twice** without moving the mouse.

Compare with Figure 8.6.

This is the body of the arrow. You'll now create the tip and the fins. This is a good time to use the mirror modifier so that you only have to make the fins on one side. The other side will be created for you automatically.

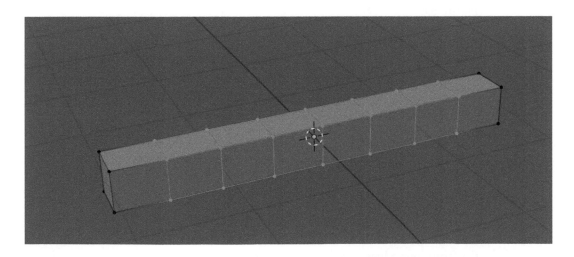

FIGURE 8.6   Seven loop cuts for the arrow.

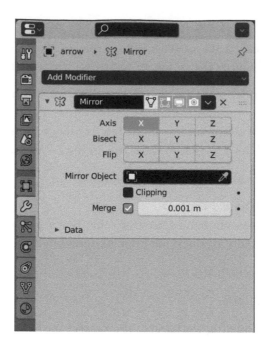

FIGURE 8.7   Using the mirror modifier.

<Step 8> **Select** the **modifier properties** in the properties editor and add the **Mirror modifier. Choose** the **X axis only** as shown in Figure 8.7.

<Step 9> **Verify** that **Edit Mode** and **Realtime** are **turned on** to the right of the Mirror name. You can tell by their blue color. They are turned on in Figure 8.7 above the Y axis button.

You are now ready to make the fins at the back end of the arrow.

<Step 10> Use **face select mode** and **select** the **left-most face** in front as shown in Figure 8.8.

<Step 11> Type **e0.5<enter>**.

Notice the mirror modifier in action. As you work on the fin on the right side of the arrow, the fin on the left side will be built for you and you can see the result in real time. This is a very useful and common modifier because so many models, both mechanical and organic, are symmetric.

<Step 12> With the extruded face still selected, type **gy-0.2<enter>**.

<Step 13> Go to **edge select** mode, **select** the **right edge** of the extruded face. You're going to move this one to the left as well. Type **gy-0.4<enter>**.

Compare with Figure 8.9.

<Step 14> Still in edge select mode, turn the view by **dragging MMB**, and then select the front four edges as shown in Figure 8.10.

<Step 15> Type **gy0.4<enter>**.

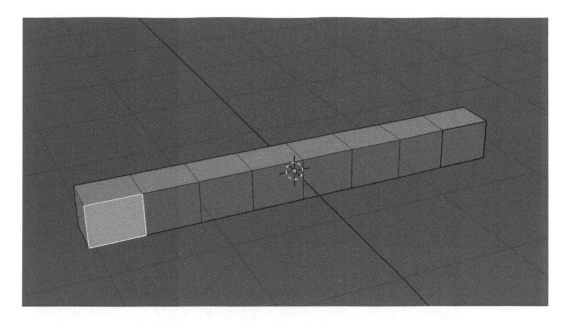

FIGURE 8.8   Select this face.

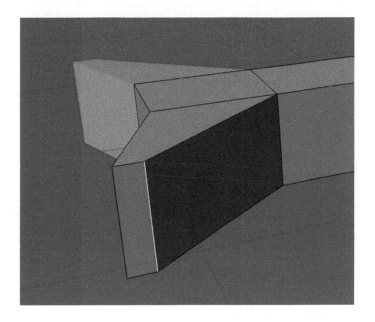

FIGURE 8.9   Back fins for the arrow.

<Step 16>   In **face select mode, select** the **front large face** and type **e0.6<enter>**.

<Step 17>   In **edge select mode, adjust edges** to match Figure 8.11. You can use the **gy** command and **move the mouse** to move two vertical edges to do this.

All that's left to do now is to sharpen the tip of the arrow. You will apply the mirror modifier, which can only be done in object mode.

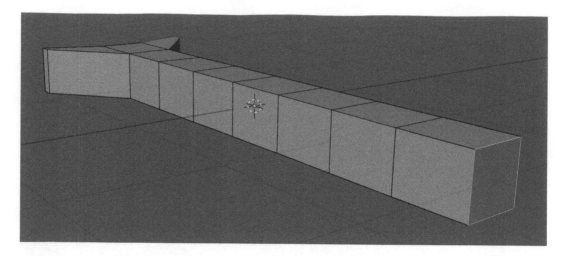

FIGURE 8.10 Front edges selected.

FIGURE 8.11 Shaping the arrowhead.

\<Step 18\> Use the **layout** workspace.

\<Step 19\> Select the **modifier properties** in the properties editor.

\<Step 20\> **Apply** the **mirror modifier** as shown in Figure 8.12.
This has the effect of stopping the mirroring process and finalizing the creation of the mirrored geometry.

\<Step 21\> Back in the **modeling** workspace, go into **vertex select mode**.

\<Step 22\> Use **wireframe viewport shading**, toggle **x-ray on**.

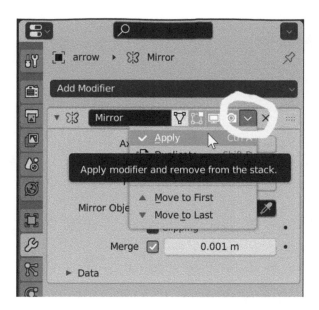

FIGURE 8.12   Applying the mirror modifier.

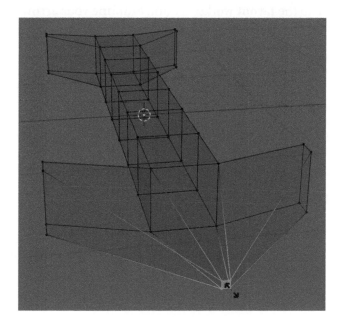

FIGURE 8.13   Sharpening the tip of the arrow.

<Step 23> **Rotate the view, Box-Select** the **front four vertices,** and **scale** them to a very small square as shown in Figure 8.13.

    This step is tricky. You need to carefully use box-select to select the four vertices in front all at once with x-ray on, because that way you actually get the two sets of four vertices that are overlaid on one another there. If you click-select the vertices instead you won't get all eight vertices and the scale operation won't work properly.

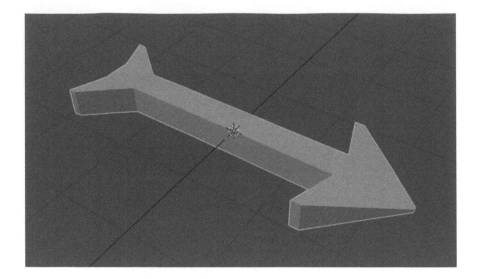

FIGURE 8.14   The 3D arrow model.

<Step 24>   Go back to the **layout** workspace and **examine** your **arrow**. Compare with
Figure 8.14.

<Step 25>   **Save** the **Blend** file.
You're going to let Unity handle making the arrow red.

ARROWS IN UNITY: DOTTIMA INSTANTIATES ARROWS

In this section you'll bring the 3D arrow from the previous section into Unity, add a spinning animation, and create a prefab for it. Then you'll look at the arrow shooting code in
the 2D game and port some of it into DotGame3D.

<Step 1>   Load **DotGame3D** into Unity.

<Step 2>   **Select** the **arrow** model in **Assets/models**.

<Step 3>   In the inspector, **uncheck Import Cameras** and **Import Lights**, set the scale
factor to **0.07**, and **apply**.

<Step 4>   Go to the **staging scene** and put an **arrow** into the scene.

<Step 5>   **Create** a **red material** in the **models** folder, **rename** it to **Arrow Material**,
assign it to the **arrow model**. Your scene should look something like
Figure 8.15.
The arrow is now ready to be turned into a prefab.

<Step 6>   Go to the **3dprefabs** folder and **drag** the **arrow** into that folder.

<Step 7>   **Save** the **staging scene** and go to the **3DLevel 2** scene.
A fast way to do that is to use File – Open Recent Scene and select the
desired recent scene.

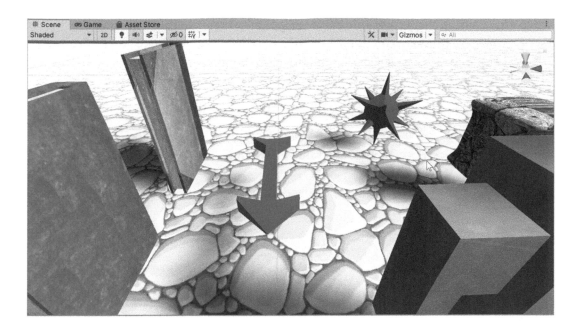

FIGURE 8.15   A red arrow in the staging scene.

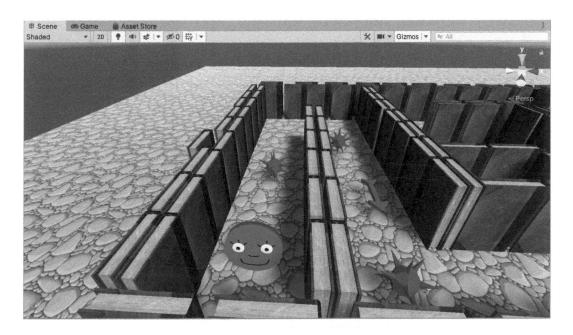

FIGURE 8.16   An arrow sitting in 3D level 2.

<Step 8>   Put an **arrow** into the scene and **adjust** the **view** to look like Figure 8.16.
In the game, the arrows won't be initialized into scenes like this. Rather, they'll be created when the player presses the "shoot" button or "shoot" key. For now, this is only a test.

<Step 9>   **Create** a **new script** for the arrow called **ArrowAnimation**.

<Step 10> **Assign** the **ArrowAnimation** script to the **arrow** in the hierarchy.

Next, you're going to do something rather strange. You're going to copy and paste the class Spiker3D from the script Spiker3D, but not all of it, just the contents inside the curly brackets.

<Step 11> **Open** the script **Spiker3D, highlight** the **contents** of the **Spiker3D class** by dragging the mouse.

<Step 12> Type **<ctrl>c,** then **do the same highlighting** in **ArrowAnimation.cs** and type **<ctrl>v.**

You should have the following code in ArrowAnimation.cs:

```
using System.Collections;
using System.Collections.Generic;
using UnityEngine;

public class ArrowAnimation : MonoBehaviour
{
    private Rigidbody rb;
    private Vector3 eulervel;

    // Start is called before the first frame update
    void Start()
    {
        rb = GetComponent<Rigidbody>();
        eulervel = new Vector3(0, 100.0f, 0);
    }

    // Update is called once per frame
    void FixedUpdate()
    {
        Quaternion deltaRotation =
          Quaternion.Euler(eulervel * Time.fixedDeltaTime);
        rb.MoveRotation(rb.rotation * deltaRotation);
    }
}
```

Your plan is to rotate the arrow along it's z-axis. You're almost there. This code rotates the arrow along the y-axis. Just for fun, try it out:

<Step 13> **Save ArrowAnimation.cs** and **test** the game.

Well, it didn't work. No rotation is visible. Can you guess why? Actually, there is no guessing here. You should see an error message at the bottom of the screen, in red letters. It's telling you that the arrow doesn't have a rigid-body component!

<Step 14> **Add a rigidbody component** to the **arrow. Turn off gravity, freeze the y position.**

You're using the same rigidbody settings as for the spiker.

<Step 15> **Test** the game again.

That's better, the arrow is now rotating, although not the way you want.

<Step 16> In line 14, where eulerlevel is set, change the Vector3 to **(0, 0, 100.0f)**, and **test** again.

Yes, the arrow is now spinning along its z-axis at 100 degrees per second. That's what you wanted, but maybe the arrow should spin faster.

As an aside, you might be wondering why there's an f for some constants but not others. Here's what you need to know. Integer constants don't need the f, but constants with a decimal period like 1.3f and, yes, even 1.0f require that f afterward. You can be lazy and type 0 instead of 0.0f, or even 100 instead of 100.0f.

<Step 17> Change the spin rate of the arrow from 100 degrees per second to **500** deg/s.

Awesome! That arrow looks like it's going to do some damage.

Next, you're going to have Dottima launch an arrow. The 2D code does that already, so you'll take a closer look at how it's done there. In the script DottimaController.cs look for GetKeyDown("space") and examine the code after that. There is a single statement that creates the arrow. You'll start by making that statement work in DottimaScript.

<Step 18> Insert the following code at the end of the Update function in **DottimaScript.cs**:

```
if (Input.GetKeyDown("space"))
{
    GameObject ar = Instantiate(
    shot,
    new Vector3(
        transform.position.x,
        transform.position.y,
        transform.position.z ),
        Quaternion.Euler(0, 0, 0)
        );
}
```

<Step 19> Declare the variable shot as a public GameObject after the rb declaration. The beginning of the DottimaScript class should look like this:

```
private Rigidbody rb;
public GameObject shot;
```

You are now ready to test this:

<Step 20> Test. When testing, press the space bar while moving Dottima around the maze.

The space bar doesn't work. Instead, you will get the following error messages in the Console panel.

```
UnassignedReferenceException: The variable shot of DottimaScript has not been assigned.
You probably need to assign the shot variable of the DottimaScript script in the
inspector.
```

You also got the exception message in red letters at the bottom of the Unity window. As the second error message tells you, this has an easy fix:

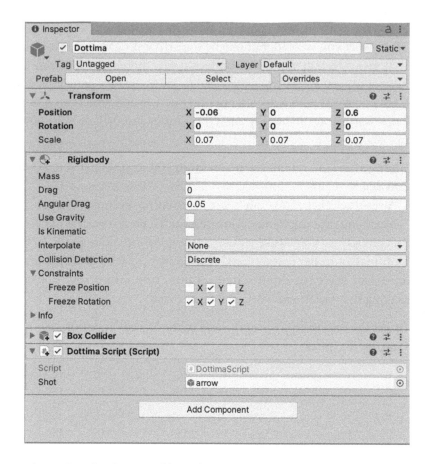

FIGURE 8.17   Assigning the shot variable in the inspector.

<Step 21> Select **Dottima** in the hierarchy, then **drag** the **arrow** game object to the Shot section in the inspector.

The inspector now looks like Figure 8.17.

<Step 22> **Test** again, then **save**.

Well, it's a start. Whenever you press the space bar, a spinning, stationary arrow is placed into the maze. You have some work to do to get that arrow flying. You'll do that in the next section.

ARROWS IN UNITY: ARROW MOVEMENT AND DIRECTION

In this section you'll put in code to make the arrows move in a specified direction. You'll also need to determine the correct direction depending on Dottima's movement direction.

<Step 1> **Examine** the direction code in **Arrow.cs**.

As you can see, there is a direction variable that stores a code for one of four possible directions. In the FixedUpdate function, a dirVector variable is computed, followed by setting the velocity vector for the arrow. Note that the rigidbody rb is of the 2D variety. Next, you will create a 3D version of this code.

\<Step 2\> **Create** a script with the name **Arrow3D** in the **scripts** folder and **assign** it to the **arrow**.

The arrow game object now has two scripts, ArrowAnimation and Arrow3D.

\<Step 3\> **Insert** the following lines at the beginning of the Arrow3D class:

```
public float speed;
private Rigidbody rb;
public int direction; // four directions 0,1,2,3
                      // down, left, up, right
```

This is similar to the beginning of Arrow.cs, except that you no longer need the animation variable, and rb is now a 3D rigidbody.

\<Step 4\> In the Start function, insert the following line:

```
rb = GetComponent<Rigidbody>();
```

Again, notice that GetComponent is no longer 2D when compared to Arrow.cs.

\<Step 5\> **Replace** the Update function with this:

```
private Vector3 dirVector;
private void FixedUpdate()
{
    if (direction == 0) dirVector = new Vector3(0.0f, 0.0f, -1.0f);
    if (direction == 1) dirVector = new Vector3(-1.0f, 0.0f, 0.0f);
    if (direction == 2) dirVector = new Vector3(0.0f, 0.0f, 1.0f);
    if (direction == 3) dirVector = new Vector3(1.0f, 0.0f, 0.0f);

    rb.velocity = dirVector.normalized * speed;
}
```

The code chooses a velocity vector for the arrow depending on the direction.

\<Step 6\> **Save in Visual Studio**. In the inspector, set the **speed** to **0.3**, the **direction** to **0**.

\<Step 7\> **Test**.

The arrow now flies in a down direction.

\<Step 8\> **Test** the other three directions by setting the direction to **1**, **2**, and **3**, and by adjusting the **Y Rotation** to **90**, **180**, and **270**.

The speed is set to a very low number for testing purposes. You'll increase the speed later on when the game is playable.

Next, you'll launch the arrow depending on Dottima's direction.

\<Step 9\> Edit DottimaScript to match the following code:

```
using System.Collections;
using System.Collections.Generic;
using UnityEngine;
```

```
public class DottimaScript : MonoBehaviour
{
    private Rigidbody rb;
    public GameObject shot;
    private int direction;
    private float yrot;

    // Start is called before the first frame update
    void Start()
    {
        rb = GetComponent<Rigidbody>();
    }

    // Update is called once per frame
    void Update()
    {
        float speed = 2.0f;
        Vector3 moveInput = new Vector3(
          Input.GetAxisRaw("Horizontal"),
          0.0f,
          Input.GetAxisRaw("Vertical"));
        rb.velocity = moveInput.normalized * speed;

        float x, z;
        x = rb.velocity.x;
        z = rb.velocity.z;
        if (x != 0 || z != 0)
        {
            if (z < x) if (z < -x) direction = 0;
            if (z > x) if (z < -x) direction = 1;
            if (z > x) if (z > -x) direction = 2;
            if (z < x) if (z > -x) direction = 3;
        }

        if (Input.GetKeyDown("space"))
        {
            if (direction == 0) yrot = 0.0f;
            if (direction == 1) yrot = 90.0f;
            if (direction == 2) yrot = 180.0f;
            if (direction == 3) yrot = 270.0f;

            GameObject ar = Instantiate(
                shot,
                new Vector3(
                    transform.position.x,
                    transform.position.y + 0.2f,
                    transform.position.z),
                    Quaternion.Euler(0, yrot, 0)
                );

            ar.GetComponent<Arrow3D>().direction = direction;
            if (x != 0 || z != 0)
                ar.GetComponent<Arrow3D>().speed += speed;
        }
    }
}
```

Compare this code with the code in DottimaController. There are some subtle differences, but the logic is very similar. You're computing the direction of Dottima, given the x and z components of Dottima's velocity vector. You then Instantiate an arrow facing that direction.

<Step 10> For the arrow game object in the hierarchy, **change** the **speed** to **1** and the **direction** to **0** in the inspector.

<Step 11> **Test** and **save**.

Next, you'll do some housecleaning. The prefab for the arrow needs to be updated.

<Step 12> **Drag** the **arrow** in the hierarchy on top of the **arrow prefab** in **3dprefabs**.

<Step 13> **Delete** the **arrow** in the hierarchy.

If you were to test the game now, you'd get an error because the shot variable is no longer assigned. You can check this by looking at Dottima in the inspector.

<Step 14> **Drag** the **arrow prefab** from **3dprefabs** to the **shot variable** for Dottima.

<Step 15> **Test** and **save**.

This should work exactly the same as earlier, but you are no longer dependent on having an arrow game object in the scene.

In the following section you'll put in code for collision detection for the arrows.

ARROWS IN UNITY: COLLISION DETECTION FOR ARROWS

Currently those arrows fly right through the books and the spikers. Of course, that's not correct. First, you'll have the arrows collide with the books.

<Step 1> **Create** an **instance** of your **arrow prefab** as shown in Figure 8.18. Change the Y position to 0.1.

FIGURE 8.18   Testing setup for arrow collision.

You are using an orthographic view and placing the arrow in a position where it should hit a book below and stop. The speed of the arrow should be 1, the direction 0, the code for down. You lifted the arrow up a little, so it won't collide with the floor.

<Step 2> **Test** this.

The arrow flies through the book below and keeps going.

<Step 3> **Add** a **box collider** to the arrow and **adjust** it to **fit the head of the arrow** as shown in Figure 8.19.

<Step 4> **Adjust** the **box collider** in the **y direction** as well, as shown in Figure 8.20, by using the front orthographic view.

<Step 5> In the inspector, **freeze all three rotations** in the Constraints section.

You don't want the physics engine rotating the arrow.

<Step 6> **Test**.

The arrow now hits the book and stops there but continues to spin. Probably what you'll want the arrow to disappear after a fixed time. You'll implement this shortly.

<Step 7> **Move** a spiker in the arrow's path and **test** that.

This also appears to work. The arrow bounces off any spikers it encounters and keeps going. You might have noticed that the arrows that are shot by Dottima don't collide with books or anything else. That's because you haven't updated the prefab yet.

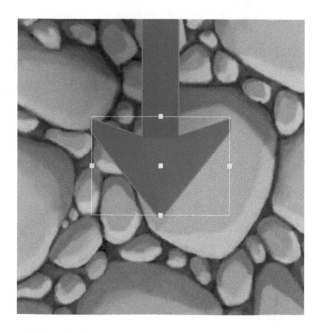

FIGURE 8.19   3D Box collider for the arrow.

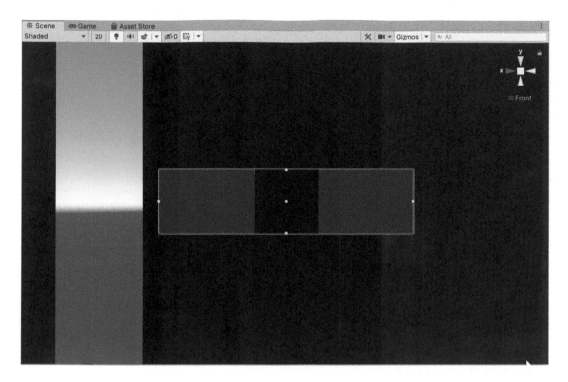

FIGURE 8.20   3D Box collider for the arrow in the y direction.

<Step 8>   **Update** the **arrow prefab** in **3dprefabs** and **test** that.

It bears repeating that you are continuing to follow the "implement small changes and test right away" philosophy of game development. Not only is that a very reliable way of creating solid games, it's also much more fun because you get to play your game a lot. And, if that's not fun you're getting valuable feedback on how the game needs to be improved.

Next, you'll bring in the deathTimer code from the 2D project. That code is simple enough. You add a state variable called **state**, 0 for alive, 1 for dying. Well, that seems backwards, but it doesn't matter. When the arrow is in the *dying* state the deathTimer decreases, and when the deathTimer reaches zero the arrow gets destroyed. Here's the code for that:

<Step 9>   In **Arrow3D declare** the two variables by inserting their declarations at the top as follows:

```
private float deathTimer;
private int state;  // 0 = alive, 1 = dying
```

These variables are declared private because you're pretty sure that they won't need to be accessed by any other game objects.

<Step 10>   **Initialize** them in `Start` as follows:

```
deathTimer = 1.0f;
state = 0;
```

<Step 11> **Insert** this code into `Update`:

```
if (state == 1)
{
    deathTimer -= Time.deltaTime;
}
if (deathTimer < 0.0f) Destroy(gameObject);
```

<Step 12> **Insert** the following function at the bottom of the class, but before the closing bracket for the class:

```
private void OnCollisionEnter(Collision collision)
{
    if (state == 1) return;
    state = 1;
}
```

This isn't exactly the best code. You just realized that you can just remove the first of these two lines, and the code does exactly the same thing. This sort of thing can happen in the heat of battle. You're going to leave it, because that's less work than changing it, and because a few steps from now you'll need that line.

<Step 13> **Test** and **save**.

As soon as the arrow collides with anything the deathTimer starts and 1 second later that arrow is destroyed. You could add an arrow dissolve animation here, but you'll put that off for another day.

Next, you'll destroy any spikers that collide with arrows. To do that you will first *tag* them.

<Step 14> **Select** the **Spiker prefab** in **3dprefabs**. Click on **Open Prefab**.

<Step 15> In the inspector, **select** the **Spiker tag** in the Tag section.

Normally you'd have to create a new tag in this situation, but you already have a Spiker tag. It was created for the 2D project.

<Step 16> **Change** the `OnCollisionEnter` function to this:

```
private void OnCollisionEnter(Collision collision)
{
    if (state == 1) return;

    if (collision.gameObject.tag == "Spiker")
    {
        Destroy(collision.gameObject);
    }
    state = 1;
}
```

This code checks whether the arrow is colliding with is a spiker, and if it is, the spiker gets destroyed.

<Step 17> **Test**.

This works, but the arrow keeps going after colliding with and destroying the spiker. To fix this do the following:

<Step 18> At the beginning of the FixedUpdate function, **insert** the following:

```
if (state == 1)
{
    rb.velocity = Vector3.zero;
    return;
}
```

This checks to see if the arrow is dying, and if so, it sets the velocity to zero.

<Step 19> **Test** again and **save**.

The arrow behavior now matches the 2D game fairly closely. You can run around with Dottima and destroy spikers. It's starting to feel like a real game. You could probably stop now and call this the first playable version. Still, it'll be pretty easy to add the 3D Blockade, so you might as well do that.

3D BLOCKADE

In this section you'll add a 3D blockade. The blockade is a large rock that can be pushed around by having Dottima run into it. It can also be nudged by shooting it with an arrow.

<Step 1> **Load Level 3** (the 2D version) and **test** it.

This is to remind yourself how the 2D game works. There is one blockade in this scene, and your goal is simply for Dottima to push it out of her way so she can get to the exit.

<Step 2> **Examine** the **Blockade** game object in the inspector.

As you might expect, the blockade has a rigidbody 2D and a box collider 2D. In the 3D version you plan to add rigidbody and box collider components. Notice also that it has no script! This is going to be easy.

<Step 3> Go to **3DLevel 3** and **test** it.

It works, except that you get an error when trying to shoot arrows. The Dottima object is out of date.

<Step 4> Go back to **3DLevel 2** and **create** a **Dottima prefab** in **3dprefabs** using the Dottima game object in this scene.

<Step 5> Back in **3DLevel 3**, **delete** the existing **Dottima** game object and **replace** it with an instance of the new prefab in 3dprefabs.

<Step 6> **Test** this.

Dottima can now shoot arrows, but there's nothing to shoot at in this level. You'll put some spikers into this level later on. You might notice a problem with shooting left-right. This will be fixed in a future chapter.

First, you'll put in a blockade.

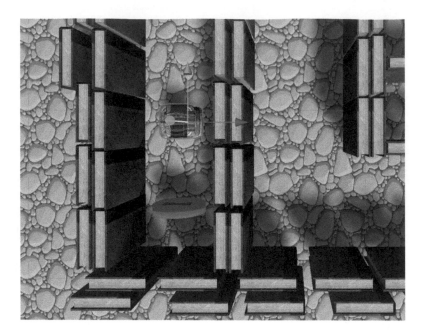

FIGURE 8.21   Blockade instance in 3D level 3.

\<Step 7\>   **Create a blockade** instance from **3dprefabs** as shown in Figure 8.21.
This blockade is too small, so let's scale it up.

\<Step 8\>   **Change** the **scale** of the **blockade** to **(2, 2, 2)**. **Test** the game.
As you would expect, there is no collision between the blockade and Dottima.

\<Step 9\>   **Add a Rigidbody component** to blockade. Turn off Gravity, Freeze the y position and all rotations.

\<Step 10\>   **Add** a **Box Collider** component and **edit** the **collider to fit**. You can get a head start by typing in the size of the box collider as **(0.2, 0.2, 0.2)** with center at **(0, 0.1, 0)**.

\<Step 11\>   **Test** again.
The blockade appears to be working just as in the 2D game.

\<Step 12\>   **Update** the **prefab** for the **blockade**.

\<Step 13\>   **Delete** the **blockade** game object in the scene, then **create** a new one from the **prefab**, as shown in Figure 8.22.

\<Step 14\>   **Test** to see if you can push away the blockade and get to the exit.

\<Step 15\>   **Place** some **spikers** into the level, **test** and **save**.
You're calling it. The game is playable, in a manner of speaking. Many essential elements are still missing, things like sound, a game structure, and interesting enemies. You'll tackle these issues in the following chapters.

FIGURE 8.22   **Placing a new blockade.**

CHAPTER 9

Game Structure

I N THIS SHORT CHAPTER you'll port most of the game structure from the 2D game. You'll put in code to go from level to level. You'll add a lives counter for Dottima and a Game Over message when she runs out of lives. You'll also put in a simple score display.

GAME STATE

In this section you'll bring in the GameState game object from the 2D game. You will see how this game object keeps track of the state of the game. It is independent of 2D vs. 3D considerations, so you can just use it as is. The 2D game doesn't have a prefab for it, so you'll make one.

<Step 1> Go to the **Level 1** scene.

<Step 2> Select **GameState** in the hierarchy and **make** a **prefab** for it in 3dprefabs.

<Step 3> In **3DLevel 1 create** an **instance** of the **GameState prefab**.

<Step 4> Test.

Creating that GameState shouldn't have any effect, so it seems unnecessary to test this. Nevertheless, testing only takes a few seconds, so why not? You're checking to see if you're getting any unexpected error messages. You didn't, so it's OK to move on.

But wait, possibly you got an error when shooting arrows. To fix that, delete Dottima on this level and replace it with an instance of the Dottima prefab from 3dprefabs. Then check all the other levels for this issue.

<Step 5> Go back to **Level 1**, and make a **prefab** for **Scoring**, again in 3dprefabs.

<Step 6> As you did before with GameState, **create** an **instance** of **Scoring** in 3DLevel 1.

<Step 7> Test.

This time you see a score, a lives counter, and a level display, just as in the 2D game. All of this is handled in the Scoring script. You can see the timer counting down from 100, five lives for Dottima, and a level indicator.

DOI: 10.1201/9780429328725-10

Your next goal is to have Dottima go from level to level. To do this you'll need to change the build settings.

<Step 8> **File – Build Settings…**

There you see the build settings left over from the 2D game. You're about to remove the six 2D scenes and replace them with the three 3D scenes.

<Step 9> **Select** all **six levels** in the **Scenes in Build** panel, **right-click**, and **remove** them.

You now just have two scenes in this build, the TitleScene and the Menus.

<Step 10> Make sure you still have **3DLevel 1** as your current scene, then **click** on **Add Open** Scenes.

<Step 11> **Add 3DLevel 2** and **3DLevel 3** in a similar manner and then **exit** the Build Settings pop-up.

<Step 12> Select the **TitleScene** and **test** the game from there. Important: **File – Save Project**.

Amazingly, when you **click** on **Play DotGame** in the Menus scene you end up playing 3DLevel 1. Moving on the 3DLevel 2 isn't working yet though. You will need to put in a 3D version of the ExitLocation object from the 2D game. You also noticed that on 3DLevel 1 the screen is darker when getting there from the options screen. You'll chase down that bug later.

<Step 13> **Examine** the **ExitLocation** game object in **Level 1**.

As you can see it is simply a Box Collider 2D placed near the exit for the level.

<Step 14> Go to **3DLevel 1**.

<Step 15> **GameObject – Create Empty**, name it **ExitLocation**, and **drag** it near the exit as shown in Figure 9.1.

<Step 16> **Add** a **Box Collider Component** and **edit** it to match Figure 9.2.

This figure has the floor game object turned off temporarily to make the box collider easier to see. The size for the box collider in the version from this book is (0.67, 1, 0.29). Your sizes may differ. The y size should remain at 1.

You're now going to bring in pieces of code from the script DottimaController from the 2D game and adjust, as necessary.

<Step 17> Insert the following declarations at the top of DottimaScript:

```
public float levelCompleteTimer = 2.0f;
public const int lastLevel = 3;
```

You had to change the lastLevel value to 3 from 6 because you currently only have three levels.

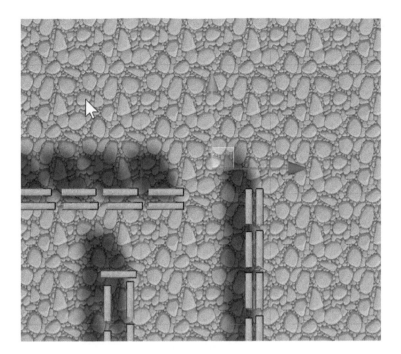

FIGURE 9.1   Placing the ExitLocation Game Object.

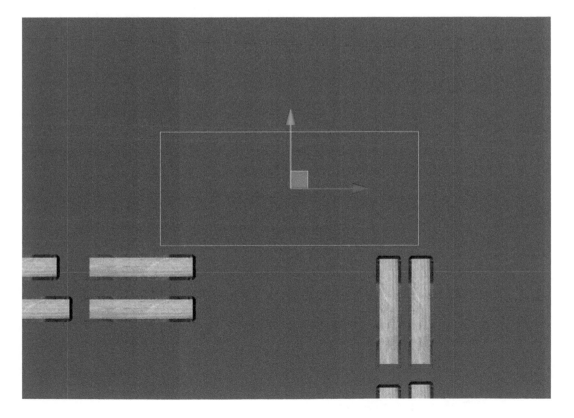

FIGURE 9.2   Editing the box collider for ExitLocation.

\<Step 18\> At the beginning of Update, **insert** this:

```
if (GameState.state == GameState.levelComplete)
{
    rb.velocity = Vector3.zero;
    levelCompleteTimer -= Time.deltaTime;
    if (levelCompleteTimer < 0.0f)
    {
        Scoring.gamescore += 500;
        GameState.level++;
        SceneManager.LoadScene(GameState.level +
            GameState.SceneOffset);
    }
}
```

\<Step 19\> At the end of the script, insert the following collision code:

```
private void OnCollisionEnter(Collision collision)
{
    if (collision.gameObject.name == "ExitLocation")
    {
        Scoring.gamescore += (int)Scoring.levelTimer;
        Scoring.levelTimer = 100.0f;

        if (GameState.level < lastLevel)
            GameState.state = GameState.levelComplete;
        else
            GameState.state = GameState.theEnd;
    }
}
```

\<Step 20\> In the using section at the top, insert this line:

```
using UnityEngine.SceneManagement;
```

This is necessary to get access to the SceneManagement functions.

\<Step 21\> **Test**, starting from the Menus scene.
You should be able to go all the way to 3DLevel 2, but then you'll be stuck because that level doesn't have an ExitLocation yet.

\<Step 22\> Go to **3DLevel 1** and **create** a prefab for **ExitLocation**, as usual in **3dprefabs**.

\<Step 23\> **Add ExitLocation**, **GameState**, and **Scoring** in **3DLevel** 2 and **3DLevel** 3.

\<Step 24\> **Test**, starting from the Menus Scene.
This should work now all the way to the end of level 3. The code for handling the end of the game isn't in there yet, so that's what's next.

\<Step 25\> **Insert** the following code after the levelComplete section in the Update function of **DottimaScript**:

```
if (GameState.state == GameState.gameOver)
{
    rb.velocity = Vector3.zero;
    levelCompleteTimer -= Time.deltaTime;
    if (levelCompleteTimer < 0.0f)
```

```
        {
            Scoring.lives = 5;
            GameState.level = 1;
            GameState.state = GameState.gamePlay;
            SceneManager.LoadScene(GameState.MenuScene);
        }
    }

    if (GameState.state == GameState.theEnd)
    {
        rb.velocity = Vector3.zero;
        levelCompleteTimer -= Time.deltaTime;
        if (levelCompleteTimer < 0.0f)
        {
            Scoring.lives = 5;
            Scoring.gamescore += 1000;
            GameState.level = 1;
            GameState.state = GameState.gamePlay;
            SceneManager.LoadScene(GameState.MenuScene);
        }
    }

    // At the end of a level, stop updating Dottima
    if (GameState.state == GameState.theEnd) return;
    if (GameState.state == GameState.levelComplete) return;
    if (GameState.state == GameState.gameOver) return;
```

<Step 26> **Test** this, once again starting from the menu scene.

You now have a pretty good game structure. You can play through all three levels and get to the end. There is a bit of a problem in that Dottima is immortal right now. You put in code for "Game Over," but you have no way of triggering it. You will deal with this in the next section.

<Step 27> **Save.**

Oh wait, there is an easy fix for that darkness. Do the following:

<Step 28> Go to **3DLevel 1. Window – Rendering – Lighting. Click** on **Generate Lighting.**

Now, when you play from the Menu Scene this level should be as bright as usual.

<Step 29> **Repeat** the previous step for levels 2 and 3. **Test** and **Save.**

GAME OVER

In this section you will make it possible for Dottima to lose lives, and if she runs out of lives it's Game Over. You'll be able to reuse the 2D code for this.

<Step 1> Load **3DLevel 2.**

In this level Dottima first encounters the spikers. You want Dottima to lose a life when she collides with them.

<Step 2> **Insert** these declarations into the **DottimaScript** class:

```
private int dottimaState = 0;  // 0 no bomb, 1 with bomb, 2 dying
private float deathTimer = 1.0f;
```

\<Step 3\> **Insert** this code into the `OnCollisionEnter` function:

```
if (collision.gameObject.tag == "Spiker")
{
    dottimaState = 2;
}
```

\<Step 4\> **Insert** this code into the `Update` function:

```
if (dottimaState == 2)
{
    float shrink = 1.0f - 2.0f * Time.deltaTime;
    transform.localScale = (
        new Vector3(
        transform.localScale.x * shrink,
        transform.localScale.y * shrink,
        transform.localScale.z * shrink));
    deathTimer -= Time.deltaTime;
    if (deathTimer < 0.0f)
    {
        deathTimer = 1.0f;
        Scoring.lives--;
        dottimaState = 0;
        gameObject.transform.localScale =
            new Vector3(0.07f, 0.07f, 0.07f);
        gameObject.transform.position =
            new Vector3(-0.06f, 0.0f, 0.6f);
        if (Scoring.lives == 0)
        {
            GameState.state = GameState.gameOver;
        }
    }
}
```

This code was mostly copied from the 2D version, except that the rotation code was removed because that no longer works in 3D and it's not really necessary. The magic numbers for resetting Dottima are different in the 3D version because the initial position and scale for Dottima are different.

\<Step 5\> **Test** the game.

You should be able to kill Dottima five times by running her into spikers, and then you'll get the Game Over display, followed by a chance to play the game again. When Dottima dies she just shrinks for 1 second and then gets reset at her initial position.

In order for this code to work, Dottima has to start at the same initial position at each level. You'll make a mental note to make this code handle different initial positions if and when that should become necessary.

Author's Note: Yes, this code is ugly in places, especially for publication in a textbook. This is done on purpose, not just because the author is lazy. It's a dose of reality. When you're trying to write games on a self-imposed or external deadline, */&(#) happens. When developing a game, you're constantly balancing the quality of your code with the necessity of getting it done yesterday. Sometimes it's clearer and better to write your code quickly and simply.

On the other hand, if you know what the future will bring it's often good to prepare for it by making your code suitable for general use, not just for the necessities of the moment.

You can call it a day for this chapter.

<Step 6>   **Save, exit Unity** and **backup**.

Yes, you need to back up your work periodically. Even better would be to set up a source control system. This book doesn't deal with the intricacies of source control, but by all means, use source control if you're so inclined.

CHAPTER 10

More Game Objects and a Large Level

I N THIS CHAPTER YOU'LL bring in the code for DotRobot and Bombs from the 2D game. You finally get to try out the new DotRobot model. You'll incorporate code for Dottima picking up and dropping bombs so she can destroy DotRobots. Also, you'll create a brand new and much larger level.

DOTROBOT

You built a DotRobotRigged prefab in the 3dprefabs folder a few chapters ago. Before you continue your work on the DotRobot game objects you'll create some new levels for them. You'll use the same technique as in Chapter 8 and make copies of the existing 3DLevel 3 to create levels 4, 5, and 6.

<Step 1> **Select 3DLevel 3. Save** this scene as **3DLevel 4, 3DLevel 5**, and **3DLevel 6**, all in the Assets/Scenes folder.

<Step 2> In **DottimaScript** set the constant **lastLevel** to **6**.

<Step 3> In the **build settings**, **add** the **new levels** making sure to have them arranged in sequence.

<Step 4> **Build** and **test** the game starting from the TitleScene.
  Assuming that worked you'll be ready to put a DotRobot into 3DLevel 4.

<Step 5> **Select 3DLevel 4** and place a **DotRobotRigged** instance from the prefab in **3dprefabs**, as shown in Figure 10.1.

<Step 6> **Test** and observe the DotRobot animation.
  The robot doesn't interact with the environment yet. It simply loops through its animation.

<Step 7> **Examine** the 2D **DotRobot prefab** in the **prefabs** folder.

DOI: 10.1201/9780429328725-11

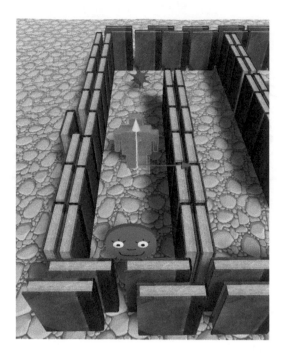

FIGURE 10.1   Placing a DotRobotRigged into 3DLevel 4.

As you can see, the 2D DotRobot has an Animator, a script, a Rigidbody 2D, and a Box Collider 2D component. You will create similar components for the 3D DotRobot, except for the Animator.

<Step 8>   **Add** a **Rigidbody** component and a **Box Collider** component to the **DotRobotRigged** game object. For the **Rigidbody, freeze** the **y position** and **all three rotations**.

<Step 9>   **Edit** the **Box Collider** to fit the DotRobot. The Box collider should surround DotRobot as shown in Figure 10.2.

<Step 10> **Test**.
Dottima can now push the DotRobot around the level just like the block-ade. The spikers collide with the DotRobot correctly, and DotRobot collides with the books. So far so good.

<Step 11> **Create** a new script with the name **DotRobot3D** and **assign** it to **DotRobotRigged**.

<Step 12> **Type** in the following code for **DotRobot3D.cs**:

```
using System.Collections;
using System.Collections.Generic;
using UnityEngine;

public class DotRobot3D : MonoBehaviour
{
```

```
public float speed;
private Rigidbody rb;
public int direction; // four directions 0,1,2,3
                      // down, left, up, right
public Vector3 dirVector;

void Start()
{
    rb = GetComponent<Rigidbody>();
    direction = 0;
    dirVector = new Vector3(0.0f, 0.0f, -1.0f);
}

 private void FixedUpdate()
{
    if (direction == 0) dirVector = new Vector3(0.0f, 0.0f, -1.0f);
    if (direction == 1) dirVector = new Vector3(-1.0f, 0.0f, 0.0f);
    if (direction == 2) dirVector = new Vector3(0.0f, 0.0f, 1.0f);
    if (direction == 3) dirVector = new Vector3(1.0f, 0.0f, 0.0f);

    if (direction == 0) rb.MoveRotation(Quaternion.Euler(
        0.0f, 180.0f, 0.0f));
    if (direction == 1) rb.MoveRotation(Quaternion.Euler(
        0.0f, 270.0f, 0.0f));
    if (direction == 2) rb.MoveRotation(Quaternion.Euler(
        0.0f, 0.0f, 0.0f));
    if (direction == 3) rb.MoveRotation(Quaternion.Euler(
        0.0f, 90.0f, 0.0f));

    rb.velocity = dirVector.normalized * speed;
 }

private void OnCollisionEnter(Collision collision)
{

    Vector3 newPosition = new Vector3(
        transform.position.x - dirVector.x * 0.02f,
        transform.position.y,
        transform.position.z - dirVector.z * 0.02f);

    rb.MovePosition(newPosition);
    direction = (direction + 1) % 4;
 }
}
```

This code needs explanation. The script name and the matching class name are DotRobot3D. The name needed to be changed because you still have the old DotRobot.cs script active in this project. Having two scripts with the same name in a project is possible, but it causes problems, so it's best to avoid that. The author found out about that one the hard way.

The direction and dirVector variables are public because that's one way to enable you to observe them while playing the game. This can help with debugging and with understanding the code. Of course, you are using Vector3 vectors rather than the Vector2 vectors in the old 2D code. The big difference between this 3D code and the 2D code is the way the DotRobot orientation is handled. In the 3D code you set the appropriate rotation quaternion depending on the current direction. The old 2D code chooses one of the four animations.

FIGURE 10.2   A 3D box collider for DotRobot.

<Step 13> **Set** the **speed** to **0.3** and **test** the game.

Dottima can now change the orientation of a DotRobot by colliding with it or by shooting it. Dottima doesn't die when running into a DotRobot, so let's put in the code for that. Can you guess where and how to do this?

<Step 14> In **DottimaScript, change** the **Spiker collision code** to this:

```
if (collision.gameObject.tag == "Spiker" ||
    collision.gameObject.tag == "Robot")
{
    dottimaState = 2;
}
```

Those vertical bars are the built-in C# "logical or" operator. You read this code as follows: if Dottima collides with a spiker or a robot, put Dottima into the *dying* state, which happens to be 2.

<Step 15> **Tag DotRobotRigged** with the "**Robot**" tag.

The Robot tag is defined already, so all you need to do is to select DotRobot in the hierarchy, and then set the tag in the inspector. You probably should have called that tag DotRobot, but it doesn't matter as long as it matches the reference in the code.

<Step 16> **Test**.

This should just work. If Dottima collides with the DotRobot in the scene she dies.

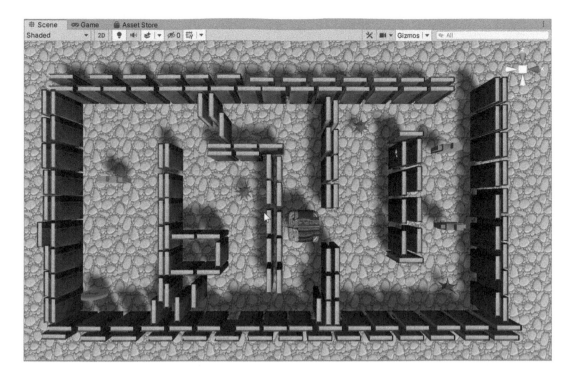

FIGURE 10.3   Rearranging your books in level 4.

<Step 17> Update the **prefab** for **DotRobotRigged** in **Assets/3dprefabs**.

<Step 18> **Rearrange** the books to match Figure 10.3. Also **put** a few **additional robots** into the right corridor.

<Step 19> **Try** to get to the exit on this level.

It can get difficult near the exit. It's certainly challenging when dealing with several invincible robots.

While you're at it, it's time to deal with a fairly serious bug. When Dottima tries to shoot an arrow to the right or left, the arrow gets stuck. This was a problem in the 2D game as well, and the code to fix it is in Arrow.cs. That code needs to be modified.

<Step 20> In **Arrow3D.cs, replace** the OnCollisionEnter function with this code:

```
private void OnCollisionEnter (Collision collision)
{
    if (state == 1) return;

    if (collision.gameObject.tag == "Player"
    || collision.gameObject.tag == "Arrow")
    {
        Physics.IgnoreCollision(
            collision.collider,
            gameObject.GetComponent<Collider>()
            );
        return;
    }
```

```
if  (collision.gameObject.tag == "Spiker")
{
    Destroy(collision.gameObject);
}
state = 1;
}
```

This is pretty much the same as the 2D version, except that the 2D Unity functions have been replaced with their 3D counterparts. This code ensures that arrows don't collide with the player or with other arrows. Of course, you'll need to have a tag for Dottima:

<Step 21> **Tag Dottima** with the Player tag and **update** the **prefab** for **Dottima** in **3dprefabs. Check** that **Dottima** is tagged on each of the six levels.

If you find a Dottima that's not tagged with the Player tag, delete it and instantiate the newly updated Dottima prefab.

<Step 22> **Update** the **prefab** for **DotRobotRigged** in **3dprefabs**. Also, **tag** the **arrow prefab** with the **Arrow** tag.

<Step 23> **Test 3DLevel 4**.

You've done a lot of testing, but you are finally happy with Level 4.

<Step 24> **Save**.

In the next section you'll introduce bombs, which will be the only way to destroy those robots.

BOMBS

As before, you'll start by looking at the bomb game object in the 2D game.

<Step 1> **Examine** the **bomb** game object **in Level 5** of the 2D game.

This game object has a circle collider 2D, a rigidbody 2D, a script, and two child objects called sparks and explosion. The child objects are particle systems, and you'll try to make them compatible with 3D geometry later on. First, it's time to make a 3D prefab for the bomb.

<Step 2> Go to **3DLevel 5**.

You may need to turn off the 2D mode in the Scene panel if you used 2D mode to examine the 2D level in the previous step.

<Step 3> **Place** a **bomb** into **3DLevel 5** from **Assets/models**, as shown in Figure 10.4.

<Step 4> **Test**.

This is an easy one. The bomb sits there, and the other game objects don't interact with it. You did notice that the bomb is sunk into the floor, so you'll need to move it up to fix that.

<Step 5> **Move** the **bomb up** so it no longer intersects the floor.

Next, you'll put in the rigidbody and the collider.

FIGURE 10.4   Placing a bomb into 3D level 5.

<Step 6> Add a **rigidbody** component, **turn off gravity**.

You may rethink the gravity setting later on, but for now you'll reimplement the 2D version. In that version Dottima simply places the bomb and runs away before the explosion happens.

<Step 7> Add a **sphere collider** and change the **radius** to **0.1**.

The adjusted sphere collider should fit the bomb perfectly, as shown in Figure 10.5.

<Step 8> In the **rigidbody**, **check Is Kinematic**.

<Step 9> **Freeze** the **Y position** for **Dottima**. **Update** the **Dottima prefab**. **Test**.

Next, you're going to put in the particle systems for the bomb. At least for now you'll live with the 2D particle systems from the 2D game. To learn about particle systems in Unity, and particle systems in general, read the particle system section in the Unity manual.

<Step 10> **Save** your scene and then go to **Level 5**.

<Step 11> In the hierarchy, **select** the **bomb** game object (at the top) and **expand** it. Then **select Sparks** and **shift-select Explosion**. **Right-click** and **copy**, as shown in Figure 10.6.

<Step 12> Back in **3DLevel 5**, **paste** the particle systems into the hierarchy, then drag them on top of the bomb, as shown in Figure 10.7.

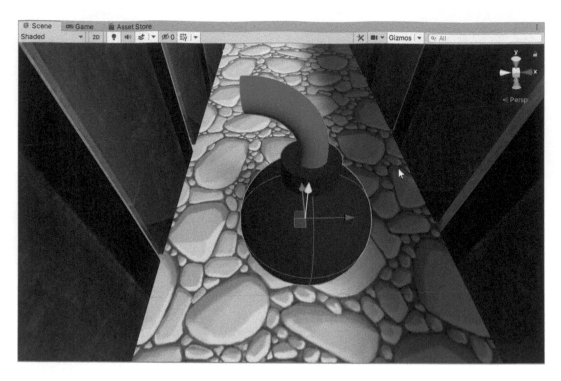

FIGURE 10.5 Sphere collider for the bomb.

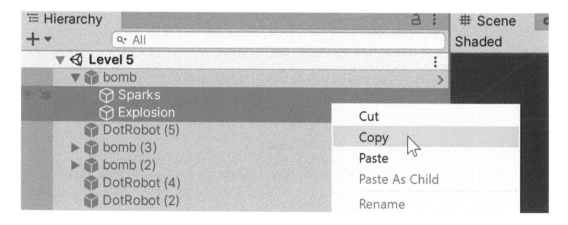

FIGURE 10.6 Copying two particle systems.

<Step 13> Select **Sparks**, and in the Transform section, set the **position to** **(−0.07, 0.2, 0)** and the **scale** to **(0.25, 0.25, 0.25)**.

These adjustments were determined by experimenting with the position and scale to line up the sparks with the end of the fuse.

<Step 14> Test.

The sparks are running continuously, which is fine for now.

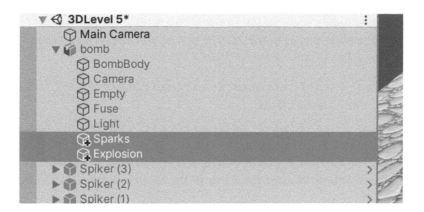

FIGURE 10.7   Particle systems pasted.

<Step 15> Select the **Explosion**, and change the **position** to **(0, 0, 0)**, **scale** to **(0.25, 0.25, 0.25)**. Press **Play** in the particle effect pop-up, as shown in Figure 10.8.

The explosion doesn't play in the game itself because "Play on Awake" is turned off. This effect is designed to be triggered by code after the fuse sparkles for a while. You can temporarily turn on "Play on Awake" to see what it looks like in the game. This explosion is a bit strange in 3D, but it does work, so it's good enough for now. Remember, these particle effects are cosmetic, in other words, they don't affect gameplay directly.

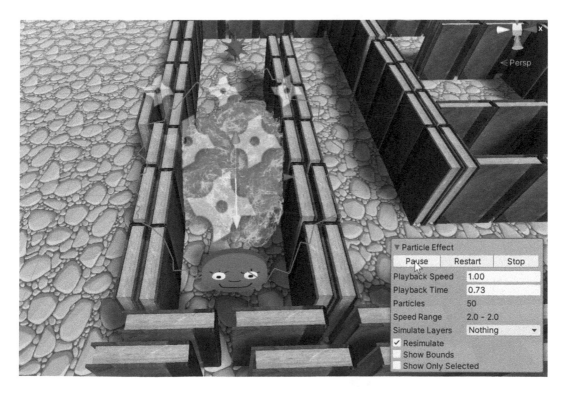

FIGURE 10.8   Explosion.

You're finally ready to put in the bomb script. The 3D version of the bomb script is very similar to the 2D version, so you'll save yourself some typing by copying and pasting.

<Step 16> **Add** a **new script component** to the **bomb** game object, call it **Bomb3D** and store it in **Assets/Scripts**.

<Step 17> **Open** both **Bomb** and **Bomb3D** in Visual Studio.

<Step 18> **Copy** the **Bomb class** from Bomb.cs, **select** the **Bomb3D class** in Bomb3D.cs, and paste. Then **change** the **name** of the class in Bomb3D.cs to Bomb3D.

<Step 19> **Comment out** all **audio references**.
You'll bring back the audio later on.

<Step 20> **Replace** the **Physics2D.OverlapCircle statement** with this:

```
Collider[] colliders = Physics.OverlapSphere(tr.position, 1.5f);
```

Notice that you had to change the Collider2D to Collider, Physics2D to Physics, and Circle to Sphere. If you did this all correctly your bomb3D.cs file should look like this:

```
using System.Collections;
using System.Collections.Generic;
using UnityEngine;

public class Bomb3D : MonoBehaviour
{
    public int bombState = 0; // 0=idle, 1=fuse
    private float fuseTimer;
    public float fuseLength = 2.0f;
    private ParticleSystem sparks;
    private ParticleSystem explosion;
    private Component[] comparray;
//    public AudioClip clip;
//    public AudioClip fuse;

    // Start is called before the first frame update
    void Start()
    {
        comparray = GetComponentsInChildren<ParticleSystem>();
        foreach (ParticleSystem p in comparray)
        {
            if (p.gameObject.name == "Explosion") explosion = p;
            if (p.gameObject.name == "Sparks") sparks = p;
        }
        bombState = 0;
        fuseTimer = fuseLength;
        sparks.Stop();
    }

    // Update is called once per frame
    void Update()
    {
        if (bombState == 1)
        {
            if (sparks.isStopped)
            {
```

```
                    sparks.Play();
//   AudioSource.PlayClipAtPoint(fuse, Camera.main.transform.position);
            }

            fuseTimer -= Time.deltaTime;
            if (fuseTimer <= 0.0f)
            {
//   AudioSource.PlayClipAtPoint(clip, Camera.main.transform.position);
                explosion.transform.SetParent(null);
                explosion.Play();
                DamageNearbyObjects(gameObject.transform);
                Destroy(gameObject);
            }
        }
    }

    void DamageNearbyObjects(Transform tr)
    {
        Collider[] colliders = Physics.OverlapSphere(tr.position, 1.5f);
        for (int i = 0; i < colliders.Length; i++)
        {
            if (colliders[i].gameObject.tag == "Spiker")
            {
                Scoring.gamescore += 50;
                Destroy(colliders[i].gameObject);
            }
            if (colliders[i].gameObject.tag == "Robot")
            {
                Scoring.gamescore += 100;
                Destroy(colliders[i].gameObject);
            }
        }
    }
}
```

You are now ready to test this. The code initializes the bomb to be idle, so the first test is pretty boring:

<Step 21> **Test.**

The bomb sits there, and there are no sparks.

<Step 22> In the `Start` function, **initialize** `bombState` to **1** and **test**.

Now the sparks go for 2 seconds and then the bomb explodes. Maybe you also tried to kill Dottima with the bomb, but that didn't work. That's OK. The bomb is there for Dottima to pick up and set down and start the fuse. You may wish to have the explosion damage or kill Dottima, but the 2D game doesn't do that, so you'll just keep that the same in the 3D game. It's a time-honored tradition in video games to have the player's weapons be harmless for the player even though in the real world that's certainly not true.

Next, you'll put in code for Dottima to pick up, carry, and drop those bombs.

<Step 23> **Examine DottimaController.cs** and look for bomb references.

You can see that there are several of those. You are now going to transfer and possibly change bomb-related code from DottimaController. The result is the code in the next step.

<Step 24> Change DottimaScript.cs to look like this:

```
using System.Collections;
using System.Collections.Generic;
using UnityEngine;
using UnityEngine.SceneManagement;

public class DottimaScript : MonoBehaviour
{
    private Rigidbody rb;
    public GameObject shot;
    private int direction;
    private float yrot;

    public float levelCompleteTimer = 2.0f;
    public const int lastLevel = 6;

    public int dottimaState = 0;   // 0 no bomb, 1 with bomb, 2 dying
    private float deathTimer = 1.0f;

    private GameObject bomb;

    // Start is called before the first frame update
    void Start()
    {
        rb = GetComponent<Rigidbody>();
    }


    // Update is called once per frame
    void Update()
    {
        if (GameState.state == GameState.levelComplete)
        {
            rb.velocity = Vector3.zero;
            levelCompleteTimer -= Time.deltaTime;
            if (levelCompleteTimer < 0.0f)
            {
                Scoring.gamescore += 500;
                GameState.level++;
                SceneManager.LoadScene(
                    GameState.level + GameState.SceneOffset);
            }
        }
        if (GameState.state == GameState.gameOver)
        {
            rb.velocity = Vector3.zero;
            levelCompleteTimer -= Time.deltaTime;
            if (levelCompleteTimer < 0.0f)
            {
                Scoring.lives = 5;
                GameState.level = 1;
                GameState.state = GameState.gamePlay;
                SceneManager.LoadScene(GameState.MenuScene);
            }
        }

        if (GameState.state == GameState.theEnd)
        {
            rb.velocity = Vector3.zero;
            levelCompleteTimer -= Time.deltaTime;
            if (levelCompleteTimer < 0.0f)
            {
                Scoring.lives = 5;
                Scoring.gamescore += 1000;
```

```
            GameState.level = 1;
            GameState.state = GameState.gamePlay;
            SceneManager.LoadScene(GameState.MenuScene);
        }
    }

    // At the end of a level, stop updating Dottima
    if (GameState.state == GameState.theEnd) return;
    if (GameState.state == GameState.levelComplete) return;
    if (GameState.state == GameState.gameOver) return;


    float speed = 2.0f;
    Vector3 moveInput = new Vector3(
        Input.GetAxisRaw("Horizontal"),
        0.0f,
        Input.GetAxisRaw("Vertical"));
    rb.velocity = moveInput.normalized * speed;

    float x, z;
    x = rb.velocity.x;
    z = rb.velocity.z;
    if (x != 0 || z != 0)
    {
        if (z < x) if (z < -x) direction = 0;
        if (z > x) if (z < -x) direction = 1;
        if (z > x) if (z > -x) direction = 2;
        if (z < x) if (z > -x) direction = 3;
    }

    if (dottimaState == 0)
    if (Input.GetKeyDown("space"))
    {
        if (direction == 0) yrot = 0.0f;
        if (direction == 1) yrot = 90.0f;
        if (direction == 2) yrot = 180.0f;
        if (direction == 3) yrot = 270.0f;

        GameObject ar = Instantiate(
            shot,
            new Vector3(
                transform.position.x,
                transform.position.y + 0.2f,
                transform.position.z),
                Quaternion.Euler(0, yrot, 0)
            );
        ar.GetComponent<Arrow3D>().direction = direction;
        if (x != 0 || z != 0) ar.GetComponent<Arrow3D>().speed += speed;
    }

    if (dottimaState == 1)
    {
        if (Input.GetKeyDown("space"))
        {
            bomb.GetComponent<Bomb3D>().bombState = 1;
            bomb.transform.SetParent(null);
            dottimaState = 0;
        }
    }

    if (dottimaState == 2)
    {
        float shrink = 1.0f - 2.0f * Time.deltaTime;
        transform.localScale = (
            new Vector3(
                transform.localScale.x * shrink,
```

```
                    transform.localScale.y * shrink,
                    transform.localScale.z * shrink));
            deathTimer -= Time.deltaTime;
            if (deathTimer < 0.0f)
            {
                deathTimer = 1.0f;
                Scoring.lives--;
                dottimaState = 0;
                gameObject.transform.localScale =
                    new Vector3(0.07f, 0.07f, 0.07f);
                gameObject.transform.position =
                    new Vector3(-0.06f, 0.0f, 0.6f);
                if (Scoring.lives == 0)
                {
                    GameState.state = GameState.gameOver;
                }
            }
        }

    }

    private void OnCollisionEnter(Collision collision)
    {
        if (dottimaState == 2) return;

        if (dottimaState == 0)
            if (collision.gameObject.tag == "Bomb")
            {
                bomb = collision.gameObject;
                bomb.transform.SetParent(gameObject.transform);

                bomb.transform.localPosition =
                    new Vector3(0.0f, 5.0f, 0.0f);

                Physics.IgnoreCollision(
                  collision.collider,
                  gameObject.GetComponent<Collider>()
                  );
                dottimaState = 1;
            }


        if (collision.gameObject.name == "ExitLocation")
        {
            Scoring.gamescore += (int)Scoring.levelTimer;
            Scoring.levelTimer = 100.0f;

            if (GameState.level < lastLevel)
                GameState.state = GameState.levelComplete;
            else
                GameState.state = GameState.theEnd;
        }

        if (collision.gameObject.tag == "Spiker" ||
            collision.gameObject.tag == "Robot")
        {
            // drop the bomb first
            if (dottimaState == 1)
            {
                bomb.GetComponent<Bomb>().bombState = 1;
                bomb.transform.SetParent(null);
            }           .
            dottimaState = 2;
        }
    }
}
```

Yes, that's a lot of code, but with so many changes it's easier and safer to just list the entire class. It's a good exercise to go through this code again and make sure you understand it.

<Step 25> Test.

Dottima can now pick up the bomb, put it on top of her head, and then drop it, which triggers the fuse and causes an explosion 2 seconds later. The bomb doesn't actually drop but just floats in space, but that actually looks OK, so you'll leave the code like that.

<Step 26> Update the **bomb prefab** in **3dprefabs**.

<Step 27> Put a **DotRobotRigged** into **3DLevel 5** and another **bomb** or two. **Test** to see if you can destroy the DotRobot.

You have now reached another important milestone. The game has all the features and characters of the 2D game, except for the question mark, which you're going to ignore because it wasn't very interesting, and you don't really need it.

<Step 28> Save.

In the next section you'll build a large level, just because you can.

A LARGE LEVEL

The first five levels of DotGame3D are very similar in size and layout. In this section you'll create a much larger level. There's no hard limit to how large you can make levels in this game. It'll be fun to do this and see if the game can handle it. As you add more and more game objects to your scene you always run the risk of breaking your game or simply slowing it down. In general, it's a good idea to make large scenes early on during development to test the technical limits of your game.

<Step 1> Go to **3DLevel 6** and **test** it.

This level should still work, but you made a lot of changes to the game since you last played this level so testing it is definitely necessary. Next, you'll play the game all the way through.

<Step 2> Go to the **TitleScene** and **play** the game through to the end.

Levels 1–5 need some work to make them better, and level 6 will be transformed into that much larger level.

<Step 3> Go back to **3DLevel 6** and **select** the **playfield**.

<Step 4> **Expand** the **playfield** in the hierarchy and **move** the **floor** to the top as shown in Figure 10.9.

You did that last step to make it easier to find the floor game object later on.

<Step 5> **Select** the **floor** and change the **scale** to **(5, 1, 5)**.

This has the unfortunate effect of scaling the texture as well, which you don't want.

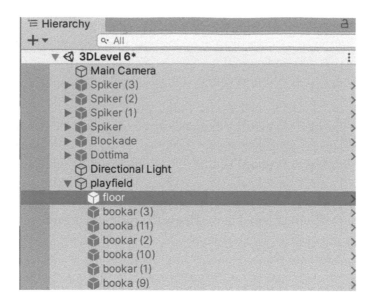

FIGURE 10.9   Rearranging the playfield game object.

<Step 6>   Go to **Assets/Five Seamless Tileable Ground Textures/Materials**.

<Step 7>   **Create** a new material with the name **GS2**.

<Step 8>   **Change** the **Albedo** to the **Grey Stones Texture**.

<Step 9>   **Change** the **Tiling** to **(100, 100)**.

<Step 10> **Change** the **Smoothness** to **0**, **turn on Emission, Global Illumination Realtime**.

<Step 11> **Select** the **floor** in the hierarchy, if necessary, and **drag** the **GS2** material to the floor.

<Step 12> **Zoom out** and compare with Figure 10.10.
     As you can see, you now have plenty of room to build a large level.

<Step 13> Look at Figure 10.11 and **build something similar**.
     You can use **<ctrl>c <ctrl>v** to copy and paste sections of existing rows of books. You can also use that technique to copy and paste spikers, bombs, and DotRobots. You will need to leave the starting position of Dottima the same and you'll need to move the ExitLocation game object to the exit. You can even have multiple ExitLocation objects if you wish.
     In order to see the placement of the objects a little better, Figure 10.11 was created with the floor turned off and the 3D Icons scaled down. Scaling the 3D Icons is controlled with a slider at the top of the Gizmos dropdown.

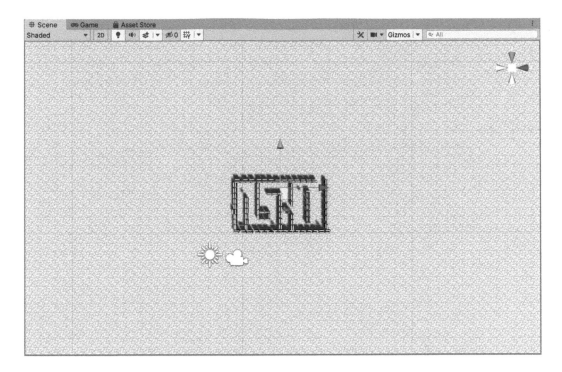

FIGURE 10.10 Making room for a large level.

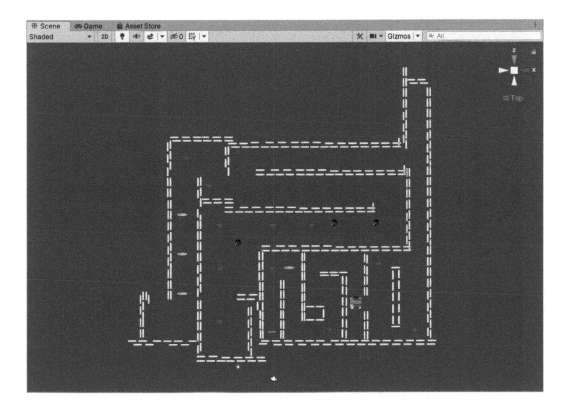

FIGURE 10.11 Layout for a large level.

\<Step 14\> Test the level, then **test** the entire game from the beginning.

Depending on the 3D graphics capabilities of your system you might get a noticeable drop in frame rate on this level. To see your frame rate, turn on Stats in the Game panel. You might also want to do a build and test the game standalone rather than within Unity.

\<Step 15\> Save and **exit** Unity.

In the next chapter you'll finally work on sound and music.

CHAPTER 11

Sound and Music

I N THIS CHAPTER YOU'LL bring in the sound and music from the 2D game. Then you'll create a new sound effect with Audacity and a new music track with MuseScore. Finally, you'll explore 3D audio and surround sound.

REVIEWING SOUND AND MUSIC FROM THE 2D GAME

DotGame3D, in its current form, simply plays a music track throughout the game. The sound effects are missing, so in this section you'll bring them back. The code to do this is mostly the same as in the 2D game. Before you do any of this, look at the Audio assets:

<Step 1>   In Unity, load **DotGame3D** and go to **Assets/Audio**.

There you'll see ten sound effects plus a Music Folder. The Music Folder has just one music track, Scott Joplin's Peacherine Rag.

<Step 2>   **Listen** to all **audio assets**.

To do that, select each audio asset in turn, then play it in the inspector. Be sure to have speakers or headphones connected with the volume turned loud enough. It's a good idea to listen to something else outside of Unity first and adjust the volume there.

Next, you'll try to understand the music code. It's pretty simple.

<Step 3>   **Test** the game from the **TitleScene** through the **beginning of Level 2** and listen to the audio.

You noticed that the music started at the menu scene and then continued from level to level without interruption. How does this code do that?

<Step 4>   In the **Menus Scene** select the **MusicLoop** game object and look at it in the inspector.

Aha, that's where you'll find the Audio Source object that refers to the Peacherine Rag audio clip. "Play On Awake" is checked. That's what triggers playing this clip. Also, "Loop" is checked, so this music simply loops over and over.

DOI: 10.1201/9780429328725-12

You may wish to add additional music tracks so that the players don't get tired of the same music over and over.

There's also a Music Loop script. Here is what it looks like:

```
void Start()
{
    DontDestroyOnLoad(gameObject);
}

// Update is called once per frame
void Update()
{
    if (GameState.state == GameState.gameOver)
    {
        Destroy(gameObject);
    }
    if (GameState.state == GameState.theEnd)
    {
        Destroy(gameObject);
    }
}
```

The Update is easy to understand. When the game ends, either with a Game Over or Dottima finishing the last level, the MusicLoop game object is destroyed. The game then goes to the menu scene, which brings back the music from the beginning. DontDestroyOnLoad() is a special built-in Unity function that keeps the music loop game object alive when loading another scene. This is necessary because, by default, Unity destroys all existing game objects upon loading a new scene.

Next, you'll bring in the arrow sound effects. You're going through all the scripts in order and searching for audio code in the corresponding 2D code.

<Step 5> Look for sound effect code in **Arrow.cs**.

You see a declaration for *whoosh* and *bounce*. In the Start() function you see where whoosh and bounce are defined, and whoosh is played. In the collision code there's a call to bounce.Play().

<Step 6> Copy the sound effect code from **arrow.cs** into **arrow3D.cs**.

<Step 7> Examine the **arrow** prefab in the prefabs folder and look for audio source components.

You will find two Audio Source components, Whoosh and Bounce. Notice that Play on Awake is off for both of them.

<Step 8> Add two **Audio Source components** to the **arrow** prefab in **3dprefabs**. The first one should reference the **whoosh** audio clip, the second one the **bounce** audio clip.

When inserting audio clips choose the second of the two successive choices in the pop-up. The first one points to the reference folder, which you don't want.

<Step 9> Turn off **Play on Awake** for both audio source components.

<Step 10> **Test** by playing **3DLevel 1** and shooting arrows.

You should hear the whoosh sound when launching arrows, and the bounce sound when arrows hit something, just as specified in the code in arrow3d. Next, you'll look at sound for those bombs. There is no music because you didn't start from the menu scene.

<Step 11> **Uncomment** the audio code in **Bomb3d.cs**.

There are just four lines to uncomment: two lines of declarations and two lines that play the sounds.

<Step 12> **Look** at the **bomb** prefab in **Assets/prefabs**.

You can see in the inspector that the Bomb script assigns the Explosion sound to the Clip variable, and the fuse sound to the Fuse variable.

<Step 13> **Save** your changes to **Bomb3d.cs** and go to the **bomb** prefab in **Assets/3dprefabs**.

<Step 14> **Assign Explosion** to **Clip** and **fuse** to **Fuse**. Don't assign the reference sounds from the reference folder.

<Step 15> **Test** this by playing **3Dlevel 5**.

There's a fuse sound when you drop the bomb, and a very cool explosion sound when the bomb explodes.

<Step 16> **Examine DotRobot.cs** and look for sound code.

This is pretty easy. There's an `AudioSource` thud, initialization of thud in `Start()`, and `thud.Play` in the collision code.

<Step 17> **Copy** the thud code into **DotRobot3D.cs**.

<Step 18> **Look** at the **DotRobot prefab** in **Assets/prefabs**.

There's an Audio Source for it using the Thud AudioClip.

<Step 19> **Add** an **AudioSource component** to **Assets/3dprefabs/DotRobot** with a **Thud** AudioClip, **no Play on Awake.**

<Step 20> **Test** this on **3DLevel 4**.

You will hear a bunch of thuds because the thud sound is played every time any DotRobot collides with anything. This can be annoying, but you'll leave this alone for now. Later in this chapter you'll learn how to use 3D sound to make the thud sound softer for DotRobots that are far away from Dottima. Next, you'll put in the speech sounds.

<Step 21> **Look** for audio code in **DottimaController.cs**.

There are four sounds. They are declared at the top of the file and referenced at four different locations throughout.

<Step 22> **Copy** the audio code from **DottimaController.cs** into **DottimaScript.cs**.

<Step 23> **Update** the audio clips for **Dottima** in **3dprefabs**.

<Step 24> **Test** from the Menu and **Save**.

You just brought in all the sounds from the 2D game, except for the Ding sound associated with the question mark, which you're no longer using. In the next section you'll add a new sound effect using Audacity.

ANOTHER SOUND EFFECT

As described in more detail in the 2D book, there are multiple ways of obtaining sound effects for your games, including recording them with a microphone, synthesizing them with software, letting someone else make them for you, or, easiest of all, finding them online. In this section you'll create an additional sound effect using Audacity. You installed Audacity way back in Chapter 1.

Are you missing any obvious sound effects that would make DotGame3D better? You noticed that there is no sound effect when you kill a spiker or DotRobot. You'd also like to have a scraping sound effect when the Blockade is in motion. You'll start by making the scraping sound. This will be done with generating white noise in Audacity and manipulating the sound to get something workable. The death sounds for spikers and DotRobots aren't really necessary because other sound effects are happening then anyhow.

<Step 1> **Launch Audacity** and do **Generate – Noise** … with **Noise Type White, Amplitude 0.7**, and **Duration 1s**, as shown in Figure 11.1.

<Step 2> Click on **OK**.

You now have a 1 second stereo track of white noise. It's a start. You can listen to it if you wish. As you do the following steps, listen to how the various effects change the track.

<Step 3> **Effect – Change Pitch**… and change the **pitch** by **–90%**.

<Step 4> **Effect – Normalize…** and click **OK**.

The next step makes the sound less distorted.

<Step 5> **Effect – Distortion**… and use the distortion type **Soft Overdrive. Apply**.

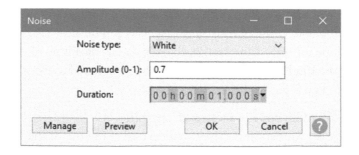

FIGURE 11.1   Making some noise.

<Step 6> **Effect – Reverb…**

<Step 7> **Test** the sound by typing **<shift><spacebar>**.

This was an example of a quick and easy sound effect. It may not be recognizable as a blockade scraping along a stone floor, but you'll put this into the game to see how it fits in with everything else. You can always replace it later on, if necessary.

<Step 8> **File – Save Project – Save Project As…** and save it as **Scrape.aup** in the **Reference** folder in **Assets/Audio** of the DotGame 3D project.

<Step 9> **File – Export – Export as Wav** and **save as Scrape.wav** in **Assets/Audio**.

<Step 10> **Exit Audacity** and **save** the project again when prompted.

<Step 11> **Back in Unity, load DotGame3D** and look at the **Blockade prefab** in **3dprefabs**.

Yes, that prefab still doesn't have a script. You will want a script that plays the Scrape sound loop where the volume is a function of the speed of the object.

<Step 12> For the **Blockade** prefab in **3dprefabs, add** an **Audio Source Component** with the **Scrape audio clip, Loop turned on, Play on Awake on, volume 0**.

<Step 13> **Create** the following script for the **Blockade prefab** in **3dprefabs**.

```
using System.Collections;
using System.Collections.Generic;
using UnityEngine;

public class Blockade : MonoBehaviour
{
    private Rigidbody rb;
    AudioSource scrape;
    private float vol;

    // Start is called before the first frame update
    void Start()
    {
        rb = GetComponent<Rigidbody>();
        scrape = GetComponent<AudioSource>();
    }

    // Update is called once per frame
    void Update()
    {
        vol = rb.velocity.x * rb.velocity.x +
              rb.velocity.y * rb.velocity.y +
              rb.velocity.z * rb.velocity.z;

        if (vol > 0.01f) vol = 1.0f; else vol = 0.0f;

        scrape.volume = vol;
    }
}
```

The Update function computes the square of the speed of Blockade, and if that is even slightly above zero the volume of the scrape sound is set to 1, else 0.

<Step 14> **Test, save,** and **exit** Unity.

That was relatively easy. You could have computed the speed of the Blockade by taking the square root of the sum of the squares, but you got lazy and realized that that square root isn't necessary here. Also, you could have avoided the computation using the y coordinate because you know that the y coordinate of the velocity will always be zero, or close to zero.

It's worth commenting on that 0.01f magic number. When testing whether a floating point number is equal to zero, it is often better to check whether it is very small instead. The reason for this is that floating point numbers in a game are often the result of computations with potential roundoff errors. The built-in physics engine might make the velocity of the Blockade object (0.00001, 0.00001, 0), for example, which would result in a tiny speed, but it wouldn't be exactly zero.

In the next section you'll create some new music with MuseScore.

MORE MUSIC WITH MUSESCORE

In this chapter you'll create additional music with MuseScore. First, you'll install MuseScore, then you'll use the MuseScore website to download a classical music track, make some changes to it, and finally put it into DotGame3D.

<Step 1> If necessary, **install MuseScore** on your system from **musescore.org**. MuseScore 3.6.2 or later is fine.

MuseScore is open source and completely free. The website musescore.org contains thousands of free, public domain scores of music that you can use in your games. It's a fantastic resource for musicians and composers. There is also an inexpensive subscription if you wish to have access to the premium music, but that isn't necessary for this book.

<Step 2> **Create a free account at musescore.org** to be able to download scores.

<Step 3> **Find** the **Bach Invention number 13 in a minor** by **BreezePiano, download** and **play** it in **MuseScore.**

This is a very popular Bach composition and if you're a pianist you might be familiar with it. This version sounds good because the creator of the score put in tempo variations, dynamics, and staccatos to give the music expression. You have the option of changing the tempo and dynamics if you wish to make it your own. This music is in the public domain because it was composed over 250 years ago, so it's definitely OK for you to use it.

<Step 4> Optional: **change** the **tempo** and **dynamics** slightly.

<Step 5> **Save** the **MuseScore** file (with the.mscz extension) in **Assets/Audio/Music.**

<Step 6> **Export** an **mp3 file** with the name **Bach Invention 13.mp3** to **Assets/Audio/ Music.**

This may take a few seconds, depending on the speed of your system.

How and where should this Bach Prelude be used in your game? After some thought you've decided to make this the intro and menu music. You'll start the ragtime music at level 1.

<Step 7> Back in Unity, go to the **Menus scene** and **right-click** on **MusicLoop**.

<Step 8> In the popup menu, choose **Copy**.

<Step 9> Go to **3DLevel 1, right-click** in the hierarchy, and do a **paste**.

<Step 10> Save the **scene** and go back to the **Menus scene**.

<Step 11> Delete the **MusicLoop** object.

<Step 12> Test the game, starting from **TitleScene**.
You should now have silence until the game starts. The music starts simultaneously with the phrase "Find the exit, Dottima." This doesn't sound very good. The simple way to fix this is to simply get rid of that somewhat annoying speech. It was put into the 2D game to explain how to play the game. This really isn't necessary. On level 1 the player has nothing else to do except to wander around the level and find the exit. You may put in graphics that say "Exit" in the future to make this clearer.

<Step 13> In **DottimaScript.cs comment out** the `AudioSource.Play` call in the `Start` function.
You're keeping this code in the form of a comment just in case you change your mind later.

<Step 14> Test again from the **TitleScene**.
That sounds much better.

<Step 15> Copy the **MusicLoop** object from **3DLevel 1** to the **TitleScene** hierarchy.

<Step 16> Remove the **MusicLoop** script from the **MusicLoop** game object in the TitleScene.

<Step 17> Change the **AudioClip** in the AudioSource component to the **Bach** music.

<Step 18> Add the following Script, named **BachLoop.cs**, to **MusicLoop** in the TitleScene.

```
using System.Collections;
using System.Collections.Generic;
using UnityEngine;

public class BachLoop : MonoBehaviour
{
    // Start is called before the first frame update
    void Start()
    {
        DontDestroyOnLoad(gameObject);
    }

    // Update is called once per frame
```

```
void Update()
{
    if (GameState.state == GameState.gamePlay)
    {
        Destroy(gameObject);
    }

}
}
```

This code is structured very much like the MusicLoop.cs script. The Bach music will play until the gameplay starts, then it is destroyed.

<Step 19> **Test** this and see what happens after game over.

You now have a problem. After game over you don't have any music for the menu. The simplest way to fix this is to simply move the MusicLoop object from the TitleScene to the Menus scene. You will lose the music for the Title, but you can live with that. Time permitting you'll find a better solution later.

<Step 20> **Move** the **MusicLoop** object from **TitleScene** to the **Menus** scene.

<Step 21> **Test** and **Save**.

Upon further reflection, you'll be able to fix the silence during the TitleScene by creating a custom audio clip of the correct length. You could even put in the "Find the Exit, Dottima!" clip for the TitleScene. You'll keep the title silent for now.

In the next section you'll explore 3D audio. This is a built-in feature of Unity that allows you to use the 3D geometry of your scene to affect audio in a realistic manner.

3D AUDIO

The term "3D Audio" in Unity refers to the synthesis of an audio experience for the player given a single *Audio Listener* and one or more *Audio Sources*. By default, the Audio Listener is attached to the Main Camera, but you will attach the Audio Listener to Dottima instead from now on. The 3D position and velocities of the audio listener and the audio sources are used to create a realistic audio experience for the player.

In this section you will use 3D Audio to fix the problem noted earlier in this chapter regarding the "thud" sounds being too loud and annoying when the DotRobots are colliding with books. First, you'll move the audio listener to Dottima.

<Step 1> **Create** a **prefab** for the **Main Camera** on **3DLevel 1** and store it in **3dprefabs**.

<Step 2> **Turn off** the **Audio Listener** in the **Main Camera prefab**.

You could also just remove the audio listener, but it's easier to just uncheck it. This also makes it easier to bring it back in the future if you should wish to do that.

<Step 3> **Delete** the **Main Camera** in **all other 3D levels** and **replace with** an instance of the **main camera prefab**.

<Step 4> **Test** the game.

Since you now have no audio listeners in the scenes you should have no audio at all on those scenes.

<Step 5> **Add** an **Audio Listener component** to the **Dottima** prefab in **3dprefabs** and **test** again.

Amazingly, that brings back all of the audio. The audio will sound the same because you're still not using 3D audio.

<Step 6> **Edit** the **Audio Source settings** for the **DotRobotRigged prefab** in **3dprefabs**. Aim to match the settings in Figure 11.2.

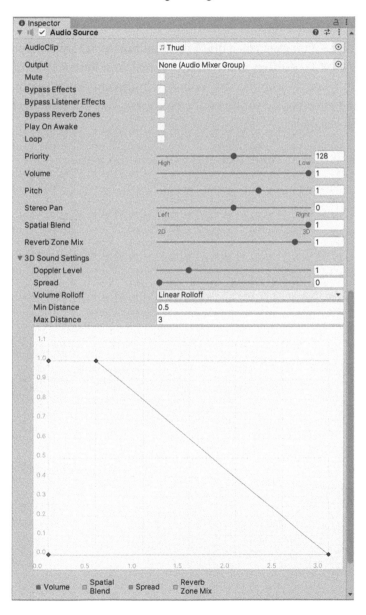

FIGURE 11.2 Audio source settings for DotRobot.

You changed just three settings. You made the **Spatial Blend 1**, changed the **Volume Rolloff** to be a **Linear Rolloff**, and changed the **Min/Max Distance** from **(1, 500)** to **(0.5, 3)**.

You want the volume of the "thud" sound to decrease linearly with the distance between Dottima and the DotRobot, with a zero volume when that distance is more than 3.0. The other settings can be left alone.

<Step 7> **Test** this by playing 3DLevel 4, or any other level with DotRobots in them.

The thud sounds should be inaudible when Dottima is more than 3 units away from the DotRobot making the sound, and at full volume when Dottima is next to the DotRobot.

<Step 8> **Save** and **exit** Unity.

This section gave you a quick introduction to 3D sound. You can read about the other 3D settings in the Unity Manual. You noticed that the spikers are silent when they bounce off walls, so a bouncing sound might make a possible sound effect to add in the future. Of course, you would make those 3D sound effects as well.

The next chapter will take a closer look at the GUI for this game.

CHAPTER 12

GUI and Cutscenes

I N THIS CHAPTER YOU'LL take a closer look at your GUI, the graphical user interface for DotGame3D as well as some related topics. You transferred the GUI from the 2D game to make the game playable and updated the title in the Title Screen. You'll now go through the GUI one more time to make it better. You'll update the title screen, add additional menu items, improve the scoring display, remove the mouse cursor during gameplay, and finally, you'll use Timeline and Cinemachine to make an ending cutscene.

THE TITLE SCREEN

The title screen should convey something about the game, not just the title. In this section you'll learn how to grab a screenshot from the game and make it the background image for the title screen. You will add a fog effect to the screenshot in GIMP to make it look like a distant background.

There are many ways of getting screenshots from your game. First, you'll build a special version of the game with an invisible Dottima, thus only showing the world when you do the screenshot.

<Step 1> Load **DotGame3D** into Unity.

<Step 2> Select **3Dlevel 6**.

<Step 3> **Play** the game and **pause** the game at a "good" spot.
It's up to you to select a good place to pause. You'll want to show DotRobot and a spiker.

<Step 4> With the game paused, **maximize** the **game** panel.
You do this by clicking on the three dots at the top right corner to activate the pop-up menu shown in Figure 12.1. Then you click on Maximize.
If you're not happy with your result you can just go back to playing the game and try again. The next step hides Dottima.

<Step 5> **Uncheck** the **Maximize** checkmark, and then select **Dottima** in the hierarchy.

DOI: 10.1201/9780429328725-13

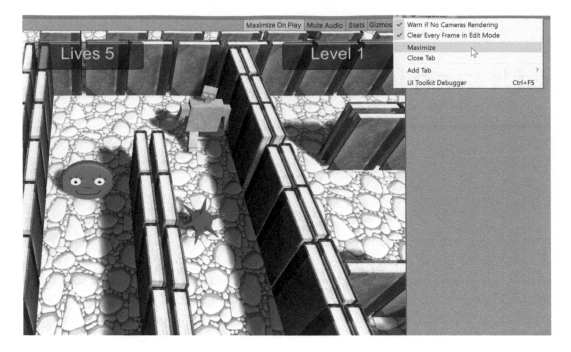

FIGURE 12.1   Maximizing the game panel for a screen capture.

<Step 6> **Uncheck Dottima** in the inspector.
     With Dottima no longer in the scene you're now ready to take the screenshot.

<Step 7> **Maximize** the **game panel** again as you did before.

<Step 8> **Minimize** Unity.

This step isn't necessary if you have two monitors.

<Step 9> **Launch** GIMP.

<Step 10> **File – Create – Screenshot…**

<Step 11> **Enter** a **delay** of **10 seconds** and **click on Snap**.
     You will get a crosshair pop-up. Before you drag the crosshair, do the following.

<Step 12> **Maximize** Unity.

<Step 13> **Move** the **Unity** window out of the way so you can see the crosshair pop-up.

<Step 14> **Drag** the **crosshair** to **select** the **Unity** window.

<Step 15> **Wait 10 seconds** for the screenshot to happen.

<Step 16> Back in **GIMP observe** the **screenshot** similar to Figure 12.2.
     Next, you're going to trim the screenshot to remove the GUI overlays.

FIGURE 12.2 Screenshot in GIMP.

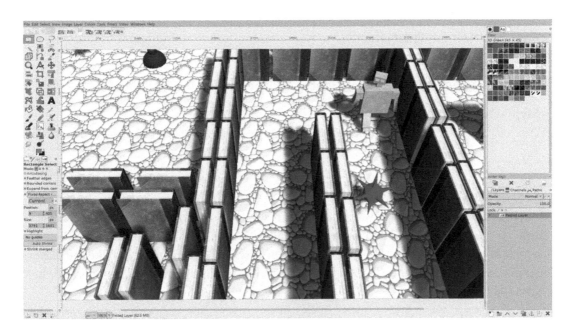

FIGURE 12.3 Screenshot without GUI.

<Step 17> In GIMP, **select** the **rectangle select tool** and **select** most of the screen with it, but not the score, lives, and level indicators at the top.

<Step 18> **Edit – Copy, Edit – Paste as – New Image**. Compare with Figure 12.3.

<Step 19> **Colors – Hue-Saturation…**

<Step 20> In the pop-up, select **Lightness** of **75**, **Saturation** of **−30**. Approximate numbers are OK.

You got a faded version of the screenshot, just what you wanted.

<Step 21> **File – Export As…** to **Assets/art/ScreenShot.jpg** in the **DotGame3D** folder.

Next, you'll need to display this screenshot as a background image on the title scene.

<Step 22> In Unity, **stop playing**, **uncheck Maximize** in the three-dot menu, and go to the **Scene** panel.

<Step 23> **Select** the **TitleScene**.

<Step 24> **Change** the **Scene** panel to **2D mode**.

<Step 25> **GameObject – 3D Object – Quad**.

<Step 26> **Rename** the **Quad** to **ScreenShot**.

<Step 27> **Stretch** the **ScreenShot** object to fit the screen.

In the Inspector you should see the Scale at about (22, 10, 1).

<Step 28> **Drag** the **ScreenShot** from Assets/art on top of the **ScreenShot** object.

<Step 29> **Test** the **TitleScene**.

It appears somewhat too bright, so do this:

<Step 30> **Select** the **Directional Light** and change the **Intensity** to about **0.8**.

<Step 31> **Test** and **Save**.

This makes the title scene much more interesting. You are ready to work on the Menus next.

MENUS

The current option screen only supports the resolution settings and a full-screen checkmark. In this section you'll add a graphics quality setting. This is important for 3D games because 3D games often have a trade-off of quality vs. frame rate, and you'd like the players help make that choice depending on the 3D graphics capabilities of their systems and their individual preferences.

<Step 1> **Select** the **Menus** scene.

<Step 2> Select **2D mode** for the Scene panel, if necessary.

<Step 3> **Expand** the **Canvas** game object in the hierarchy.

<Step 4> **Uncheck** the **MainMenu** and **check** the **SettingsMenu**.

<Step 5> **Select Menus** in the hierarchy.

<Step 6> **GameObject – UI – Dropdown – TextMeshPro**.

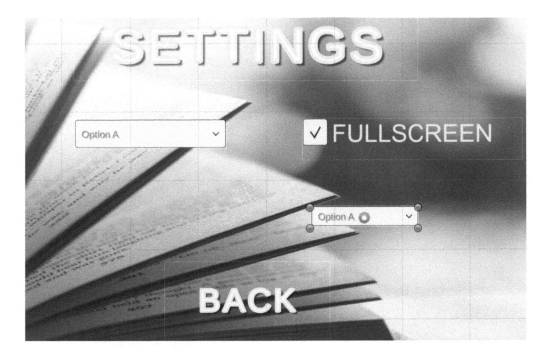

FIGURE 12.4   Inserting a TextMeshPro dropdown.

<Step 7> **Rename Dropdown** to **GraphicsQuality**.

<Step 8> **Adjust Pos X** and **Pos Y** to line up the dropdown object, as shown in Figure 12.4.

<Step 9> Select **GraphicsQuality** in the hierarchy and **drag** it on top of the **SettingsMenu** object.

This should make the new GraphicsQuality dropdown a child of the SettingsMenu, just like the ResolutionDropdown and the other children of the SettingsMenu object.

<Step 10> With the **GraphicsQuality** object **selected**, **scroll down** the inspector to the Options section. Change **Option A** to **Low**, **Option B** to **Medium**, **Option C** to **High**.

It's time to test this.

<Step 11> **Test**.

You're missing a label, and the size of the surrounding box is too small.

<Step 12> **Select** the **Canvas** in the hierarchy.

<Step 13> **GameObject – UI – Text – TextMeshPro**.

<Step 14> **Adjust** the **position** by changing **Pos X** and **Pos Y** in the inspector. **Change** the **Text Input** to **Graphics Quality**. Change the **Font Size** to **24**. Compare with Figure 12.5.

FIGURE 12.5   Graphics quality dropdown.

<Step 15> **Select** the **GraphicsQuality** object and change the **Height** to **42** in the inspector.

<Step 16> **Test**.
     This looks good, but the GraphicsQuality setting doesn't do anything yet. You can make this happen very easily.

<Step 17> **Edit** SettingsMenu.cs in Visual Studio.

<Step 18> **Insert** the following code immediately above the SetFullscreen function.

```
public void SetQuality(int qi)
{
    QualitySettings.SetQualityLevel(qi);
}
```

<Step 19> **Save** this and go to **Unity**. **Select GraphicsQuality** in the hierarchy.

<Step 20> In the inspector, look for **On Value Changed**, and **click** on the + sign.

<Step 21> **Drag** the **SettingsMenu** object from the hierarchy to the **None (Object)** box.

<Step 22> **Change No Function** to **SettingsMenu** and then **SettingsMenu.SetQuality**. The **On Value Changed (int32)** box should look like Figure 12.6.

<Step 23> **Test** this by opening **Edit – Project Settings – Quality** and running the game.

FIGURE 12.6   Setting up on value changed.

When you're changing the graphics quality settings in the game the Project Settings window will update. You won't see the update unless the mouse is hovering over the Project Settings panel. You noticed that you have six quality settings in the Project Settings window, but your dropdown only supports three settings. Also, the initial settings don't match.

<Step 24> **Select GraphicsQuality** in the hierarchy and **update** the **Options** to match the six Project Settings Quality settings.

<Step 25> **Test** again.
It should work now, at least when you're testing within the Menus scene.

<Step 26> **Uncheck** the **SettingsMenu, check** the **MainMenu** and **test** again.
The "graphics quality" text is showing up on the Main Menu. This is easily fixed.

<Step 27> **Move** the **Text (TMP)** object to be a **child** of the **SettingsMenu**.

<Step 28> **Test** again.
The only problem now is that upon initialization the setting appears as "very low." When the player first looks at the settings menu the "very low" setting is incorrect. Instead, the game will be using the default setting. You will live with this for now, but you'll make a mental note that this needs to be fixed before releasing this game to an unsuspecting public.

<Step 29> Go to the **TitleScene** and **test** the **very low** and the **ultra graphics** quality settings.
You should see no shadows for very low quality, and soft shadows in ultra. You plan to revisit these settings later on when the game is closer to completion.

<Step 30> **Save**.
In this section you improved the Settings Menu by adding graphics quality. Of course, you may wish to add more settings in a similar manner as your game becomes more complex. For example, you may wish to add a difficulty setting.

SCORING

In this short section you'll improve the existing display of the score, timer, level, and lives. The code for this is, unsurprisingly, in the Scoring.cs script.

FIGURE 12.7   Yellow scoring using GUI.Label.

<Step 1>   Edit **Scoring.cs** in Visual Studio.

In the OnGUI function you see at the beginning, code that displays the gamescore, levelTimer, level, and lives. This code uses the GUI . Box function. Upon reflection, you decided that the box isn't really necessary. Instead, you want a label.

<Step 2>   Replace the beginning of OnGUI with this code:

```
GUI.skin.label.fontSize = 30;
GUI.color = Color.yellow;
GUI.Label(new Rect(20, 20, 400, 50), "Score: " + gamescore +
             " Timer: " + (int)levelTimer);
GUI.Label(new Rect(Screen.width - 220, 20, 200, 50),
             "Level " + GameState.level);
GUI.Label(new Rect(Screen.width / 2 - 100, 20, 200, 50),
             "Lives " + lives);
```

<Step 3>   **Test** this and compare with Figure 12.7.

The text is difficult to read superimposed over the floor but looks good in contrast with the books. You may adjust the text color to something else later on.

<Step 4>   **Save**.

You have just scratched the surface of what's possible with the Unity GUI system. In a commercial release you would need to spend more time polishing and adjusting the GUI, but the current GUI is good enough for this small prototype.

HIDING THE MOUSE CURSOR

You've probably noticed that the mouse cursor is visible during gameplay. The game doesn't support the mouse, so it would be best to just turn it off and on when entering and leaving gameplay. The following lines of code will do that:

```
Cursor.visible = false;
Cursor.visible = true;
```

So now you need to decide where to do this.

<Step 1>   In **DottimaScript.cs** make the cursor invisible in the `Start` function.

<Step 2>   In **MainMenu.cs**, insert a `Start` function and make the cursor visible in it.

<Step 3>   **Test** by playing the game from the TitleScene. Then **Save**.
     Well, that should have been done long ago, but better late than never. It's common to notice small cosmetic flaws during development. If there's an easy fix it's best to do it right away.

In the next sections you'll create an ending cutscene using Timeline and Cinemachine.

ENDING CUTSCENE AND TIMELINE

DotGame simply displays "The End" when the player reaches the ending of the game. Decades ago, when arcade video games were in their infancy, endings didn't exist, and the games simply repeated themselves until the arcade shut down. Instead of an ending the games got more difficult until the player couldn't handle it anymore. At least that was the theory. Now, in the 21st century, video games are expected to have an ending, often consisting of elaborate and lengthy cutscenes, followed by a credits roll and a chance to play again.

In this section you'll create a short ending cutscene, featuring Dottima at the end of her adventure. In this scene Dottima will simply move along a straight line. The camera will show a closeup of Dottima, then a side shot of Dottima moving along, and then a shot of Dottima moving toward the horizon. You'll create three different cameras to do that.

Unity has very good support for creating cutscenes like this via Timeline and Cinemachine. First, you'll need to build the scene, and then you'll use Timeline to animate Dottima and control the cameras. In the subsequent section you'll use Cinemachine to improve the cameras.

<Step 1>   **Create** a new Scene in **Assets/Scenes** with the name **Ending** and **select** it.
     As usual, the scene just contains the Main Camera object and Directional Light object. Expand the Ending object in the hierarchy if necessary.

<Step 2>   **Instantiate** a **floor** prefab in from **Assets/prefabs**, and **Dottima** from **Assets/3dprefabs**. **Turn off 2D mode** in the Scene panel.

<Step 3>   **Move Dottima** to **(0, 0, 4)** and the **floor** to **(0, 0, 0)**.

<Step 4>   **Change** to the **Default Layout** if necessary and adjust the view to match Figure 12.8.
     You see Dottima in her starting position for the ending cutscene. First, you'll animate Dottima to simply be stationary for a few seconds, and then slowly move straight ahead to the other side of the floor. You could do this by writing a script, but it's easier to use Unity animation, thus avoiding having to write code altogether. In fact, you won't be writing any code at all to create this cutscene.

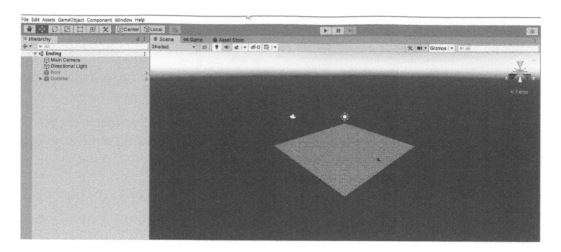

FIGURE 12.8 Starting to set up the ending scene.

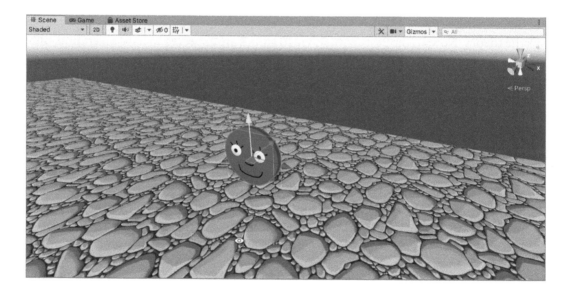

FIGURE 12.9 A better view of Dottima.

\<Step 5\> **Hold** the **RMB** and use **WASD controls** and the **mouse** to fly around the scene until it looks about like Figure 12.9. **Then zoom out** until you see most of the floor.

Notice that while you're flying around this very simple scene, the mouse cursor changes to an eye icon with a tiny WASD key configuration below it. Be sure to become familiar with this way of controlling the scene view in Unity.

\<Step 6\> With **Dottima selected**, do **Window – Animation – Animation**.

You will get a pop-up animation window.

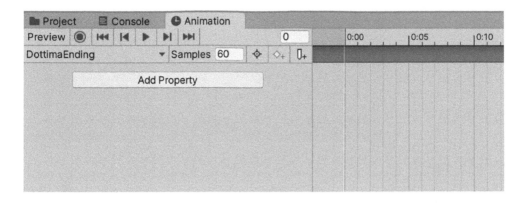

FIGURE 12.10   Docking the animation window.

<Step 7>   **Expand** the right panel and **click** on the **Create** button. Find the **Assets/ animations** folder, change the name to **DottimaEnding.anim** and then **Save.**

<Step 8>   **Dock** the **animation window** into the bottom panel as shown in Figure 12.10 by **dragging** the **Animation tab next to the Console tab**.

Next, you'll do the animation for Dottima using the Animation window recording feature.

<Step 9>   **Click** on the **red record button** next to Preview.

Notice the red shading in the time scale. That's a reminder that you're now in recording mode.

<Step 10>   **Drag Dottima** in the **Z direction** a little, then **reenter 4** for the **Z position** in the inspector.

You're not actually moving Dottima, but this maneuver creates a keyframe at the start.

<Step 11>   Type **720<enter>** in the **current frame** box and move Dottima to **(0,0 –4)**.

This creates a new keyframe at frame 720. This represents 12 seconds into the animation clip at 60 frames a second.

<Step 12>   Use the mouse-wheel to **zoom out** the Animation time display and compare with Figure 12.11.

<Step 13>   **Stop recording** and then **press** the **preview play** button to **watch** the **animation**.

Dottima takes 12 seconds to move across the floor. She doesn't do this at a constant speed, but rather she speeds up and slows down.

<Step 14>   **Select floor, remove Animator component** in the inspector, if it exists. **Test**.

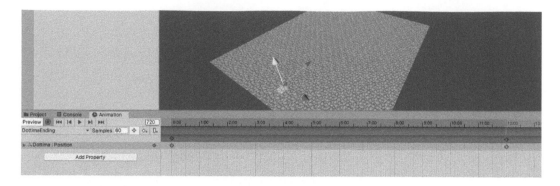

FIGURE 12.11 Inserting a keyframe at frame 720, time 12 seconds.

This is quite strange here. Dottima is tiny and moves towards the camera. The cursor is invisible, which makes it difficult to turn off play mode. You'll need to press the <esc> key to get the mouse cursor to show up so you can then stop playing the game.

And yes, Dottima can shoot arrows here, but her movement is controlled by the Animator controller, not the Dottima Script. You can leave this as is. This cutscene shouldn't really allow user interactions, but this doesn't harm anything, so you'll leave this alone as a hidden feature. Optionally you can turn off the Dottima Script. There's an old saying for situations like this: It's not a bug, it's a feature.

It's time for the timeline. The timeline window coordinates multiple animations and can adjust them more easily than within the Animation window.

<Step 15> **Window – Sequencing – Timeline**.

This will create a timeline window on top of the scene in the center of the Unity display.

<Step 16> **Move** the **Timeline tab** next to the Animation tab below, as shown in Figure 12.12.

Before you create a new timeline, do this:

<Step 17> **Create** an **empty GameObject**, name it **timeline**.

<Step 18> **Select** the **timeline** GameObject, and then **click** on **Create** in the Timeline window. Put it into **Assets**.

Normally you might wish to make a Timelines folder, but you'll only have one timeline in this project, so the root area of Assets is fine.

<Step 19> **Right-click** in the left empty panel of the Timeline and choose **Animation Track** from the pop-up, as shown in Figure 12.13.

<Step 20> **Select** the **new track**, **right-click** in the right panel, and choose **Add from Animation Clip** and choose **DottimaEnding**. **Zoom out** the **timeline** so you can see the entire DottimaEnding clip.

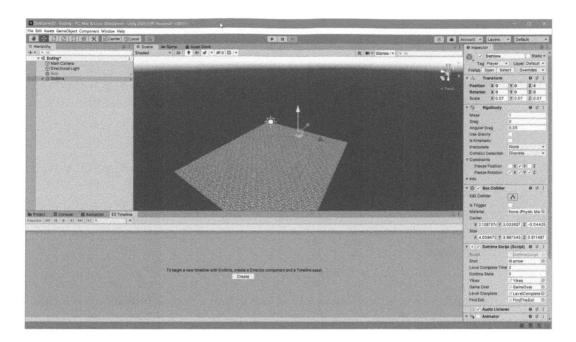

FIGURE 12.12   Creating a timeline window.

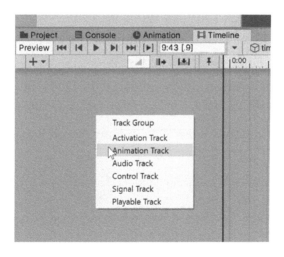

FIGURE 12.13   Adding an animation track to Timeline.

<Step 21> **Click** on the **bullseye icon** for the new track and select **Dottima**. Compare your screen with Figure 12.14.

<Step 22> **Preview** the timeline.
  Dottima starts moving at time 3:00. The initial position of Dottima has changed. To fix the initial position do the following.

<Step 23> **Select** the **Dottima** timeline in the Timeline panel. In the inspector **set** the **Z position** to **4** and **Preview** again.

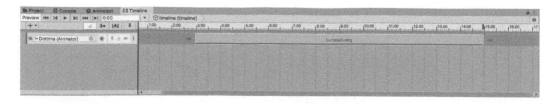

FIGURE 12.14   Bullseye used to add Dottima (Animator) to timeline track.

This time Dottima starts at the proper initial position. However, Dottima is facing the wrong way. The following step fixes that.

<Step 24> In the hierarchy, **expand Dottima, select the Dottima child** and **change the Y rotation to 180** in the inspector. **Select** the **timeline** object and **preview**, then **test**.

Next, you'll set up the three cameras.

<Step 25> **Create two** more **cameras** and **name** the three cameras **Initial Camera, Side Camera**, and **End Camera**.

<Step 26> **Place** the **initial camera** to **Position (0, 1, 2), Rotation (20, 0, 0)** with **Field of View 20**.

<Step 27> **Uncheck** the **other two cameras** and **test**.

You should see a close up of Dottima in place for 3 seconds and then move on. Next, you'll set up the side camera.

<Step 28> **Uncheck** the **Initial Camera** and **check** the **Side Camera** in the inspector. **Select** the **Side Camera. Change Dottima's Y Rotation to 0.**

<Step 29> Use **WASD** and the **mouse** while holding the RMB and fly the scene view to approximately match Figure 12.15.

<Step 30> With the side camera still selected, do **GameObject – Align With View** (or **<ctrl><shift> F**).

This matches the currently selected camera with the scene view.

<Step 31> **Test.**

As before, Dottima waits 3 seconds then moves, this time as seen using the side camera.

<Step 32> **Set up** the **end camera** as shown in Figure 12.16 and **test** it.

All that's left to do is to switch among the three cameras. This can be done using the timeline.

<Step 33> **Select** the **timeline** object in the hierarchy.

<Step 34> **Drag** the **Initial Camera** into the **Timeline** and **select Add Activation Track** in the pop-up.

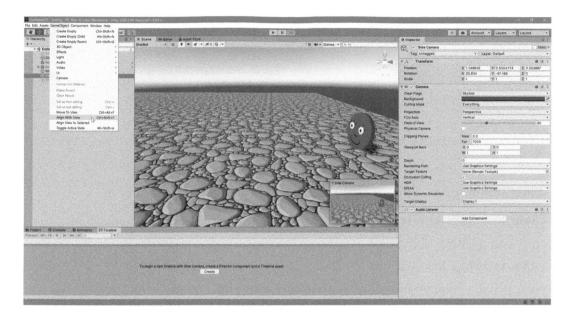

FIGURE 12.15   Setting up the side camera.

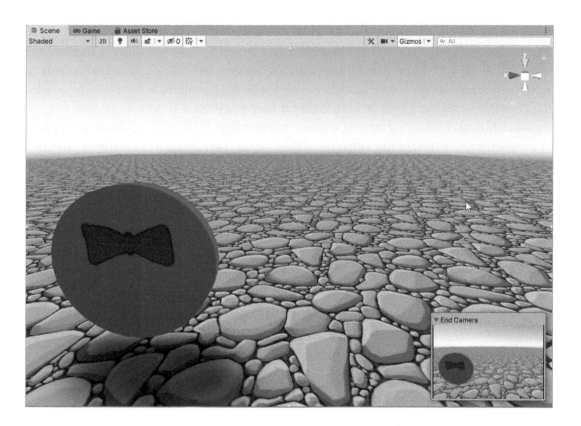

FIGURE 12.16   Setting up the end camera.

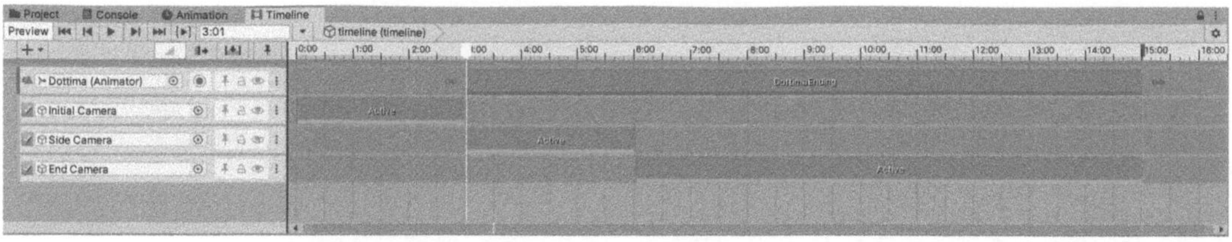

FIGURE 12.17   Activation tracks for the three cameras.

<Step 35> Repeat for the other two cameras.

<Step 36> Adjust the **lengths** and **positions** of the Activation tracks as shown in Figure 12.17.

<Step 37> Test and **save**.
You now have the Initial Camera active for 3 seconds, then the Side Camera for another 3 seconds and then the End Camera for 9 seconds.

You already have an acceptable ending cutscene, but you can do much better. This is the perfect opportunity to learn about Cinemachine, featured in the next section.

CINEMACHINE

The Emmy-winning Cinemachine is a relatively recent feature for Unity. Cinemachine supports advanced camera handling with an easy-to-use interface, allowing you to achieve spectacular cinematic camera control without having to write code. In combination with Timeline, Cinemachine makes it easy to create elaborate cutscenes or even movies. This section will give you a basic introduction by replacing the three stationary cameras from the ending cutscene in DotGame3D with more interesting, animated cameras.

<Step 1> Install the **Cinemachine package**, if necessary.
Cinemachine is one of many free, optional add-ons for Unity. To install it, go to the package manager and select Packages: Unity Registry to see all available packages. Scroll down to find Cinemachine in the alphabetical list of packages, select it and click on Install. The installation takes about 30 seconds. You will notice a new Cinemachine menu entry at the top.

<Step 2> Click on **Cinemachine** and look at the choices, as shown in Figure 12.18.
This menu allows you to create a wide variety of cameras. Before you use Cinemachine there's some housekeeping to do in the project.

<Step 3> In the Timeline, **remove** the **three activation tracks** for the cameras.
You'll be redoing these tracks using Cinemachine.

<Step 4> Uncheck the **Side Camera** and **End Camera**, **check** the **Initial Camera** and **test**.

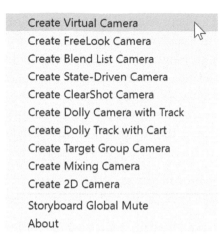

FIGURE 12.18 Cinemachine menu

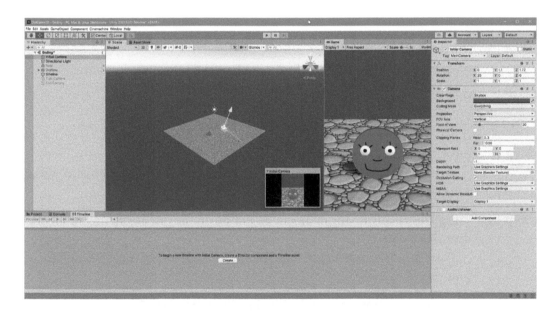

FIGURE 12.19 Setting up the game and scene windows simultaneously.

In this test you just have the Initial Camera active. In order to work with multiple cameras, it's convenient to see the Scene and the Game windows simultaneously. Here's how to do that:

<Step 5> Grab the **Game tab** with the **mouse** and **drag** it **to the right** until you see something like Figure 12.19.

<Step 6> Carefully **drag** the **border** between the Scene and Game windows and make these windows about the same size.

<Step 7> Select the **Initial Camera** and do **GameObject – Align View to Selected.** The two views are now similar to one another.

\<Step 8\>   With the Initial Camera selected, do **Cinemachine – Create Virtual Camera**. You now notice a couple of things. The Initial Camera in the Hierarchy shows a strange grey and red icon. This indicates that the Initial Camera object now has a CinemachineBrain. In the Inspector you'll see the CinemachineBrain at the bottom as a new Component. This means that Cinemachine is now in control of this camera. As you add more virtual cameras to the scene, they all will have the ability to control the Initial Camera.

\<Step 9\>   **Select** the **CM vcam1** object in the hierarchy. This is the first virtual camera. You will now change the settings for it.

\<Step 10\>   **Verify** that you have the setting **Do nothing** for both the **Body** and the **Aim**.

\<Step 11\>   **Test** with **Maximize on Play** turned **on**. This is just a "sanity" test to make sure everything still works. Use \<esc\> to stop playback, as usual.

\<Step 12\>   **Turn off Maximize on Play**, **select timeline** in the hierarchy, and **test** again. As long as you don't move the mouse into the Game window the mouse stays visible. Watch the time progression in the Timeline window. You will now convert the three Unity cameras from the previous section into Cinemachine Virtual Cameras. You'll start with the Initial Camera.

\<Step 13\>   Select **CM vcam1** in the hierarchy. Because you had the Initial Camera active this virtual camera matched the setup for it.

\<Step 14\>   **Drag Dottima** from the hierarchy to **Follow** in the inspector. Then do that again for **Look At**. These settings make the virtual camera follow Dottima and also look at Dottima.

\<Step 15\>   In the **Lens** section, change the **Field of View** (FOV) to **75**. You did this because you couldn't see Dottima at all with a low FOV setting.

\<Step 16\>   Change **Body** to **3rd Person Follow** and **Shoulder Offset** to (**0, 0.16, 1**).

\<Step 15\>   **Test**. You just turned this virtual camera into a "follow" camera. These next steps give you better control over what's happening.

\<Step 16\>   **Stop running** the **game**, then **change** the **Aim** to **Composer** and check **Game Window Guides** at the top of the CinemachineVirtualCamera in the Inspector. Compare with Figure 12.20. The blue box shows the *Soft Zone* area of the screen. The camera will attempt to keep Dottima within the soft zone and away from the red zone.

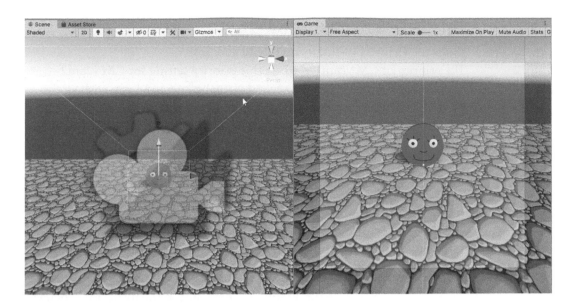

FIGURE 12.20   Guides for Cinemachine.

<Step 17> In the inspector **expand** the **Aim** section and set the **Dead Zone Width** and **Height** to **0.2**.

You can now see a grey square in the middle of the Game window. This is the *Dead Zone*, an area where Dottima, the object being aimed at, can move without affecting the camera.

<Step 18> **Change** the **Damping** setting in the **Body** section to (**0.5, 0.5, 3**) and **test**.

At the beginning of the movement of Dottima the yellow aimpoint slowly moves towards the bottom of the dead zone. The aimpoint is always inside of the dead zone. At the end of the animation Dottima resets and this follow camera smoothly continues to follow. You won't be using this part of the camera animation in the cutscene, but it's instructive to watch it and learn how the follow camera operates.

Next, you'll create a second virtual camera and have it match the Side Camera.

<Step 19> **Disable** the **Initial Camera** and enable the **Side Camera** in the Inspector.

<Step 20> **Select** the **Side Camera** and do **GameObject – Align View to Selected**.

Both the Scene and the Game window now show the view from the Side Camera.

<Step 21> **Cinemachine – Create Virtual Camera**. Make sure that **CM vcam2** is **selected.**

You wish to make this camera simply look at Dottima but not follow her.

<Step 22> **Drag Dottima** to **Look At** in the inspector.

<Step 23> Change the **Body setting** to **Do Nothing**.

<Step 24> Change the **Priority** of **CM vcam2** to **20** and **Test**.

The priority of CM vcam1 is 10, so this priority setting for CM vcam2 makes Cinemachine use just the second virtual camera. As you wished, the camera is stationary and aims at Dottima as she moves away. You now want to automatically switch from the first to the second virtual camera. This is done in the timeline.

<Step 25> Select **timeline** in the hierarchy.

<Step 26> Drag the **Initial Camera** into the **Timeline** and select **Add Cinemachine Track**.

<Step 27> Right-click in the **Initial Camera Track** and select **Add Cinemachine Shot**.

<Step 28> Select the **Cinemachine Shot** and set up the Virtual Camera by **dragging** the **CM vcam1** object into the **Virtual Camera slot** in the inspector. Change the **priority** for **CM vcam2** to **5** and select **CM vcam1** in the timeline. Your screen should look like Figure 12.21.

The Game window shows the vcam1 view.

<Step 29> Adjust the **CM vcam1 shot** in the **Timeline** to **start** at time **0:00** and **end** at time **4:00**.

<Step 30> Add another **Cinemachine shot**, and this time **use CM vcam2**.

<Step 31> Slide the second shot to the left so that it runs from time 4:00 to time 9:00, as shown in Figure 12.22.

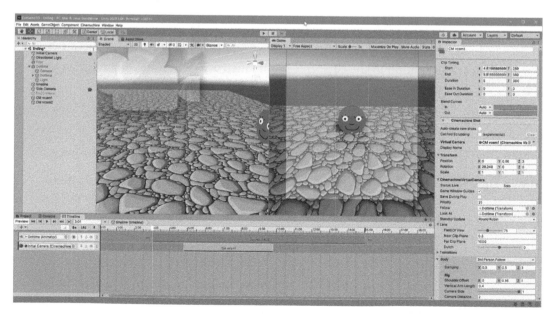

FIGURE 12.21 Setting up the timeline for Cinemachine.

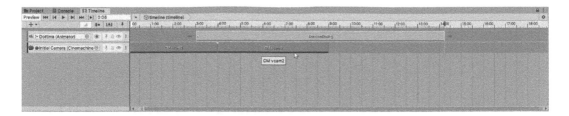

FIGURE 12.22   Two shot clips in the Cinemachine track.

<Step 32> **Disable** the **Side Camera** and **enable** the **Initial Camera**.

<Step 33> **Scrub** the **time** to see the effect of having two clips. Then **test** it by running the game.

Scrubbing means to hold the LMB in the time ruler, and then move the mouse left and right to see the display at any moment in time that you choose. You see that at time 4:00 the cameras abruptly switch. It will look better to *blend* the cameras as follows:

<Step 34> **Overlap** the **camera clips** in the time from 4:00 to 5:00 by dragging the left clip over to the right by 1 second, and then readjusting the start. The overlapped region is displayed with a diagonal line.

<Step 35> **Test** by scrubbing and/or playing the scene.

You will see a very nice, blended transition from the first to the second virtual camera. To finish things off you'll set up a third virtual camera for the end of this cutscene.

<Step 36> **Disable** the **Initial Camera** and **enable** the **End Camera**.

<Step 37> **Select** the **End Camera** and do **GameObject – Align View to Selected**.

<Step 38> **Cinemachine – Create Virtual Camera**.

<Step 39> Change the **Priority** for **CM vcam3** to **20**.

<Step 40> **Change Body** to **Do nothing**.

<Step 41> **Drag Dottima** to **Look At** and **test**.

Because the End Camera is selected and the priority for CM vcam3 is 20, all you see is CM vcam3 in action.

<Step 42> **Disable** the **End Camera**, **enable** the **Initial Camera**, and **test**.

This time you see all three cameras, one after the other. In the timeline at time 9:00 the third virtual camera takes over because it has the highest priority. That transition is jarring, so you'll create a blend as follows:

<Step 43> **Right-click** in the **Initial Camera track** and select **Add Cinemachine Shot**.

<Step 44> **Drag CM vcam3** to the **Virtual Camera slot** in the inspector.

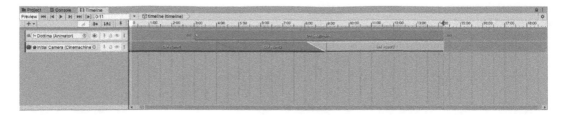

FIGURE 12.23   Three blended virtual cameras in the timeline.

<Step 45> **Blend** the **CM vcam2** and **CM vcam3** shots, as shown in Figure 12.23.

<Step 46> **Test** once again and **save**.

This time you finally have the cutscene you wanted. Dottima moves toward the horizon and the three virtual cameras follow her. In the next section you'll integrate this cutscene into the game.

INTEGRATING THE ENDING CUTSCENE

You still have some work to do. The cutscene needs to exit before reaching time 14.00. Also, the ending cutscene needs to actually be played at the end of the game, and then the game should go back to the main menu to allow the player to play another game.

<Step 1> **File – Build Settings – Add Open Scenes**.

You should now have the Scenes/Ending scene inserted as Scene 8.

<Step 2> In **GameState.cs** insert the following line:

```
public const int EndScene = 8;
```

<Step 3> In **DottimaScript.cs**, in the GameState.theEnd section, replace
`GameState.MenuScene` with `GameState.EndScene`.

<Step 4> **Play** the game from the beginning and try to get to the ending.

As you expected, the game gets stuck in the ending cutscene, but otherwise it's OK. To make testing easier, change the definition of lastLevel:

<Step 5> In DottimaScript.cs, **set** `lastLevel` to 1 rather than 6 near line 14.

Remember to undo this when you're done testing the ending.

<Step 6> **Select 3Dlevel 1** and test from there.

After you quickly play 3Dlevel 1 you immediately go to the ending. You're now ready to fix the ending.

<Step 7> In the Ending scene, add the following script to Dottima and name it DottimaEndingScript.cs.

```
using System.Collections;
using System.Collections.Generic;
using UnityEngine;
using UnityEngine.SceneManagement;
```

```
public class DottimaEndingScript : MonoBehaviour
{
    private float TotalTime;
    // Start is called before the first frame update
    void Start()
    {
        TotalTime = 0.0f;
    }

    // Update is called once per frame
    void Update()
    {
        TotalTime += Time.deltaTime;
        if (TotalTime > 13.5f)
            SceneManager.LoadScene(GameState.MenuScene);
    }
}
```

<Step 8> **Test.**

It worked!

<Step 9> **Change** `lastLevel` in DottimaScript back to **6.**

You really should test this one more time. Yes, you have no music during the ending cutscene. That's something for another day.

<Step 10> **Save** and **exit** Unity.

CHAPTER 13

Testing and Debugging

OR MANY PROGRAMMERS, TESTING and debugging can take just as much time as writing code. If that's you, don't panic. Testing and debugging are normal parts of the process. In this chapter you'll start by exploring testing techniques and then you'll learn about the debugging features built into Unity and Visual Studio.

You probably would have benefitted by learning about debugging earlier in this book, but it's a little bit of a chicken and egg problem. You needed to learn about the basics of Unity first before taking a dive into debugging. Nevertheless, this chapter is standalone, in the sense that it doesn't depend on your progress in the Dottima3D project. So, if you're reading this because you managed to create some bugs in the earlier chapters, that's fine. Just save your work and follow along with this chapter, then go back, and with any luck you'll know how to find those bugs and fix them.

TESTING

In this section you'll explore some basic game testing techniques. Testing is the single most important development technique for achieving reliability. You can write poor code, but if you test it well and fix all the bugs, you'll end up with something that can be released. Conversely, even if you're very experienced and use best practices when writing your code, you'll almost certainly create disastrous bugs if you don't bother to test.

You'll start by building a simple project and testing it.

<Step 1> **Create** a **new 3D project** with the name **TestAndDebug**.
　　　If you worked through the previous chapter, you'll notice that the Cinemachine menu entry is gone and you're back to the Default Layout.

<Step 2> **GameObject – 3D Object – Plane. Change** the **scale** to (**10, 10, 10**).

<Step 3> In Assets, **create** a **green material**, name it **Green**, and **drag it** onto the **Plane**.

<Step 4> **Create** an **empty GameObject** and name it **GenerateSpheres**.

<Step 5> **Create** a **new script**, **BuildSpheres.cs** with the code below and assign it to GenerateSpheres:

DOI: 10.1201/9780429328725-14

```
using System.Collections;
using System.Collections.Generic;
using UnityEngine;

public class BuildSpheres : MonoBehaviour
{
    public GameObject block;
    public int width = 10;
    public int height = 4;

    // Start is called before the first frame update
    void Start()
    {
        for (int y = 0; y < height; y++)
        {
            for (int x = 0; x < width; x++)
            {
                Instantiate(block,
                    new Vector3(x, y, 0),
                    Quaternion.identity);
            }
        }
    }
}
```

<Step 6> **Save** in Visual Studio.

This code should create a 10 by 4 array of Spheres floating above the plane.

<Step 7> **Run** the game.

Nothing happens, no spheres are visible.

<Step 8> **Stop** running the game.

Look at the Unity Screen as shown in Figure 13.1.

Notice the red text at the bottom? That's the problem. It's a good habit to often look there and see if you're getting any error messages. To see the full error messages in all of their glory, do this:

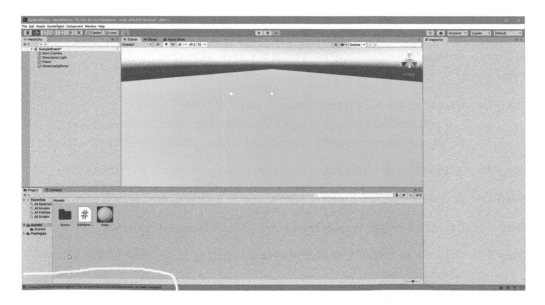

FIGURE 13.1   **Error!**

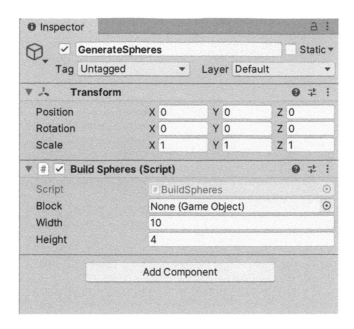

FIGURE 13.2   Missing assignment shown in the inspector.

<Step 9>   **Click** on the **Console Tab**.
You can now see the full error message.

<Step 10>   Select **GenerateSpheres** and look in the **inspector**. Compare with Figure 13.2.
You forgot to create the Sphere prefab from which to instantiate.

<Step 11>   **GameObject – 3D Object – Sphere**.

<Step 12>   **Click** on the **Project Tab**.

<Step 13>   **Drag** the **Sphere** to the **Assets** window.
You now have a Sphere prefab in Assets.

<Step 14>   Select **GenerateSpheres** and drag the **Sphere** from the **Assets** to the **Block** slot in the inspector.

<Step 15>   **Run** the game and compare with Figure 13.3. Then **stop** the game.
So far so good. Now the question arises, where did the original sphere go? Is it still there? You can see the 40 generated spheres, but the original sphere is not visible.

<Step 16>   **Go** to the **2 by 3 layout**.
This layout shows both the Scene and the Game windows, which can be very useful for testing.

<Step 17>   **Run** the game and take a look. Don't stop running the game for now.
You now see the block of spheres both in the Scene and in the Game window. In the Hierarchy you see a Sphere object and many clones, presumably 40 of them.

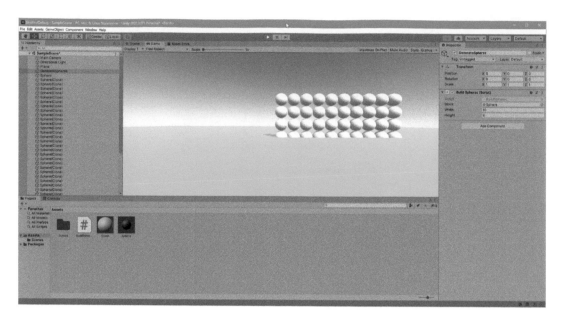

FIGURE 13.3 A block of 40 spheres.

<Step 18> **Select** the **Sphere** object in the hierarchy, then **drag** it to the **right** and **up** in the scene window. Compare with Figure 13.4.

Aha! That original Sphere was at the origin, overlapping with one of the generated spheres. You just experienced one of the really great features of Unity: allowing you to change the game while it's running. Sometimes this method can reveal bugs that would otherwise be very difficult to find. Be careful when

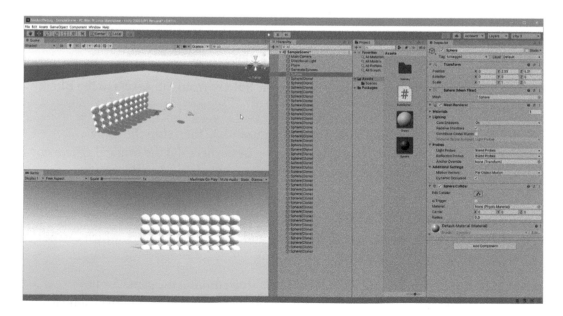

FIGURE 13.4 Finding the original sphere.

doing this though. Any changes made while the game is running are only temporary and will undo themselves when you stop running the game.

<Step 19> **Stop** running the game. Note that the Sphere is back at (0,0,0). **Delete** the **Sphere** in the hierarchy and run the game again.

That's better. That left over sphere didn't really harm anything, but it's gone now, and the scene is a little cleaner.

Did you notice that the 2 by 3 layout doesn't have a Console? You can bring one into this layout by doing Window – General – Console and then dragging the Console Tab around the Unity layout to a convenient place. Alternatively, you could just go back to the Default layout. You'll stay in the 2 by 3 layout for now.

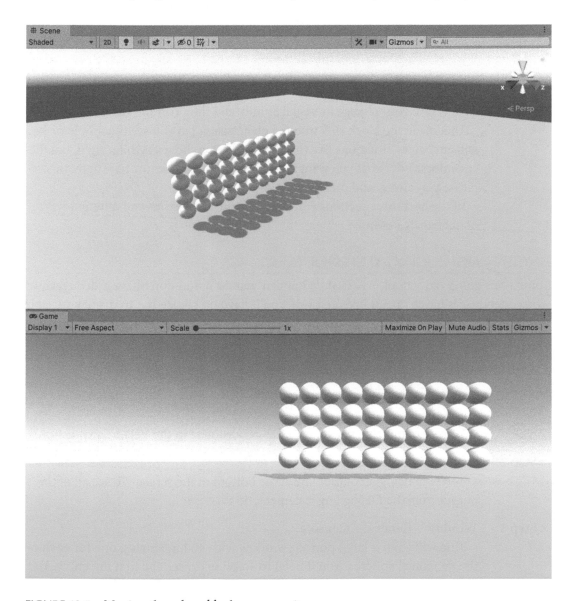

FIGURE 13.5   Moving the sphere block up one unit.

Your next goal is to move that block of spheres up by 0.5 units so that the bottom row doesn't intersect with the plane.

<Step 20> **Replace** the Vector3 line in BuildSpheres.cs with this:

```
new Vector3(x, y + 1, 0),
```

This will move the spheres up by one unit. Remember that the y-axis in Unity points up.

<Step 21> Remember to **save** your change in Visual Studio, then **run** the game and compare with Figure 13.5.

That worked, but you would like the sphere block to sit exactly on the plane. You'll do that by making the offset ½ unit rather than one unit.

<Step 22> Replace the Vector3 line with this one:

```
new Vector3(x, y + 1/2, 0),
```

<Step 23> Again, **save** your change in Visual Studio, and then **run** the game.

That made the block sink into the plane again. Do you see the problem? You will encounter situations like this: You think you did everything right, but the code doesn't do what you want it to do. If you already know how to fix this, please play along, and pretend that you're stumped.

In the next three sections you'll learn about and use several different ways of debugging in Unity.

ANCIENT DEBUGGING TECHNIQUES

Sometimes going old school is easiest. What can you do if you don't have a debugger, or worse, debuggers haven't been invented yet? You'll have no choice but to display variable values using explicit code. This can be effective and easy to do. Decades ago, this was often the only way to track down those elusive bugs.

<Step 1> After the Instantiate statement, insert this:

```
Debug.Log("Y value: " + (y + 1/2));
```

You are outputting the value of the y coordinate in the Vector3 expression.

<Step 2> **Save, Run** the game, and **stop**.

You're noticing an output line at the bottom of the screen. To see all of the output from the Debug.Log statement, do this:

<Step 3> **Window – General – Console**.

This will open a large pop-up window with 40 log entries, one for each of the generated spheres. You'll need to scroll up to see the first log entry. You don't know it yet, but each log entry has three lines. To see all three lines, do this:

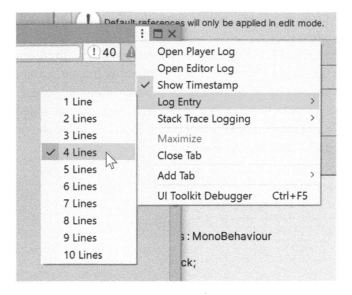

FIGURE 13.6   Setting the number of lines per log entry to 4.

<Step 4>   In the top right corner of the Console Window, **open** the **Console menu** by clicking on the three vertical dots, as shown in Figure 13.6.

<Step 5>   **Click** on **Log Entry** and **4 Lines**.

In Figure 13.7 you see the first three full Log entries including Line Number 20. This can be useful when you have multiple Debug.Log statements in your code.

<Step 6>   Click on **Collapse** in the Console Window.

This collapses any repeating statements. The number of repeats is shown on the right side of the console window.

So, what have you discovered? Apparently $0 + 1/2$ evaluates to 0. If you're still stumped on why this is happening, at this point you should ask for help from an experienced C# programmer. There are internet forums where your

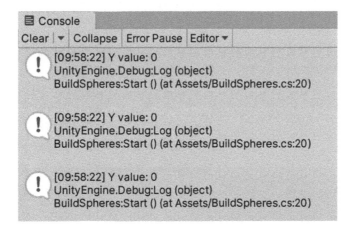

FIGURE 13.7   Full debug log statements.

fellow game developers will be more than happy to help out with a short question such as this.

The problem is the mixing of integers and floats. The Vector3 statement needs floating point values, but you are using integer computations. When using integers in C# or most other programming languages, 1 divided by 2 results in 0 with a remainder of 1, which then gets discarded. What you want is the floating point constant of 0.5. A good lesson for the future is this: Be very careful with integer division!

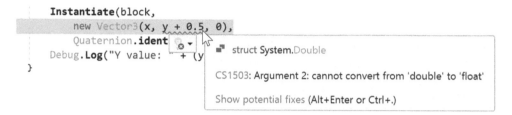

```
Instantiate(block,
    new Vector3(x, y + 0.5, 0),
    Quaternion.ident
    Debug.Log("Y value:        + (y
}
```

    struct System.Double

    CS1503: Argument 2: cannot convert from 'double' to 'float'

    Show potential fixes (Alt+Enter or Ctrl+.)

FIGURE 13.8 Double vs. float.

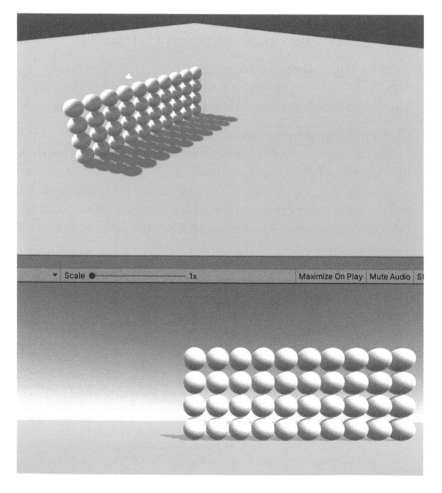

FIGURE 13.9 The block of spheres on the plane.

<Step 7> **Replace** the `Vector3` statement with this:

```
new Vector3(x, y + 0.5, 0),
```

Visual C doesn't like this and puts in a squiggly red line under the y+0.5. If you hover the mouse over the red line, you'll see something like Figure 13.8.

This is a common issue when coding in Unity. Floating point constants are, by default, doubles, but Unity usually operates with floats. To fix this, do this:

<Step 8> **Change** the `0.5` to `0.5f` in the `Vector3` statement, **save** and **run**. Compare with Figure 13.9.

<Step 9> **Save**.

In the next section you'll continue to learn about debugging C# in Unity.

DEBUGGING C# IN UNITY

You spent the last section debugging C# in Unity. This section continues to explore additional Unity debugging features.

<Step 1> **Remove** the `Debug.Log` line in the `Start` function of **BuildSpheres.cs.** You no longer need this log statement.

<Step 2> Insert the following three lines at the beginning of the Start function.

```
Debug.Log("Starting");
Debug.LogWarning("This is a Warning");
Debug.LogError("Error");
```

That's right, you can put in your own warning and error messages.

<Step 3> **Save** and **run** the game. Look at the **console** window.

You may or may not see the three Log entries. The visibility of these three types of log messages is controlled by three buttons at the top right of the console window, as shown in Figure 13.10.

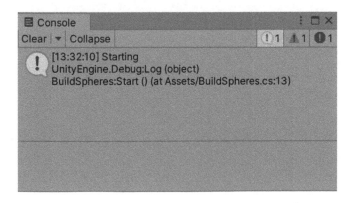

FIGURE 13.10   Console window settings.

You can see that the white exclamation mark is selected, but the yellow and red are not. All three have a 1 next to them. This means that you have one ordinary log message, one warning, and one error, but the warnings and errors aren't visible.

<Step 4> **Enable** the **warnings** and **errors** by clicking on the buttons at the top right of the console window, if necessary. Compare with Figure 13.11.

Next, you'll try out the Debug.DrawLine feature. This member of the Debug class allows you to temporarily draw lines in the Scene View to help you visualize your objects.

<Step 5> GameObject – 3D Object – Cylinder. **Position** this cylinder at (−5, 5, 5).

That cylinder is floating in your scene and it's difficult to know where it is. You're going to add a debug line to help visualize the position of the cylinder.

<Step 6> **Add** a script component to the Cylinder, call it **CylinderScript** with the following code: (Note: the code continues after Figure 13.12)

```
using System.Collections;
using System.Collections.Generic;
using UnityEngine;

public class CylinderScript : MonoBehaviour
{
    // Start is called before the first frame update
    void Start()
    {
        float height = transform.position.y;
        Debug.DrawLine(
```

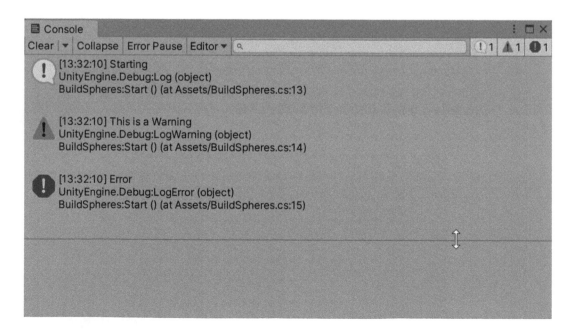

FIGURE 13.11   Warnings and Errors visible in the Console.

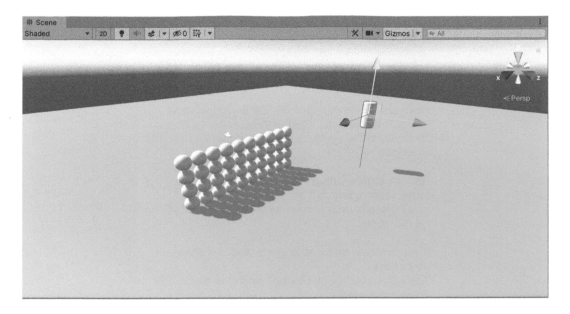

FIGURE 13.12   Debug.DrawLine in action.

```
                transform.position,
                transform.position - Vector3.up * height,
                Color.red, 5);
        }
    }
```

<Step 7> Run the game and compare with Figure 13.12.

That number 5 in the `Debug.DrawLine` function call indicates that the line should disappear after 5 seconds. To further explore the methods for the Debug class, go to the Unity documentation, click on **Scripting API**, and then search for **debug**.

<Step 8> Save.

The next section gives you a short introduction to the Visual Studio Debugger.

THE VISUAL STUDIO DEBUGGER

Visual Studio has a built-in debugger that will allow you to step through your code, examine memory, and gain a better understanding of what's happening. This can be much easier and faster for the developer when compared to putting in Debug statements.

Even though there are no known bugs in the TestAndDebug project, you're going to do a quick debugging session with it to learn how to set it up.

<Step 1> Exit Unity, **launch** it again and **load TestAndDebug**.

This is so your steps will match what's written in this book.

<Step 2> Double-click on **BuildSpheres** in **Assets**.

You now have Visual Studio showing BuildSpheres.cs.

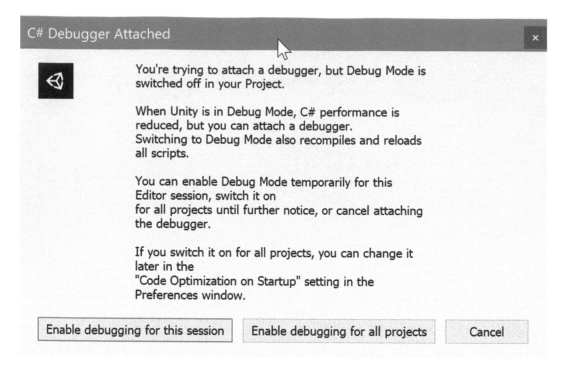

C# Debugger Attached   ✕

You're trying to attach a debugger, but Debug Mode is
switched off in your Project.

When Unity is in Debug Mode, C# performance is
reduced, but you can attach a debugger.
Switching to Debug Mode also recompiles and reloads
all scripts.

You can enable Debug Mode temporarily for this
Editor session, switch it on
for all projects until further notice, or cancel attaching
the debugger.

If you switch it on for all projects, you can change it
later in the
"Code Optimization on Startup" setting in the
Preferences window.

| Enable debugging for this session | Enable debugging for all projects | Cancel |

FIGURE 13.13   Pop-up for attaching the debugger.

<Step 3>   In Visual Studio do **Debug – Attach Unity Debugger**.

<Step 4>   In the popup, select the **TestAndDebug** Unity instance and click on **OK**.
Now you get another pop-up, as shown in Figure 13.13.
You're going to enable debugging for this session in the next step. This step
may reduce performance, so generally you will only take this step when actually debugging. Chances are good that C# performance won't matter for the
projects in this book, but you do wish to have C# performance during development match performance at release.

<Step 5>   Click on **Enable Debugging for this session**.
You are now ready to use the Visual Studio Debugger.

<Step 6>   Put a **breakpoint** at **line 13**, the line with Debug.Log("Starting").
You do that by **clicking** on line 13 within the **gray vertical strip** on the left.
Compare with Figure 13.14.
If you have two screens, something that is highly recommended, especially
for game development, put the Visual Studio window and the Unity window
on separate screens.
You can also simulate this with virtual desktops.

<Step 7>   **Run** the **game** in **Unity**.
The Visual Studio window will get focus and you'll see an arrow inside the
red dot for the breakpoint. Meanwhile in Unity nothing has happened so far
because execution was halted at the breakpoint.

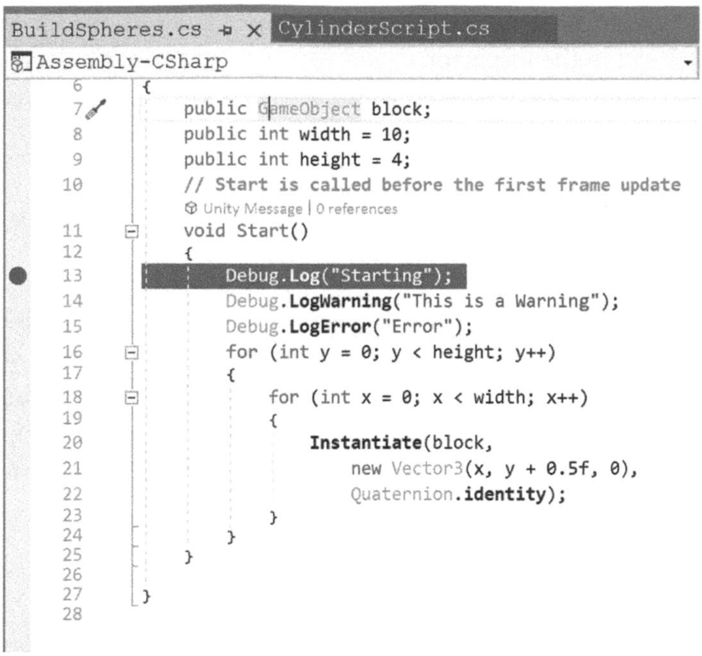

```
BuildSpheres.cs  ⊕ ×  CylinderScript.cs
⚙ Assembly-CSharp
      6        {
      7 ✏          public GameObject block;
      8            public int width = 10;
      9            public int height = 4;
     10            // Start is called before the first frame update
              ⚙ Unity Message | 0 references
     11            void Start()
     12            {
  ●  13                Debug.Log("Starting");
     14                Debug.LogWarning("This is a Warning");
     15                Debug.LogError("Error");
     16                for (int y = 0; y < height; y++)
     17                {
     18                    for (int x = 0; x < width; x++)
     19                    {
     20                        Instantiate(block,
     21                            new Vector3(x, y + 0.5f, 0),
     22                            Quaternion.identity);
     23                    }
     24                }
     25            }
     26
     27        }
     28
```

FIGURE 13.14 Setting a breakpoint.

\<Step 8\> **Repeatedly** type the **\<F10\>** key to start stepping through the program. As you do this look in the **Autos** section below and notice that various variables are getting updated.

\<Step 9\> Once you see the **block** variable in the Autos section, **expand** it to take a look. You can see quite a bit of information about the Sphere prefab that's assigned to block.

\<Step 10\> Type the \<F5\> key. This continues the execution. You can now see the result in the Unity window.

\<Step 11\> **Stop** running the game in Unity. That breakpoint is still visible in Visual Studio.

\<Step 12\> **Run** the game again. You are once again stuck at the breakpoint. This time you'll just give up and stop running the game right away. Unfortunately, when you're stuck on a breakpoint the Unity window is dead.

\<Step 13\> Do **Debug – Stop Debugging**, or type **\<shift\>\<F5\>**. This automatically stopped running the game in Unity and detached the debugger from Unity. So, if you want to continue to debug, you'll need to attach it again.

\<Step 14\> In Visual Studio, **attach** the Unity debugger again as you did before. You are in the same Unity session, so you are still in debug mode. This time you'll create a bug and try out the debugger with it.

<Step 15> In Unity, **select** the **GenerateSpheres** object and **remove** the **Sphere** from the **Block** slot in the inspector.

As you know, this will cause an error. Let's see what happens when you try to run the game now.

<Step 16> **Run** the game.

Aha, no error yet. You are stuck at that breakpoint again. The problem will occur at the `Instantiate` statement.

<Step 17> **Start stepping** through the program with **<F10>** as you did before.

When you get to the `Instantiate` statement execution you get thrown back to Unity with the Exception error on display at the bottom. The program is unable to continue. Back in Visual Studio you can't do a whole lot, except look at the Autos. The error message in the Console in Unity tells you where the exception occurred.

<Step 18> **Stop** running the game, **remove** the **breakpoint** in Visual Studio and run the game again.

The Visual Studio debugger isn't much help here as well. You're still in Unity. The lesson here is that you need to find the location of any exceptions by reading the error messages in the console in Unity and take it from there.

<Step 19> **Fix** the bug, **save**, and **exit** Unity.

The Visual Studio debugger isn't just for debugging. It's also extremely useful for trying to understand somebody else's code or even your own old code. You can just put a breakpoint at the beginning and start stepping through while looking at the data and watching what happens. The Unity environment makes it easy to do something quite similar by pausing play and examining the Hierarchy and the Scene View.

In this chapter you examined some of the common techniques for testing and debugging in Unity. There is quite a bit more for you to learn about testing and debugging, but this was a good start.

CHAPTER 14

Input

I N THIS VERY SHORT chapter, you'll explore game input. So far in this book all input has been achieved mainly via the keyboard. It's time to consider gamepad controllers because they have become quite common on PCs. These controllers were designed specifically for consoles such as Xboxes, PlayStations, or the Switch, so you'll find that they work very well for most 3D games.

If you wish to support mobile devices with touchscreen controls, laptops with touchscreens, or similar input systems, you'll need to find that information online. Unity supports a wide variety of inputs, even accelerometers, temperature, and humidity inputs, but in this chapter, you're only going to deal with keyboards, mice, and gamepads.

UNITY INPUT SYSTEMS

All input in Unity games gets handled via the built-in Input system. Alternatively, there is a newer Input System available via the Package Manager. To keep things simple, you're going to stick with the tried and true existing Input System. It is possible that you'll need to switch over to the new Input System eventually in future Unity versions. Yes, the new system is better in many ways, but for the games in this book the old Input System is just fine and definitely easier to set up.

<Step 1> **Load DotGame3D** into Unity.

<Step 2> **Find** the places in the code using the Input class.
You do that by opening one of the scripts in the project, typing **<ctrl>f** to open the find dialog, and then searching the entire project for the string "Input" and a period after it. You'll find that the only places where the Input class is used is in DottimaScript.cs and DottimaController.cs. You may recall that those files are fairly similar to each other with DottimaController being used for the 2D game and DottimaScript for the 3D game.
Your next step is to make the DottimaScript Input calls more general. You will use the Input Manager to define an Action button, and then you'll check the virtual Action button rather than the physical space key in the code.

DOI: 10.1201/9780429328725-15

<Step 3> Edit – **Project Settings**… and choose the **Input Manager** and expand Axes if needed.

<Step 4> **Change** the **Size** from **18** to **19**.
This creates another input at the bottom. You now have two inputs, both called Cancel.

<Step 5> **Expand** the bottom input and **edit** it to match Figure 14.1.
You named this new input "Action", gave it a descriptive name, set the positive button to "space" and left everything else the same.

<Step 6> In DottimaScript.cs **replace** `Input.GetKeyDown("space")` with `Input.GetButtonDown("Action")` in the two places in the file.

<Step 7> **Save** in Visual Studio and **test** in Unity.

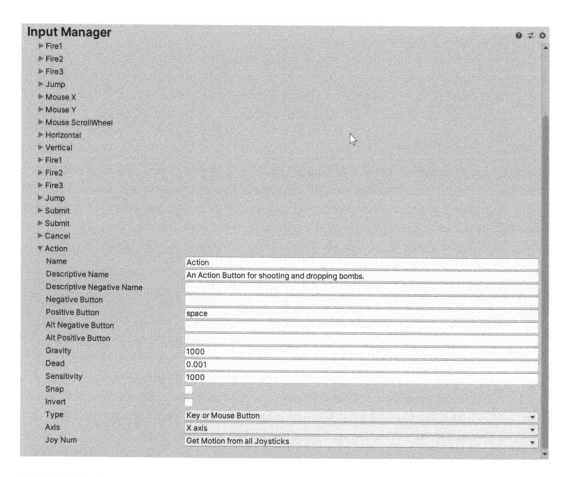

FIGURE 14.1   Input system in project settings.

The controls should work exactly the same way as before with the four arrow keys and the space bar. The only difference is that now your code refers to the "Action" button, a virtual button, rather than the physical "space" button.

<Step 8> **Save.**

You'll now be able to support gamepads by altering the virtual button.

GAMEPAD SUPPORT IN DOTGAME3D

Gamepads are used by console game systems and can also be connected to PCs and Macs. In this section you'll support gamepads for DotGame. You'll start by attaching a generic gamepad made by Logitech or a similar device. Most gamepads should be compatible with the code in this section. In a commercial release you would have a problem on your hands: How do you support and test the large variety of gamepads on the market? You're going to keep things simple for now and start by supporting just one gamepad, yours. Later on, you'll surf the web and try to get help with this issue. One approach is to simply release the game with support for a few major gamepads and then add support for more of them as requested by your players.

<Step 1> **Attach a gamepad** to your **computer**.

Chances are you have one already. If not, buy one or skip this section. You will be able to work through this book without owning a gamepad, but it'll be more fun for you if you have access to one.

<Step 2> In the **Input Manager**, fill in the **alt Positive Button** slot with **joystick button 0.**

Amazingly, that's all you had to do to support firing with your gamepad.

<Step 3> **Test** playing the game with your gamepad.

You can now play the game all the way through with just your gamepad. Unfortunately, you still can't operate the menus with your gamepad. Fortunately, there's a fix for this.

<Step 4> **Go** to the **Menus** scene.

<Step 5> **Select** the **EventSystem** in the Hierarchy.

In the Inspector you can see that there is a slot called First Selected, which is empty.

<Step 6> **Expand** the **Canvas** in the hierarchy, then **expand** the **MainMenu**, and **drag** the **PlayButton** into the **First Selected** slot in the inspector. The EventSystem should now look like Figure 14.2.

<Step 7> **Play** the game from the **Title Scene**.

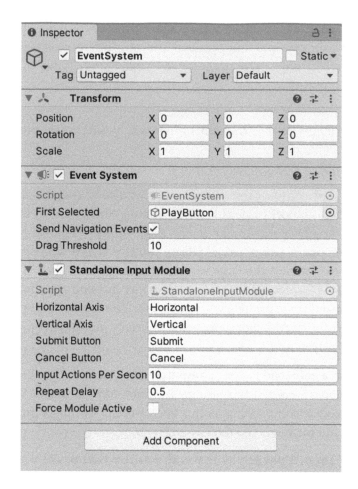

FIGURE 14.2   EventSystem for the menus scene.

Well, that's better. You can select different menu items on the Main Menu, and you can play the game, but the Options Menu doesn't work with the gamepad. You're stumped on how to fix this, so you're going to call it a bug and move on. Sometimes bugs such as this fix themselves when you rework the scenes later on during development, or maybe when you upgrade to a newer version of Unity. There is a good chance that Unity will provide easy gamepad support for GUI elements in the future. This will likely require the new Input System mentioned above.

In the following chapter you'll test and prepare DotGame3D for release.

CHAPTER 15

Preparing DotGame3D for Release

Releasing a game can be a time-consuming and arduous process, especially if you haven't done it before. The process depends heavily on your target platforms. In this chapter you'll prepare DotGame3D for release on Windows PC. You'll test the game, tie up loose ends, fix any leftover bugs, and do some performance testing. Finally, you'll do a *postmortem*: a review of the development process and a summary of what you learned.

This book won't cover all of the details of releasing and publishing for any particular platform, such as a PC, Mac, Xbox, or Android, just to name a few. This information changes frequently, so it'll be up to you to get current instructions from your publisher and online stores.

TESTING FOR RELEASE: BUILD AND RUN

The goal for this section is to make a Windows build for DotGame3D and then install and run it on one or more of your other PCs. As state above, this chapter only covers planning for a release on Windows PC. Preparing for a Mac release should be similar.

You're going to look at the build settings in more detail.

<Step 1> **Load DotGame3D** into Unity and do **File – Build Settings**…

You should have nine scenes set up right now for this build: TitleScene, Menus, six levels, and Ending, in that order. All scenes are in the Assets/Scenes folder. The platform is PC, Mac, and Linux Standalone. In the Target Platform dropdown, you have Windows selected. There are no other choices because you haven't installed Mac nor Linux support in your current Unity version. For architecture you chose x86 rather than x86_64. 64-bit support isn't necessary for this small game and potentially gives you access to running the game on older 32-bit Windows installations. The other setting can be safely ignored for now.

DOI: 10.1201/9780429328725-16

<Step 2> Click on **Player Settings**, **do a Reset**, and type in your **Company Name**, **Product Name**, and **Version**.

The reset is done, as usual, by selecting it from the Setting Icon at the top right of the Player section.

You'll need to decide on a versioning scheme. Typically, when testing the version numbers are less than 1.0, something like 0.1, 0.2, or even 0.2.12. When you finally release to the general public you would use 1.0 or 1.0.0. It is critically important to always change the version number every time you release a build to anyone. The Version can be any string, such as 0.3BetaTest.

When you release to the public you might wish to develop a custom Icon and Cursor. These are set below the Version setting. There's also an Icon section where you can put in overrides.

<Step 3> Expand **Resolution and Presentation**. If you did a reset properly you should have **Fullscreen Mode** set to **FullScreen Window**.

Feel free to explore the Splash Image and Other Settings. There's a lot of settings there, and it's best to leave those alone unless you know what you're doing. And no, you can't turn off the Unity Splash Screen unless you're using a paid Unity version.

<Step 4> **Close** the project settings pop-up.

<Step 5> Click on **Build**. **Create** a new folder with a name of your choice to build in. **Select Folder**.

This build should take less than a minute, depending on the speed of your system.

<Step 6> Find the .exe file in the folder for your new build, and double click on it to run it from the operating system.

The game should work as usual. It's time to copy this build to another system or two and try it out there.

TESTING ON DIFFERENT PLATFORMS

In this section you'll test the game on a typical laptop. Find a Windows laptop and make sure it's charged and updated.

<Step 1> Copy the entire build directory to a USB flash drive.

It should be about 75 MB, which is fairly small these days.

<Step 2> **Plug the USB** drive into your laptop and run the game on it.

Notice if the game is playable. Try to play the game all the way through.

<Step 3> Have someone else play the game on the laptop and try to get feedback from them. You'll have to explain the controls to them because this game doesn't display control instructions yet.

\<Step 4\> Copy the build directory to yet another system and try it out there.
At this point you probably have some feedback, from your own experience playing the game on other systems, as well as from other people. You'll sleep on it and then decide what to do with the game.

Meanwhile, you're going back to your development computer and try the profiler to get some technical details on how the game performs.

THE UNITY PROFILER

The Unity Profiler allows you to visualize where your game is spending its time. This can help you make your game perform better. DotGame3D doesn't need to perform better, so you don't really need to do this, but it's good to learn about the Profiler now. That way you'll be ready to use and understand it later on with more complex games in the future.

\<Step 1\> Load **DotGame3D** into Unity as usual.

\<Step 2\> **Select 3DLevel 6** in **Assets/Scenes**

\<Step 3\> **Window – Analysis – Profiler**.
This opens the profile window. Move it to another screen, or if you don't have one, move it out of the way.

\<Step 4\> **Play 3DLevel 6** for a few seconds, then **stop**.

\<Step 5\> **Maximize** the **Profiler** window and **drag** the **timeline** to the middle.
Compare with Figure 15.1.
You can see Profiler Modules at the top left.

\<Step 6\> With the mouse hovering in the top half of the window, **move** the **scroll-wheel** to see all of the Profiler Modules.

\<Step 7\> **Click** on the **Memory Module**.
You will see useful information about your memory usage. The Total Used Memory in the Author's version of the game is 424.3 MB. Below you see how much memory each of your main systems are using. The System Used Memory is about 1 GB.

As you can see, there is a lot of info available via the profiler, much more than you need. The profiler is there to help if you have performance issues, or even a particularly nasty bug.

For more info about the profiler, start by looking at the Unity Manual, and maybe watch a video tutorial about it online.

This section was a quick intro to the Unity Profiler. You now know what it is and how to run it. Running the profiler does slow down your game, but only slightly, so it's still very useful even if it's not completely precise.

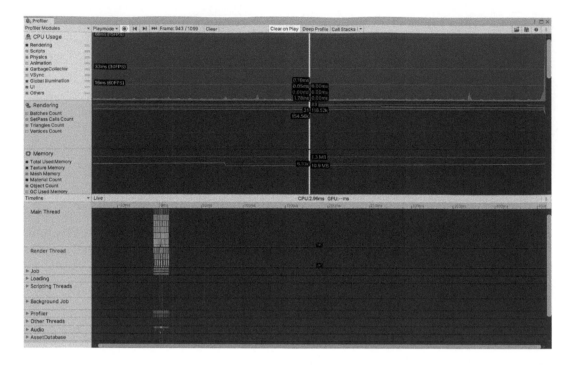

FIGURE 15.1   The Unity profiler in action.

RELEASE AND POSTMORTEM

This is a very small game. Once you know how to play it, it will take you 2 minutes or so to play it from beginning to end. Clearly it would help to add another five to ten larger levels. You've decided to think about this some more, before going down that road.

The good news is that this game is kind of fun, just the way it is. You could release it as a free demo game, an ad for something bigger and better. Before you do that, you need to make list of existing problems, bugs, and issues, and then work on the list. Here it is:

- Missing legal information, a copyright message, and credits.

- Add a text scene that explains the controls and the goal of the game.

- The early levels need to be more interesting and different from one another.

- The bombs need to be moved up, so they don't intersect the floor.

- The bomb explosion is too small.

- Books need to be aligned better with one another.

- The arrows get stuck sometimes when launching them quickly, one after another.

These issues are fairly easy to fix. They are left as exercises for the reader.

It's time for the *postmortem*, a review of the game development process and the game itself. The word postmortem literally means "after death," an examination by a roomful of doctors to study what happened to the deceased patient, and what could have been improved during treatment.

DotGame3D originated as a 2D game, and then was remade as a 3D game. Along the way you learned techniques for 2D and 3D game development, and the process of turning a 2D game into a 3D game in Unity. The game is fairly simple and short, perfect for learning about Unity and game development. The controls feel good, and it's fun to play the game. The game isn't deep enough for a commercial release, but it served its purpose of teaching the basics of 3D game development. You are now ready to move on and make a larger, original 3D game.

II

A 3D Adventure

IN PART II OF *3D Game Development with Unity* you'll build a 3D Adventure game from scratch. You'll continue to learn about the awesome tools and resources available in Unity. As in Part I, you'll follow along in this book and build the game step by step. The step descriptions are slightly less explicit because you're now more experienced and can handle that.

DOI: 10.1201/9780429328725-17

CHAPTER 16

FPS, Etc.

I N THIS CHAPTER YOU'LL think about the game concept for your new game and create a simple design for it. Your goal is to make a prototype FPS-style game with emphasis on exploration and puzzles, with a little bit of shooting as well. You'll release the prototype to friends and family and then maybe take it to production.

A BRIEF HISTORY OF FPS GAMES

No book about 3D game design would be complete without discussing one of the most influential and successful genres of 3D games: first-person shooters. FPSs have a reputation for violence, but the genre is large, and the violence can be anywhere from nonexistent to disturbing and all-encompassing. Many FPSs aren't so much about the shooting but about experiencing a story and living an adventure. You've decided to make your game appropriate for all audiences, including children, so the violence will be minimal.

Before diving in and designing your new creation it's well worth it to look at the history of FPS games.

<Step 1> **Search** the web for **History of FPS** games and read one or two of the search results.

If you're an avid and experienced FPS player you'll know this history already, but it's still worthwhile to get an overview of the past.

Game genre terminology changes frequently, at least every decade. Way back in 1982, when FPSs were just a distant dream, Chris Crawford, the foremost expert on game design at the time, wrote in his book *The Art of Computer Game Design* that all skill and action computer games fall into the following categories: Combat Games, Maze Games, Sports Games, Paddle Games, Race Games, and Miscellaneous Games. We've come a long way in 40 years. It's probably safe to say that 40 years from now, FPS games may seem a relic of the past, just as maze games and paddle games do now. To quote Yogi Berra: "It's tough to make predictions, especially about the future."

In recent years, major hit console games have tended toward supporting a third-person perspective rather than just a first-person view. This allows the player character to be visible.

DOI: 10.1201/9780429328725-18

These games lie someplace in between first person and third person, with the shooting only part of the gameplay. You've decided, right or wrong, to use a broad definition of FPS: Any game where the camera closely follows the player character is an FPS game for you, even if the game has little or no shooting and even if it looks more like a third-person game.

DESIGNING AN FPS ADVENTURE

All game designs start with a short concept. Here is the concept for your new game, *FPSAdventure*. There is a single large world for the hero character to explore, with puzzle rooms hidden here and there. Solving all the puzzle rooms unlocks the final boss battle to finish the game. The hero will start out weak but will get stronger as they discover items to help them.

First, let's start with the world. You're going to face a stark reality of making large worlds: you can't just build it all and load it into a single scene. If you do that, you'll either run out of memory or slow down your game to a crawl. Over the years game developers have had to deal with this issue and solved it in a number of ways.

The most common technique is to break up the world into chunks and to then only display the chunks that are near the player. You can then use fog to hide when chunks are loaded into a scene. Another way to deal with this is LOD, or level of detail, in your models. This means that you have multiple versions of your meshes and show low detail versions for models that are far away, and higher-detail models as they get closer. This can look jarring, but it can work very well when done carefully.

Of course, the easiest way to make large worlds is to simply break your game into separate levels that are loaded independently. This is what you did in DotGame3D. As long as each level is small enough you won't have a problem.

In this game you've decided to build a large overworld, which you're just going to call the world scene, break it into chunks if necessary, and display the chunks only when they are close to the player. You'll also experiment with fog to hide the popping in and out of those chunks. The puzzle rooms will be their own scenes and small enough to load in their entirety when the player enters.

To visualize this, take a look at Figure 16.1.

The stars indicate where you'll place the entrances to the puzzle rooms. You're going to have to make 30 chunks and lay them out in a 5 by 6 grid as shown in the sketch. You'll also put down some simple geometry on the outside border area, for example, some sand dunes or hills. You'll need to keep the player from exploring beyond the borders of the world. Most games handle this by simply making that terrain uninteresting and placing an invisible fence some distance into the border area. You'll also need to design a skybox with clouds and maybe some mountains in the far distance.

Next, you'll need to make some characters, including the main hero character and some enemies. Before you go much further, you'll need names for the characters, and the game itself. Because this is a prototype, you're going to use some purposely poor names. The game name is FPSAdventure, the main character is MyHero. You did a quick web search and didn't find any other major games using these words, so you're OK with these names

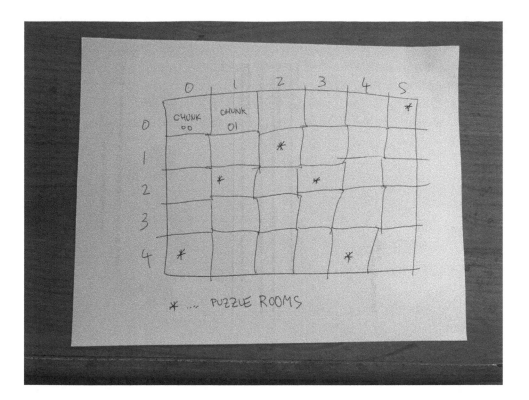

FIGURE 16.1   Sketch of world layout.

for now. You plan to change these names before going into production. This is akin to having a working title for a movie or novel.

Because this is a prototype, you're going to use premade characters, courtesy of the Unity Asset Store or possibly other free sources of 3D characters on the web. This will make development much faster and easier. Once the game is playable you will think about how and when to create original graphics for the characters in this game. Your focus will be on gameplay and not so much on artistic style.

The single weapon for MyHero will be arrows, much like the ones in DotGame3D. They will follow a slightly parabolic arc rather than the linear path in DotGame3D. When an arrow hits an enemy, it will cause damage depending on the speed of the arrow. The arrow speed depends on the strength of MyHero.

You will also bring in some decorative and functional game objects such as buildings, benches, animals, etc. The environment should be interesting and rich, and you'll develop interactions between MyHero and the environment. For example, you'll be able to shoot some of the game objects with your arrows to damage them or move them around.

The puzzle rooms will be major components of the game, with a significant reward for MyHero when a puzzle is solved. Keeping things simple, you'll just increase the strength of MyHero by one strength unit for each solved puzzle. You'll show the strength in a graphical GUI overlay. Increased strength will improve the character's abilities, including the jumping height, the running speed, and the launch speed of the arrows.

The puzzle rooms will all have as the goal to reach a treasure chest by manipulating the environment in some way to be able to reach and open the chest by touching it.

Now that you have a somewhat vague and incomplete design you'll dive in and start development. As you do that, you'll get more ideas and get invaluable feedback on how the game looks and feels. In the next two chapters you'll build the world, put MyHero into the world, and create some of the game objects, so you can better visualize what this game will look like.

CHAPTER 17

Worldbuilding

W HEN STARTING DEVELOPMENT OF a brand new game it's often best to create the environment first, then a few characters, and then the basic gameplay. If it's not fun at that point, cancel the project and start over with something else. If you like the game yourself and enjoy playing it you'll likely have no shortage of ideas on how to make the game bigger and better.

In this chapter you'll start this process by trying out the worldbuilding tools available in Blender and Unity. Your goal is to build two fairly large environments, one with Blender landscape tools and another entirely within Unity. You'll then decide which of the two approaches works better. Possibly you'll use both.

USING BLENDER FOR TERRAIN GENERATION

In this section you'll experiment with Blender's built-in terrain generator. Way back in Chapter 2 you used the A.N.T. Landscape add-on in Blender to make a quick and easy landscape for the toycar game. You'll explore this add-on a bit more in this section. First though it's time to set up the project in Unity.

<Step 1> **Create** a **new 3D project** with the name **FPSAdventure** using **Unity 2020.3.0f1**.

This is the same version of Unity that you used earlier in this book.

<Step 2> In **Assets**, create the following folders: **Models, Scripts, World, Audio, Art, Prefabs**.

It's a good idea to get used to a standard folder structure in the Assets folder. A good rule to follow is this: always put new assets into an appropriate folder. If something doesn't really fit anywhere, create a new folder for it. Oh, and you're going to capitalize all those folder names from now on, just because that looks better.

<Step 3> **Rename** the **SampleScene** to **WorldScene**.

DOI: 10.1201/9780429328725-19

You plan on having a relatively large world for your single player character to run around in. The puzzle rooms will each have their own scenes, and you'll have some GUI scenes as well.

\<Step 4\> **Save** and **exit** Unity.

You'll spend the rest of this section in Blender, so you might as well close Unity for now.

\<Step 5\> **Open** up **Blender 2.92.0**, the same version as you used before.

Author's Note: The author of this book (that's me) is using 2.92.0, so it's probably best if you use the same exact version. In general, it's a good policy to resist upgrading your tools during development, as tempting as that may be. If you decide to use a later version, for example, 2.93.0 LTS, then the steps in this book should work, but the figures might not match exactly, and there's always the chance that adjustments to a step or two would be necessary if, for example, a menu layout changed along the way.

\<Step 6\> **File – Save As…**, navigate to **Assets/World** in your new Unity Project entitled **FPSAdventure**, and **save as world1.blend**.

\<Step 7\> **Delete** the default **Cube**.

\<Step 8\> **\<shift\>\<A\> Mesh – Landscape**.

This step assumes that you installed the landscape add-on in Chapter 2 and that it's still installed. If not, install it by following the instructions in Chapter 2.

\<Step 9\> At the bottom left, **expand Another Noise Tool – Landscape**, if necessary. Zoom in, and compare your screen with Figure 17.1.

\<Step 10\> **Collapse** the **A.N.T. menu** and **expand it again**.

This is just to see how that interface works.

\<Step 11\> **Click** in the **3D Viewport**.

The menu disappears. And no, you can't get it back. You'll have to start over!

\<Step 12\> **Delete** the **landscape** in the outliner, then do **\<shift\>\<A\> Mesh – Landscape** again.

Blender remembered that you had the menu open last time, so it's there again. You may be doing this again if you accidentally click in the 3D Viewport, so be careful about that.

\<Step 13\> **Try** out some, or even all, of the **Operator Presets**. Do that by clicking on the down arrow on the right side, immediately to the left of the + and – buttons, and then exploring those presets. Before you do that make sure that you're still zoomed in on the landscape.

As you can see, there are quite a few presets for this add-on. Once you choose a preset you can still make some adjustments. Here's an example.

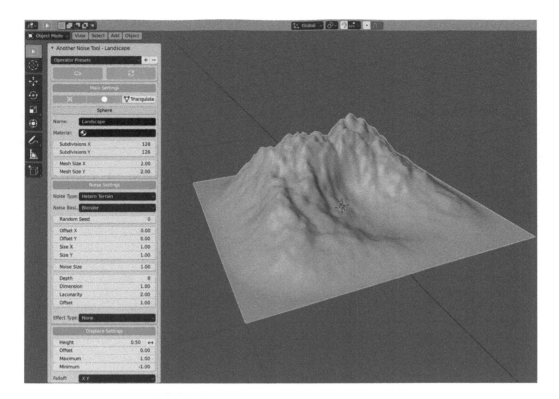

FIGURE 17.1   A.N.T. – landscape menu.

<Step 14> **Choose** the **Lakes 2 preset**, change the **Noise Type** to **Shattered hTerrain**, and then **drag** the **Random Seed setting** to try out several random seeds.

The Random Seed setting is an integer that initializes the random number generator. Changing the random seed will cause a different terrain to be generated, so you can quickly try out several terrains until you find one that you like.

You probably don't realize it, but you're just a few keystrokes away from slowing down or even freezing Blender. You need to be aware of this potentially nasty situation, as shown in the following steps.

<Step 15> **Select** the **Canyons** preset.

<Step 16> **Choose Wireframe Viewport shading** and **turn off X-ray**.

<Step 17> **Change Subdivisions X** and **Y** to **256.**

Notice that there's a delay when you enter these numbers, depending on the performance of your system. Compare with Figure 17.2.

Once the landscape is generated there should be no performance issues, though that probably depends on the graphics capabilities of your system. The current settings generate 65025 faces.

<Step 18> **Warning**: this step may freeze your system. **Increase** the **Subdivisions** by powers of 2 until your system takes more than 2 minutes to generate the landscape.

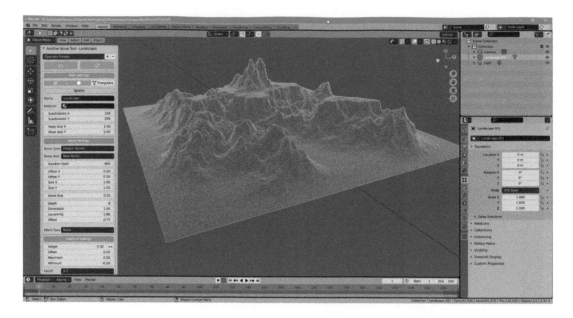

FIGURE 17.2   Pushing the envelope in Blender.

This could be anywhere from 512 to 4096. When you use your system to generate millions of faces it'll try to do that, but it could take a very long time, or even freeze your system. When you push the limits of performance of your system, be prepared to shut down or even unplug your computer because that may be the only way to escape. Welcome to the world of 3D graphics!

Next, you'll go back to a more reasonable grid size.

<Step 19> Set the **subdivisions** to **128** by **128**.

Your plan is to use this landscape as border terrain for your world. You'll use texture painting to draw in snowcaps, forest, and rock colors to make the landscape look more realistic.

<Step 20> **File – Save**.

This is to save the mesh just in case you need to start over at this spot.

These next few steps are a setup for texture painting.

<Step 21> **Go** to **Edit Mode**.

<Step 22> **UV Editing** workspace. **Zoom in** on both panels with the mouse wheel and compare with Figure 17.3.

<Step 23> **Hover** over the **right 3D viewport** and type **U** to get the unwrap pop-up.

<Step 24> **Select Unwrap**.

After a short delay you'll get the unwrapped mesh showing in the left panel, the UV editor.

<Step 25> **Zoom** the **UV editor** and compare with Figure 17.4.

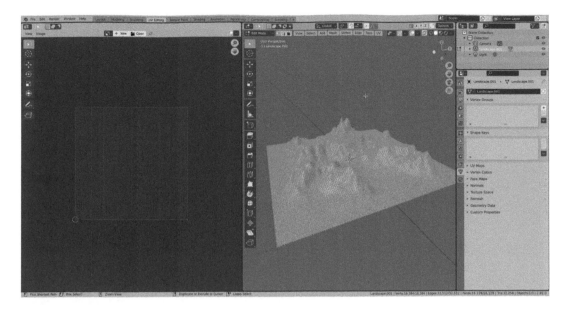

FIGURE 17.3 Setting up for texture painting a landscape.

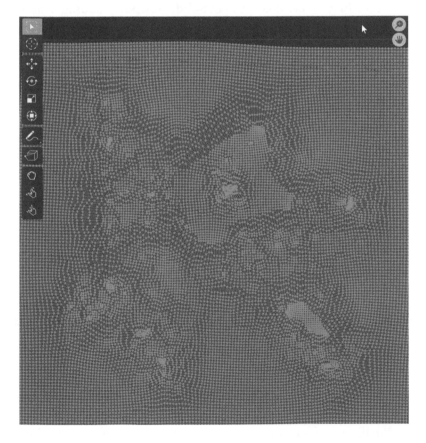

FIGURE 17.4 Unwrapped landscape mesh.

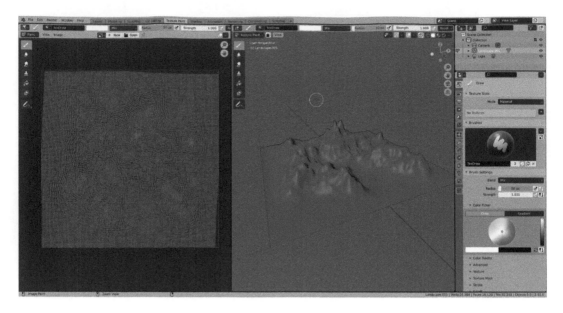

FIGURE 17.5   Texture painting setup continued.

<Step 26> **Texture Paint Workspace. Select Solid Viewport Shading. Zoom in** and **pan** as shown in Figure 17.5.

The landscape is purple because it has no assigned texture. Make sure you have the "Active Tool and Workspace settings" selected in the Properties editor on the right. You'll notice that it says "No Textures" in the Texture Slots section.

<Step 27> **Click** on the+**sign** next to **No Textures** and select **Base Color**.

<Step 28> Make the **Color** a **dark green**, as shown in Figure 17.6.

<Step 29> **Click** on **OK**.

As you can see, the landscape is now dark green. You could now paint in the Texture Paint window. But wait! You still need to set up the UV paint window.

<Step 30> In the **Image Editor** on the left, **hover** the mouse over the "Browse Image to be Linked" icon. It's to the right of Image.

<Step 31> **Click** on the **downward arrow** and then **click** on **Material.001 Base Color**.

<Step 32> **Zoom out** with the mouse wheel to see the entire UV image. It should be dark green.

<Step 33> At the top left, if necessary, **select Paint** as the **Editing context being displayed** as shown in Figure 17.7.

Finally, you are ready to Texture Paint. Your current paint color is white.

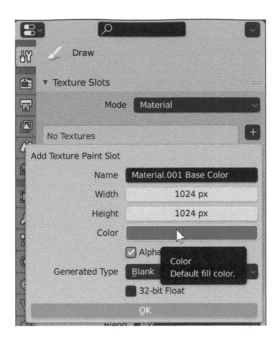

FIGURE 17.6 Setting the default fill color for texture painting.

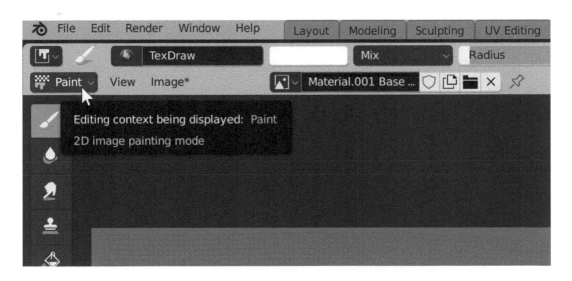

FIGURE 17.7 Setting the "Editing context being displayed" in the UV editor.

<Step 34> Start **painting** some snow on the peaks. You can change colors in the Properties editor. Try to have green colors at low elevations, dark grey at steep higher elevations for cliffs and rocks, and a few reddish browns here and there.

You don't need to get this perfect here. You'll be able to touch this up after you've seen what it looks like in the game. Compare with Figure 17.8.

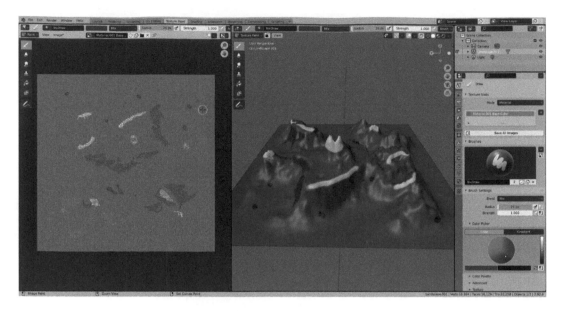

FIGURE 17.8   Texture painting completed.

Yes, this could be quite a bit better, but this is just a prototype, so it's good enough for now.

You notice a star next to the word "Image" in the UV editor menu. The star tells you that the image has been changed and possibly needs to be saved.

<Step 35> **Image*** – **Save** and use the default settings.

You will get a png file in the Assets/World folder. This is the texture file that you will need to associate with the mesh in Unity.

<Step 36> **Look** at the mesh in the **Layout Workspace** using the **Rendered Viewport Shading**.

Don't worry about minor flaws in this model. You'll fix those later on, if and when you decide to use this model. Chances are that in production this model will be replaced with a higher resolution version, but it's a good placeholder.

<Step 37> **Save** and **exit** Blender.

As you just witnessed, the A.N.T. Landscape addon can be useful for quickly making a detailed mesh, but of course there are many other ways of generating landscapes in Blender. If you're interested, search the internet for alternative techniques including real-world data, sculpting, or using procedural textures as height maps.

In the next section you'll look at this blend file in Unity.

BLENDER LANDSCAPE IN UNITY

In this section you'll make multiple copies of the landscape you just created in Blender.

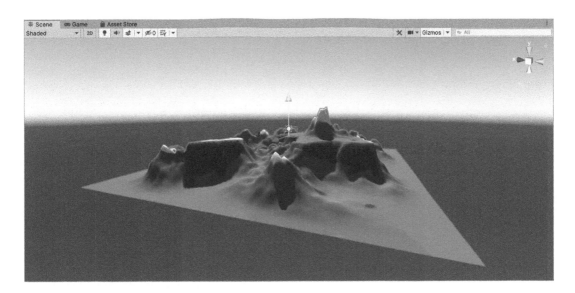

FIGURE 17.9   Blender landscape in Unity.

<Step 1> **Open** the **FPSAdventure** project in Unity.

<Step 2> **Select world1** in Assets/World.

<Step 3> In the inspector, **change** the **Scale Factor** to **10** and **uncheck Import Cameras** and **Import Lights. Click** on **Apply**.

<Step 4> **Drag world1** into the **hierarchy**.

<Step 5> **Hover** the mouse in the **Scene window** and type **f** to do a **Frame Selected**. Compare with Figure 17.9.

Next you're going to do preliminary performance testing to see if Unity can handle ten copies of this Landscape.

<Step 6> In the hierarchy, **make nine copies** of **world1** using **<ctrl>d**, and spread the copies out so they don't overlap.

<Step 7> **Maximize** the **Scene view** and compare it with Figure 17.10. Then **unmaximize**.

<Step 8> **Select** the **Main Camera** and do **GameObject – Align With View**.

<Step 9> In the **Game Window**, Select **Stats** and **Maximize on Play**.

<Step 10> **Test** the game and take a look at the stats.

You're displaying 1.5 million triangles and probably getting a decent frame rate. The author's system is getting 600 frames per second. Your frame rate will probably be different, depending on your system performance. Any frame rate over 60 is acceptable.

What do you have to do to slow things down? You can do a temporary experiment if you wish. Do a select all, unselect the Camera and Light, then

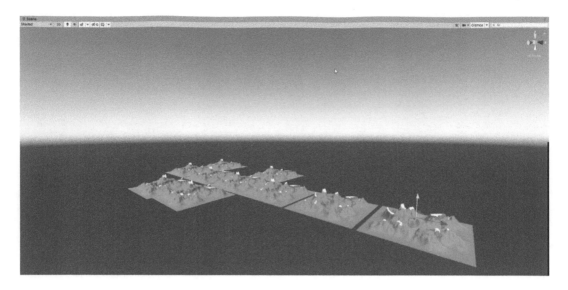

FIGURE 17.10   Ten landscapes.

use <ctrl>D to make ten copies or the ten landscapes, getting you over 100 landscapes. If you then run the game you'll have 15 million triangles and you'll almost certainly see some slowdown, though you might still be over 60 fps.

<Step 11> **Delete** all but one of the world1 objects in the Hierarchy.

<Step 12> **Save**.

So far your worldbuilding was a simple exercise. You plan on using the world1 object, and copies of it, in the background. Next, you'll take a look at the Terrain Tools in Unity.

USING UNITY FOR TERRAIN GENERATION

Blender isn't the only way to create terrains. In Blender you have all of the Blender tools available to make custom terrains just the way you want, but this can be very time consuming. Unity provides a good alternative.

This section was inspired by the YouTube video "How to Make Beautiful Terrain in Unity 2020" by UGuruz. As of January 2022, this video has more than one million views, accumulated in about 1 year. You are not alone. Just remember that most of those views are from tourists, and only the truly dedicated developers such as you actually worked through it. This video is 16 minutes long, but it will take you much longer than that to duplicate the work. By all means, watch the video first before attempting to do the steps in this section, although that isn't necessary.

The first hurdle is obtaining the required assets from the Unity Asset Store. It is possible, though unlikely, that the assets in the following steps are no longer available. Maybe they have moved, or they might have been renamed. If this is the case, go to franzlanzinger.com and look for replacement links in the resource section for this book. Alternately, contact the author and he (that's me) will gladly help you.

Before building your new terrain in Unity, you will need terrain textures, tree meshes, and grass textures. The terrain will consist of some gently rolling hills populated by tall trees, lush grass, and flowers, and carving through it all you'll have a network of dirt paths. Later on when you play the game your game characters will be able to wander through this terrain, collide with the trees, but other than that they'll be able to wander through the terrain freely. When you place the trees you're going to carefully avoid having trees in the paths, though nothing really bad will happen if there's a tree or two on a path someplace.

For me, the author, this realizes a vision from about 20 years ago when I was hiking in a local county park with a similar landscape. Back then I thought that just maybe, in the distant future, it'll be possibly to build a 3D game that looks like that. Amazingly, not only is this possible now, but it's also easy to build a game just like that, at home, and run it on a readily available gaming system.

<Step 1> With FPSAdventure still loaded in Unity do **Window – Package Manager**.

<Step 2> **Window – Asset Store** and **click** on **Search online**.
Your browser will open assetstore.unity.com. Because you got there via Unity you are signed in.

<Step 3> **Search** for **Outdoor Ground Textures** by A Dog's Life Software.

<Step 4> **Download** and **import** this free asset using the package manager.
Be aware that this is a 300 MB download, so it might take a few minutes. When importing choose all the textures.

<Step 5> Look for **ADG_Textures** in the Assets folder. **Try** out the **DemoScene**.
The sample scene shows the 14 textures. This will give you an idea of what's in this package. Take a look at the texture files. You'll see that each texture consists of a material and five image files: ambient, diffuse, height, metallic, and normal. This is a common setup for PBR textures. For more information on PBR textures, search online. You don't need to know how this works, just that the five textures are displayed overlayed on each other using a PBR shader within the Unity render process. PBR textures tend to look realistic, especially in response to changes in lighting.

<Step 6> In the Asset Store, get **Conifers [BOTD]** by FORST.
You can, if you wish, look at the documentation for this package. It's a rather extensive and advanced pdf file: Conifers [BOTD] Documentation. pdf at the top level of Assets/Conifers [BOTD]. It's definitely worthwhile to try out the demo scene. Look for it in **Conifers {BOTD}/Render Pipeline Support/Built-in RP/Demo/Conifers Cast**. Just select the scene and play it. You'll see four trees responding to wind – very cool.

<Step 7> Get **Grass Flowers Pack Free** by ALP8310 in the Asset Store.
As before, look for a demo and run it. You'll see a nice field of flowers moving in the wind.

FIGURE 17.11   Setting up a terrain in Unity.

Next, you're going to create a single large terrain. You'll need a new scene for this.

<Step 8>   **Create** a **new scene** in **Assets/Scenes** and name it **UnityTerrain**.

<Step 9>   **GameObject – 3D Object – Terrain**. Compare with Figure 17.11.

You'll need to adjust the Scene view. On the right the inspector shows the settings and adjustments for the Unity terrain system. This is where you'll build the terrain. The first thing to note is the terrain menu.

<Step 10>   **Click** on the **settings icon** near the top of the inspector. It's the rightmost icon of five and looks like a gear with eight teeth.

Near the bottom of the settings is the Mesh Resolution section. Notice that the default is 1000 by 1000. That's quite large. Typically the units for this are meters, so this terrain is 1 km by 1 km. You're going to leave well enough alone for now. You may need to make this terrain smaller in the future depending on your performance statistics.

This isn't much of a terrain just yet. Rather than generating the terrain procedurally as you did in Blender, using this tool you will be able to manually sculpt it.

<Step 11>   **Select** the **Paint Terrain** icon, the second from the left, and below it, select **Raise or Lower Terrain**, as shown in Figure 17.12.

You can now see 12 brushes and sliders for Brush Size and Opacity.

<Step 12>   **Experiment** with the **brushes**, **brush size**, and **opacity** by **dragging** the brushes around in the terrain.

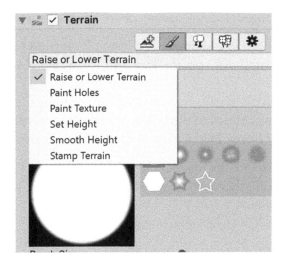

FIGURE 17.12 Setting up to paint the terrain in Unity.

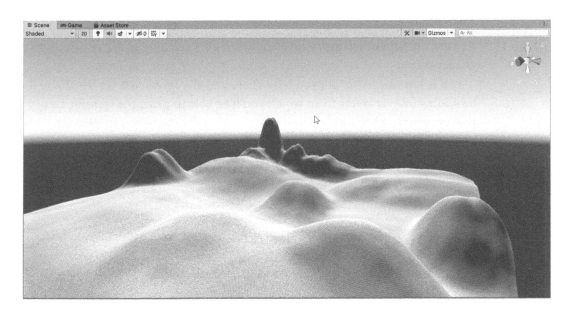

FIGURE 17.13 Terrain painting complete.

Here's a few tips. You can hold <shift> to lower terrain. To start over, just lower the entire terrain down to zero with the first brush and a large brush size. You can undo with <ctrl>z as usual. Useful keyboard shortcuts are [ ] for brush size and - = for brush opacity.

<Step 13> Paint a terrain similar to Figure 17.13.

Unity has some additional terrain tools that can be useful. First, if you haven't done so already, you'll need to **enable preview packages** as follows:

<Step 14> Edit – Project Settings… and select **Package Manager**.

<Step 15> In the Advanced Settings section, **check Enable Preview Packages**.

<Step 16> **Window – Package Manager** and search for **terrain tools** in the Unity Registry. **Install**. Also **get** the **Terrain Tools Sample Asset Pack** from the Asset Store.

This installation will give you additional brushes and features in the terrain system. Once this is installed the keyboard shortcuts are different. To change the size of a brush, hold S and use the mouse to change the size.

<Step 17> **Experiment** with the new brushes and new features. Feel free to change the Terrain a little when doing this. You'll need to set **Raise or Lower Terrain** again.

Next, you'll bring in some textures.

<Step 18> Still in the Paint Texture section, choose **Paint Texture** from the dropdown shown in Figure 17.12.

That dropdown has obtained additional entries when you installed the Terrain Tools in Step 16. You'll still find the Paint Texture entry.

<Step 19> Expand the **Layers** section, where you will find a warning about not having any layers yet.

This is just fine. After all, you haven't created any layers just yet. Next you'll be adding several layers from which you'll be able to paint the terrain. This process will be quite similar to texture painting the landscape in Blender, earlier in this chapter.

<Step 20> **Click** on **Add Layer** and select **moss** and **close** the pop-up.

You automatically had the moss applied to the entire terrain. Now you'll make some adjustments.

<Step 21> **Click** on the name **moss** in the inspector. Then, **click** on **moss** in the project window.

You now see some settings for moss in the inspector.

<Step 22> **Change** the **Tiling Settings** to **50,50** instead of **10,10** and change the **Normal Scale** to **3**. Compare with Figure 17.14.

<Step 23> **Use** the **right mouse button** and **WASD** control to fly closely to the terrain to see the very detailed moss texture, as shown in Figure 17.15.

As nice as this looks, you're going to remove it and instead create your own grass texture.

<Step 24> **Select Terrain** in the hierarchy, in the inspector choose **Paint Texture**, then below click on **Remove Layer**, and **confirm** that you're OK with losing the splatmap.

A splatmap is a single control texture that controls the combination of the other textures in a multitexture material, such as the moss material you just deleted. You're basically losing those adjustments you made a few steps back.

FIGURE 17.14   Moss texture applied to terrain.

FIGURE 17.15   Moss texture closeup.

That's OK as you won't need them any more in this project and they're easy to recreate if needed. For more information about this, search the web for texture splatting.

<Step 25>   In **Create New Layer** rename the new layer to **MyGrass**, click on **Create…**, and select **ground6_Diffuse**. **Close** the pop-up, click on **MyGrass** in the inspector, s**elect** the **MtGrass** in the **Project** panel and **click** on **Select** for a **Normal Map**. Choose **ground6_Normal**.

FIGURE 17.16   Custom grass texture.

<Step 26> Change the **Tiling Settings Size** to **20** by **20** and compare with Figure 17.16.

<Step 27> **Create** a **3D Cube** with y **scale 2**.
　　This is to simulate a human character in this terrain to get a sense of scale. This is a tall 2 meter human.

<Step 28> **Move** the **cube** toward a somewhat flat part of the middle of the terrain. Align it with the terrain.
　　The position of this cube should be near (500, 10, 500). You can use the RMB WASD control to fly the camera around to do this. You'll notice that the texture scale is off, so do this:

<Step 29> **Select** the **MyGrass** layer and **change** the **Tiling Settings** back to where they were, **2 by 2**. Compare with Figure 17.17.
　　Next, you'll make a ground texture, just as you did with the grass.

<Step 30> **Select Terrain** in the hierarchy, **Paint Texture** in the inspector, then **create** a new layer with the name **MyGround** and choose **ground1_Diffuse**.

<Step 31> Select **MyGround** in **Assets** and in the inspector **add** the **Normal Map** as you did before.

<Step 32> **Select Terrain** in the hierarchy, **select** the **MyGround** layer in the inspector.
　　You do this by clicking on the bullseye menu for MyGround and selecting MyGround.

<Step 33> **Select** the **second brush** in the list of brushes in the Brush Mask section, **change** the **Brush Size** to about **6** and start **drawing a path** near the cube. Compare with Figure 17.18.

FIGURE 17.17 Simulated character on the grassy terrain.

FIGURE 17.18 Drawing a path with the MyGround layer.

<Step 34> Continue to **draw a network of paths** to span the entire terrain. This is a large
terrain, so it may take a while. Compare with Figure 17.19. It's OK if your
network looks different.

   Be sure to also look at the path closeup near the cube. Use **frame selected**
to find the cube. Maybe this shouldn't be called a cube anymore since it's not a
cube! You'll resist calling it a refrigerator…

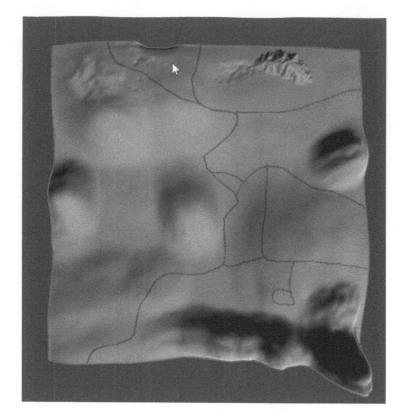

FIGURE 17.19   A path network.

<Step 35> **Rename** the **Cube** object to **PlayerBlock** and **Save**.

It's looking kind of barren out there. How about some trees?

<Step 36> **Select Terrain** in the hierarchy, then **select Paint Trees**, the middle icon in the icon strip below the Terrain section in the inspector.

You can see that you have no trees defined. Fortunately you downloaded those very nice trees earlier in this section.

<Step 37> In the Trees section, **click** on **Edit Trees…** and select **Add Tree**.

<Step 38> In the Add Tree popup, **click** on the **bullseye icon** for the Tree Prefab and select the **medium conifer**. **Close** the **pop-up** and then **click** on **Add**.

You can now place trees in the terrain with your brush.

<Step 39> **Try placing** trees with the **brush**. **Change** the **Brush size** and the **Tree Density** to see the effect of that.

<Step 40> **Click** on **Mass Place Trees** and **place 10000** trees. **Don't keep** the **existing trees. Check** the **frame rate** by **running** the **game** with **Stats turned on**.

If you get a strange camera view, set up a view that you like by doing a frame selected on the PlayerBlock, adjust, and then do an Align With View for the Main Camera.

This works but it might result in a low frame rate unless you have a high-end graphics card and system. You're going to try this again, but this time with the bare trees that will not use up quite so many graphics resources.

<Step 41> Click on **Edit Trees…**, **Add Tree**, and add the **Conifer Bare tree**.

<Step 42> Select the **Conifer Bare** tree and do **Mass Place Trees** with **10,000** trees. Again, don't keep the existing trees, and check the frame rate.

That's better. On most gaming PCs you'll see better than 60 fps. The author got about 200 fps on his 2060 Nvidia card and fairly slow I5 CPU, shown in Figure 17.20.

Wow, this scene has 3 million triangles running at 170 fps. That's an embarrassment of computing riches. In a few years this will probably seem like nothing special. As game developers, it pays to keep in mind that technology will likely improve exponentially, at least in the foreseeable future.

You are doing some very preliminary performance testing. To get the real performance of your game you'll need to have actual gameplay and be running a build rather than inside Unity. Still, it's good to get an approximate feel for where you stand.

You've noticed that some of those trees are on a path, so next, you're going to fix that.

<Step 43> Start at the PlayerBlock and move along the path in one direction. Whenever you see a tree on the path, remove it by **<shift> clicking** on it. Use a smaller brush to make this easier.

FIGURE 17.20　Some of the 10,000 trees.

It could take you an hour or two to do this along the entire path network, so you're going to just learn how to do this for a few minutes and procrastinate this job for production. This is a prototype after all.

Next, you'll learn how to add some fog.

\<Step 44\> **Window – Rendering – Lighting**. Drag the tab of this window next to the inspector.

\<Step 45\> **Select Environment** in the **Lighting** window.

\<Step 46\> **Turn on Fog**, change the **color** to a **light green**, and change the **Density** to **0.002**.

Compare with Figure 17.21.

You will be adjusting the fog later during development once all the graphics are in the game. For now, it helps to add a little bit of fog for a more realistic look.

Next, it's time to add grass, weeds, and flowers. Yes, you have a grass texture already, but the terrain will look much better with more detailed grass, etc.

\<Step 47\> Go back to the **PlayerBlock**, then **select** the **Terrain**, and in the inspector select the **Paint Details** icon, the fourth of the five Terrain icons.

Just as was the case for the trees, you don't have any Detail objects defined.

\<Step 48\> Click on **Edit Details…** and then **Add Grass Texture**. Select **grass2** for the Detail Texture.

\<Step 49\> Make the **Healthy Color** and the **Dry Color** somewhat **darker**.

FIGURE 17.21 Fog.

FIGURE 17.22   Adding grass detail.

<Step 50> **Change** the **Max Height** to **1**, Min **Height** to **0.2**. Then click on **Add**.

You can change these setting any time by going back and editing.

<Step 51> **Draw** some **grass**. **Experiment** with the **brush settings**. It helps to have lower Opacity and Target Strength. Compare with Figure 17.22.

These details will fade out when they move far away from the camera. Try it!

This grass texture works similarly to a particle system. Each chunk of grass is a single quad with a texture that shows some vegetation. Optionally, the quad can turn to face the camera, a process called billboarding. Try turning billboarding on and off to see the difference.

A more expensive but better-looking way to have grass in your scene is with grass meshes. As an optional exercise, load the Flooded Grounds asset from the Asset Store where you will find Grass Meshes. It's a 1 gig download, so feel free to skip this if that's too large a download for you.

The Asset Store has additional textures and meshes for you to try out. Many are free or very low cost, so with a little bit of effort you can make a very nice terrain for your game.

Obviously, this terrain system is superior to the A.N.T. landscape add-on in Blender. For now, you've decided to shelve the Blender terrain and use only the Unity terrain. Also, the original idea of creating 30 terrains stitched together is overly complicated. It would be much too much work to build 30 terrains of similar size and scope to the one you just started to build.

<Step 52> **Save**.

You built a reasonable terrain with which to experiment. In the next section you'll add a better skybox.

SKYBOXES

A Skybox is a large cube with inward-facing textures. The textures are stretched using a mathematical formula so that the inside of the box appears to look just like the sky. If the skybox is built correctly you won't be able to see the edges of the box. The Unity Asset Store has a wide variety of skyboxes to choose from. So far you've used the very simple built-in default skybox. It's time get one of those better skyboxes from the Asset Store.

<Step 1> Get the **10 Skyboxes Pack: Day – Night** by Wello Soft from the **Unity Asset Store**.

<Step 2> Go to the **Lighting** window and click on **Environment**.

<Step 3> For the **Skybox Material, click on** the **bullseye menu** and select one of the materials that start with Sky, for example, **SkyCloudy**.

That was easy. Compare with Figure 17.23.

So far you have ten skyboxes to choose from, which is plenty. You'll make the final skybox choice later. And yes, it's possibly to make your own skyboxes. The Unity manual has explicit instructions on how to make your own skyboxes, but it's much easier to just use a skybox built by somebody else.

It's useful to learn how to adjust the lighting to match your skybox. Here's an example.

<Step 4> **Select** the **SkyMorning** skybox.

FIGURE 17.23   A cloudy skybox.

FIGURE 17.24 Sunrise.

<Step 5>   **Adjust** the **Directional Light** rotation so that the tree shadow points away from the yellow sun. Try **(10, 90, 0)** as a starting point for the **Rotation** setting. Then Compare with Figure 17.24.

<Step 6>   **Save** and **exit** Unity.

In this chapter you learned how to build a rather large section of a game world. You're not finished yet, because there's more items to be added. Your world isn't going to be just a forest with paths. In the next chapter you'll bring in some game objects and, of course, MyHero.

CHAPTER 18

Character Controller

I N THIS CHAPTER YOU'LL make a character controller for your 3D adventure game. Character controllers contain the code that reads controller inputs and uses them to move and rotate your character in your game world.

You'll start by getting a free, premade character from the Unity Asset Store. Later you may decide to replace it with another character, or even build a custom character. Unity contains a Character Controller class, but that's just the starting point. You'll need to write code to have your character behave the way you want.

This chapter follows fairly closely the YouTube video titled "Character Controller in Unity" by PabloMakes. Pablo's excellent video was made with a slightly older version of Unity and a different Unity layout. One possible approach for you would be to watch that YouTube video first, and then work through the steps in this chapter. When everything works and you think you understand it all, watch the video again to solidify your understanding. Of course, you can also just follow the steps in this chapter as usual.

Be aware that while the code in this book is similar to the code in the video, there are quite a few changes and adjustments, so be sure to carefully follow the book rather than the video when typing in code. The figures will also look very different because you'll be working in the newly constructed terrain from the last chapter rather than Pablo's background world.

IMPORTING A CHARACTER FROM THE ASSET STORE

You'll start by getting Ellen, a free character from the Unity Asset Store. Your plan is to replace Ellen with another character in the future, but for now Ellen is a good placeholder. The following download is 357.99 MB. Downloading and installing can take several minutes. As always, the time for that depends on your internet speed and system performance.

\<Step 1\>   Load **FPSAdventure**, and then go to the **Asset Store** and get **3D Game Kit –
            Character Pack. Only Import Ellen**. Do that by **unchecking Characters**,
            then **checking Ellen** in the import pop-up.

            Once you're finished installing, you'll find Ellen in Assets/3D Game Kit –
            Character Pack/Characters/Ellen/Models. For now, Ellen will be the hero of
            the game, with the name Ellen rather than MyHero.

DOI: 10.1201/9780429328725-20

FIGURE 18.1   Introducing Ellen.

<Step 2>   **Drag Ellen** next to the PlayerBlock in the scene.

The scene should still be looking at the PlayerBlock, which is where you left things in the last chapter.

<Step 3>   Change the **Directional Light Rotation** to (**20, 90, 0**) and compare with Figure 18.1.

You rotated the directional light so you can get better lighting and shadows. Feel free to make additional adjustments to the light rotation if you wish.

Ellen is in the T-pose. Humanoid characters are usually presented in this pose at first. When you imported this character, you also got dozens of animations for Ellen. You'll only be using a few of them. But before you deal with animating Ellen, you'll start to build the character controller, which will allow you to move Ellen around the terrain with a camera following her.

Speaking of cameras, you'll once again use Cinemachine. You downloaded it in Part I, but because this is a different project, you'll need to also install it into this project.

<Step 4>   In the **Package Manager**, **select Packages**: **Unity Registry**, find **Cinemachine**, and **install** it.

This will be quick because you already downloaded it in Part I. If you skipped that somehow, or you're on another computer now, no problem, just download it first before installing. You don't need the Sample Scenes.

In the top menu for Unity, you now see Cinemachine between Component and Window. This tells you that Cinemachine has finished installing and is ready to be used.

<Step 5>   **Cinemachine – Create FreeLook Camera**.

<Step 6> Select **CM FreeLook1** in the hierarchy and explore in the inspector by scrolling through it.

You'll see that this virtual camera has three rigs called TopRig, MiddleRig, and BottomRig. These are three concentric circles, a small circle near the feet of Ellen, a larger one above her head, and an even larger one high up above Ellen. This virtual camera moves among those three circles. The Orbits section lists the three rigs and there you can adjust the settings for them if you wish. You've decided to use the default settings.

You'll need to set the Follow and Look At slots before this camera becomes operational.

<Step 7> Set **Follow** to **Ellen**, **Look At** to **Ellen Neck**. **Test** the game by **moving** the mouse around. Compare with Figure 18.2.

As you move the mouse you can feel the three orbits as described above. You can't move Ellen around yet, just the camera.

<Step 8> **Uncheck** the **PlayerBlock**.

You'll probably never need this object again, but just in case it's convenient to uncheck it so you can easily get it back and quickly get back to the center of the world.

FIGURE 18.2   Cinemachine camera using the BottomRig orbit.

FIGURE 18.3   Adjusting the character controller for Ellen.

<Step 9>   **Select Ellen**, and in the inspector click on **Add Component** and select **Character Controller**.

This controller uses a capsule collider that should envelope the character. The collisions that happen in the game are with this capsule, and the animations are just there for decoration. You'll need to adjust the settings of the Character Controller, so it fits Ellen better.

<Step 10> Change the **Center Y** to **0.85**, **Radius 0.3**, **Height 1.7**. Compare with Figure 18.3.

You're now ready to write a script to move Ellen in response to your controls.

CHARACTER MOVEMENT

In this section you'll start to write a rather extensive script for controlling the Character Controller. Your first goal is to move Ellen around the terrain without animation.

<Step 1>   Create a **New Script** for **Ellen**, named **ThirdPersonController. Move** the new script into the **Assets/Scripts** folder as usual.

From now on, in order to save space, the three default "using" statements will not be printed in the code listings. It is assumed that those three "using" statements are still at the beginning of the file.

<Step 2>   **Type** in the following code for **ThirdPersonController**:

```
public class ThirdPersonController : MonoBehaviour
{
    CharacterController MyController;
    // Start is called before the first frame update
    void Start()
    {
        MyController = GetComponent<CharacterController>();
    }
```

```
// Update is called once per frame
void Update()
{
    float x = Input.GetAxisRaw("Horizontal");
    float z = Input.GetAxisRaw("Vertical");

    Vector3 movement = new Vector3(x, 0, z);
    MyController.Move(movement * Time.deltaTime);
}
}
```

<Step 3> **Read** the code and try to **understand** it.

This should be familiar territory for you. You're reading the input as you did in Part I, and then creating a movement vector. In Unity the y-axis points up, so movement usually occurs in the x-z plane. You put in the Time.deltaTime adjustment to make your code frame rate independent.

<Step 4> **Save** your code in Visual Studio and **test** the game. **Move** Ellen with **WASD** or the **arrow** keys, all the while moving the camera with the mouse.

Congratulations! You're finally able to move around in that large world while running the game. There are quite a few issues, though, and you'll tackle them one by one. The first thing to fix is the movement speed. It's much too slow.

<Step 5> **Add** a public float with name `Speed`, set it to `5.0f`, and change the `MyController.Move` line to this:

```
MyController.Move(movement * Speed * Time.deltaTime);
```

<Step 6> **Test** the game. Have Ellen move around a little bit to get a feel. Use the mouse to adjust the camera while moving. Try out the arrow keys, WASD, and the gamepad. Try to collide with a tree.

Collision with the trees is working. You see that Ellen can go up a hill, but when moving down the altitude stays constant, resulting in having Ellen flying. You're going to fix that later in this chapter in the gravity section.

Next, you'll improve the code so that Ellen moves in the camera coordinate system rather than the world coordinate system. This will feel more natural to the player.

<Step 7> **Insert** the following line in the public section at the top:

```
public Camera MyCamera;
```

<Step 8> Replace the `MyController.Move` line at the very end with these two lines of code:

```
Vector3 rotatedMovement = MyCamera.transform.rotation * movement;
MyController.Move(rotatedMovement * Speed * Time.deltaTime);
```

This code rotates the movement vector using the camera's rotation. To rotate a vector3 you multiply it by the rotation.

<Step 9> **Save** the code in Visual Studio, then in Unity, **assign** the **Main Camera** to the **MyCamera** slot for Ellen in the inspector.

<Step 10> **Test.**

This almost works. If you rotate the camera with the mouse, Ellen moves away from you and toward you in response to the up-down controls. There is a problem though: Ellen doesn't stay on the ground when you point the camera up and move away. You'll need to use a different rotation as follows.

<Step 11> **Replace** the `Update` function with this:

```
void Update ()
{
    float  x = Input.GetAxisRaw("Horizontal");
    float z = Input.GetAxisRaw("Vertical");

    Vector3 movement = new Vector3(x, 0, z);
    Quaternion cameraYrotation =
        Quaternion.Euler(
            0.0f,
            MyCamera.transform.rotation.eulerAngles.y,
            0.0f);
    Vector3 rotatedMovement = cameraYrotation * movement;
    MyController.Move(rotatedMovement * Speed * Time.deltaTime);
}
```

Yes, the top of the function is the same, but this was the easiest way to explain this change. This new code zeroes out the x and z parts of the camera rotation, leaving just the y rotation, which it then applies to the movement vector.

<Step 12> **Test** again.

This time Ellen stays on the ground when you go back and forth, as long as you stay in a flat part of the terrain. No, this doesn't fix the missing gravity issue, but as stated above, that will be fixed later on.

Next, you're going to make Ellen face her direction of movement.

<Step 13> **Insert** the following three lines at the end of the Update function:

```
float angleOfMovement = Mathf.Atan2(rotatedMovement.x, rotatedMovement.z);
angleOfMovement *= Mathf.Rad2Deg;
transform.rotation = Quaternion.Euler(0.0f, angleOfMovement, 0.0f);
```

This code computes the angle that the rotated movement vector makes with the x axis, converts it to degrees, and then uses Euler angles to set the rotation quaternion for Ellen. That *= multiplies the angleOfMovement by the conversion factor Mathf.Rad2Deg. You pronounce that "Rad to degrees," which is the built-in float of 180/pi. This is necessary because Mathf.Atan2 returns radians, but the Quaternion.Euler function requires degrees.

<Step 14> Check that the **Binding Mode** in the **Orbits** section for your freelook camera is **Simple Follow with World Up**.

Depending on your Unity usage history, this is probably set already, but if it's not this is the time to change it.

<Step 15> **Test**.

Ellen now faces the direction of movement, except when she's stationary. To handle that case, do the following:

<Step 16> **Surround** those last three lines with this if statement:

```
if (rotatedMovement.magnitude > 0.0f)
{
  // three lines of code go here //
}
```

<Step 17> **Test** again.

This time Ellen stays facing the most recent rotatedMovement vector. You can just hold the up arrow key and steer Ellen with the mouse.

The rotation of Ellen is very jerky when you change direction, so the following code will smooth this using the Mathf.Lerp linear interpolation function.

<Step 18> **Insert** a new public float called `RotationSpeed` with default value of `15.0f`.

<Step 19> Above the `Start` function, **insert** this line:

```
float mDesiredRotation = 0.0f;
```

Your code will smoothly change the actual rotation toward the desired rotation.

<Step 20> **Replace** the **six line if statement** at the bottom of the `Update` function with this:

```
if (rotatedMovement.magnitude > 0.0f)
{
    mDesiredRotation = Mathf.Atan2(rotatedMovement.x, rotatedMovement.z);
    mDesiredRotation *= Mathf.Rad2Deg;
}
Quaternion currentRotation = transform.rotation;
Quaternion targetRotation = Quaternion.Euler(0.0f, mDesiredRotation, 0.0f);
transform.rotation = Quaternion.Lerp(
    currentRotation,
    targetRotation,
    RotationSpeed * Time.deltaTime);
```

That last statement, spread out over four lines, nudges the current rotation in the direction of the target Rotation by using the Lerp function. This is a commonly used technique for smoothing out jerky transitions. The RotationSpeed variable controls the size of the nudge.

<Step 21> **Test** this with different values for RotationSpeed.

A very high RotationSpeed degenerates (yes, that's the correct technical term) to the snapping rotation change you had earlier. A low RotationSpeed is still workable but will feel sluggish. 15 seems about right. You can now easily move around the terrain with just the gamepad.

You've noticed that Ellen covers more ground when moving along a diagonal. When you press both up and right, for example, the movement vector has a length of about the squareroot of 2, or about 1.41. This is a bug, but it's easily fixed with the following:

<Step 22> **Replace** the **movement declaration and initialization** with this new version:

```
Vector3 movement = new Vector3(x, 0, z).normalized;
```

The built-in function `Normalized` changes the length of the input vector to 1 while preserving the angle. For example:

```
(3.0f, 0.0f, 4.0f).normalized == (0.6f, 0.0f, 0.8f).
```

<Step 23> **Test** and notice that Ellen now moves at a constant speed regardless of her direction.

Overall, the control feels very smooth, especially with a gamepad.

<Step 24> **Save.**

In the next section you'll animate Ellen.

IDLE, WALK, AND RUN ANIMATIONS

You already accomplished the hard part, creating (actually downloading) the basic movement animation loops for your character. For starters, all you really need is an idle and a walk animation. You don't need the idle animation either, but these idle animations are so common now in just about every game, so it just looks wrong that your characters don't have one.

<Step 1> **Select Ellen** and in the **Animator** component, **uncheck Apply Root Motion**.

This **Apply Root Motion** feature automatically moves the game object using the animation motion, but you're already moving the gameobject using the script, so this needs to be turned off.

<Step 2> In the **Art** folder, **create** an **animator controller** with the name **EllenAnimC**.

<Step 3> For Ellen, in the inspector, select **EllenAnimC** as the **Controller** in the **Animator component**.

<Step 4> **Double-click** on **EllenAnimC** in **Assets/Art**.

<Step 5> **Undock** the **Animator window** and stretch it to match Figure 18.4.

This is the starting setup for the animator. It's not doing anything yet. You can verify this by running the game. This kind of testing is called a *sanity test*. It just makes sure that the changes in the previous steps didn't break anything even though the changes didn't actually make any detectable changes during play. It's a good idea to do frequent sanity testing when making unfamiliar changes to your project.

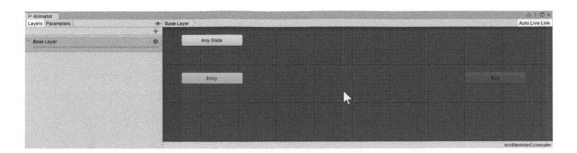

FIGURE 18.4   Animator window for EllenAnimC.

\<Step 6\>   In the **Animator** window, **right-click, Create State – Empty**.

\<Step 7\>   **Click** on **New State**, then in the inspector choose **EllenIdle** as the Motion.
When you run the game now you see the EllenIdle in action, even when you move Ellen around the terrain.

\<Step 8\>   In the **Animator** window, select **Parameters** and add a **float parameter** with name **Speed**. The initial value is 0.0, which is fine.

\<Step 9\>   **Rename New State** to **Movement** in the inspector.
The Animator window will show the new name.

\<Step 10\>   **Right-click** on **Movement** and select **Create New BlendTree** in **State**.

\<Step 11\>   **Double-Click** on **Movement** to see the Blend Tree.
There's a slider that allows you to adjust the Speed parameter. Currently it's at 0. The idea behind all this is as follows. The script for Ellen will set the Speed parameter depending on Ellen's physical speed. You'll use the convention that 0 means idle, 0.5 means walking, and 1.0 means sprinting. The Animation controller will use the Speed parameter, as determined by your script, and use it to run a blend of three animations: Idle, Walk, and Sprint. You will now set up the Blend Tree to set this up in the Animator Window.

\<Step 12\>   **Click** on the **Blend Tree** to see the Blend Tree in the inspector.

\<Step 13\>   Make sure that the **Blend Type** is **1D**, as in one-dimensional.

\<Step 14\>   In the **Motion Section**, add three motion fields and use **EllenIdle**, **EllenWalkForward** and **EllenRunForward** as the Motions. Compare your Blend Tree with Figure 18.5.

\<Step 15\>   At the bottom of the Blend Tree in the inspector, **enlarge** the **preview pane**, **click** on the **run icon**, and **slide** the **Speed** in the **Blend Tree** in the **Animator** window.
You'll see Ellen doing a blend of animations ranging from Idle when the Speed is 0, walk at 0.5 and run at 1. Those Thresholds can be adjusted in the inspector, but you'll leave them at the current default settings.

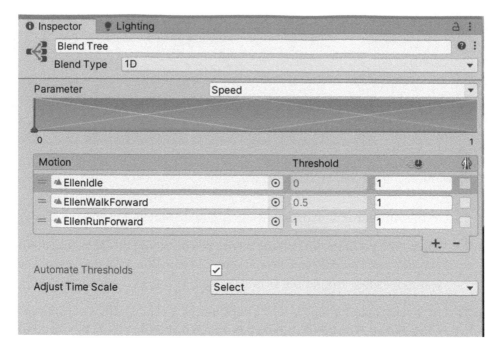

FIGURE 18.5   A blend tree for Ellen.

You have here a really good way of visualizing how blending works. For example, put the Speed at 0.1 and you'll see Ellen doing her idle animation, but at the same time walking forward very slowly. The Parameter section in the inspector shows a graph for this.

<Step 16> In **ThirdPersonController.cs insert** the following in the declaration section on top:

Animator MyAnimator;

<Step 17> **Insert** at the end of the `Start` function:

```
MyAnimator = GetComponent<Animator>();
```

<Step 18> At the bottom of `Update` **insert**:

```
// Animation code
if (rotatedMovement.magnitude > 0.0f)
{
    MyAnimator.SetFloat("Speed", 1.0f);
} else
{
    MyAnimator.SetFloat("Speed", 0.0f);
}
```

<Step 19> **Test.**

It's not as smooth as you'd like, but it works. The code isn't taking advantage of blending and simply snapping from 0.0 to 1.0. These next changes smooth it all out using Lerp just as you did before for the rotations.

<Step 20> **Insert** this at the top:

```
public float AnimationBlendSpeed = 2.0f;
```

<Step 21> Insert above the `Start` function:

```
float mDesiredAnimationSpeed = 0.0f;
```

<Step 22> **Replace** the animation code with this:

```
// Animation code
if (rotatedMovement.magnitude > 0.0f)
{
    mDesiredAnimationSpeed = 1.0f;
} else
{
    mDesiredAnimationSpeed = 0.0f;
}

float actualAnimationSpeed;
actualAnimationSpeed = Mathf.Lerp(
    MyAnimator.GetFloat("Speed"),
    mDesiredAnimationSpeed,
    AnimationBlendSpeed * Time.deltaTime
    );
MyAnimator.SetFloat("Speed", actualAnimationSpeed);
```

The `actualAnimationSpeed` variable is a local variable used only one time. Yes, you could eliminate that variable and simply substitute the calculation for it into the `SetFloat` call, but that really wouldn't make your code more efficient. By using this local variable, you made the code more readable.

<Step 23> **Test**.

That's much better. Next, you'll add a run button to control running vs. walking.

<Step 24> **Replace** the `Speed` declaration with the following:

```
public float Speed = 2.0f;
public float RunSpeed = 6.0f;
```

Alert! You are about to change a default value for a public variable. When you do that, you'll need to also change it in the inspector. You'll do that right now, so you won't forget later on.

<Step 25> **Save** the .cs file in Visual Studio, then **select Ellen** and **update** the **Run Speed** and **Speed** settings in the inspector, as shown in Figure 18.6.

Back in Visual Studio do this:

<Step 26> Insert these lines above the `Start` function:

```
bool mRunning = false;
float mSpeed;
```

<Step 27> In `Update` after the first two Input statements at the beginning, **insert** this:

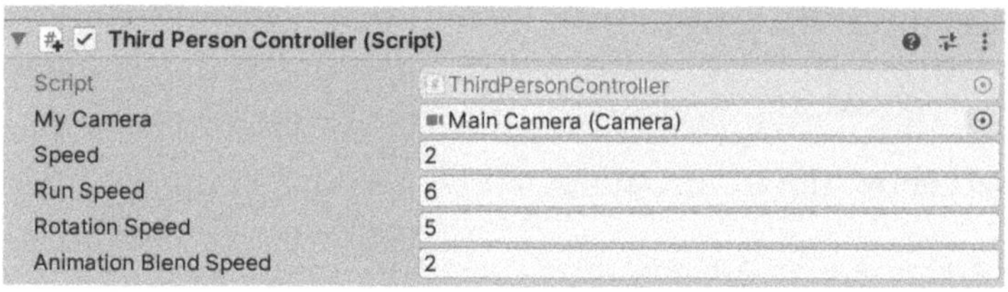

FIGURE 18.6   Default settings for public variables for Ellen.

```
mRunning = Input.GetButton("Fire1");
```

This Fire1 button is set up in the default Input Manager settings. You get the left <ctrl> keyboard button as well as button 0 on your gamepad. You should probably rename Fire1 to Run Button, but you're too lazy to do that right now. Maybe you'll do that in production.

<Step 28> Replace the `MyController.Move` statement with this:

```
mSpeed = mRunning ? RunSpeed : Speed;
MyController.Move(rotatedMovement * mSpeed * Time.deltaTime);
```

This code speeds up Ellen's movement in response to the Fire1 button.

<Step 29> Replace the `mDesiredAnimationSpeed = 1.0f` statement with this:

```
mDesiredAnimationSpeed = mRunning ? 1.0f : 0.5f;
```

This looks funny, but it does the right thing. It sets the "Speed" parameter in the Animator to the correct value, depending on the `mRunning` bool.

<Step 30> Test with a gamepad and with arrow keys.

Wow, this is really starting to make progress. It took some work to build this Character Controller, and you're not finished yet. In the next section you'll add gravity, a long overdue feature.

GRAVITY

This is going to be short and sweet. You'll have a vertical speed variable, called `mSpeedY`. It will keep track of your vertical speed, which is zero when Ellen is stationary, but when she moves above the terrain her vertical speed will become negative due to the influence of, you guessed it, gravity. You'll use the earth's gravity of $-9.8\,m/s^2$, but you could, if you wanted, change that.

<Step 1> Before the `Start` function, **insert** these lines:

```
float mSpeedY = 0.0f;
float mGravity = -9.8f;
```

<Step 2> After the Input lines in `Update`, **insert** this:

```
mSpeedY += mGravity * Time.deltaTime;
Vector3 verticalMovement = Vector3.up * mSpeedY;
```

<Step 3>   **Replace** the `MyController.Move` function call with this:

```
MyController.Move((verticalMovement +
    rotatedMovement * mSpeed) * Time.deltaTime);
```

<Step 4>   **Test**.

Ellen can now run around the entire terrain, except where it's too steep. When she moves down, the new gravity code moves her down toward the terrain surface.

Ellen, when moving up a steep hill, tends to have her feet disappear. This has to do with the capsule collider. The following small change fixes this.

<Step 5>   **Select Ellen**, and for the Character Controller Component, **change** the **Center Y** to **0.9**, **Center Z** to **0.1**.

<Step 6>   **Test** again.

That's going to be good enough for now. You'd like to do a real test of gravity by having Ellen jump off a ramp.

<Step 7>   **Create a cube** near Ellen with **rotation (−25, 0, 0)** and **scale (1, 1, 10)**.

This will get you a ramp near Ellen. You can use **frame selected** to find the ramp and adjust it.

<Step 8>   **Test** Ellen jumping off the ramp, as shown in Figure 18.7. Do this several times without restarting the game.

FIGURE 18.7   Ellen ready to jump off the ramp.

You may notice that the drop gets faster over time. This is a subtle bug. You're never resetting mSpeedY. A quick way to verify this is to use Debug mode in the inspector.

<Step 9> **Turn off Maximize on Play** in the **Game** window, and in the inspector **click** on the three-dot menu at the top right and **select Debug**, as shown in Figure 18.8.

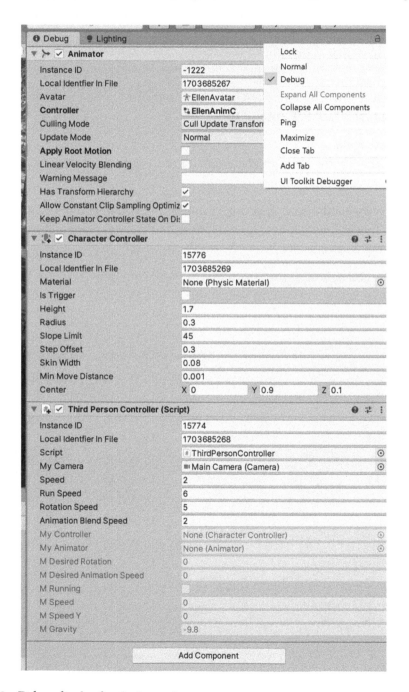

FIGURE 18.8   Debug display for the Inspector.

When you select Ellen you will see the internal variables at the bottom, among them M Speed Y.

<Step 10> **Test** the game and watch mSpeedY in the Debug Inspector.

Sure enough, it just keeps getting larger and larger. This was not your intention. Fortunately, there's an easy fix for this.

<Step 11> In Update, immediately before the verticalMovement calculation, insert this:

```
if (MyController.isGrounded) mSpeedY = 0.0f;
```

<Step 12> **Test** again and check that mSpeedY now stays at or near 0 most of the time. Also fall off that ramp again a few times.

<Step 13> **Save**.

You now have a pretty good character controller for moving your player character around the terrain. It took some work, but it was an educational experience, which is really your goal here after all.

You still don't have a game, so in the next chapter you'll put in same gameplay involving interactions with enemy characters. Before that you'll explore the 3D Game Kit from the Unity Asset Store.

CHAPTER 19

First Playable

I N THIS CHAPTER YOU'LL make your game playable. It's already playable in the sense that your character can move around in a fairly large level, but there really is no game there just yet. You're missing quite a few elements, so it seems like a tall order. Before you continue development with this project, you're going to go on a side quest. You have discovered that Ellen is part of the Unity 3D Game Kit, a very extensive, free demo game. You'll try this out, even though it's a 2 Gig download. You're going to explore this Game Kit and try to use what you can in your own game. You already have Ellen, and maybe some other parts of the 3D game kit will prove useful.

3D GAME KIT

The 3D game kit was originally released by Unity in 2018 to show off some of the new features of Unity at that time. It looks like a published, commercial game with beautiful graphics, some great assets, code, audio, GUI, etc. It's well worth your time to look at this, even though it's promoted as a way to make games without coding. While that's true, you will have access to the code behind the scenes and hope to be able to use pieces of this project in FPSAdventure.

\<Step 1\>   Make sure everything is **saved** in your project and **exit** Unity.

\<Step 2\>   **Make a backup copy of FPSAdventure**.

\<Step 3\>   Use the **Unity Hub** to create a new **3D project** using Unity 2020.3.0f1 as usual with the name **GameKitTest**.

\<Step 4\>   Go to the **Asset Store** and search for **3D Game Kit**. This book uses version 1.9.4, released April 9, 2021. It should be OK to use a more recent version if 1.9.4 isn't available.

\<Step 5\>   **Download** and **Install 3D Game Kit**.
    This may take about an hour, so if you don't have an hour right now, do something else and come back and do this another time. At first, the download speed simply depends on how quickly you can download 2 GB. After the

download is complete, you'll start the import, which takes much longer than the download. Fortunately, you'll only need to do this once and that part is automatic.

<Step 6> **Look** at the **console**.

There you'll see some messages regarding additional packages that needed to be added.

<Step 7> **Save**, **exit** Unity, then **start** the project again.

This is just to see if there's any errors, and to see how long saving and loading takes. Fortunately, this is quite fast.

<Step 8> **Explore** the files and folders in **Assets/3DGamekit**. **Read** the **Readme** file.

<Step 9> **Turn on Maximize on Play**, then load the **Start scene** in 3DGamekit/Scenes.

<Step 10> **Play** the game and look at the Menu at the very beginning. Compare with Figure 19.1.

Ask yourself: what do you see and hear? Don't touch those controls just yet. Be sure to have audio on.

You've got some very nice atmospheric orchestral music. It's not something you'd be able to produce yourself. There's an animated alien monster of some kind in the bottom left. It might be a fish? There are some glowing insects flying around randomly. You have a menu with three items, Start, Options, and Exit Game.

<Step 11> Try **exiting** the game with the **mouse**.

Note that the arrow keys don't work. This menu requires the mouse. The gamepad also doesn't work. There's a click sound when you change from one menu selection to another.

FIGURE 19.1   Main menu for 3D game kit: The Explorer.

\<Step 12\> **Run** the game again. This time **try** the **options**.

This is an interesting menu screen. You see a nice scrolling credits screen on the right. It's good to see credits in this game, accessible right away, not just after the player completes the game. It's interesting that over ten people worked on this game.

\<Step 13\> **Click** on **Controls**.

There's a text file showing the controls for the game. As expected, this is a mouse-and-keyboard-only game. The mouse is used to look at the scene, and the LMB is a melee attack. You can also move with the usual WASD, and the space bar jumps. There's no mention of left control doing a run. You'll try that out in the game.

\<Step 14\> Go **back** and **back** again, then **start** the game. Don't touch the controls after that.

You see a loading screen, then the character stands there. If you patiently wait, you'll see Ellen doing her idle animation (the same one from FPSAdventure) and then some "I'm bored" animations. It looks like you're on a strange alien world. Oh, and earlier you noticed the name of the game, The Explorer.

There are five hearts on the top left. Maybe they indicate your health. It's time to explore.

\<Step 15\> **Look** around with the **mouse**, then **start moving** with the **WASD** keys. Try out the **melee** attack. Also, try the **arrow keys** and the **gamepad**.

Well, the melee doesn't do anything. Just as in FPSAdventure, the arrow keys and the gamepad work. Also, you're stuck in the game. There's no obvious way to leave the game.

\<Step 16\> Try **typing** \<esc\>.

OK, that works, but the game really should have told you about that. Figure 19.2 shows the Paused menu.

\<Step 17\> **Click** on the **X** at the top right.

Sure enough, that takes you back to the game.

\<Step 18\> **Pause** again, this time **restart** the level.

You once again are at the beginning, as shown in Figure 19.3.

You're ready to actually play the game. In real life you'd just dive in and play the game right away without doing all this careful analysis of the menus. In this situation, because you are a game developer, and you're not just playing this game for fun, you're examining it and comparing it to your own efforts. And, since you have access to all the source code, you're making mental notes of systems that you can possibly use, like the menu system, for example.

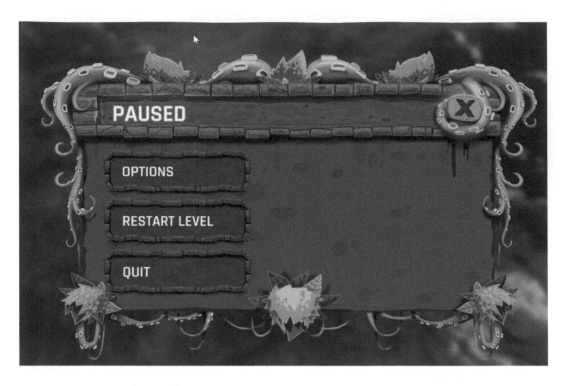

FIGURE 19.2   Paused in Explorer.

\<Step 19\>   **Play** the game for a short while. **Don't play for too long if you are prone to motion sickness.**

Unfortunately, this game can cause motion sickness for some people, so if you feel it coming on, stop and play again a day later. The cause is likely the fact that the camera is controlled by the mouse rather than by following the

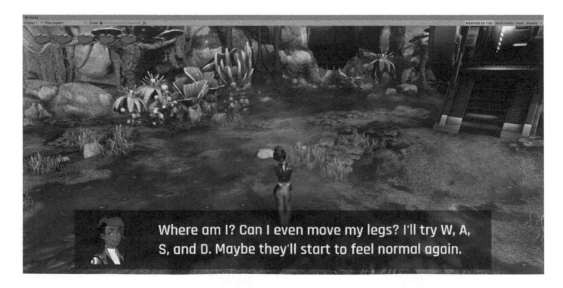

FIGURE 19.3   Starting the first level of The Explorer.

player. For example, if you're like the author, who is very sensitive to motion sickness, you might be fine when playing FPSAdventure, but have trouble with The Explorer. If you do have a motion sickness problem, don't let that stop you from being a game developer. Just don't play games that make you sick, and tweak the camera motion, the most likely cause of motion sickness, when you're developing 3D games.

In The Explorer, there are two levels. In the first you simply try to find the entrance to a dungeon, which then comprises the second level. The first level is an open world level with a skybox. The second level is an interior puzzle level, very much like what you'd like to do with the puzzle rooms in FPSAdventure. You get to the entrance of the second level by opening a few doors while trying to stay alive. The game is tuned to be very easy for experienced players, though it might be difficult for beginners.

Now that you have a feel for this game, you'll make your own level using the built-in tools in 3D Game Kit. To learn how to do that you'll work through one of the many tutorials available at learn.unity.com. First read the following instructions, then go on to Step 20.

You already did the tough part, which was to download and install the 3D Game Kit. Notice that in the intro video there are some obsolete comments. No, the 3D Game Kit is no longer a 4 GB download, it's only 2 GB at this time. Also, the Asset Store looks different in Unity 2020.3. Do not follow the instructions from the introductory video. It's better for you to just watch and absorb. After the video you'll start with the interactive portion of the tutorial.

\<Step 20\> Go to **learn.unity.com**, **sign in** with your Unity Id, and search for **The Explorer**. Select **The Explorer: 3D Game Kit**. The entire tutorial takes 4 hours and 40 minutes. You'll start with the first section, Quick Start, which only takes 1 hour 15 minutes. Don't forget to set your Unity Version to 2020.3, then watch the 13-minute intro video. After that, continue to work through the tutorial.

\<Step 21\> **Optional**: Do the **Walkthrough tutorial** and explore the many other tutorials at learn.unity.com.

\<Step 22\> **Save** and **exit** Unity.

It is useful to find out what's available at learn.unity.com. Those tutorials were paid content at one time, but they are now free to anyone. There's even an experience points system which keeps track of your progress.

After learning about the 3D Game Kit, you're now full of new ideas about how to continue with the FPSAdventure project. You're going to bring in some enemy characters. You'll create some buildings to make your world more interesting. You'll also learn how to have your enemy characters use a *navmesh* to help them navigate your levels.

In the next section you'll search for enemies in the Unity Asset Store and in Mixamo and bring them into your game.

ENEMIES

In this section you'll build a small test scene and use it to display and test out enemies. You'll grab one enemy from the Unity Asset Store and another from Mixamo.

<Step 1> **Load FPSAdventure** and **play** it for a few seconds.

It's been a while, so it's good to play the game to remember the state of things. You still have Ellen in a large forest with a ramp. Your current scene is UnityTerrain. To make things easier you'll create a test scene.

<Step 2> In **Assets/Scenes** create a new scene and name it **TestEnemies,** then **select** it.

<Step 3> **Create** a **plane, rename** it to **Ground,** and do a **frame selected** to show it.

<Step 4> **Scale** the **Ground** with **(3, 1, 3).**

<Step 5> Go to **Assets/ADG_Textures/ground_vol1/ground6** and **drag ground6** to **Ground**.

<Step 6> **Delete Main Camera.**

<Step 7> **Save** this scene and **load** the **UnityTerrain** scene.

<Step 8> Select **Ellen,** then <ctrl> **select Main Camera** and **CM FreeLook1.** Type <ctrl>c.

<Step 9> Go back to **TestEnemies, click** on the hierarchy, and type **<ctrl>V.**

<Step 10> **Move Ellen** to **(0, 0, 0)** and do a **frame selected.**

<Step 11> **Test**.

You now have Ellen moving in your test scene with the Cinemachine Camera and the Character Controller working as you developed it in UnityTerrain. The stage is set for bringing in more characters.

<Step 12> In the **Unity Asset Store,** get **Monster Orc by VK GameDev** in the usual manner.

You'll find your Orc in Assets/Monster_Orc(Troll).

<Step 13> **Try** out the **Demo_Scene** if you wish.

You'll see two versions of the Orc, somewhat far away. One is animated the other isn't.

<Step 14> Back in the **TestEnemies** scene, **drag** the **monster_orc prefab** near Ellen on the Ground.

<Step 15> **Test** the game and compare with Figure 19.4.

The Orc stays in one place and does a sequence of animations, one after another. Before you make the orc move and behave the way you want, you'll get another character, this time from Mixamo.com.

Mixamo is an extensive free resource, available at Mixamo.com. You'll need a free Adobe account, log in with it, and you'll immediately get access to more

FIGURE 19.4   Ellen meets the Orc.

than 100 3D humanoid models, and more than 2000 animations. It's fun just to look at them. All animations are compatible with all the Mixamo characters. You're going to choose one of the characters and bring it into your scene with an idle and a walking animation.

<Step 16> **Get** a free **Adobe** account, go to **Mixamo.com** and **sign in** with your Adobe account.

<Step 17> **Explore** the characters and animations, just for fun.

<Step 18> **Click** on **Characters** and choose the **Maw J Laygo** character.
To help find this character, search for **Maw**. It should be the first search result.

<Step 19> **Click** on **Animations** and search for **walk with swagger**. **Choose** the **first** of the three search results.

<Step 20> On the right, **checkmark In Place**. Compare with Figure 19.5.
You can use the mouse scroll wheel to make the animation appear larger. There are some settings on the right. Overdrive controls the speed of the animation, Character Arm-Space moves the arms away or toward the character. Trim lets you remove or add animation frames at the beginning or the end of animations. Some of the animations are quite long so Trim can be useful in that case. For this animation you'll just leave the settings at their defaults.

FIGURE 19.5   Maw swagger animations.

<Step 21> **Click** on **Download**. For **Format**, choose **FBX for Unity (.fbx)**. Use **With Skin**. **Click** on **Download**. Make a note of where the download file is stored in your system.

The download location depends on your browser setting. A common location is the standard **Downloads** folder.

<Step 22> Search for **standing short idle** and **click** on **Download**. Choose **Without Skin**, keep the **FBX for Unity** Format, and then **click** on **Download**.

Because you didn't include the skin (that's the model) this download is only about 400 KB instead of 15 MB.

<Step 23> Also, **download** a **Zombie Punching** and a **Zombie Running** animation. Be sure to **click** on **In Place** for the Zombie Running animation.

You now have a fairly impressive character with four scary animations. You're done with Mixamo for now so you may exit your browser.

<Step 24> In **Assets**, create a folder called **MixamoCharacter** and **copy** the **four fbx files** you just downloaded into that folder. You can do that by dragging the files into it, or by right-clicking in the **MixamoCharacter** folder in Unity and choosing **Open in Explorer**. You can then use your operating system to copy the files to there with **<ctrl>c <ctrl>v**.

<Step 25> In **Assets/MixamoCharacter** look for the slider at the bottom right corner. **Slide** it all the way to the **left**.

The file names are long, so this slider lets you see the names in full, but not the fbx extensions.

<Step 26> Click on **maw_j_laygo@Walking** and in the inspector select **Materials**.

In the preview pane at the bottom of the inspector you see that you don't have a material for this object. To get the materials and textures set up, do the following:

<Step 27> In **Assets/MixamoCharacter**, create a **Textures** and a **Materials** folder.

<Step 28> **Select** the **walking animation** again, then in the inspector, click on **Extract Textures…**

<Step 29> Select the **Textures** folder, then **click** on **Fix Now** in the pop-up.
You can now see the textures displayed in the preview pane. You still need to extract the Materials as well.

<Step 30> In the inspector, click on **Extract Materials…**, then select the **Materials** folder.
You will get an error in the Console window. Ignore this and make a mental note that this should be investigated in the future if you have any issues with this model.

<Step 31> In the inspector, click on **Animation**, and **play** the animation in the preview pane.
You will see your character walking in place.
Next, you'll make an avatar for this model.

<Step 32> In the inspector, click on **Rig** and change the Animation Type to **Humanoid**. Click **Apply**.

<Step 33> Drag **maw_j_laygo@walking** to the **scene** next to Ellen and the orc.
If you play the game now, the maw character doesn't animate. That's because he doesn't have an animation controller set up yet.

<Step 34> In the **MixamoCharacter** folder, **create** a **new animation controller**. Name it **MawAnimationController**.
A bare Animator window appears with Any State and Entry.

<Step 35> **Select** the new **animation controller** and **drag maw_j_laygo@Walking** from the Project window to the Animator window.

<Step 36> **Select maw_j_laygo@Walking** in the hierarchy, then in the inspector set the **controller** in the Animator component to **MawAnimationController**.

<Step 37> **Select maw_j_laygo@Walking** in the Project window, and in the inspector select **Animation**, then **check Loop Time** below in the inspector for the Walking animation.

<Step 38> **Click** on **Apply** in the inspector. You may need to scroll down to see the apply button.

<Step 39> **Test** the game and, if it all worked, you'll have Maw walking in place. Compare with Figure 19.6. **Save**.
In the next section you'll get those enemies to do some basic movement. Your goal is to have them slowly walk toward Ellen.

FIGURE 19.6 Maw walking in place.

ENEMY MOVEMENT

In this section you'll build character controllers for the orc and the maw. First, you'll put in the movement logic, then you'll work on animations. Later in this chapter you'll use a navmesh to guide enemy movement.

<Step 1> Select **monster_orc** and **rename** it to **enemy_orc**.

<Step 2> Drag **enemy_orc** into **Assets/Prefabs**, choose **original prefab** when prompted.

<Step 3> Add a **character controller** component to **enemy_orc** in the hierarchy.

<Step 4> **Adjust Center Y** to **1.0**.

<Step 5> **Add** a **new script** to the **enemy_orc** prefab, call it **OrcScript**. **Move OrcScript** to the **Scripts** folder and **edit** it in Visual Studio.

<Step 6> Enter the following code for **OrcScript** and **test**.

```
public class OrcScript : MonoBehaviour
{
    public float speed = 1.0f;
    CharacterController MyController;
```

```
    // Start is called before the first frame update
    void Start()
    {
        MyController = GetComponent<CharacterController>();
    }

    // Update is called once per frame
    void Update()
    {
        MyController.Move(Vector3.forward * speed * Time.deltaTime);
    }
}
```

This is about as simple as it gets for a character controller. The orc simply moves forward at a speed of 1.0f. The animation runs through its sequence regardless of the movement. What you'd like is for the orc to immediately go into his walk animation. You'll do that by creating a new Animator Controller for it.

<Step 7> In **Assets/Prefabs**, create a new **Animator Controller, call** it **enemy_orc_controller**.

<Step 8> Select **enemy_orc** in the hierarchy, then in the inspector, click on **Monster_orc** in the **Animator** section next to **Controller**.

<Step 9> In the Project window, **double-click** on **Monster_orc**. Zoom out in the Animator window and compare with Figure 19.7.

<Step 10> Select the bottom box entitled **Monster_anim|Walk**, then **right-click** and **select Copy**.

<Step 11> Go to **enemy_orc_controller** in **Assets/Prefabs**, **right-click** in the **Animator window**, and **select Paste**. Compare with Figure 19.8.

<Step 12> Select **enemy_orc** in the hierarchy. In the inspector **change** the **Animator Controller** to **enemy_orc_controller**.

<Step 13> **Test** and **watch** the orc's walk.
It's getting better. The orc is floating above the ground, so make the following adjustment.

<Step 14> **Change** the **Center Y** in the **Character Controller** from **1.0** to **1.1** and **test**.
This lowers the orc down to the ground. He's still slipping a little, but you'll accept that for now. Next, you'll make the orc move to his left.

<Step 15> In **OrcScript**, change **forward to left**. **Test** it.
The orc is moving to his left, but he's still facing forward. The following step fixes that. The code is similar to the ThirdPersonController script. It basically works the same way, except that instead of reading inputs to control the character a fixed direction is hardcoded by setting x to 1.0f and z to 0.0f.

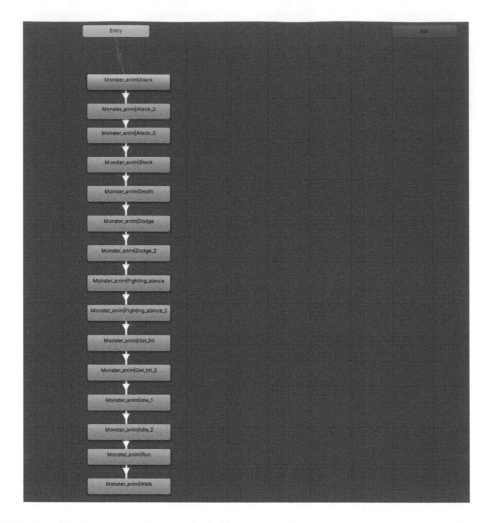

FIGURE 19.7   **Monster_orc animator controller.**

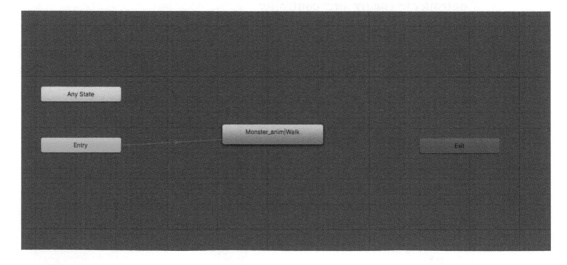

FIGURE 19.8   **Putting the walk into the enemy_orc_controller.**

<Step 16> **Replace** the **OrcScript class** with this and **test**.

```
public class OrcScript : MonoBehaviour
{
    public float Speed = 2.0f;
    public float RotationSpeed = 15.0f;

    CharacterController MyController;

    float mDesiredRotation = 0.0f;

    float mSpeedY = 0.0f;
    float mGravity = -9.8f;

    // Start is called before the first frame update
    void Start()
    {
        MyController = GetComponent<CharacterController>();

    }

    // Update is called once per frame
    void Update()
    {
        float x = -1.0f;
        float z = 0.0f;

        mSpeedY += mGravity * Time.deltaTime;
        if (MyController.isGrounded) mSpeedY = 0.0f;
        Vector3 verticalMovement = Vector3.up * mSpeedY;

        Vector3 movement = new Vector3(x, 0, z).normalized;
        mDesiredRotation = Mathf.Atan2(movement.x, movement.z)
            * Mathf.Rad2Deg;
        MyController.Move(verticalMovement +
            movement * Speed * Time.deltaTime);

        Quaternion currentRotation = transform.rotation;
        Quaternion targetRotation = Quaternion.Euler(
            0.0f, mDesiredRotation, 0.0f);
        transform.rotation = Quaternion.Lerp(
            currentRotation,
            targetRotation,
            RotationSpeed * Time.deltaTime);
    }
}
```

The orc now faces along the movement vector's direction. This code also includes some as yet unnecessary code for handling gravity. Time to test that out.

<Step 17> As you did for testing gravity for Ellen, **put** in a **ramp**, as shown in Figure 19.9, and **test** it.

The orc walks up the ramp and falls off the end, just as you would expect.

You're now ready for your first baby-step toward AI coding: making a character find the player and walk toward her. This is fairly simple. You'll need to build a vector that points from the character at the player, normalize it, and then use that as the movement vector. To do that, find the player location, subtract the character location, normalize, and you're done. Here is the code for all that:

FIGURE 19.9 Orc on a ramp.

<Step 18> In **OrcScript**, **replace** the **x** and **z definitions** with the following four lines:

```
GameObject target;
target = GameObject.FindGameObjectWithTag("Player");
Vector3 movement = target.transform.position - transform.position;
movement = movement.normalized;
```

In this code you're finding Ellen's position, subtracting the character's position, and then normalizing the resulting vector. The use of a tag to find Ellen is inefficient, and not recommended when performance matters.

<Step 19> **Remove** the **movement** definition later on in the code.

<Step 20> Give **Ellen** a **Player tag** and **test**.
The orc follows Ellen around as she moves. Try running to see how the Orc always faces Ellen and moves toward her.

<Step 21> **Add** a **character controller** and **OrcScript** to **maw_j_laygo@Walking.**
Adjust the character controller **Center Y to 1. Uncheck Apply Root Motion in Animator. Test.**
Now the maw monster follows Ellen around as well. This is a good place to stop. You still don't have gameplay but you're slowly converging toward it.

<Step 22> Save and **exit**.

You don't really need to exit Unity here, but it's a good habit to periodically exit. In this way you can be confident that saving is working properly and you're resetting Unity to a fresh state when you load the project again. Doing this can have beneficial effects for the internal state of the Unity editor.

In the next section you'll make the TestEnemies scene more interesting.

MEDIEVAL TOWN

In this section you'll install a small medieval town from the Asset Store. You'll put some buildings and other items into the Test scene and see how your simple enemy AI deals with this scene.

<Step 1> Launch Unity and **load FPSAdventure**.

<Step 2> In the **Asset Store,** find the free asset entitled **Midieval Town Exteriors** by **Lylek Games,** and **install** it into your project. **Check** the **Free Assets checkbox** to help find it.

<Step 3> Read the **Read me First** document and follow the instructions for the standard render pipeline.

Yes, you are currently using the standard render pipeline. Later on, you'll learn about alternatives.

<Step 4> Look at the **Demo scene** and compare with Figure 19.10.

As you can see, there are a few buildings, a well, some barrels, and chests, perfect for trying out a few things. Best of all, these assets don't use up a lot of memory, and the package is quick to download and install.

<Step 5> Load the **TestEnemies** scene. In the **Project** window go to **MidievalTownExteriors/Prefabs** and place a **Building_a** and a **Building_d** into your scene, as shown in Figure 19.11.

FIGURE 19.10   A Medieval Town from the Asset Store.

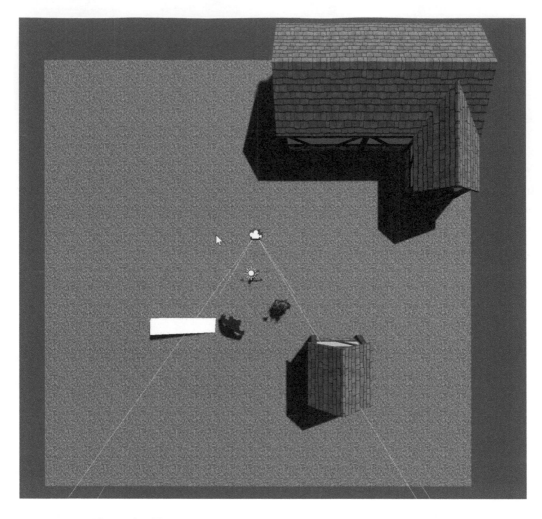

FIGURE 19.11   Placing buildings.

<Step 6>   **Test** this by trying to get the enemies stuck.
　　　　This isn't hard to do. Just run to a far side of a building, and the enemies will get stuck on the other side. You're going to want the enemies to be smarter than that. But first you're going to improve your village.

<Step 7>   **Increase** the **Ground scale** to **(10, 1, 10)**.

<Step 8>   **Place** about **20** more of the **village prefabs** onto your larger **ground**. Create something similar to Figure 19.12.

<Step 9>   **Test** it by **running** around the village and observing the enemies.
　　　　Again, it'll be pretty easy to get the enemies stuck behind a building.
　　　　In the next section you'll create a navmesh and put in better enemy AI.

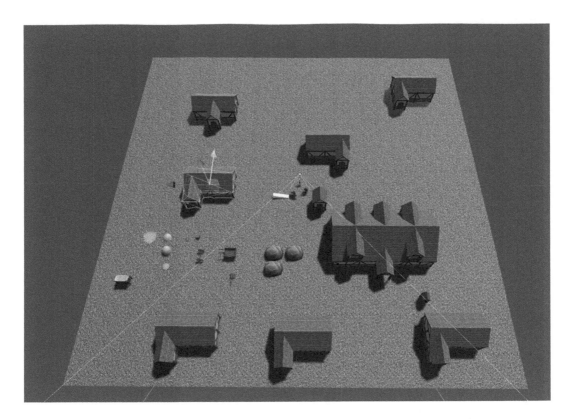

FIGURE 19.12   A larger village.

NAVMESH AND ENEMY AI

Your goal in this section is to have your enemies find a path to the player regardless of the layout of the scene. You'll need to create a *navmesh* to do this. A navmesh, short for navigation mesh, is a mesh of triangles that can be used to efficiently traverse a complex scene. It is especially useful for path-finding algorithms.

Fortunately, all the difficult work will be done for you by Unity, and you won't have to actually write any path-finding algorithms yourself.

\<Step 1\>   **Window – AI – Navigation**.
           This brings up a new window for you. It's on a tab next to the Inspector and the Lighting tabs.

\<Step 2\>   If necessary, select **Object**, and select the **All** Scene Filter.

\<Step 3\>   **Rearrange** the **TestEnemies** game objects in the hierarchy as follows: Bring the cameras and the Directional Light to the top, then below it the Ground object followed by Ellen and the enemies.
           This makes them easier to find.

\<Step 4\>   Select **Ground,** then in the navigation window check **Navigation Static**. **Select Walkable** for the **Navigation Area**.

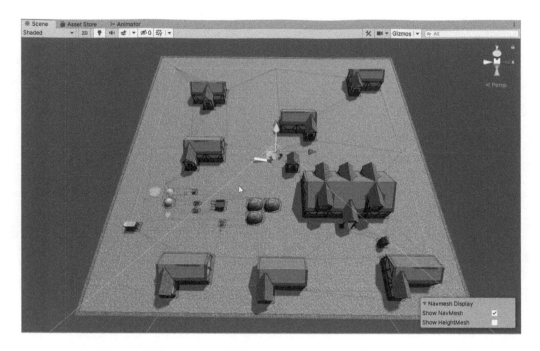

FIGURE 19.13   Navmesh displayed in the scene.

<Step 5>   In the navigation window, select **Bake**, and then click on **Bake**. Compare your Scene with Figure 19.13.

The tinted areas constitute the Navmesh. Notice that most of the roofs of the houses are also tinted. You don't want characters walking on the roofs in this game, so do the following.

<Step 6>   **Select** all the **village objects**, the ones below the enemies in the hierarchy.

<Step 7>   In the **Navigation Window**, select **Object**, then select **Navigation Static** and **Not Walkable**. When asked, make the child objects not walkable as well.

<Step 8>   **Bake** the **navmesh**.

Notice that the roofs are now no longer shaded blue. If you zoom in on the buildings and other village objects, you'll notice that they are surrounded by a grassy border. This is on purpose to keep navmesh agents a fixed distance away from obstacles.

To see this more clearly, do the following.

<Step 9>   In the **Bake** panel, set the **Agent Radius** to **1** and the **Max Slope** to **30**. **Bake** again. Next, you'll wish to test out this navmesh in the game.

<Step 10>   Edit **OrcScript** with the following changes:

Insert "using UnityEngine.AI;" in the using section.
Insert "public NavMeshAgent agent;" near the top.
Comment out the MyController.Move statement and **insert** this instead:

```
agent.SetDestination(target.transform.position);
```

This code replaces the movement of the enemy with a navmesh agent and sets the destination to the player, thus causing the enemy to always traverse the navmesh and find a short path toward the player.

<Step 11> **Save** the code in Visual Studio, then **add** a **Nav Mesh Agent** component to **enemy_orc** and also **maw_j_laygo@Walking**. In the Nav Mesh Agent section, change the **Speed** to **1.0** for enemy_orc, and **2.0** for **maw_j_laygo@Walking**.

<Step 12> **Set Agent to enemy_orc** in the Orc Script section for enemy_orc. Similarly do that for **maw_j_laygo@Walking**. **Test** this by running around the scene and watching how the enemies follow Ellen.

By watching from above in the Scene window you see that the orc is slower, but otherwise the enemies are using the same pathfinding algorithm. The important, and disturbing, part is that there is nowhere for Ellen to hide now.

<Step 13> **Save**.

You achieved your goal for this section, so next you'll go back to the UnityTerrain scene and give it a navmesh, a small village and enemies.

CREATING A LARGE LEVEL

In this section you will work with the UnityTerrain scene. You'll build a small village, bake a navmesh, and then bring in some enemies.

<Step 1> **Load** the **UnityTerrain** scene and **test**.

You should have Ellen, a ramp, and a large terrain with lots of trees. You should remove any enemies in the scene.

<Step 2> **Choose** an area of the terrain to flatten so you can put some buildings there.

<Step 3> In the hierarchy, select **Terrain.** In the inspector choose **Paint Terrain** and use the dropdown at the top of the Terrain section to select **Effects/Slope Flatten**, as shown in Figure 19.14.

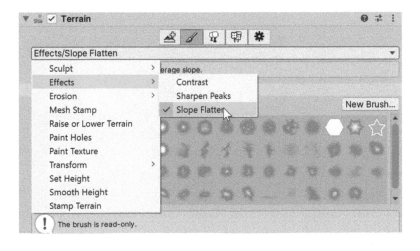

FIGURE 19.14   Choosing the Effects/Slope Flatten terrain tool.

<Step 4>   **Create** a **flat area** near a path in the terrain large enough for a few buildings similar to Figure 19.15. Clear the trees from the flat area.

<Step 5>   **Place** a few **village prefabs** into the flat area similar to Figure 19.16.

<Step 6>   **Delete** the **ramp**.

<Step 7>   **Move Ellen** to the **village** and **test**.
You'll probably see some buildings and items floating above the terrain.

FIGURE 19.15   Creating a flat area for a small village.

FIGURE 19.16   A small village in a large forest.

<Step 8> In the **Scene** window, check the village buildings and other items. **Adjust** their **positions** so they are all seated properly on the terrain.
You are now ready to create a navmesh for this scene.

<Step 9> **Select all village objects** and in the **navigation** window make them **not walkable**.

<Step 10> In the **bake** section of the navigation window, click on **Bake**.
This will take a minute or so. There's a progress bar at the bottom.

<Step 11> When you have a navmesh, **explore** the scene and look at the result. Compare with Figure 19.17.
This looks like it'll work. There are some oddities in this navmesh, but you won't worry about that just yet. It's time to bring in some enemies.

<Step 12> **Save** and go back to the **TestEnemies** scene.

<Step 13> **Select** the **two enemies** in the **hierarchy**, then **right-click** and select **Copy**.

<Step 14> Back on the **UnityTerrain** scene, in the hierarchy, **right-click** and **Paste**.

<Step 15> **Move** the **enemies** near Ellen.
You can do that easily by selecting Ellen, and in the inspector, right-click on **Transform** and select **Copy Position**. Then select the enemies and do a **Paste Position** for their transforms. This will put the enemies on top of Ellen. You can then easily move the enemies to separate them from Ellen.

<Step 16> **Test** this to see if the enemies are following Ellen.

FIGURE 19.17 A navmesh in the forest.

This is not going to work. Can you diagnose the problem? That's right, you're getting null reference errors in the Console. When you click on the Errors you are taken to the OrcScript script, and you see that the script isn't finding the Player tag. Aha!

<Step 17> **Select** Ellen and set her tag to **Player**. Then **test** again.

This should fix the problem. Just for fun you'll test to see if these enemies can find Ellen if she's far away.

<Step 18> **Place Ellen** far away from the village **somewhere in the forest**. **Test** to see if the enemies can find her there.

This may take a few minutes. It's a good exercise to see if you can follow the enemies using **WASD** controls and **right-click** on the mouse in the scene window.

<Step 19> When you're finished testing, **undo** the **move of Ellen** to get her back to the village. You may have to undo several times.

<Step 20> **Save** and **Exit** Unity.

Do you have a playable game here? Not really, but you're getting closer. In the next section you'll add a simple GUI to keep track of the health of Ellen.

GUI AND SCORING

Because this is a prototype, you're going to make it easy for yourself and have a very simple GUI, even simpler than in Part I. You'll display the health of Ellen as a number overlay. You'll leave the real health display with hearts for later. You'll also display a score, but you'll leave it at zero for now.

You already did a simple GUI in DotGame3D, so this is a good time to learn how to use package export and import to transfer assets from one project to another.

<Step 1> **Launch Unity** and **load** the **DotGame3D** project from Part I. Do you still have that? If not, you can download it at franzlanzinger.com.

<Step 2> In the hierarchy, **select** the **Main Camera**.

Most any other object in the hierarchy would work as well. This is just to get asset-exporting to work properly.

<Step 3> **Assets – Export Package…**

You will see a pop-up listing all the possible assets to export. Select only the items as shown in Figure 19.18.

<Step 4> **Click** on **Export** and export to the file **DotGameAssets.unitypackage** in the **FPSAdventure/Assets** folder.

<Step 5> **Exit** Unity, **load FPSAdventure**, and do **Assets – Import Package – Custom Package**. Select the package you just created above. Click on **Import**.

<Step 6> **Select Assets/DotgameAssets** and in the inspector **click** on **Open**. Compare with Figure 19.18.

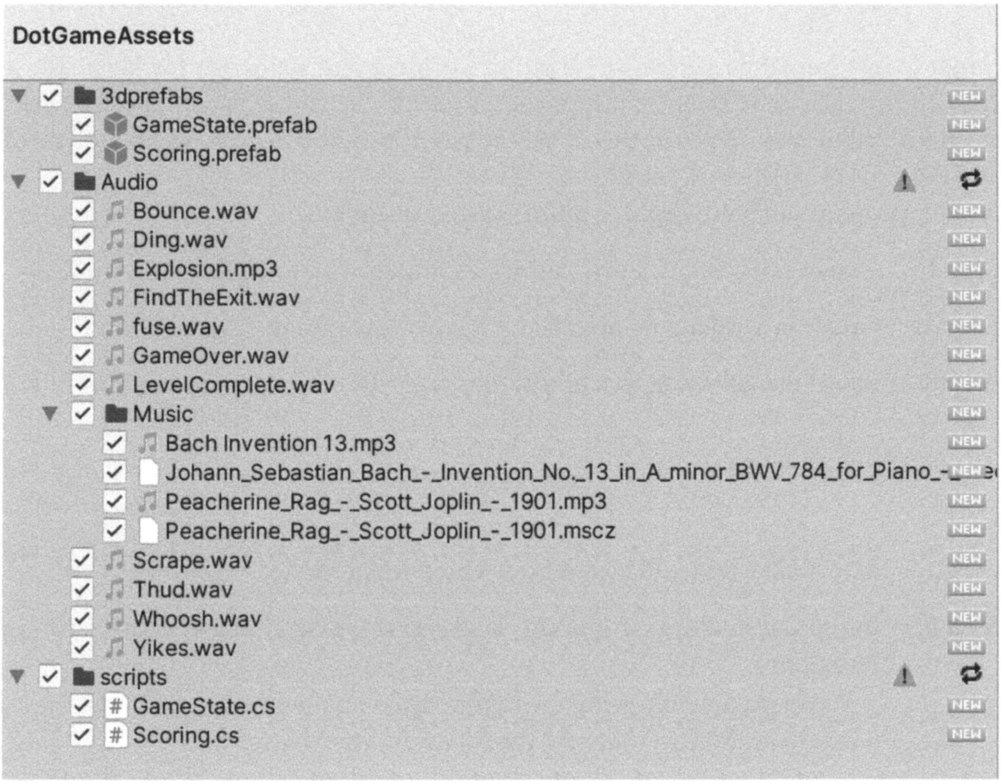

FIGURE 19.18   Importing some DotGame assets.

> You are importing two scripts, the associated prefabs, and all of the Audio for later use.
>
> You can ignore the two warning triangles because it will be OK to merge the package contents with the Audio and the Scripts folders.

<Step 7>   **Click** on **Import**.

<Step 8>   From **Assets/3dprefabs drag GameState** and **Scoring** into the hierarchy.

<Step 9>   **Test**.

> You'll see the familiar GUI from DotGame3D. It's the wrong GUI, but it works, and you'll fix it easily enough in the following step.

<Step 10>   In **Scoring.cs** replace `lives` with `health` and `Lives` with `Health`. Initialize `health` to 9. **Test**.

> You still have a score, a level timer, and a level display in the GUI, in addition to the health display in the top middle. You'll leave those intact for now even though they're not being used for anything. You'll probably remove the scoring entirely in this game, but it's not harming anything right now.
>
> In this very short section, you used the package manager to bring in the GUI from your previous project and made a slight adjustment to make it fit your game. In the next section you'll have the enemies affect Ellen's health.

ENEMY COLLISIONS

In order to have actual gameplay, you'll put in a collider and rigidbody for Ellen. The idea is that if Ellen collides with an enemy, she loses health. When her health goes to zero, she dies and it's game over. You can then tune the game by adjusting the number of enemies and the speeds of enemies vs. Ellen.

You'll use the Unity Tag system to quickly detect enemies.

<Step 1> **Create** a new tag "enemy" and assign it to the two enemies.

<Step 2> **Create or Update** the **prefabs** for the two enemies in Assets/Prefabs.

<Step 3> **Insert** the following function at the end of ThirdPersonController.cs:

```
private void OnCollisionEnter (Collision collision)
{
    if  (collision.gameObject.tag == "enemy") Scoring.health--;
}
```

<Step 4> **Select Ellen** and **add** a **rigidbody component** for her.

<Step 5> In the **Constraints** section, **check all six freeze checkmarks** for Position and Rotation.

You're not actually using the rigidbody component as a rigid body, but it needs to be there in order for the collision detection to work.

<Step 6> **Add** a **Box Collider** for **Ellen** and **adjust** it.

This is easier to do if you turn off the display of the character controller. That can be done by collapsing it in the inspector. Compare the box collider for Ellen with Figure 19.19.

Ellen already has a capsule collider, but this box collider is necessary to work with the code from step 3.

<Step 7> **Test** this by **colliding Ellen** with **enemies** and watching the **health GUI display**. The health should decrease by one for every collision.

<Step 8> **Add** two **orcs** and one more **maw** from the **prefabs** into the scene, and **test** again.

The enemies will all attack Ellen at once. It won't take long for Ellen's health to go negative.

<Step 9> **Experiment** with different speeds for Ellen and the enemies.

This last step is somewhat open ended. Imagine that you're not following steps in a book but rather creating a brand new game of your own invention. What would you do next?

<Step 10> **Save** and **exit** Unity.

The game is basically playable, but you still have a long way to go toward a releasable game. For a prototype you're in great shape. In this chapter you made a lot of progress. It's a stretch, but you've decided to call what you have the first playable version. In the next chapter you're going to create a puzzle room.

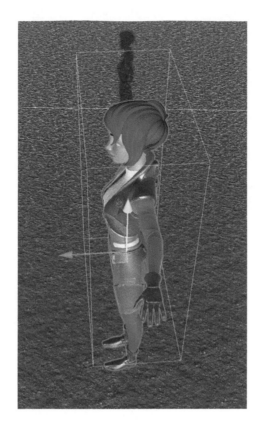

FIGURE 19.19   A box collider for Ellen.

CHAPTER 20

A 3D Puzzle Room

IN THIS CHAPTER YOU'LL build a puzzle room for Ellen. The final game should have a lot of these, at least ten, and possibly many more. In your prototype version you'll just build a single, simple puzzle room to get a feel for what this looks like.

PUZZLE DESIGN RULES

Taking a step back, you've decided to think about puzzles in general. What are some good design rules for puzzle games? As usual, the web has a lot of answers, but you're going to resist googling for it at first. Instead, you're going to contemplate the problem, write down a few ideas, and then search for "puzzle game design rules." Did your ideas overlap the collective wisdom of the internet?

If you haven't already, read the article titled "13 Rules for Escape Room Puzzle Design" at the website thecodex.ca. The very first rule is this:

Puzzles Should Be Fair – You are on the Player's Side!

If you follow no other rules, this is the one to keep in mind at all times. Your goal isn't to make the puzzles so difficult that only a select few, or even nobody, can solve them. On the other hand, there's a fine line between easy and too easy.

As always, but especially for puzzles, testing is critical. As the puzzle designer you're not able to test your puzzles yourself because, well, you already know the solution. So, you'll need to make sure to test all of the puzzles with noobs.

Getting back to actually designing your first puzzle, you start by writing down some basic ideas for possible puzzles using your existing game mechanics.

Your puzzle room will be, in essence, an escape room. You'll solve one or more simple puzzles to get to a treasure chest. When you get close enough to the treasure chest it opens, revealing a key or other treasure and you get transported back to the main game.

Your development plan is simple. First, you'll collect some useful assets from the Asset Store. You'll look for walls, staircases, movable ramps, and of course an animatable treasure chest. Afterward you'll build the room scene and write some simple scripts as needed.

DOI: 10.1201/9780429328725-22

PUZZLE ROOM GRAPHICS

In this section you'll explore the Asset Store for items that you might be able to use when making your puzzle rooms. Because of possible incompatibilities you're going to create yet another project.

<Step 1> **Create** a new 3D Unity Project titled **PuzzleTest**.

<Step 2> In the **Unity Asset Store**, get the **Lowpoly Dungeon Assets by Kunniki**.

This asset is very small and simple. The art style is low poly, which isn't really what you want, but it's fine for a prototype. You plan to replace the graphics in the puzzle room with higher detailed graphics later on during production. Time and budget permitting, you may create your own custom graphics using Blender, or purchase something in the Unity Asset Store, or one of the many other internet stores for 3D graphics assets.

If you try to run the demo, you'll get a compiler error. This isn't really a problem because you don't need the demo. You are interested in looking at the demo though, so the following steps fix this bug.

<Step 3> In **Assets/LowpolyDungeonAssets/Demo Scene**, **load** the **Demo Scene**.

<Step 4> Go to the **Console** and **double-click** on the **error**.

Unity will show you the error in Visual Studio by editing the file MinDrawer.cs.

<Step 5> **Comment out** the **second line** by adding two slashes in front of it like this:

```
// using UnityEngine.PostProcessing
```

<Step 6> **Save** in Visual Studio and **go back to Unity**.

This will fix the bug. You may have a warning, but you can ignore it. You can now run the demo.

<Step 7> **Test** the game in Unity. You'll get a mostly static view of the scene, as shown in Figure 20.1.

There are quite a few other free and inexpensive dungeon assets in the Unity Asset Store. You chose this one because it's a small download and has all the elements you want for now. You're not quite finished trying it out.

<Step 8> Go to **Assets/Scenes** and **load** the **SampleScene**.

This is the mostly empty scene that came with the project when you created it.

<Step 9> **Create** a **3D plane** and **scale** it to (**2, 1, 2**).

<Step 10> **Place** some of the **prefabs** in **LowpolyDungeonAssets** into this scene, maybe something like Figure 20.2.

This looks like it's going to work in FPSAdventure, so it's time to transition back to that project.

FIGURE 20.1   Low-poly dungeon assets.

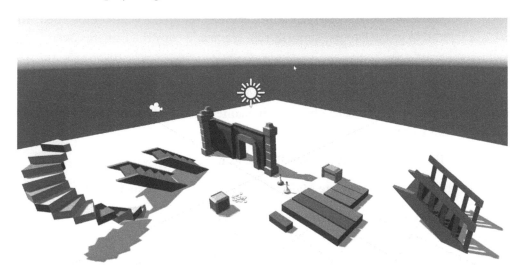

FIGURE 20.2   Placing some dungeon assets into the PuzzleTest project.

<Step 11> **Save, exit Unity,** and use UnityHub to **load FPSAdventure** into Unity.

<Step 12> **Window – Package Manager** and **import Lowpoly Dungeon Assets**. Import everything.

<Step 13> As before, **fix the error** in the file **Mindrawer.cs**. Then run the game to make sure it still works.

That's right, importing packages can sometime break your game, so it's a good habit to do a quick test before using the package. If there is a problem caused by importing a package you can simply delete the package or try to debug it.

<Step 14> **Create** a new scene in **Assets/Scenes** and name it **PuzzleScene1**.

Yes, you're putting in the digit 1 to keep track of future multiple puzzle scenes.

<Step 15> **Select PuzzleScene1, create a plane, rename it** to **Floor, scale** it to (**3, 1, 3**), and do a **frame selected**. Then adjust the view to your liking.

You're going to start by putting Ellen into the center. You still don't have a prefab for Ellen, so you'll make one.

<Step 16> **Save, go to UnityTerrain, select Ellen**, do a **frame selected**.

<Step 17> **Drag Ellen** into **Assets/Prefabs** and **create** an original prefab.

<Step 18> **Test** the game, then **save** and go back to **PuzzleScene1**.

<Step 19> **Drag** the **Ellen prefab** to the center of the **Floor**.

An easy way to do this is to drag Ellen anyplace, then in the inspector, find the Transform Menu, those three dots on the right, and select Reset.

If you run the game here, you will get an error called UnassignedReferenceException. You didn't set up the Camera for Ellen. You'll need to go back to the UnityTerrain scene and copy the cameras over.

<Step 20> **File – Open Recent Scene – UnityTerrain. Save** the **PuzzleScene1** scene when prompted.

<Step 21> In the hierarchy, **select** both **Main Camera** and **CM FreeLook1, right-click** and **Copy**.

<Step 22> **File – Open Recent Scene – PuzzleScene1**.

<Step 23> In the hierarchy, **delete Main Camera, <ctrl>v** to paste the cameras.

<Step 24> **Assign** the **Main Camera** to **My Camera** for **Ellen** to fix the error.

This time you get a different error: Failed to create agent because there is no valid NavMesh.

<Step 25> **Select** the **Floor** object, go to the **Navigation** window, check **Navigation Static** in the Object Tab, then go to **Bake** and **Bake**.

<Step 26> **Test**.

This won't work yet. You'll get a static view of the sky dome. Do you know what's wrong? There are no error messages.

When you look at the CM FreeLook1 camera in the Inspector you notice that the Follow and Look At slots aren't set.

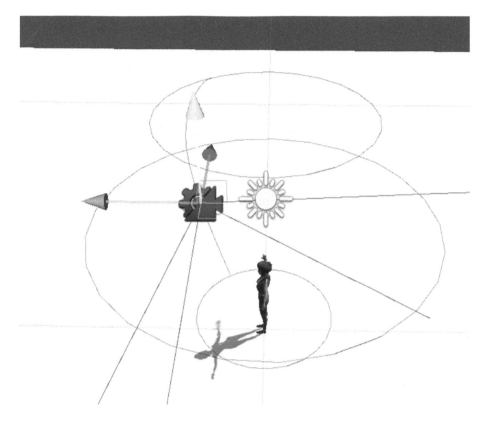

FIGURE 20.3   Three orbits for CM FreeLook1.

<Step 27> **Assign Ellen** to **Follow** and **Ellen_Neck** to **Look At** for **CM FreeLook1**.
   In the Scene window you'll see the three orbit circles, as shown in
   Figure 20.3.

<Step 28> **Test.**
   Finally! Ellen is able to run around the Floor. Sometimes the simplest
   things take the most work.

In the next section you'll build the first puzzle.

BUILDING THE PUZZLE ROOM

You're going to make a very simple puzzle at first where the only problem is navigating
Ellen toward a very obviously placed treasure chest.

<Step 1> **Create a folder** called **PuzzlePrefabs** in **Assets**.
   You will collect your puzzle pieces there.

<Step 2> Go to **Assets/LowpolyDungeonAssets/Assets/Prefabs/Floor**.

<Step 3> **Slide** the **icon slider to the left** so you can see the full names of the Floor
   prefabs.

There are 12 floor assets including five flat planks and seven stairs. You'll start by taking Floor_3Plank_Stone_Big.

\<Step 4\> **Drag Floor_3Plank_Stone_Big** into the scene near Ellen.

\<Step 5\> Test **Ellen** walking on top to the planks.
Ellen sinks into the planks, which is not realistic at all. The 3Plank object is missing a collider.

\<Step 6\> **Add** a **box collider** to the 3Plank object and **test**.
That was easy. You didn't need to adjust the box collider, it just worked. Ellen is able to step onto the planks. Before you go on, let's make a new prefab for the planks.

\<Step 7\> **Rename Floor_3Plank_Stone_Big** to **Planks**, then **drag** it into to **PuzzlePrefabs** as an original prefab.
This prefab is basically the same as the one you downloaded, except that it has a box collider.

\<Step 8\> **Build** a 3 by 4 arrangement of planks, as shown in Figure 20.4.
You do this by using **\<ctrl\>d** to make duplicates and arranging them carefully.

\<Step 9\> **Move** the **Plank objects** to match Figure 20.5, **test** and have **Ellen walk** to the **top**.
The vertical gap from one Plank to the next must be relatively small or Ellen won't be able to traverse it.

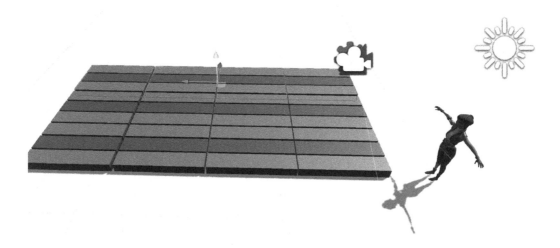

FIGURE 20.4   Planks arranged in a 3 by 4 pattern.

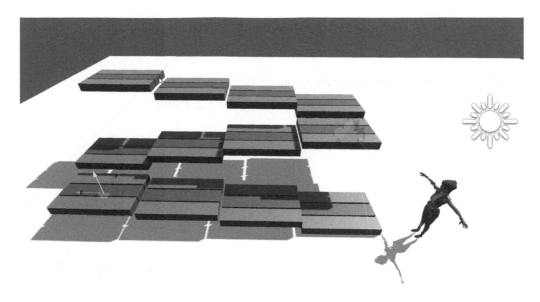

FIGURE 20.5   A ramp for Ellen.

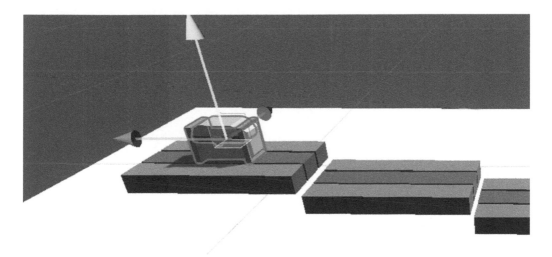

FIGURE 20.6   A treasure chest.

<Step 10> Put a **chest** on the top Planks object, as shown in Figure 20.6.

You'll find the chest in the **Prefabs/Props** folder named **Props_Chest**.

<Step 11> Rename Props_Chest in the hierarchy to **Chest** and give it a **box collider**.

<Step 12> Test it.

You'll find that Ellen can walk on top of the Chest, but that's OK for now because as soon as Ellen touches the Chest you'll freeze Ellen, open the chest, and then leave the scene to go back to the main game. At least, that's what you intend to do...

<Step 13> Make a **Chest prefab** in **PuzzlePrefabs**.

<Step 14> Save.

You have a start here. You still need to integrate this with the rest of the game, but that can be done later. In the next chapter you'll explore lighting in Unity.

CHAPTER 21

Shaders and Lighting in Unity

THIS CHAPTER IS AN introduction to shaders and lighting in Unity. First, you'll take a quick look at the wide variety of built-in shaders. Then you'll learn about direct and indirect lighting by experimenting with these features in the puzzle room. At the end of this chapter you'll explore the more advanced topic of raytracing.

INTRODUCTION

It can be a full-time job to work on shaders and the lighting for a large commercial game. Even for a small prototype, one or two custom shaders plus some effort on the lighting can have a dramatic effect on the visual quality of the game.

What are shaders and lighting? As is often the case, the Unity manual has answers. But, before you try to read that part of the manual it helps to get an overview. A shader is a program that runs on a GPU. When you encounter a shader it will usually be part of the graphics pipeline, and it will help compute the colors of pixels using the massive compute power of GPUs. Modern graphics cards can have as many as 10000 shader hardware units, all operating simultaneously! Occasionally you'll encounter what are called *compute shaders*, which perform calculations on the GPU, outside of the graphics pipeline.

Lighting in Unity approximates how light behaves in the real world. You will encounter direct and indirect lighting. Direct lighting simulates light emanating from a light source and directly hitting a material. Indirect lighting bounces one or more times in the scene before hitting a material. As the light bounces it changes color, intensity, and direction depending on the surface.

Lighting can be performed in real time, or it may be precomputed, a process that is called baking, similar to the baking of navmeshes. The result of this baking is one or more textures called lightmaps. You will learn how to bake lightmaps later on in this chapter.

In the final section in this chapter you'll learn about raytracing. Raytracing is an advanced and new feature for Unity, so you'll simply look at some sample output and weigh the pros and cons of using raytracing. You won't be using raytracing in this game, but you need to know what it is for your future games. Raytracing is a high-end or nonexistent feature for most current platforms, but just a few years from now it'll be everywhere.

DOI: 10.1201/9780429328725-23

SHADERS IN UNITY

In this section you'll take a quick look at shaders in Unity. You'll learn the very basics about what they are and how to learn more about them. You won't need to learn how to create your own shaders just yet.

Before you begin with shaders in Unity you'll need to know about Unity's render pipelines. So far you've been using the Built-in Render Pipeline. Render pipelines take the contents of a scene and display them on a screen. Two other Unity render pipelines are the Universal Render Pipeline (URP) designed for a wide range of platforms, and the High Definition Render Pipeline (HDRP) designed for high-end platforms. For more details on this, read the Render pipelines introduction in the Unity manual.

As stated in the introduction, shaders are programs that run on the GPU. Shaders are part of your chosen render pipeline. For now, you've decided to simply continue to use the shaders that come with the Built-in Render Pipeline. That's right, you've been using shaders on your projects already. Look at any material in the inspector, and you'll see a shader dropdown menu with Standard selected by default. Later in this section you'll experiment with this dropdown to get a feel for what these shaders are and what they do.

<Step 1> **Load FPSAdventure** into Unity and go to **PuzzleScene1**.

<Step 2> In **Assets/Art, create** a **material** and give it a **light brown** color. Change the **Smoothness** to **0.9**. Rename it to **FloorMaterial**.

<Step 3> **Assign** it to the **Floor**.

<Step 4> Adjust your view of the scene to approximately match Figure 21.1. That bright circular area is the reflection of the directional light.

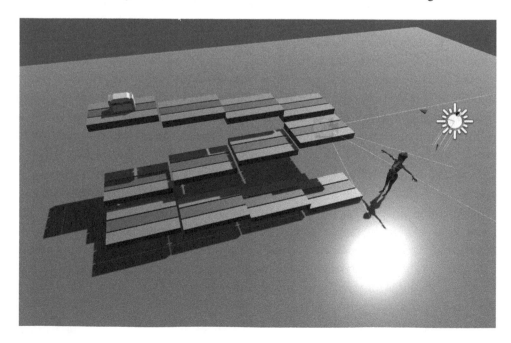

FIGURE 21.1 Using the standard shader.

<Step 5> In the **Metallic** section of the Standard Shader settings, **slide** the **Smoothness slider** and observe the effect. **Undo** the change and **revert** to a **smoothness** of about **0.9**.

<Step 6> **Change** the **Shader** to **Standard (Specular Setup)**.

Specular lighting is characterized by bright highlights on shiny objects. To see examples, search the internet for **specular highlights**.

<Step 7> **Change** the **Specular** color to a **dark yellow**. Compare with Figure 21.2.

There is quite a dramatic effect, with the yellow and the brown combining to form a green color.

<Step 8> Change the **Shader** to **Unlit – Color**.

This time you get a flat brown color for the floor and the shadows are missing for the floor, but they are still visible on the Planks. As you can see, setup and options of the shaders is critical for creating the look of your scene. It's good to know that each material has its own shader settings.

<Step 9> Change the **Shader** to **Legacy Shaders/Bumped Specular**.

These legacy shaders should probably no longer be used in new projects, but it's still interesting to see what they can do.

<Step 10> Go back to the **Standard shader**. **Save**.

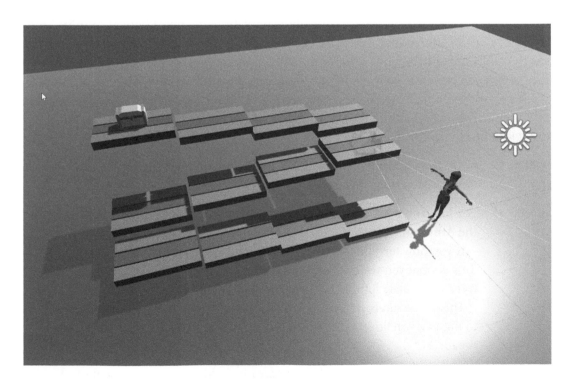

FIGURE 21.2   Using a dark yellow specular color.

If, in the future you feel the need to write your own shaders there are two possible ways to do that. First, you can use what's called the *Shader Graph*. This is a built-in tool that comes with Unity and allows you to quickly put together fairly complex shaders without coding. It's definitely the way to go if you're new to shaders. Just be aware that the shader graph is only compatible with URP and HDRP, so you will have to convert your project to one of those render pipelines.

Another possibility is to write your own shaders from scratch using a programming language designed for that, for example, Cg. This is an advanced topic, but you can find online tutorials accessible to beginners if you're interested. Also, there is information on this in the Unity manual. You won't be creating shaders in this book, but it's good to be aware of this possibility for your future projects.

YouTube has a large number of videos and tutorials on Unity shaders, so feel free to browse around to see what you can do with them. A great example is an ice shader, which can make a simple mesh look like ice. Usually, shaders are used for special visual effects. They give you access to the GPUs on your system with their amazing compute power. And yes, those GPUs can also be programmed to do scientific computing, AI, and crypto-mining, but those topics are way beyond the scope of this book.

In the next section you'll work on improving your puzzle scene by making it an interior room and adding better lighting. Along the way you'll learn about various direct lighting options.

DIRECT LIGHTING

In this section you'll try out some of the lighting options in Unity. So far you've only used the default directional light. This is basically a simulation of a point light at infinity. Thus, the light rays are all parallel. For practical purposes, a directional light acts the same as sunlight. The default Directional lights in Unity are examples of real-time lighting, which means that you can animate those lights to simulate the movement of the sun, for example.

To get ready you'll change the lighting settings for your current puzzle scene. If you're missing the lighting window, you can get it by doing Window – Rendering – Lighting and dragging the tab next to the inspector tab.

<Step 1> Go to the **Lighting** window, select **Environment**, and choose **None** for the **Skybox Material**.

<Step 2> For **Environment Lighting**, choose **Color** for the Source and a **dark grey** for the **Ambient Color**.

If you now turn off the Directional Light you'll get a mostly black scene. This is what you want for an initial setup for an indoor scene. Unity keeps track of separate lighting settings for different scenes.

This scene surely doesn't look like an interior scene yet, so you're going to put in a real floor, walls, and a ceiling. Take a peek at Figure 21.3 to get the idea.

<Step 3> **Create four walls** and a **ceiling** by creating additional planes. **Scale** and **rotate them** to line up with the existing floor.

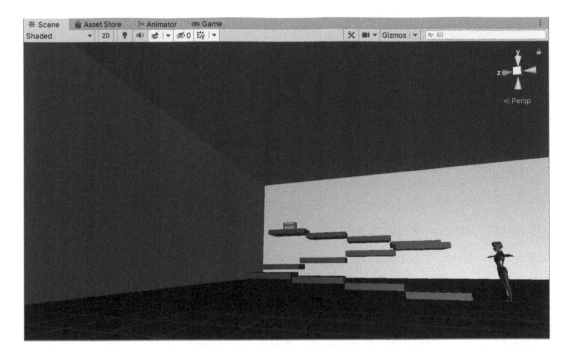

FIGURE 21.3   Building walls and a ceiling.

<Step 4>   Create a new **material** called **WallMaterial** with a **light tan color** and **assign** it to the walls and the ceiling.

You may need to flip the walls or the ceiling by 180 degrees to make the material visible from the inside of the puzzle room. Remember that by default, all materials are one-sided and thus are only visible from one side.

<Step 5> Turn off the **scene lighting** icon at the top of the scene window and check that all the walls and the ceiling are using the **WallMaterial**. Compare with Figure 21.3.

You turned off the scene lighting so you could see better when putting in the new objects. You're ready to try out the different lights. You'll start with the existing directional light.

<Step 6>   Turn on scene lighting again, then **select** the **Directional Light** object.

<Step 7>   In the inspector, **experiment** with the **color**. The existing color is a faint yellow. Try out different colors and watch the effect in the scene window. When you've had enough, set the **color** to **white**.

<Step 8>   Click on **Intensity** and **drag** to try out different intensities. **Leave** it at **1**.

The indirect multiplier setting has no effect right now, so leave it at 1.

<Step 9>   Try setting the **Shadow Type** to **No Shadows,** then back to **Soft Shadows.**

This is easy enough. Notice that the other shadow settings in the inspector disappear when you do this.

Now you'll explore the shadow settings. As a side note, a few years back shadows were considered an advanced feature of Unity and they weren't included in the free Unity version. Thankfully, the free version of Unity is now mostly equivalent to the paid version, so you no longer need to worry about this. Not only does the Unity render engine generate shadows, when enabled, you also have quite a few settings to control them.

<Step 10> **Reduce** the **strength** of the **Realtime Shadows** to **0.2**. Compare with Figure 21.4.

This setting is mostly an artistic choice. The default setting is 1. You've decided that you'd prefer something between 0.2 and 1, so how about 0.5?

<Step 11> Set the **strength** to **0.5**.

<Step 12> Set the **Resolution** to **Very High Resolution**, if necessary.

This is probably your default setting. Notice that you can have this setting depend on the quality settings. High-resolution shadows use up more graphics memory and rendering time.

<Step 13> **Try** out the other **Realtime Shadow Resolutions**.

The low-resolution settings give Ellen a somewhat fuzzy shadow. Again, this is an artistic choice, depending on whether you're going for realism or a particular unrealistic art style. You're going to leave this setting at Very High Resolution.

FIGURE 21.4   Shadows with an intensity of 0.2.

<Step 14> **Experiment** with **Bias**, **Normal Bias**, and **Near Plane**, read the explanations by hovering the mouse over the titles of these settings.

You will leave those settings at their default settings of 0, 0.36 and 0.1. The reset of the settings in the inspector can be ignored for now.

<Step 15> **Explore** the **settings** for **Hard Shadows**.

Particularly interesting are hard shadows at low resolution. This setting reveals what's going on under the hood, so to speak. The renderer creates a shadow map at a particular resolution. When the resolution is low you can see the pixels of the shadow map. Such a shadow setting combination doesn't look good, but on low-end hardware that may be the only choice. You've decided to keep soft shadows and the highest available resolution.

<Step 16> **Choose soft shadows** and the **highest available shadow resolution**.

Next you'll try out point lights.

<Step 17> **Create eight point lights**, one for each corner of the room. Compare with Figure 21.5.

An efficient way to do this is to create just one point light in one corner, then use **<ctrl>d** to duplicate it and move the duplicate to a nearby corner. Then you can select both point lights, duplicate them, move both duplicates, select four point lights, duplicate, and move.

<Step 18> **Turn** off the **directional light**.

That will give you a very dark room. You wish to use just the eight point lights, so you'll need to increase their range.

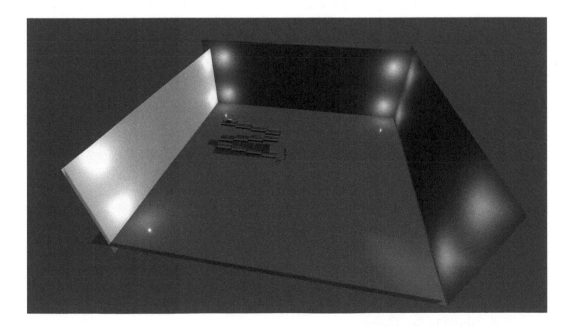

FIGURE 21.5   Eight point lights, initial setup.

FIGURE 21.6   Eight point lights illuminating the room.

<Step 19> **Select** all **eight point lights**, change the **range** to **170, intensity** to **0.5**. Change the **shadow type** to **Soft Shadows** and compare with Figure 21.6.

<Step 20> **Test** the game, **turn on Stats** to check the **frame rate**.

With a high-end graphics card you'll get a very high frame rate. Take a look at the shadows as Ellen moves around. You have eight lights, so eight shadows, although they are difficult to see. When Ellen walks near one of the corners you'll get a nice shadow on the wall from the light in that corner, but the shadows from the other lights are fainter. All in all the scene looks interesting this way.

Next you're going to put a spotlight on that treasure chest.

<Step 21> **Reduce** the **intensity** of the **point lights** to **0.4**.

<Step 22> **Create** a **spotlight, place** it above the treasure chest pointing down, **pink color, intensity 10. Adjust** the **Spot Angle**. Compare with Figure 21.7.

<Step 23> **Turn on hard shadows** for the **spotlight**, and **test**.

<Step 24> **Save**.

You'll see that nice pink lighting when Ellen walks up the ramp to the treasure, and a harsh shadow from the spotlight as Ellen gets close to the treasure chest.

In this section you tried out three of the most commonly used direct lights: directional lights, point lights, and a spotlight. In the next section you'll learn about indirect lighting.

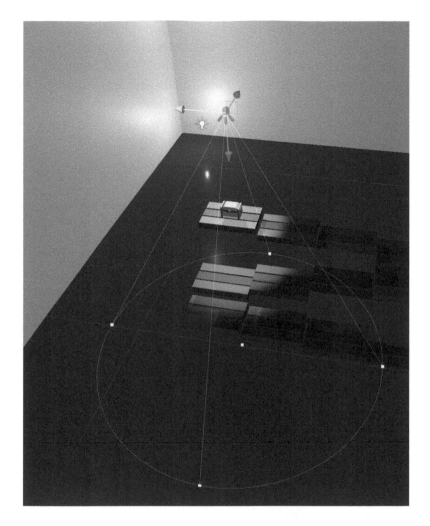

FIGURE 21.7 Spotlight on the treasure.

INDIRECT LIGHTING

Indirect lighting simulates light rays that don't come directly from a direct light source. This is much closer to the real world where light rays bounce many times from one surface to another before finally reaching our eyes. In this section you'll set up indirect lighting for the puzzle scene.

First you'll adjust the settings in the lighting window.

<Step 1> **Lighting window** and select the **Scene** button if necessary.

<Step 2> **Create** new **lighting settings** with the name **PuzzleSceneLightingSettings** and store them in **Assets/Art**.

<Step 3> **Expand** the **Realtime Lighting** section, **disable Realtime Global Illumination (Deprecated)**.

Remember that the word *deprecated* within the context of Unity means that a feature is scheduled for replacement or deletion in future versions of Unity. It's a good policy to avoid deprecated features. Occasionally, as you upgrade to newer versions of Unity, you will find that some features have become deprecated. This gives you fair warning to find a way to replace your use of those features. The good news is that as long as you don't upgrade Unity those deprecated features will continue to work.

<Step 4> **Check Baked Global Illumination** in the **Mixed Lighting** section. Use the **Shadowmask Lighting Mode**.

You may wish to revisit this setting in the future, but for now the Shadowmask setting is good.

<Step 5> In the **Lightmapping Settings**, set the **Lightmapper** to **Progressive GPU (Preview)**.

Assuming that you have a fairly recent graphics card, this setting will vastly speed up your baking, typically by a factor of 20 or more. It really depends on which specific graphics card you have. The default Progressive CPU setting causes Unity to generate the lightmap using only your CPUs, which might be more reliable, but much slower.

<Step 6> **Disable Progressive Updates**.

This setting can be useful once you're more familiar with lightmap baking. For beginners, it can be easier to follow what's happening when you have this turned off.

<Step 7> **Disable Compress Lightmaps**.

This setting can save some memory, but can cause artifacts, so for now it's best to turn it off because memory usage is not a problem for this small project. As you can see, there are quite a few settings here. The default settings are a good starting point. As you get more experienced with lightmaps, and depending on the particular layout of your scene, you may wish to experiment with the other Lightmapping Settings.

<Step 8> **Enable Ambient Occlusion. Change** the **Max Distance** to **3**.

This setting creates shadows in those portions of your scene where two surfaces meet at sharp angles, for example, where the ceiling and the walls meet. This is a very popular setting, especially for interior scenes, and can greatly improve realism.

<Step 9> In the **Workflow Setting, disable Auto Generate**.

To fully understand what's happening you're turning off Auto Generate. This is somewhat of a personal choice, and you may prefer to turn this on again once you understand the baking process.

All these settings will have no effect just yet. You now need to adjust the lights and most of the game objects in the scene.

<Step 10> **Make** all your **lights static**.

You do this by selecting them in the hierarchy. Then you check the Static checkmark at the top right, also in the inspector.

<Step 11> **Change** the **mode** of all of your lights to **Mixed**.

The mode setting is also in the inspector about halfway down in the Light section. The mixed setting allows for baked and real-time lighting to operate simultaneously.

<Step 12> **Select** the **Walls, Ceiling, Floor, Chest**, and **Planks** and make them **static**.

If you're asked about whether you wish the children to be static as well, select yes.

<Step 13> **Change** the **intensity** of the **point lights** to **0.3**.

<Step 14> In the **Lighting** Window, click on **Generate Lighting**.

You now need to wait, anywhere from a few seconds to an hour, depending on your computer and graphics card. The author's computer did this in less than a minute using a GeForce RTX 2060 Super card. If your system takes a long time to do this you may decide to work on other things within Unity. The baking process will continue in the background. When baking is complete your scene should look like Figure 21.8.

To see the actual lightmap, do this:

<Step 15> In the **Scene** window, where it says Shaded in the top left corner, and **select** the **Baked Lightmap shading mode**. **Adjust** the **Lighting Exposure** slider. Compare with Figure 21.9.

FIGURE 21.8 Lightmap baking result with ambient occlusion.

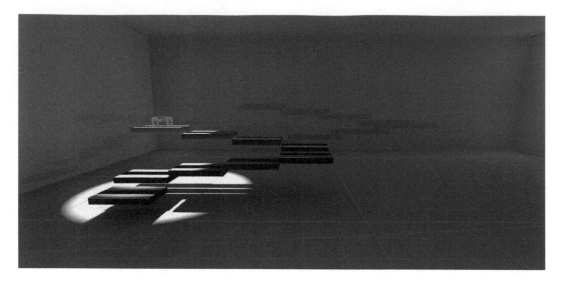

FIGURE 21.9   Baked lightmap shading mode.

To see even more detail, in the Lighting Window, select Baked Lightmaps and notice that you have in fact six lightmaps. You can click on the "Open Preview" buttons to see each of the lightmaps in a preview window. In general you won't need to look at these lightmaps directly, but it's good to know about this in case you run into a problem. At the bottom of the Baked Lightmaps panel you can see some interesting statistics, in particular how many light-maps you have, how large they are, the total bake time, and the name of the device that did the baking.

<Step 16> Test it and **save**.

Aside from having a more realistic look in your scene, there's another, sometimes huge, benefit to the use of lightmaps. As you add more lights to your scene, performance doesn't get worse, just the baking time. This way you can have realistic shadows and lighting on low-end devices.

So far you have just scratched the surface of the subject of lighting. To learn more, try one of the many Unity lighting tutorials available online. Be aware that the lighting features in Unity have changed somewhat over the years, so avoid obsolete tutorials.

In the next section you'll take a look at raytracing.

RAYTRACING

This section covers *raytracing*. Raytracing is an advanced way to model lighting by creat-ing a large number of simulated light rays that mimic the real-world behavior of light. Recently, consumer graphics cards have started to include real-time raytracing features. To follow along with some of the later steps in this section you'll need to use one of these graphics cards. This is a standalone section, so feel free to skip this section if you don't wish to learn about raytracing at this time.

Before diving in and experimenting with raytracing you'll watch an introductory video, first created for the Unite Now conference.

<Step 1> Search for **Activate ray tracing in Unity** on YouTube. Select the video entitled **Activate ray tracing with Unity's High Definition Render Pipeline** from June 2021, and watch at least half of the video.

Starting at Step 2 you'll duplicate some of the steps in this video on your system, but for now, just watching this video will give you a great overview of ray tracing in Unity. As always, be sure to watch in full-screen mode with at least 1080p resolution, if possible. You don't need to understand everything in the video. It's good to follow along as best you can first before you dive in and try this out for yourself.

The following steps closely follow the video mentioned in Step 1 with additional comments and activities to help you understand what's happening.

<Step 2> **Create a new project** from the **Unity Hub** with **Unity Version 2020.3.0f1** and using the **High Definition RP pipeline**. Use the name **RayTracingTest.**

It will take some time for Unity to set this up. Recall that throughout this book you've been using Unity's built-in render pipeline, so this may be your first attempt at using the more advanced HDRP. In order to use real-time raytracing in Unity it is required to use HDRP.

<Step 3> **Read** the explanation of the template in the **Readme** document as displayed in the inspector.

As you can see, there is quite a bit of content here for you to explore before you even start to add raytracing. In the inspector there are also several links to additional documentation and projects. You will bypass that for now and dive into the existing scene instead.

<Step 4> **Play** the game with **Maximize on Play** and **Stats** turned on.

Notice the frame rate. With a modern graphics card capable of RTX (real-time raytracing) you should get at least 100 FPS. Use the usual WASD controls with the mouse and visit the three rooms described in the Readme. The gamepad can let you move around but you'll still need the mouse to point the camera. You'll now go back to following along with the video.

<Step 5> **Edit – Project Settings… Quality.**

There are three settings so far, but none of them use raytracing. You will create a new quality setting with the name Raytracing.

<Step 6> **Click** on **Add Quality Level.**

<Step 7> **Change** the **name** from **Level 3** to **Raytracing.**

\<Step 8\> Go to **Assets/Settings**, Select **HDRPHighQuality**, and type **\<ctrl\>d** to duplicate it.

\<Step 9\> Change the **name** of the **duplicate** to **HDRPRTXQuality** and **drag** it into the **first slot** under Rendering in the quality window with Raytracing still selected. Your Project Settings Window should now look like Figure 21.10.

\<Step 10\> With **HDRPRTXQuality** selected in **Assets/Settings**, look at the inspector, **expand Rendering**, and **turn on Realtime Raytracing (Preview)**.

That's right, Realtime Raytracing is still in Preview in your current version of Unity. This means that this feature is new and may change drastically in the future. That's fine because you're merely trying out raytracing in a test project.

If you get a warning, and probably you will, do the next step.

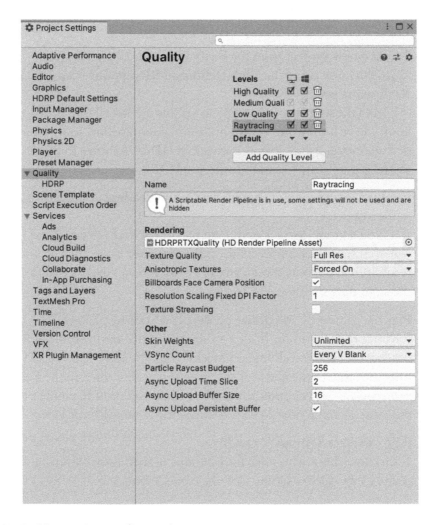

FIGURE 21.10 New project quality settings.

<Step 11> **Window – Render Pipeline – HD Render Pipeline Wizard**.

<Step 12> **Select HDRP + DXR**.

If you get any errors on this window, **click** on **Fix All**, and follow the instructions. You are now set up for Realtime Raytracing.

<Step 13> **Select** the **Scene Camera**, next to the Gizmos icon, and for **Camera Anti-aliasing** select **Temporal Antialiasing**.

This feature smooths out jittering from frame to frame, something that can occur when doing real-time raytracing. In order for this to work in the scene view, do the following as well.

<Step 14> **Turn on Always Refresh** in the Scene view, as shown in Figure 21.11.

Next, you're going to change some settings in the project settings.

<Step 15> **Edit – Project Settings – Quality – HDRP** and **choose** the **Raytracing quality setting**, stored in **HDRPRTXQuality**.

<Step 16> **Verify** that in the **Rendering** section you have **Realtime Raytracing checked**.

<Step 17> In the **Lighting** section, choose **Screen Space Ambient Occlusion** and **Screen Space Global Illumination**.

<Step 18> In **Reflections**, choose **Screen Space Reflection** and **Transparent** below that.

<Step 19> In **Shadows**, check **Screen Space Shadows**.

<Step 20> **Play** the game.

Wow, it looks better. You can see reflections on the floor, better shadows, better lights, and the frame rate is still fast.

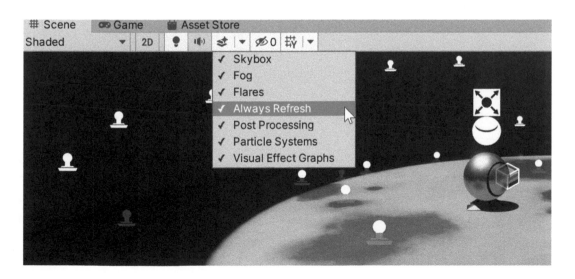

FIGURE 21.11   Turning on always refresh.

You are now at about minute 8 in the video. As an optional exercise you may wish to follow along with the rest of the video on your own, or you can just watch the video from here to get a sense of what's possible with raytracing.

\<Step 21\> Save.

In this chapter you learned the basics of lighting in Unity as well as the exciting prospect of using raytracing. In the next chapter you'll take a closer look at physics in Unity.

CHAPTER 22

Physics

I N THIS CHAPTER YOU'LL learn more about the Unity physics engines. Yes, that's right, you might be surprised to learn that Unity has several physics engines available. Earlier in this book you used physics components without worrying too much about how they work. Next, you'll start with a Unity physics overview section, followed by the creation of a simple physics scene for one of your puzzle rooms. Just for fun, you'll also explore the cloth component and the ragdoll wizard.

UNITY PHYSICS OVERVIEW

Unity has several ways to simulate physics in your projects. You may also bypass Unity's physics entirely and compute your own physics simulation by writing your own scripts to do that. If your project uses strange, unrealistic physics you'll need to write your own scripts, but usually it's much easier to use Unity's built-in physics.

First, you need to be aware of the four different physics engines in Unity 2020.3:

- Built-in 3D physics

- Built-in 2D physics

- DOTS physics package

- Havok physics package

This chapter only covers the built-in 3D physics for Unity. The other three possibilities are documented in the Unity documentation. For your current project, because it is a 3D project, you will only use built-in 3D physics. It is possible to mix 2D and 3D physics, but that's best avoided. Because of this you need to take care to not use any component with 2D in the name for the rest of this 3D project.

Next, you'll get a head start on your physics puzzle room.

<Step 1>   Using UnityHub load **FPSAdventure**. Create a new scene **in Assets/Scenes**, name it **PuzzleScene2**, and **select** it.

DOI: 10.1201/9780429328725-24

Your goal for this scene is to create a physics-based puzzle. You won't have Ellen in this puzzle just yet. You'll start by creating a floor and a ball.

<Step 2> **Create** a **cube** with name **Floor**, **scale (10, 1, 10), position (0, 0, 0)**.

<Step 3> **Create** a **sphere** with name **Ball, position (0,3,0)**.

<Step 4> In **Assets/Art create** a **red ball material**, name **BallMaterial**.

<Step 5> Assign **FloorMaterial** to **Floor**, **BallMaterial** to **Ball**. Compare your scene with Figure 22.1.

<Step 6> **Play** the game, then **stop**.

The ball remains suspended. You're going to take a closer look at the two game objects in the scene. Both of them have colliders, but no physics components.

Your goal is for the ball to fall due to gravity and bounce on the floor. You'll need to add physics components to the floor and the ball to do that. Furthermore, the settings need to be just right, or you'll get very strange behavior. You'll start by getting the ball to drop.

<Step 7> **Add** a **rigidbody component** to the **ball**.

You do that by clicking on Add Component, typing "rig" into the search box, and selecting Rigidbody. Do not select Rigidbody 2D. Remember, you're only using 3D physics components in your project, so you need to avoid the 2D physics components.

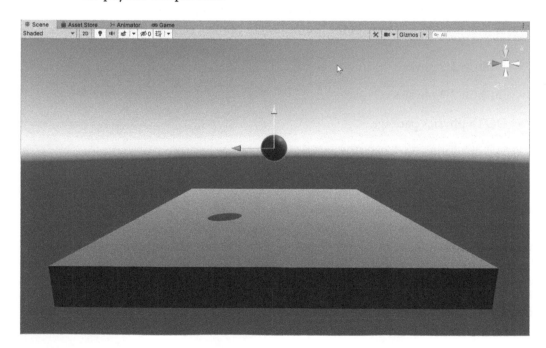

FIGURE 22.1 Ball bounce experiment setup.

<Step 8> **Reset** the **Rigidbody component**.

This is probably unnecessary, but you're ensuring a match with the settings used in the production of this book. The settings should be as follows: **Mass 1**, **Drag 0**, **Angular Drag 0.05**, Use **Gravity checked**, **Is Kinematic unchecked**, **Interpolate None**, **Collision Detection Discrete**, **no Constraints**.

The critical settings are **Gravity** and **Is Kinematic**. For the ball you want gravity turned on. Oddly, the **Is Kinematic** setting will appear to turn the physics engine off, so you want this unchecked, so that the physics engine does in fact move the ball. This setting can be confusing to the uninitiated because the word "kinematic" implies motion, just the opposite of what you would expect. In fact, kinematic objects do usually move, but the movement stems from explicit motion control in a script.

<Step 9> **Test**.

The ball falls and then gets stuck on the floor. It doesn't bounce. In order to get bouncing to happen you'll need to have a rigidbody component for the floor as well.

<Step 10> **Add** a **rigidbody component** to the **floor, turn off Use Gravity**.

This is worth a try, but it fails pretty spectacularly. When you run this, instead of bouncing the balls it makes the floor move down, with the ball stuck to the floor. Try it. The problem is the **Is Kinematic** setting. The floor is intended to be stationary, so you don't want the physics engine to move it.

<Step 11> Check **Is Kinematic** for the Rigidbody of the floor, then test again.

This still doesn't work, but at least the floor stays in place. The problem is that you're missing a bouncy physics material.

<Step 12> In **Assets, create** a **Physics** folder. In that folder create a **Physic Material** with name **Bounce**.

The word "Physic" is not a typo. Unity calls 3D Physics materials *Physic* Materials, whereas the name for 2D Physics Material has the "s" at the end of Physics. This missing s has been a part of Unity from the very beginning.

<Step 13> Set the **Bounciness** to **1** in the inspector. In the **Sphere Collider** for the **Ball**, **select** the **Bounce Material**.

<Step 14> **Test**.

The ball bounces but it's not very bouncy. This is because the floor is still missing the bounce material. The physics engine combines the physic materials from both objects involved in a collision.

<Step 15> **Add** the **Bounce material** to the **floor Box Collider**.

\<Step 16\> **Run** the game for a while, then **stop**.

If you run this long enough, you'll notice that the ball bounces higher and higher, which isn't exactly realistic.

\<Step 17\> Change the **Bounciness** of the **Bounce material** to **0.9**, and **test**.

That looks pretty good.

The time has come to learn about the three types of physical objects in Unity:

- Static

- Kinematic

- Dynamic

Whenever you use a physics engine, even in some other game engine, it's important to know these concepts. The short version is this: Static objects don't move, but still interact with other physics objects in limited ways. Kinematic objects are allowed to move, but the movement is accomplished using a custom script. Dynamic objects move under the control of the physics engine.

In order to create a static object, simply give it a collider and you're done. Static objects don't have rigidbody components. Kinematic objects have a rigidbody component, the Is Kinematic setting is turned on, and you typically move it with code. A Dynamic object has a rigidbody component with the Is Kinematic setting turned off, and Gravity turned on or off depending on the game.

In the next section you'll build a simple physics puzzle using static, kinematic, and dynamic objects.

A PHYSICS PUZZLE

Physics puzzles are quite common in larger games. They bring some welcome relief from the nonstop action and can help move the story along. You're going to design and then build a small prototype physics puzzle as part of your prototype game.

In order to keep things simple you'll build the level from scratch using boxes and spheres created in Unity. When prototyping puzzles, it's most important to make the game playable and fun first. It's fine to postpone the graphics and audio unless they are essential to the puzzle.

Your very simple design is to make the ball controllable using WASD, arrow keys, and the gamepad, just like Ellen. You'll use the ball to push items around in the room, thus clearing a path to reach the treasure chest.

You'll start by building the playfield. You already have a floor and a ball, so next you'll put in four walls.

\<Step 1\> **Duplicate** the **floor**, move it to the side and **rename** it **Wall**.

\<Step 2\> **Change** the **x rotation** to **90**, **z scale** to **5**, and line it up with the right edge of the floor, as shown in Figure 22.2.

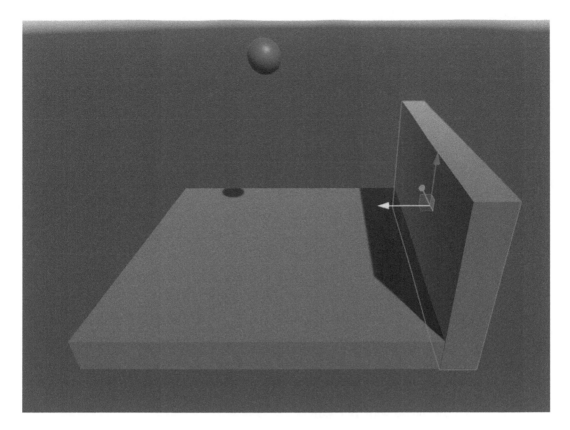

FIGURE 22.2   Adding a wall to puzzle scene 2.

<Step 3> Build the other three walls by duplicating, rotating, and moving existing walls, in a similar manner to Steps 1 and 2. Compare with Figure 22.3.

This room feels cramped. How would you make it larger? That's right, you can stretch it, but just in the x and z directions. You do that as follows.

<Step 4> **Select** the **Floor** and the **four walls simultaneously**. Use the **Scale tool** to stretch in the x and z direction. Hold **<ctrl>** down while stretching to **snap** and **scale** by a **factor of three** in each direction. Compare with Figure 22.4.

To check that it worked, look at the floor in the inspector. You should see a scale of (40, 1, 40). You should see similar whole scale numbers for the walls, for example, (5, 4, 40).

<Step 5> **Play** the game, then **stop**.

The ball is still bouncing in place. Next you'll make the ball kinematic and write a short script for moving it around the playfield.

<Step 6> Select the **ball** and change the **Y position** to **1**.

FIGURE 22.3   Puzzle room 2 with four walls.

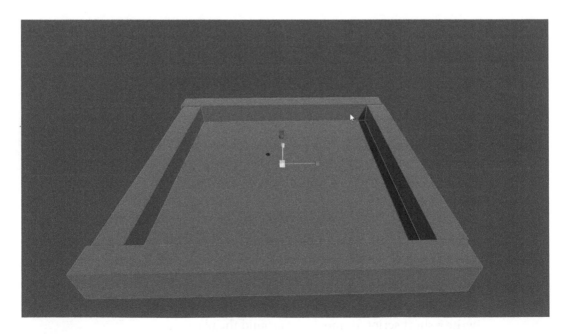

FIGURE 22.4   Floor and walls scaled by a factor of exactly 3.

<Step 7> **Create** a **new script** for the ball called **BallControl** in the scripts folder as follows:

```
public class BallControl : MonoBehaviour
{
    public float speed = 8.0f;
    // Start is called before the first frame update
    void Start()
    {

    }

    // Update is called once per frame
    void Update()
    {
        float x = Input.GetAxisRaw("Horizontal") * speed;
        float z = Input.GetAxisRaw("Vertical") * speed;
        transform.Translate(x * Time.deltaTime, 0, z * Time.deltaTime);
    }
}
```

<Step 8> **Try it**.

This feels a bit odd, and the speed is probably too low. The worst problem, however, is that the ball starts bouncing very strangely after hitting a wall. The following fixes this:

<Step 9> In the **rigidbody component** for the **ball, freeze** the **y position** and **all rotations**. Then **try it** again.

That's much better. The idea here is that you want the physics engine to deal with the collisions between the ball and other objects, but you only want to move the ball in the x and z directions. Also, you don't want the ball to rotate at all because if you let that happen the ball can start to move on its own, and you really don't want that.

<Step 10> **Create** a **cube** with **scale (2, 1, 2)**, **position (-5, 4, 0)**, and give it a **rigidbody** with **gravity, not kinematic**.

<Step 11> **Add** the **Bounce material** to the **Box Collider**.

<Step 12> **Rename** the **Cube** to **Obstacle**.

<Step 13> **Adjust** the **Main Camera** and **test**.

You can now move the obstacle around, and you have some control over where it goes.

Are you ready for a challenge? Figure 22.5 shows the completed puzzle level.

<Step 14> **Build** the level shown in Figure 22.5 using the following hints:

The thin walls are one unit thick.

The chest is from **PuzzlePrefabs** with scale **(4, 4, 4)**.

The white objects are called **sliders** with scale **(5, 1, 1)**, or similar. The tall one has **height 3**.

FIGURE 22.5   A physics puzzle level.

The sliders have a new physic material called **Slide** with both friction settings at **0.1**.

Sliders have their **rotation frozen**, and **Y position frozen** as well, just like the ball.

The point of the puzzle is that the tall slider can only be moved by removing the obstacle in front and then pushing it out of the way using another slider.

The critical setup for moving the tall slider is shown in Figure 22.6.

This puzzle is relatively easy, but it's not at all obvious, and you're going to have people getting stuck in it. As in any puzzle, testing is the key, first by you, and then by other people.

\<Step 15\> **Test** the puzzle yourself. Make sure that the tall slider can't be moved with the ball. Then push away the obstacle object and make your way to the treasure chest.

You now have the tools to make additional puzzles. The most important element is the "Eureka" or "Aha!" moment, the measure of any good puzzle. These puzzles should not depend on the physical skill of the player but rather on their insights, perseverance, and vision. This is a design choice because it is certainly possible to make physics puzzles that require exact timing by the players to achieve a solution.

Once the puzzles are finalized you should make them look and sound better. You can safely put off that work until you're in production.

\<Step 16\> **Save**.

And now, for something completely different: cloth.

FIGURE 22.6   Solving the physics puzzle.

CLOTH

The cloth component is a fun, specialized system in Unity, and fairly easy to set up. You're going to put an animated cloth into the physics puzzle scene just to try it out. You'll worry about how to use it for enhancing the puzzle another time.

<Step 1>   Still in the **PuzzleScene2** scene, **move** the **Ball** to position **(0, 1, 0)**.

<Step 2>   **GameObject – 3D Object – Plane. Rename** it to **flag**.

<Step 3>   **Change** the **X rotation** to **270, scale (0.5, 1, 1), position (–1, 6, 4)**.

<Step 4>   **Create** a **FlagMaterial** and make it **green, assign** it to the **flag**. Compare with Figure 22.7.

<Step 5>   **Add** a **Cloth Component** to the **flag. Test**.
    You can see the flag falling down. That's not what you want. Your goal is to have the flag hang there and behave like a flag when the ball interacts with it. You're almost there.

<Step 6>   **Turn** off the **Mesh Collider** for the flag.
    You won't need this collider for what you have in mind. You could delete it, but turning it off also works.

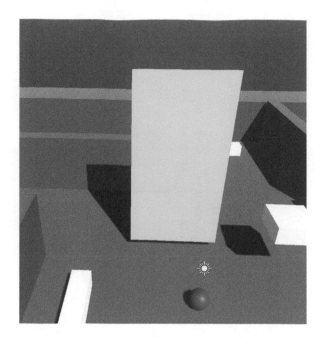

FIGURE 22.7   Setting up a green hanging flag.

<Step 7> In the **Cloth** section in the inspector click on the **Edit Cloth Constraints** icon at the top left of the section. Compare your screen with Figure 22.8.

<Step 8> **Select** the **top two rows of vertices** in the **flag**, and set the **Max Distance** for them to **0**.

<Step 9> **Expand** the **Sphere Colliders** at the bottom of the cloth section in the inspector and change the **Size** to **1**. **Expand Element 0**.

<Step 10> **Drag** the **ball** game object to the slot for the **First** slot for **Element 0**.

<Step 11> **Test** the game by **moving** the ball into the flag. **Amazing!**
    The flag responds to the ball motion but has no effect on the ball. Also, if you move a slider into the flag it doesn't respond. You could make that happen by adding capsule colliders to the sliders, and then add them to the Collider lists in the Cloth component.
    The ball sometimes pushes through the flag. The following step fixes that.

<Step 12> In the **Sphere Collider** for the **Ball**, **change** the **radius** from **0.5** to **0.57**.

<Step 13> **Test**.
    This change fixes the flag interaction, but it may have an effect on the puzzle, so be sure to test that you can still solve the puzzle.

<Step 14> **Save**.

In the next section you'll try out the ragdoll wizard.

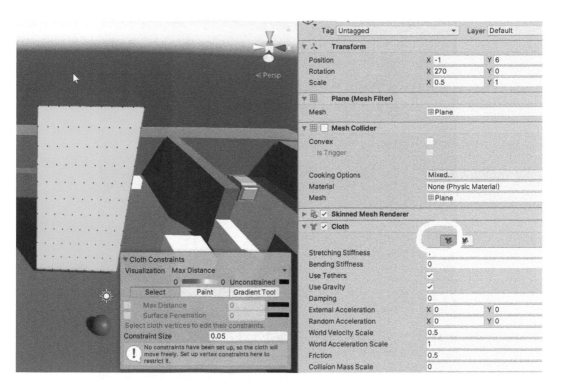

FIGURE 22.8   Editing cloth constraints.

RAGDOLL WIZARD

Ragdoll physics is a way to simulate making a humanoid character move like a ragdoll. This is a good way to animate a death sequence when a character falls down a steep slope, or after a character hits ground after a severe crash. You'll try this out in PuzzleScene1.

<Step 1> Load **PuzzleScene1**.

Feel free to brighten this scene if it feels dark. This section isn't about lighting.

<Step 2> **Drag Assets/Monster_Orc (Troll)/Prefabs/monster_non_anim_orc** into the scene.

<Step 3> Change the **rotation** to **(0, 180, 0)**, **position** to **(−3, 5, 5)**.

You can move the orc away from the planks, if necessary, but keep the y coordinate at 5.

<Step 4> **Add** a **rigidbody component**, **gravity on**.

<Step 5> **Add** a **capsule collider** and **edit** it to fit. Compare with Figure 22.9.

He's just floating up in the air and will fall, due to gravity, and sit there.

<Step 6> **Test**.

Ellen can run into the orc, and he will roll around like a static figurine. You'd rather have him behave like a ragdoll.

FIGURE 22.9   Setting up the orc in PuzzleScene1.

<Step 7> **Select** the **monster**.

<Step 8> **Save** the scene.
This is a good spot to save in case you need to redo the following steps.

<Step 9> **Remove** the **Capsule Collider**.

<Step 10> Select **monster_non_anim_orc** in the hierarchy and **expand** it.

<Step 11> **Right-click** on **Monster_rig** and do **3D Object – Ragdoll…**
You will get a sizable pop-up.

<Step 12> **Expand** the **Monster_rig** as shown in Figure 22.10.

<Step 13> Drag **spine** to **Pelvis**, etc., as shown in Figure 22.11 but don't click on create!

<Step 14> **Double check** the **bone assignments**, Change the **total mass** to **0.6**, then click on **Create**.
You immediately get colliders, Rigidbodies, and Character Joint components assigned to the bones of the Monster_rig. You will have to adjust the head sphere collider.

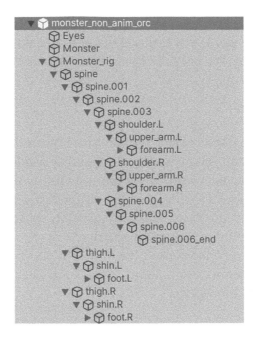

FIGURE 22.10 Setting up the ragdoll for the Monster_rig.

FIGURE 22.11 Bone assignments for ragdoll.

<Step 15> **Select** the **spine.006_end** object in the Hierarchy, then **adjust** the **Sphere collider** to fit the head. Approximately a **radius** of **0.003** will work with a center of (0, 0, 0). This can be tricky, so if you have trouble, just make the radius smaller.

<Step 16> **Test** and **save**.

This time the orc behaves like a ragdoll. You can have Ellen walk up to it to move the orc around. To see the initial fall you can watch it in the scene window.

You just tried out the ragdoll wizard on the orc, just for fun. You've decided to not use it because you don't really need it in this game, but it's good to know about it. You can leave the dead orc in this level just for decoration and to possibly confuse the players. In the production version you may remove the ragdoll entirely.

In this chapter you learned more about the Unity physics engines. They are extremely useful for many types of games, but especially for 3D character based games. In the next chapter you'll finally add some sound.

CHAPTER 23

Sound and Music, Part 2

I N THIS VERY SHORT chapter you're going to cheat. The Unity Asset Store has an incredible selection of free, high-quality sound effects and music, ready for you to use in your game projects. This is especially useful when making prototypes. You can always replace any placeholder sounds during production. For prototypes, a few sounds and a little music can go a long way.

SOUND PACKAGES FROM THE UNITY ASSET STORE

When searching for appropriate sounds for a prototype, simply search for "sound monsters free," for example. Then look for sound bundles and try out a few of them. The "Casual Kingdom World Sounds" package looks like a good candidate. You can listen to the soundtrack in a short video, and it sounds like it fits FPSAdventure.

<Step 1>   Get **Casual Kingdom World Sounds – Free** from the Unity Asset Store.

<Step 2>   **Try out** the various sounds in Unity. They are hiding in **Assets/Packages/ Casual Kingdom – Free Package**.
   You'll start by putting the soundtrack into the game. You have two choices, an MP3 version, or a Wav version. The MP3 version is smaller and sounds good, so you'll use that one.

<Step 3>   **Drag** the **MP3** soundtrack into the **PuzzleScene1** scene. **Check Loop and Play on Awake** in the inspector and **test.**
   Well, that sure was easy. This music doesn't really fit the puzzle room, but you'll leave it there and try it in the main scene instead.

<Step 4>   **Save,** then load the **UnityTerrain** scene.
   You'll probably not see Ellen in the Scene window, so do this:

<Step 5>   **Do Frame selected** for **Ellen**.

<Step 6>   **Bring** in the **Soundtrack** just as you did in the puzzle room. Then **test** the game.

DOI: 10.1201/9780429328725-25

That's better, especially when Ellen is running away from the Monsters. You're going to delay putting in sound effects because they really aren't needed just yet. It'll be easy to put them in by using the techniques you learned in DotGame3D.

It' time to take a step back and decide what to do next.

\<Step 7\> Save.

In the next chapter you'll release FPSAdventure. Maybe.

CHAPTER 24

Releasing FPSAdventure?

I S THIS GAME READY for release? In a word, no. This is just a prototype, so it's not really meant to be released. Still, while you're happy with what you've done so far, it's missing some key elements. The three scenes aren't connected, the main character has no actions other than idling, walking, and running, and the enemies just run toward you and cause damage by touching.

This situation is typical for a prototype. At any point during development of a prototype you have the option of canceling the project, shelving it, continuing development, or starting over and going to production.

STEAM EARLY ACCESS?

Until recently, releasing prototypes to the public wasn't even considered by game developers. All that changed with *Steam*'s *Early Access*. Steam, one of the top digital storefronts for games, created Early Access as a way for developers to make games available to players during development. To find out more about this, search the web for "Is Early Access Right for You 2014" or go to https://youtu.be/JRDwA3cQmlc. It's a fairly long video produced by Valve, the makers of Steam, and well worth watching.

Is FPSAdventure ready for Early Access? Not really. You want the game to be fun to play rather than an early prototype. You want about an hour of gameplay. You don't have that yet. So what are you going to do with your creation? You put a lot of time and effort into it. You surely don't want to just throw it away.

You've decided to continue to work on the game at some time in the future. Then, when the game is more fun to play, looks and sounds better, only then will you consider releasing it using Early Access or some other way. In Early Access you're inviting players to look at what you have so far and give you feedback. Think of your players as part of the production team.

It's of course OK to just save your project, back it up, and move on, but before you do that you should do some cleanup. You're going to go through the release process, fix a few simple issues, and then shelve it. A few weeks or months of shelf time can do wonders for a project and will allow you to get back to it with fresh ideas and energy.

DOI: 10.1201/9780429328725-26

TESTING AND DEBUGGING

Because you're not releasing this game very soon, you'll ignore most of the minor bugs. You do wish to test this game on other computers. That in turn means that you'll need to put together an acceptable build. To accomplish that you have two issues that need fixing. You need a way to exit the game from a build, and you need a way to access the puzzle rooms.

This is a good opportunity for you to practice what you've learned. In the UnityTerrain scene, create three spheres or different colors. Find a way to exit the game when Ellen collides with the first sphere, go to PuzzleScene1 when colliding with the second ball, etc. If you're feeling ambitious, put in code to exit the game when the player types the <esc> key.

You'll be using Application.Exit() to exit the game, just as the code in DotGame3D. You can just look at the appropriate code in DotGame3D if you need help with this. To actually try out the Application.Exit() call, you'll need create a build.

BUILD AND RUN

To set up the build you'll need to include the three scenes from this project. You probably did that already when you did the exercise in the previous section. You'll notice that it takes quite a long time to do this build, much longer than for DotGame3D. This isn't surprising given the large terrain and the advanced lighting features in this project.

As you did in DotGame3D, copy the build folder to another system or two and see if the game is playable there. You'll make a note that you have no way of knowing the frame rate when running the build, so in the future you'll try to find a way to display the frame rate when running the game in a build. As usual, the internet can help you with this.

POSTMORTEM

There is no postmortem. That's because this game is very much alive. Still, it can be useful to review what happened so far. The main purpose of this prototype was, and is, to experiment with some of the more advanced features of Unity, including terrain building, navmeshes, baked lighting, raytracing, and integrating some very interesting assets from the Asset Store and Mixamo.

The game, such as it is, definitely has potential, but it'll take more work to get it to a releasable state. Most game developers develop prototypes and experimental projects quite often. The projects that see the light of day are few and far between.

In the next and final chapter of this book you'll look toward the future and reflect once more on what you accomplished, having worked through hundreds of pages and thousands of steps.

CHAPTER 25

Epilogue

IN THIS CHAPTER YOU'LL take a look back at what you accomplished by working through this book. You'll also dream about the future.

LEARNINGS

"Learnings" is an old, but until recently obscure word. If you made it this far, worked all the steps, then, indeed, you learned something. And even after so many pages, you know that this is just the beginning of your game development journey.

If you learned one thing during this process, let it be this: Learning new things is worth it. You barely scratched the surface of C# programming and software engineering, a career onto itself. You'll never finish learning all the features of Blender, GIMP, Unity, Audacity, and MuseScore, especially since they are moving targets. Of course, there's no better way to reinforce your learnings than to apply them by creating and working on new projects.

WHAT NEXT?

In the next four sections you'll see descriptions of four possible projects for you to consider. You might not have time to do them all but pick one or more and spend some time making prototypes for them. Try to use what you learned in this book, and if you're daring, pick a new Unity, GIMP, or Blender feature or two to use in your creation. Then comes the hard part: release, shelve, or delete? Here's a hint: never delete projects that took more than a few days to do, even if you think that they're not worth saving. Storage is cheap, and you might find a use for some of those assets in a future project. If you talk with any old-time game developers, most of them will have stories of games that they wish they had backed up and saved.

PROJECT 1: CARD GAME

Do you have a favorite card game? Making a 3D card game can be an easy way to make a smallish 3D game. No, card games aren't typically done in 3D, but it would be fun to treat the cards as 3D objects, and try the physics engine on them. You could even do something like 52 Pickup. Google it if you don't know what that is.

DOI: 10.1201/9780429328725-27

PROJECT 2: RACING GAME

You already have a head start from Chapter 2. Full-featured racing games can't be made quickly, but you can try to have just one track, one type of car, and use the car physics pre-made for Unity. You can find a car physics section in the Unity manual. This could also be a way to try out two omissions in this book: networking and multiplayer.

PROJECT 3: PLATFORMER

Here is where the Unity Asset Store can really help. Grab some free assets and make a platformer. Review the assets that you already downloaded, and explore the free Unity Tutorials for additional ideas. And of course, there are always YouTube tutorials.

PROJECT 4: ROGUELIKE

Do you know the game Rogue, and any of the descendant *roguelike* games? The word "roguelike" implies that your levels will be procedurally generated. A good way to start is to watch some videos about 3D roguelike games, then try to make one yourself.

FINAL THOUGHTS

Thank you, dear reader, and fellow game developer. Please let me know about your experiences as a reader, student, and/or game developer. I can be reached at franzlanzinger.com. If you did, in fact, read the 2D book and this 3D book and worked through both of them, congratulations! Now, do it again. Yes, really. Technical material such as presented here can often only be fully digested via several passes. If you wish, try going through the steps with newer versions of the software. Get creative along the way and change a few things. You'll be astonished at just how much easier and enlightening it can seem the second or even the third time through.

I would love to hear from you, get feedback about my books and my games. As you continue in your quest for that big hit game, a quirky indie game, or a way to tell that story that needs to be told, keep playing, keep learning, and keep creating.

Appendix I

The C# Coding Standard for This Book

THIS APPENDIX PRESENTS THE coding standard for C# and Unity as used in this book. This one is fairly simple and short. More extensive and detailed C# coding standards can be found on the internet. Your organization may have its own coding standard. Even if you're a solo developer it's helpful to follow this coding standard, or something similar.

Tabs: Never use tabs. Instead, indent using spaces, either two or four spaces.

Line width: Limit line width to 72 characters. This is to help with readability.

Bracing: Open and closed braces are at the beginning of lines and are the only thing on the line. Never omit braces for blocks of just one statement. Single line blocks may have the braces on the same line.

For example:

BAD:

```
if ( x > 9 ) y = 3;
```

GOOD:

```
if (x > 9)
{
  y = 3;
}
```

ALSO OK:

```
if (x > 9){ y = 3;}
```

The bad example is shorter, but harder to maintain and just asking for someone to change the code to something like this:

REALLY BAD:

```
if (x > 9) y = 3; z = 4;
```

Why is this really bad? Well, the programmer probably wanted the z assignment statement to only be executed when x > 9. This code will, however, always do the z assignment regardless of the value of x.

Comments: Use comments only when necessary. Use the // style of comments rather than the /* */ style. Put comments above the code rather than after or on the side of it.

Why are extensive comments bad? Because in the heat of development, comments don't get maintained, and then, years later, the comments will mislead the next developer. A better approach is to write self-commenting code, code that doesn't need comments to explain it. Yes, it's OK to break this standard occasionally.

Spacing: Add spaces to improve readability where appropriate. In particular, separate arguments in function calls with spaces.

GOOD:

```
DisplayScore(score, 20, 30);
```

BAD

```
DisplayScore(score,20,30);
```

There are many such situations where adding a space can make your code look clearer. C# usually doesn't care about these extra spaces. Just don't put spaces inside of identifiers.

Vertical spacing: Add single blank lines generously to separate methods and blocks of functionality. If you have too many of these, consider refactoring them into multiple methods.

Large methods: Avoid them. Break them into smaller methods to improve clarity and readability.

Naming: Use camelCasing or PascalCasing. Avoid underscores.

GOOD:

```
public void MyFunction();
```

BAD:

```
public void my_function();
```

PascalCasing is used for functions and class names.

GameObject names should also use PascalCasing because the associated script uses the name as the class name.

Appendix II
Game Development Checklist

W HEN DEVELOPING A GAME, it pays to go through a checklist to make sure you didn't forget something along the way. Here is one possible checklist. As you gain experience as a game developer, add to this list, or change it to suit your needs and goals.

BEFORE YOU START DEVELOPMENT

Are you excited about the game? If not, toss it and do something else.

Are doing this only for the money? If so, do something else if you can afford to.

Do you have an excellent, original concept?

Does it all make sense?

What are some competing games? Did you play them? Did you at least look at videos of them?

DURING DEVELOPMENT

Is it fun?

Do you enjoy playing it yourself?

If it's not fun, what's your excuse? Don't be afraid to kill the project if it's not fun.

Are the controls responsive? If not, make them responsive ASAP. The controls should feel good all by themselves even when you're just moving a character around or driving a vehicle for no reason, for example.

Is the learning curve OK? This needs to be tested.

What rewards are you giving the player?

Good UI. Make the UI experience fast and easy to understand.

Does gameplay start ASAP?

If you have cutscenes, always make them skippable. Not everyone cares about the story, especially if they're playing the game a third time.

Do you have a schedule?

What are your platforms? For example: PC first, then Mac, then mobile.

What is the audio plan for the game? Do you have speech, music, sound effects?

MARKETING

How are you promoting this project?

When and how are you making GIFs?

Do you have domain and a website for the game?

Do you have a Twitter account, Facebook, other social media?

Trailer?

Playable demo?

Do you have cheat codes? If so, what are they and what do they do?

Who are the testers during development? Before release?

BEFORE RELEASE

Does the game use the new title everywhere, or do you have the working title in there someplace?

Do you have a copyright notice?

Trademarks?

Did you put in a developer credits screen? Did you forget anyone?

Do you have accurate names in the credits? Did you send a copy to all developers?

Did you check all licenses and observe all associated terms?

Are the developer credits easily accessible, even for players who didn't finish the game?

Is the website operational?

Index

Note: *Italic* page numbers refer to figures.

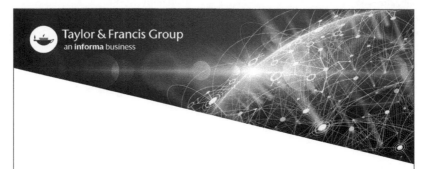

Milton Keynes UK
Ingram Content Group UK Ltd.
UKHW050440111024
449327UK00039B/24